46-99 BK Bud 7/99

What Works
on Wall Street

Other Books by James P. O'Shaughnessy

INVEST LIKE THE BEST: USING YOUR COMPUTER TO UNLOCK THE
SECRETS OF THE TOP MONEY MANAGERS

HOW TO RETIRE RICH: TIME-TESTED STRATEGIES TO BEAT THE
MARKET AND RETIRE IN STYLE

What Works on Wall Street

A Guide to the Best-Performing Investment Strategies of All Time

James P. O'Shaughnessy

Revised Edition

McGraw-Hill

New York   San Francisco   Washington, D.C.   Auckland   Bogotá
Caracas   Lisbon   London   Madrid   Mexico City   Milan
Montreal   New Delhi   San Juan   Singapore
Sydney   Tokyo   Toronto

Library of Congress Cataloging-in-Publication Data

O'Shaughnessy, James P.
    What works on Wall Street / James P. O'Shaughnessy. — revised ed.
      p.   cm.
    Includes bibliographical references and index.
    ISBN 0-07-048246-2 (alk. paper)
    1. Investments—United States.   2. Investment analysis—United
States. I. Title.
    HG4910.0828 1998
    332.6—dc21   98-5810
                                         CIP

McGraw-Hill

A Division of The McGraw·Hill Companies

1 2 3 4 5 6 7 8 9 0 DOC/DOC 9 0 3 2 1 0 9 8

ISBN 0-07-048246-2

*The sponsoring editor for this book was Susan Barry, the editing supervisor
was Bernard Onken, and the production supervisor was Tina Cameron. It was
set in Palatino by Renee Lipton of McGraw-Hill's Professional Book Group
composition unit.*

Printed and bound by R. R. Donnelley & Sons Company.

McGraw-Hill books are available at special quantity discounts to use as
premiums and sales promotions, or for use in corporate training pro-
grams. For more information, please write to the Director of Special Sales,
McGraw-Hill, 11 West 19th Street, New York, NY 10011. Or contact your
local bookstore.

This publication is designed to provide accurate and authoritative information
in regard to the subject matter covered. It is sold with the understanding that
the publisher is not engaged in rendering legal, accounting, or other professional service. If legal advice or other expert assistance is required, the services
of a competent professional person should be sought.
        —From a declaration of principles jointly adopted by a committee
            of the American Bar Association and a committee of publishers.

To Lael, Kathryn, Patrick, and Melissa

About the Author

James P. O'Shaughnessy is Chairman and CEO of O'Shaughnessy Capital Management, Inc., a widely known Greenwich, Connecticut, investment advisory firm. He also serves as the manager of the four no-load funds in the O'Shaughnessy Funds family. Long recognized as one of America's leading financial experts and a pioneer in quantitative equity analysis, he has been called a "world beater" and a "statistical guru" by *Barron's. Higher Returns* said he is "one of the most original market thinkers we've come across." *Forbes* pronounced his first book *Invest Like the Best* "awesome" and named it one of the best financial books of the year. *The Stock Trader's Almanac* called *Invest Like the Best* the "Best Investment Book of 1994." O'Shaughnessy's investment strategies have been featured in *The Wall Street Journal, The New York Times, The Washington Post, The Financial Times, The Los Angeles Times,* London's *Daily Mail,* Japan's *Nikkei Shimbun Daily, Newsweek, Barron's, Forbes, Smart Money, Worth,* and *Money.* He appears regularly on CNN and CNBC. He lives in Greenwich, Connecticut, with his wife and three children.

Wait for the wisest of all counselors, Time.
—Pericles

Contents

Preface

*The more original a discovery, the more obvious it
seems afterward.*   —ARTHUR KOESTLER

Patrick Henry was right when he proclaimed that the only way to judge
the future was by the past. To make the best investment plans for the
future, investors need access to unbiased, long-term performance
results. It doesn't matter if they are aggressive investors seeking fast
growth or conservative investors seeking low-risk, high-yielding stocks
for their retirement account. Knowing how a particular investment
strategy performed historically gives you the vital information you
need on its risk, variability, and persistence of returns. Access to long-
term performance results lets you make informed choices, based on
facts, not hype.

This book offers readers the first long-term studies of Wall Street's
most popular investment strategies. To date, there is no widely available, comprehensive guide to which strategies are long-term winners
and which are not. Although there are many studies covering short
periods of time, *What Works on Wall Street* is the first all-inclusive, defin-
itive guide to the long-term efficacy of Wall Street's favorite investment
strategies.

All the tests in this book use Standard & Poor's Compustat database,
the largest, most comprehensive database of U.S. stock market information available. This is the *first* time the historical S&P Compustat
data have been released to an outside researcher in their entirety. *What*

Works on Wall Street includes 45 years of results for Wall Street's most popular investment strategies.

Origins

It took the combination of fast computers and huge databases like Compustat to prove that a portfolio's returns are essentially determined by the factors that define the portfolio. Before computers, it was almost impossible to determine what strategy guided the development of a portfolio. The number of underlying factors (characteristics that define a portfolio, like price-to-earnings ratio and dividend yield) an investor could consider seemed endless. The best the investor could do was look at portfolios in the most general ways. Sometimes even a *professional manager* didn't know what particular factors best characterized the stocks in his or her portfolio, relying more often on general descriptions and other qualitative measures.

The computer changed this. We can now analyze a portfolio and see which factors, if any, separate the best-performing strategies from the mediocre. With computers, we can also test combinations of factors over long periods of time to gain insight into what to expect in the future from any given investment strategy.

Most Strategies Are Mediocre

What Works on Wall Street shows that most investment strategies are mediocre and the majority, *particularly those most appealing to investors over the short term*, fail to beat the simple strategy of indexing to the S&P 500. The book also provides evidence to disprove the academic theory that stock prices follow a "random walk."

Rather than moving about without rhyme or reason, the stock market methodically rewards certain investment strategies while punishing others. *What Works on Wall Street*'s 45 years of returns show that there's nothing random about long-term stock market returns. Investors can do *much better* than the market if they consistently use time-tested strategies that are based on sensible, rational methods for selecting stocks.

Discipline Is Key

What Works on Wall Street shows that the only way to beat the market over the long term is to consistently use sensible investment strategies.

Eighty percent of the mutual funds covered by Morningstar fail to beat the S&P 500 because their managers lack the discipline to stick with one strategy through thick and thin. This lack of discipline devastates long-term performance.

Highlights

After reading *What Works on Wall Street*, investors will know the following:

- Most small capitalization strategies owe their superior returns to microcap stocks with market capitalizations below $25 million. These stocks are too small for virtually any invstor to buy.

- Buying stocks with low price-to-earnings ratios is most profitable when you stick to larger, better-known issues.

- Price-to-sales ratio is the best value ratio to use for buying market-beating stocks.

- Last year's biggest losers are the *worst* stocks you can buy.

- Last years earnings gains alone are *worthless* when determining if a stock is a good investment.

- Using several factors dramatically improves long-term performance.

- You can do four times as well as the S&P 500 by concentrating on large, well-known stocks with high dividend yields.

- Relative strength is the only growth variable that consistently beats the market.

- Buying Wall Street's current darlings with the highest price-to-earnings ratios is one of the *worst* things you can do.

- A strategy's risk is one of the most important elements to consider.

- Uniting growth and value strategies is the best way to improve your investment performance.

Acknowledgments

This book would not have been possible without the help of many people. When I started this project several years ago, Jim Branscome, then head of S&P Compustat, was a champion of the project at every turn. His successor, Paul Cleckner, was also extraordinarily supportive and is an outstanding example of an executive who understands the best way to help the business bottom-line is to help the bottom-line of thousands of ordinary investors. Howard Smith, the current head of Compustat, has also been wonderful to work with on the ongoing effort to improve the strategies and data covered in the book. Thanks also to Steve Johansen, who was a Compustat PC Plus specialist when I wrote the first version of this book. Steve went above and beyond the call of duty helping me design the tests as well as doing the majority of the work for this edition's decile studies.

But this book would not have been finished without the continual help, support, and encouragement of my wife, Melissa. I am extremely indebted to her for editing every line. Her many talents were especially valuable in editing and rewriting the manuscript. Without her expert hand, this book might never have been finished. In addition to loving her dearly, I owe any success I have as an author to her.

Thanks also to my team at O'Shaughnessy Capital for putting up with me while I revised this book.

James P. O'Shaughnessy
Greenwich, Connecticut
1997

1

Stock Investment Strategies: Different Methods, Similar Goals

Good intelligence is nine-tenths of any battle.
—NAPOLEON

There are two main approaches to equity investing: active and passive. The active approach is most common. Here, managers attempt to maximize their returns at various levels of risk by buying stocks they believe superior to others. Usually the managers follow similar routes to investigating a stock. They analyze the company, interview management, talk to customers and competitors, review historical trends and current forecasts, and then decide if the stock is worth buying.

Active investors are guided by styles, broadly called *growth* and *value*. What type of stock they buy depends largely on their underlying philosophy. Growth investors buy stocks that have higher-than-average growth in sales and earnings with expectations for more of the same. A classic growth stock's earnings just keep getting better and better. Growth investors believe in a company's potential and think a stock's price will rise with its earnings.

Value investors seek stocks with current market values substantially below true or liquidating value. They use factors like price-to-earnings ratios and price-to-sales ratios to identify when a stock is selling below its intrinsic value. They bargain-hunt, looking for stocks whose underlying assets they can buy for 70 cents on the dollar. Value investors believe in a company's balance sheet, thinking a stock's price will eventually rise to meet its intrinsic value.

Many times actively managed funds use a hodgepodge of techniques from both schools of investing, but the most successful funds have strongly articulated strategies. The majority of mutual funds, professionally managed pension funds, and individual accounts are managed with an active approach.

Traditional Active Management Doesn't Work

The approach of traditional, actively managed funds makes perfect sense until you review the record. The majority do not beat the S&P 500. This is true over both short and long time periods. Figure 1-1 shows the percentage of actively managed mutual funds in Morningstar's database that beat the Vanguard Index 500, Vanguard's S&P 500 index fund. The *best* 10 years, ending December 31, 1994, saw only 26 percent of the traditionally managed active mutual funds beating the index. When you dig deeper and look at the percentage by which they beat the index, the news gets worse. As Figure 1-2 shows, of the 128 funds beating the Vanguard Index for the 10 years ending December 31, 1996, only 43 percent managed to beat the index by more than 2 percent a year on a compound basis. What's more, this record *overstates* the performance of traditionally managed active funds, since it doesn't include all the funds that failed to survive the 10 years.

Passive indexing has exploded in the past decade as a result. Here, investors buy an index they think broadly represents the market, such as the S&P 500, and let it go at that. Their objective is to match the market, not outperform it. They are willing to give up their shot at outperforming the market for the security of not underperforming it. Driven by the disappointing results of traditionally managed portfolios, index fund managers have seen their assets soar, from $10 billion in 1980 to over $250 billion in 1990, with estimates that index funds will account for more than half of all pension plan holdings by the end of the century. The pension plans lead the way, but retail investors are right on their heels. Index funds are the fastest-growing sector in the mutual fund business. Between 1986 and 1996, assets invested in index mutual funds soared from $556 million to $65 billion.

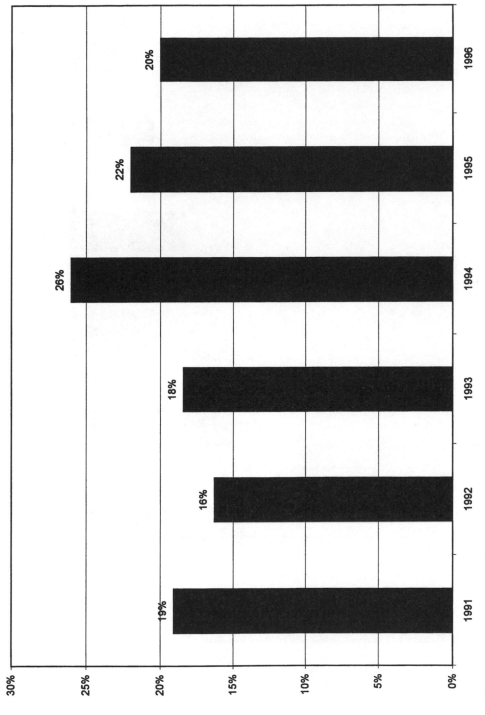

Figure 1-1. Percent of all equity funds with 10-year track records beating the Vanguard Index 500 for the 10 years ending December 31 in each year. (Source: *Morningstar OnDisc*)

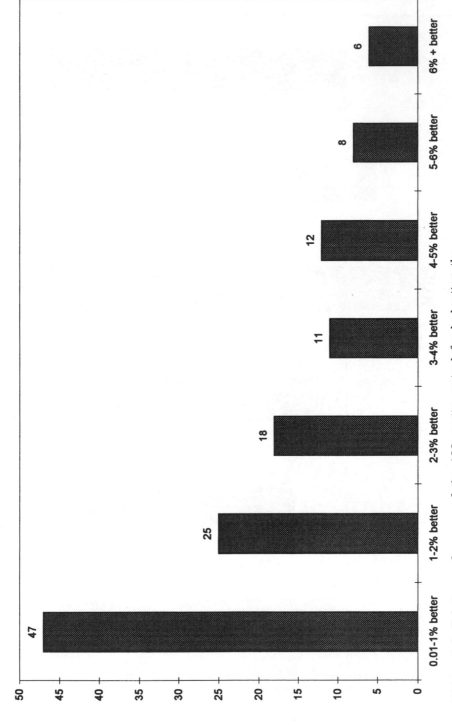

Figure 1-2. Relative performance of the 128 equity mutual funds beating the Vanguard Index 500 for the 10 years ending December 31, 1996. (Source: *Morningstar OnDisc*)

What's the Problem?

Academics aren't surprised that traditionally managed funds fail to beat the market. Most have long held that markets are efficient and that current security prices reflect all available information. They argue that prices follow a "random walk" and move without rhyme or reason. According to their theories, you might as well have a monkey throw darts at a stock page as attempt analysis, since stock prices are random and cannot be predicted.

The long-term evidence in this book contradicts the random walk theory. Far from prices following a random walk, the evidence reveals a purposeful stride. The 45 years of data found in this book prove strong return predictability. The market clearly and consistently rewards certain attributes (e.g., stocks with low price-to-sales ratios) and clearly and consistently punishes others (e.g., stocks with high price-to-sales ratios) over long periods of time. Yet the paradox remains: If the tests show such high return predictability, why do 80 percent of traditionally managed mutual funds fail to beat the S&P 500?

Finding exploitable investment opportunities does not mean it's easy to make money, however. To do so requires the ability to consistently, patiently, and slavishly stick with a strategy, even when it's performing poorly relative to other methods. Few are capable of such action. Successful investors do not comply with nature; they defy it. In the next chapter I argue that the reason traditional management doesn't work well is that human decision making is *systematically flawed and unreliable.* This weakness provides an opportunity to those who use a rational, disciplined method to buy and sell stocks on the basis of time-tested methods.

Studying the Wrong Things

It's no surprise that academics find traditionally managed stock portfolios following a random walk. Most traditional managers' past records cannot predict future returns, because their behavior is inconsistent. You cannot make forecasts on the basis of inconsistent behavior, because when you behave inconsistently, you are unpredictable. Even if a manager is a perfectly consistent investor—a hallmark of the best money managers—if *that* manager leaves the fund, all predictive ability from past performance is lost. More, if a manager changes his or her style, all predictive ability from past performance is also lost. Academics, therefore, have been measuring the *wrong* things. They assume perfect, rational behavior in a capricious environment ruled by greed, hope, and fear. They have been contrasting the returns of a passively held portfolio—the S&P 500—with the returns of portfolios managed in an inconsistent, shoot-from-the-hip style. Track records are worthless unless you know what strategy the manager uses and if it is *still* being used. When you study a traditionally managed fund, you're really looking at two things: first, the strategy used and second, the ability of the manager to implement it successfully. It makes much more sense to contrast the one-factor S&P 500 portfolio with *other* one- or multifactor portfolios.

Why Indexing Works

Indexing to the S&P 500 works because it sidesteps flawed decision making and automates the simple strategy of buying the big stocks that make up the S&P 500. The mighty S&P 500 consistently beats 80 percent of traditionally managed funds by doing nothing more than making a disciplined bet on large capitalization stocks. Figure 1-3 compares the returns on the S&P 500 with those for our Large Stocks universe, which consists of all the stocks in the Compustat database with market capitalizations greater than the database mean in any given year. This effectively limits us to the top 16 percent of the Compustat database by market capitalization. Stocks are then bought in equal dollar amounts. The returns are virtually identical. An investment of $10,000 in the S&P 500 on December 31, 1951 was worth $1,726,128 on December 31, 1996. The same $10,000 invested in our Large Stock universe was worth $1,590,667, a $135,461 difference. (Both include the reinvestment of all dividends.) And it's not just the absolute returns that are similar—risk, as measured by the standard deviation of return, is also virtually identical for the two strategies. The annual standard deviation of return for the S&P 500 was 16.65 percent, whereas that for the Large Stocks universe was 16.01 percent.

Indexing to the S&P 500 is just *one* form of passive implementation of a strategy that consistently buys big stocks. Buying the 10 highest-yielding stocks in the Dow Jones Industrial Average each year is another strategy that works consistently. From 1928—when the Dow was expanded to 30 stocks—through 1996, the strategy consistently beat the S&P 500. Indeed, it beat the S&P 500 in every decade—from the depressionary 1930s through the restructuring 1990s—and had only two 10-year rolling periods where it failed to do better than the S&P 500. You'll find a number of other winning strategies in this book.

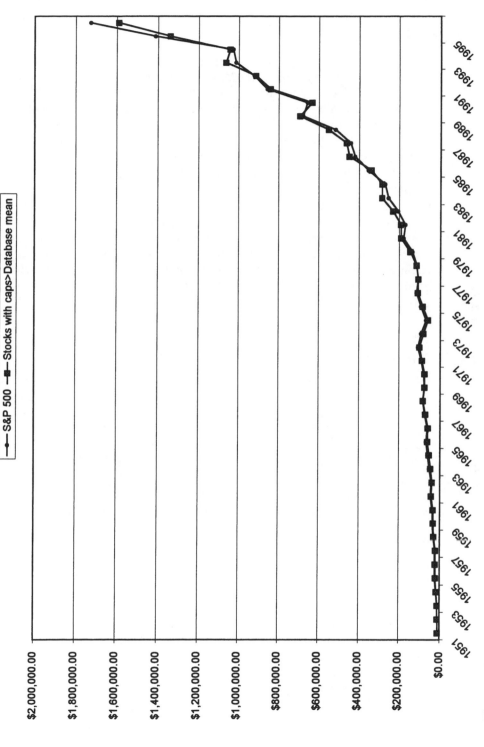

Figure 1-3. Comparative returns. December 31, 1951–December 31, 1996.

Pinpointing Performance

It took the combination of fast computers and huge databases like Compustat to prove that a portfolio's returns are essentially determined by the factors that define the portfolio. Before computers, it was virtually impossible to determine what strategy guided the development of a portfolio. The number of underlying factors (characteristics that define a portfolio like PE ratio and dividend yield) an investor could consider seemed endless. The best the investor could do was look at portfolios in the most general ways. Sometimes even a *professional manager* didn't know what particular factors best characterized the stocks in his or her portfolio, relying more often on general descriptions and other qualitative measures. The computer changed this. We can now quickly analyze the factors that define any portfolio and see which, if any, separate the best-performing funds and strategies from the mediocre. With computers, we can also test combinations of factors over long periods of time to gain insight into what to expect in the future from any given investment strategy.

Discipline Is the Key

If you use a one-factor model based on market capitalization—like the two mentioned above—you get the same results. If, however, you change a portfolio's underlying factors so that they deviate significantly from the S&P 500—say, by keeping price-to-sales ratios below 1 or dividend yields above a certain number—you can expect that portfolio to perform differently from the market. S&P 500 index funds are nothing more than *structured portfolios* that make disciplined bets on a large capitalization factor. *Many other factors perform much better.* Structured investing is a hybrid of active and passive management that automates buy and sell decisions. If a stock meets the criteria, it's bought. If not, not. No personal, emotional judgments enter the process. Disciplined implementation of active strategies is the key to performance. Traditional managers usually follow a hit-and-miss approach to investing. Their lack of discipline accounts for their inability to beat simple approaches that *never vary* from their methods.

Imagine what the market would look like today if in the 1950s the editors at Dow Jones & Company decided to revamp the Dow Jones Industrial Average, basing it on reasonably priced value stocks instead of big industrial companies. If they expanded the list to 50 names and each year simply bought the 50 stocks with the lowest price-to-sales ratio, the "market" today would be four times higher than it is!

Consistency Wins

In a study for my book *Invest Like the Best,* I found that the *one* thing uniting the best managers is consistency. I'm not alone. In the 1970s, AT&T's study of its pension fund managers found that successful investing required, at a minimum, a structured decision-making process that can be easily defined and a stated investment philosophy that is consistently applied. John Neff of the Windsor fund and Peter Lynch of Magellan became legends because their success was the result of slavish devotion to their investment strategies.

A Structured Portfolio in Action

Very few funds or managers stick with their strategies for long periods of time. One that did, the Lexington Corporate Leaders Trust, is most unusual because it's a structured portfolio in action. Formed in 1935, the trust was designed to hold 30 stocks that were leaders in their industries. The fund's portfolio is *share-weighted,* holding the same number of shares in each company regardless of price. Since 1935, seven companies have been eliminated, and two spin-offs added, so the fund currently holds 25 stocks. Yet this single-factor portfolio is a market slayer—between January 1, 1976 and December 31, 1996, $10,000 invested in the fund grew to $197,563, a compound return of 15.27 percent a year. That beat both the S&P 500's return of 14.91 percent and 90 percent of traditionally managed funds. More, Lexington's charter prevents rebalancing the portfolio, which would allow it to reflect changes in corporate leaders. Imagine how the fund would have performed if it bought today's leaders like Microsoft and Intel! Indeed, a structured strategy like the high-yielding Dow approach mentioned earlier, which allows for refreshing the stocks every year, posted *much better* returns. There, $10,000 invested on January 1, 1976 was worth $328,964 at the end of 1996, a compound return of 18.1 percent.

Overwhelmed by Our Nature

Knowing and doing are two very different things. As Goethe said, "In the realm of ideas, everything depends on enthusiasm; in the real world, all rests on perseverance." While we may *understand* what we should do, we usually are overwhelmed by our nature, allowing the intensely emotional present to overpower our better judgment. When someone questioned Mikhail Gorbachev about actions he had taken against his better judgment, he replied, "Your question is academic because it is abstract. People don't have the luxury of living in the abstract. They live in the real, emotional, full-blooded world of reality."

It is in the full-blooded world of reality that the problems begin, for both investors and other professionals. Let's see why this is so.

2

The Unreliable Experts: Getting in the Way of Outstanding Performance

What ails the truth is that it is mainly
uncomfortable, and often dull. The human mind
seeks something more amusing, and more
caressing.　　　　　—H. L. MENCKEN

Everyone is guilty of faulty decision making, not just the scions of Wall Street. An accountant must offer an opinion on the creditworthiness of a firm. A college administrator must decide which students to accept into a graduate program. A psychologist must decide if a patient's ills are neurosis or psychosis. A doctor must decide if it's liver cancer or not. More prosaically, a bookie tries to handicap the next horse race.

All these are activities in which an expert predicts an outcome. They occur every day and make up the fabric of our lives. Generally, there are two ways to make predictions. The most common way is for a person to run through a variety of possible outcomes mentally, essentially relying on knowledge, experience, and common sense to reach a decision. This is known as a "clinical" or intuitive approach, and is the way traditional active money managers make choices. The stock analyst may pour over a company's financial statements, interview management, talk to customers and competitors, and finally try to make an overall forecast. The graduate school administrator might use a host of data, from college grade point average to interviews with applicants, to determine if students should be accepted. This type of judgment relies on the perceptiveness of the forecaster.

The second general way to reach a decision is the actuarial, or quantitative, approach. Here the forecaster makes no subjective judgments. Empirical relationships between the data and the desired outcome are used to reach conclusions. This method relies solely on proven relationships, using large samples of data. It's similar to the structured process described in Chapter 1. The graduate school administrator might use a model that finds college grade point average highly correlated to graduate school success and admit only those who have made a certain grade. In almost every instance, from stock analysts to doctors, we naturally prefer qualitative, intuitive methods. In most instances, we're wrong.

Human Judgment Is Limited

David Faust writes in his revolutionary book *The Limits of Scientific Reasoning:* "Human judgment is far more limited than we think. We have a surprisingly restricted capacity to manage or interpret complex information." Studying a wide range of professionals, from medical doctors making diagnoses to experts making predictions of job success in academic or military training, Faust found that *human judges were consistently outperformed by simple actuarial models.* Like traditional money managers, most professionals cannot beat the passive implementation of time-tested formulas.

Another researcher, Paul Meehl, offered the first comprehensive review of statistical prediction (similar to a structured approach) and clinical prediction (similar to an intuitive, traditional approach) in his 1954 study *Clinical Versus Statistical Prediction: A Theoretical Analysis and Review of the Literature.* He reviewed 20 studies that compared clinical and statistical predictions for academic success, response to electroshock therapy, and criminal recidivism. In almost every instance, Meehl found that simple actuarial models outperformed the human judges. In the prediction of academic success in college, for example, a model using just high school grade point average and the level attained on an aptitude test outperformed the judgments of admissions officers at several colleges.

Robyn Dawes, in his book *House of Cards: Psychology and Psychotherapy Built on Myth,* tells us more. He refers to Jack Sawyer, a researcher who published a review of 45 studies comparing the two forecasting techniques: In *none* was the clinical, intuitive method—the one favored by most people—found to be superior. What's more, Sawyer included instances where the human judges had more information than the model *and* were given the results of the quantitative models *before* being asked for a prediction. *The human judges still failed to beat the actuarial models.*

Psychology researcher L. R. Goldberg went further. He devised a simple model based on the results of the Minnesota Multiphasic Personality Inventory (MMPI), a personality test commonly used to distinguish between neurosis and psychosis, to determine into which category a patient falls. His test achieved a success rate of 70 percent. He found that no human experts could match his model's results. The *best* judge achieved an overall success rate of 67 percent. Reasoning that his human judges might do better with practice, Goldberg gave training packets consisting of 300 additional MMPI profiles to his judges along with immediate feedback on their accuracy. Even after the practice sessions, *none* of the human judges matched the model's success rate of 70 percent.

What's the Problem?

The problem doesn't seem to be lack of insight on the part of human judges. One study of pathologists predicting survival time following the initial diagnosis of Hodgkin's disease, a form of cancer, found that the human judges were vastly outperformed by a simple actuarial formula. Oddly, the model used criteria that the judges *said* were predictive to outperform them. *The judges were largely unable to use their own ideas properly.* They used perceptive, intelligent criteria, but were unable to take advantage of their predictive ability. The judges themselves, not the value of their insights, accounted for the dismal predictive performance.

Why Models Beat Humans

In a famous cartoon, Pogo says: "We've met the enemy, and he is us." This illustrates our dilemma. Models beat human forecasters because they reliably and consistently apply the same criteria time after time. In almost every instance, *it is the total reliability of application of the model that accounts for its superior performance.* Models never vary. They are always consistent. They are never moody, never fight with their spouse, are never hung over from a night on the town, and never get bored. They don't favor vivid, interesting stories over reams of statistical data. They never take anything personally. They don't have egos. They're not out to prove anything. If they were people, they'd be the death of any party.

People, on the other hand, are far more interesting. It's more natural to react emotionally or personalize a problem than it is to dispassionately review broad statistical occurrences—and so much more fun! We are a bundle of inconsistencies, and although they make us interesting, they play havoc with our ability to invest our money successfully. In most instances, money managers, like the college administrators, doctors, and accountants mentioned above, favor the intuitive method of forecasting. They all follow the same path: Analyze the company, interview the management, talk to customers and competitors, and so forth. *All* of them think they have superior insights, intelligence, and ability to pick winning stocks, yet 80 percent are routinely outperformed by the S&P 500.

Base Rates Are Boring

The majority of investors, as well as *anyone else using traditional, intuitive forecasting methods,* are overwhelmed by their human nature. They use information unreliably, one time including a stock in a portfolio and another time excluding it, even though in each instance the information is the same. Human decision making is systematically flawed because we prefer gut reactions and individual, colorful stories to boring base rates. Base rates are among the most illuminating statistics that exist. They're just like batting averages. For example, if a town of 100,000 people has 70,000 lawyers and 30,000 librarians, the base rate for lawyers in that town is 70 percent. When used in the stock market, base rates tell you what to expect from a certain *class* of stocks (e.g., all stocks with high dividend yields) and what that variable *generally* predicts for the future. But base rates tell you *nothing* about how each *individual* member of that class will behave.

Most statistical prediction techniques use base rates. For example, 75 percent of students with grade point averages above 3.5 go on to do well in graduate school. Smokers are twice as likely to get cancer. Stocks with low price-to-earnings ratios outperform the market 65 percent of the time. The best way to predict the future is to bet with the base rate that is derived from a large sample. Yet numerous studies have found that people make full use of base rate information *only* when there is a lack of descriptive data. In one example, people are told that out of a sample of 100 people, 70 are lawyers and 30 are engineers. When provided with no additional information and asked to guess the occupation of a randomly selected 10, people use the base rate information, saying 7 are lawyers and 3 are engineers.

However, when worthless yet descriptive data are added, such as "Dick is a highly motivated 30-year-old married man who is well liked by his colleagues," people largely *ignore* the base rate information in favor of their "feel" for the person. They are *certain* that their unique insights will help them make a better forecast, even when the additional information is meaningless. We prefer descriptive data to impersonal statistics because they better represent our individual experience. When stereotypical information is added, such as "Dick is 30 years old and married, shows no interest in politics or social issues, and likes to spend free time on his many hobbies, which include carpentry and mathematical puzzles," people *totally* ignore the base rate and bet Dick is an engineer, despite the 70 percent chance that he is a lawyer.

It's difficult to blame people. Base rates are boring; experience is vivid and fun. The only way anyone will pay 100 times a company's earnings for a stock is if it's got a tremendous story. Never mind that stocks with high price-to-earnings ratios beat the market just 35 percent of the time over the last 45 years—the story is so compelling you're happy to throw the base rates out the window.

The Individual Versus the Group

Human nature makes it virtually impossible to forgo the specific information of an individual case in favor of the results of a great number of cases. We're interested in *this stock* and *this company*, not with this class of stocks or this class of companies. Large numbers mean nothing to us. As Stalin chillingly said: "One death is a tragedy, a million, a statistic." When making an investment, we almost always do so on a stock-by-stock basis, rarely thinking about an overall strategy. If a story about *one* stock is compelling enough, we're willing to ignore what the base rate tells us about an entire class of stocks.

Imagine if the insurance industry made decisions on a case-by-case basis. An agent visits you at home, interviews you, checks out your spouse and children, finally making a judgment on the basis of *gut feelings*. How many people who should get coverage would be denied and how many millions of dollars in premiums would be lost? The reverse is also true. Someone who should be denied might be extended cover-age because the agent's gut feeling was *this* individual is different, despite what actuarial tests say. The company would lose millions in additional payouts.

The same thing happens when we think in terms of individual stocks, rather than strategies. A case-by-case approach wreaks havoc with returns, since it virtually guarantees that we will base many of our choices on emotions. This is a highly unreliable, unsystematic way to buy stocks, yet it's the most natural and the most common.

Personal Experience Preferred

We always place more reliance on personal experience than impersonal base rates. An excellent example is the 1972 presidential campaign. The reporters on the campaign trail with George McGovern unanimously agreed that he could not lose by more than 10 percent, even though they knew he lagged 20 percent in the polls and that no major poll had been wrong by more than 3 percent in 24 years. These tough, intelligent people bet against the base rate because the concrete evidence of their personal experience overwhelmed them. They saw huge crowds of supporters, felt their enthusiasm, and trusted their feelings. In much the same way, a market analyst who has visited a company and knows the president may ignore the statistical information that says the company is a poor investment. In social science terms, the analyst is over-weighting the vivid and underweighting the pallid statistics.

Simple Versus Complex

We also prefer the complex and artificial to the simple and unadorned. We are certain that investment success requires an incredibly complex ability to judge a host of variables correctly and then act upon that knowledge.

Professor Alex Bavelas has designed a fascinating experiment in which two subjects, Smith and Jones, face individual projection screens. They cannot see or communicate with each other. They're told that the purpose of the experiment is to learn to recognize the difference between healthy and sick cells. They must learn to distinguish between the two using trial and error. In front of each are two buttons marked Healthy and Sick, along with two signal lights marked Right and Wrong. Every time a slide is projected, they guess if it's healthy or sick by pressing the button so marked. After they guess, their signal light will flash Right or Wrong, informing them if they have guessed correctly.

Here's the hitch. Smith gets true feedback. If he's correct, his light flashes Right; if he's wrong, it flashes Wrong. Since he's getting true feedback, Smith soon gets around 80 percent correct; it's a matter of simple discrimination.

Jones' situation is entirely different. He doesn't get true feedback on his guesses. Rather, the feedback he gets is based on Smith's guesses! It doesn't matter if he's right or wrong about a particular slide; he's told he's right if Smith guessed right and wrong if Smith guessed wrong. Of course, Jones doesn't know this. He's been told there is a true order that he can discover from the feedback. He ends up searching for order when there is no way to find it.

The moderator then asks Smith and Jones to discuss the rules they use for judging healthy and sick cells. Smith, who got true feedback, offers rules that are simple, concrete, and to the point. Jones uses rules that are, out of necessity, subtle, complex, and highly adorned. After all, he had to base his opinions on contradictory guesses and hunches.

The amazing thing is that Smith doesn't think Jones' explanations are absurd, crazy, or unnecessarily complicated. He's impressed by the "brilliance" of Jones' method and feels inferior and vulnerable because of the pedestrian simplicity of his own rules. The more complicated and ornate Jones' explanations, *the more likely they are to convince Smith.*

Before the next test with new slides, the two are asked to guess who will do better than the first time around. All Joneses and most Smiths say that Jones will. In fact, Jones shows no improvement at all. Smith, on the other hand, does significantly worse than he did the first time around, since he's now making guesses using some of the complicated rules he learned from Jones.

A Simple Solution

William of Ockham, a fourteenth-century Franciscan monk from the village of Ockham in Surrey, England, developed the "principle of parsimony," now called Ockham's Razor. For centuries it has been a guiding principle of modern science. Its axioms—such as "What can be done with fewer assumptions is done in vain with more" and "Entities are not to be multiplied without necessity"—boil down to this: Keep it simple, sweetheart. Ockham's Razor shows that most often the simplest theory is the best.

This is also the key to successful investing. However, successful investing runs contrary to human nature. We make the simple complex, follow the crowd, fall in love with the story about some stock, let our emotions dictate decisions, buy and sell on tips and hunches and approach each investment decision on a case-by-case basis, with no underlying consistency or strategy. When making decisions, we view everything in the present tense. And since we time-weight information, we give the most recent the greatest import. It's extremely difficult *not* to make decisions this way. Think about the last time you really goofed. Time passes and you say: "What was I thinking! It's so obvious that I was wrong. Why didn't I see it?" The mistake becomes obvious when you see the situation historically, drained of emotion and feeling. When the mistake was made, you had to contend with emotion. Emotion often wins, since as John Junor says, "An ounce of emotion is equal to a ton of facts."

This isn't a phenomenon reserved for the unsophisticated. Pension sponsors have access to the best research and talent that money can buy, yet they are notorious for investing heavily in stocks just as bear markets begin, and for firing managers at the absolute bottom of their cycle. Institutional investors *say* they make decisions objectively and unemotionally, but they don't. The authors of the book *Fortune & Folly* found that while institutional investor's desks are cluttered with in-depth, analytical reports, the majority of pension executives select outside managers using gut feelings and keep managers with consistently poor performance simply because they have good personal relationships with them.

The path to achieving investment success is to study long-term results and find a strategy or group of strategies that make sense. Remember to consider risk (the standard deviation of return) and choose a level that is acceptable. *Then stay on the path.*

To succeed, let history guide you. Successful investors look at history. They understand and react to the present in terms of the past. Yesterday and tomorrow, as well as today, make up their *now.* Something as simple as looking at a strategy's best and worst years is a good example. Knowing the potential parameters of a strategy gives investors a tremendous advantage over the uninformed. If the maximum expected loss is 35 percent, and the strategy is down 15 percent, instead of panicking, an informed investor can feel happy that things aren't as bad as they could be. This knowledge tempers expectations and emotions, giving informed investors a perspective that acts as an emotional pressure valve. Thinking historically, they let what they *know* transcend what they *feel.* This is the only way to perform well.

The data in this book give perspective. They help you understand that hills and valleys are part of every investment scheme and are to be expected, not feared. They tell you what to expect from various classes of stocks. Don't second-guess. Don't change your mind. Don't reject an individual stock—if it meets the criteria of your strategy—because you think it will do poorly. Don't try to outsmart. Looking over 45 years, you see that many strategies had periods where they didn't do as well as the S&P 500, but also had many that did much better. Understand, see the long-term, and let it work. If you do, you're chance of succeeding is very high. If you don't, no amount of knowledge will save you and you'll find yourself with the 80 percent of underperformers and thinking: "What went wrong?"

3
Rules of the Game

It is amazing to reflect how little systematic knowledge Wall Street has to draw upon as regards the historical behavior of securities with defined characteristics. We do, of course, have charts showing the long-term price movements of stock groups and individual stocks. But there is no real classification here, except by type of business. Where is the continuous, ever growing body of knowledge and technique handed down by the analysts of the past to those of the present and future? When we contrast the annals of medicine with those of finance, the paucity of our recorded and digested experience becomes a reproach. We lack the codified experience which will tell us whether codified experience is valuable or valueless. In the years to come we analysts must go to school to learn the older established disciplines. We must study their ways of amassing and scrutinizing facts and from this study develop methods of research suited to the peculiarities of our own field of work. —BEN GRAHAM
The father of securities analysis, 1946

We've made little progress since 1946. Many studies have found that smaller stocks (based on total market capitalization) do better than larger stocks; that stocks with low price-to-earnings ratios do better than stocks with high price-to-earnings ratios; that high-yielding stocks perform well; and so on. Yet the time periods covered by most studies remains a reproach to the money management industry. Many tests are flawlessly designed, especially after criticism of early studies sent researchers back to the drawing board to design more rigorous procedures. In almost every instance, researchers seem to have followed carefully thought out, reasonable plans. However, the time covered in most studies is far too short to reach reasonable conclusions. Many studies cover as little as three to five years, and many researchers believe a five-year track record is sufficient to judge a manager's abilities. But like Alexander Pope's maxim that a little learning is a dangerous thing, too little time gives investors extremely misleading information. One respected researcher estimated that to make reasonable assumptions about a strategy's validity (i.e., to assume it was 95 percent likely to be statistically relevant), you would need more than 25 years of data.

Short Periods Are Valueless

Consider the Soaring Sixties. The go-go growth managers of the era switched stocks so fast they were called gunslingers. Performance was the name of the game, and buying stocks with outstanding earnings growth was the way to achieve it.

Now look at how misleading a five-year period can be. Between December 31, 1963 and December 31, 1968, $10,000 invested in a portfolio which annually bought the 50 stocks in the Compustat database with the best one-year earnings-per-share percentage gains soared to almost $35,000 in value, a compound return of better than 28 percent a year. That more than doubled the S&P 500's 10.16 percent annual return, which saw $10,000 grow to just over $16,000. Unfortunately, the strategy didn't fare so well over the next five years. It went on to *lose* over half its value between 1968 and 1973, compared with a gain of 2 percent for the S&P 500.

It's Different This Time

People want to believe the present is different from the past. Markets are now computerized, block traders dominate, individual investors are gone, and in their place sit huge mutual funds to which they have given their money. Some people think these masters of money make decisions differently, and believe that looking at how a strategy performed in the 1950s or 1960s offers little insight into how it will perform in the future.

But not much has really changed since Isaac Newton—a brilliant man, indeed—lost a fortune in the South Sea Trading Company bubble of 1720. Newton lamented that he could "calculate the motions of heavenly bodies but not the madness of men." Herein lies the key to why basing investment decisions on long-term results is vital: The price of a stock is still determined by *people*. And as long as people let fear, greed, hope, and ignorance cloud their judgment, they will continue to misprice stocks and provide opportunities to those who rigorously use simple, time-tested strategies to pick stocks. Newton lost his money because he let himself get caught up in the hoopla of the moment and invested on the basis of a colorful story rather than the facts. Names change. Industries change. Styles come in and out of fashion, but the underlying characteristics that identify a good or bad investment remain the same. A long view of returns is essential, because only the fullness of time uncovers basic relationships that short-term gyrations conceal. It also lets us analyze how the market responds to a large number of events, such as inflation, stock market crashes, stagflation, recessions, wars, and new discoveries. From the past the future flows. History never repeats *exactly*, but the same *types* of events continue to occur.

Anecdotal Evidence Is Not Enough

Investment advice bombards us from many directions with little to support it but anecdotal accounts. Many managers will give a handful of stocks as examples, demonstrating how well they went on to perform. Unfortunately, these managers conveniently ignore the many *other stocks* that also possessed the preferred characteristics but *failed*. We must look at how well *strategies*, not stocks, perform. There's often a chasm of difference between what we think might work and what really works. This book's goal is to bring a more methodical, scientific method to stock market decisions and portfolio construction. To do this, I have tried to stay true to those scientific rules that distinguish a method from a less rigorous model. Here are some of them.

An Explicit Method.   All models must use explicitly stated rules. There must be no ambiguity in the statement of the rule to be tested. There is no allowance for a private or unique interpretation of the rule.

A Public Rule.   The rule must be stated explicitly and publicly so anyone with the time, money, data, equipment, and inclination can reproduce the results. The rule must make sense and must not be derived from the data.

A Reliable Method.   Someone using the same rules and the same database must get the same results. Also, the results must be consistent over time. Long-term results cannot owe all their benefit to a few years.

An Objective Rule.   I have attempted to use only rules that are intuitive and logical and that appeal to sensibility, but in all cases the rules
are objective. They are independent of the social position, financial sta-
tus, and cultural background of the investigator and do not require
superior insight, information, or interpretation.

A Reliable Database.   There are many problems with back testing,
and the quality of data is the top concern. *All* large collections of historical data contain many errors. A review of Standard & Poor's
Compustat Active and Research database reveals that the data are
remarkably clean. Nevertheless, problems remain. Undoubtedly, the
database contains stocks for which a split was unaccounted for, a bad
book value persisted for several years, earnings were misstated and
went uncorrected, a price was inverted from 31 to 13, and so on. These
problems will be present for *any* test of stock market methods and must
not be discounted, especially when a method shows just a slight advantage over the market in general.

Potential Pitfalls

Many studies of Wall Street's favorite investment methods have been
seriously flawed. Among their problems:

Data Mining.   It takes approximately 40 minutes for an express train
to go from Greenwich, Connecticut, to Grand Central Station in
Manhattan. In that time, you could look around your car and find all
sorts of statistically relevant characteristics about your fellow passen-
gers. Perhaps there are a huge number of blondes, or 75 percent have
blue eyes, or the majority were born in May. These relationships, however, are most likely the result of chance occurrences and probably
wouldn't be true for the car in front of or behind you. When you went
looking for these relationships, you went data mining. You've found a
statistical relationship that fits *one set of data very well, but will not trans-
late to another.* If you torture the data long enough, they will confess to
anything. If there is no sound theoretical or commonsense reason for
the relationship, it's most likely a chance occurrence. Thus, if you see
strategies that require you to buy stocks only on a Wednesday and hold
them for $16\frac{1}{2}$ months, you're looking at the results of data mining.

A Limited Time Period.   *Anything* can look good for 5 to 10 years.
There are innumerable strategies that look great during some time periods but perform horribly over the long term. Even zany strategies can

work in any given year. For example, a portfolio of stocks with ticker symbols that are vowels—A, E, I, O, U, and Y—beat the S&P 500 by more than 11 percent in 1996, but that doesn't make vowel selection a good strategy! It simply means that in 1996, chance led the portfolio to outperform the S&P 500. The longer the time period studied, the greater the chance a strategy will continue to work in the future. Statistically, you will always have greater confidence in results derived from large samples than in those derived from small ones.

Microcapitalization Stocks Allowed. Many studies are deeply flawed because they include tiny stocks that are nearly impossible to buy. Take stocks with a market capitalization below $25 million. During the 45 years of our study, $10,000 invested in all the stocks in the Compustat database with a market capitalization below $25 million would have grown to over $806 million dollars! Unfortunately, no one can realistically *buy* these stocks at the reported prices. They possess virtually no trading liquidity, and a large order would send their prices skyrocketing. O'Shaughnessy Capital Management commissioned Lehman Brothers to do a liquidity study of all the stocks in the Compustat with market capitalizations below $25 million in the first quarter of 1997. They found that the majority of the issues had virtually no trading volume and that the difference between the bid and the asked price was many times more than 100 percent! More, the trading costs incurred, even if the stocks could be bought, would be enormous.

Most academic studies define small capitalization stocks as those making up the fifth (smallest) market capitalization quintile of the New York Stock Exchange. Yet many of these stocks are *impossible* to trade. Indeed, on September 30, 1997, the median market cap of the 514 mutual funds in Morningstar's all-equity, small cap category was $860 million! Only 7 had median market caps below $100 million dollars, and of these, only 2 managed more than $100 million. Thus, while many small cap funds use academic studies to support their methods, no fund can manage to buy the stocks that fuel their superior performance.

Look at how a strategy's performance is affected by different levels of market capitalization. Consider 1967, a time of "go-go" growth stock investing. Had you bought the 50 stocks with the best one-year earnings-per-share gains for the previous year, the returns by market capitalization would be as follows:

- Capitalization greater than $1 million (almost all stocks in the database): +121.3 percent
- Capitalization greater than database median (the upper half of stocks in the database): +83.9 percent

■ Capitalization greater than database average (largest 16 percent): +29.6 percent

Survivorship Bias, or Then It Was There, Now It's Thin Air. Many studies don't include stocks that fail, producing an upward bias to their results. Numerous companies disappear from the database because of bankruptcy, or more brightly, takeover. While most newer studies include a research file made up of delisted stocks, many early ones did not.

Look-Ahead Bias, or Hindsight Better Than 20/20. Many studies assume that fundamental information is available when it is not. For example, researchers often assume you had annual earnings data in January; in reality the data might not be available until March. This upwardly biases results.

Rules of the Game

I have attempted to correct the above problems by using the following methodology.

Universe. Our universe is the Standard & Poor's Compustat Active and Research database from 1951 through 1996. This 45 years of data is, to my knowledge, the longest period ever used to study a variety of popular investment strategies. I cannot overstate the importance of it. Any study from the early 1970s to the early 1980s will find strong results for value investing, just as any study from the 1960s will favor growth stocks. Styles come in and out of fashion on Wall Street, so the longer the time period studied, the more illuminating the results. From a statistical viewpoint, the strangest results come from the smallest samples. Large samples always provide better conclusions than small ones. Some pension consultants use a branch of statistics called *reliability mathematics* to predict future performance from past returns. They've found that 14 periods are needed as a minimum even to *begin* making accurate predictions about the future.

To avoid *survivorship bias*, Compustat's research file includes stocks originally listed in the database but removed because of merger, bankruptcy, or other reason. Most of the models tested were developed by my firm, O'Shaughnessy Capital Management, Inc., between 1994 and 1995. Thus, the period 1950–1993 serves as the time when no modifications were made on any of the strategies. This is what other studies call the *out-of-sample* holdout period.

Market Capitalization. Except for specific small capitalization tests, I review stocks from two distinct groups. The first includes only stocks with market capitalizations in excess of $150 million (adjusted for inflation), called All Stocks throughout the book. Table 3-1 shows how I created the deflated minimums. We'll use the $150 million number until the next update of the book, when the inflation figures will be adjusted upward. The second includes larger, better-known stocks with market capitalizations greater than the database average (usually the top 16 percent of the database by market capitalization). These larger stocks are called Large Stocks throughout the book. Table 3-2 shows the number of stocks with market capitalizations above the database mean. In all cases, I removed the smallest stocks in the database from consideration. For example, at the end of 1996 more than 4400 stocks were jettisoned because their market capitalization fell below an inflation-adjusted minimum of $150 million. In the same year, only 1202 stocks had market capitalizations exceeding the database average.

I chose the $150 million value after consulting traders at several large Wall Street brokerages. They felt it was the minimum necessary for investing $100 million in 50 stocks in 1995, when I wrote the first edition of this book. I use this figure to avoid tiny stocks and to focus only on those stocks that a professional investor could buy without running into liquidity problems. Inflation has taken its toll: A stock with a market capitalization of $27 million in 1950 is the equivalent of a $150 million stock at the end of 1994.

Avoiding Look-Ahead Bias. I use only publicly available, annual information. For the period 1951–1994, I also time-lag the data by a minimum of 11 months so that only data available at the time the portfolio was constructed are used. While 11 months may seem excessive, it conforms to what you would find using the current database on an annual basis. From 1994 on, the results shown are for real-time portfolios, so no time lagging is required. For this and subsequent revisions of the book, I will use the actual portfolio that the strategy selected as of December 31 of each year.

One potential problem with the earlier data is the changing nature of the Compustat database. As Figure 3-1 shows, Standard & Poor's has continually expanded the database. Many smaller stocks have been added, including up to five years of retroactive data. And since these firms were usually added *because* they were successful, the likelihood of a look-ahead bias becomes a real concern. Though *What Works on Wall Street* may suffer from this bias, the problem is greatly diminished with the smallest stocks eliminated from consideration.

Table 3-1. Inflation-adjusted Value of $150 Million in Each Year with the Five-Year Averages Used as Minimums

Year ending	Inflation-adjustment factor	Value of $150 million	Average from previous five years
31-Dec-52	5.60	$26,763,261.88	
31-Dec-53	5.57	$26,924,919.17	
31-Dec-54	5.60	$26,799,185.73	$26,829,122.26
31-Dec-55	5.58	$26,888,995.33	
31-Dec-56	5.42	$27,661,357.92	
31-Dec-57	5.26	$28,505,568.20	
31-Dec-58	5.17	$29,008,501.98	
31-Dec-59	5.10	$29,439,588.07	$28,300,802.30
31-Dec-60	5.02	$29,870,674.17	
31-Dec-61	4.99	$30,068,255.30	
31-Dec-62	4.93	$30,445,455.63	
31-Dec-63	4.85	$30,948,389.41	
31-Dec-64	4.79	$31,307,627.83	$30,528,080.47
31-Dec-65	4.70	$31,918,333.13	
31-Dec-66	4.55	$32,978,086.46	
31-Dec-67	4.41	$33,983,954.02	
31-Dec-68	4.22	$35,582,564.96	
31-Dec-69	3.97	$37,755,957.37	$34,443,779.19
31-Dec-70	3.77	$39,839,540.17	
31-Dec-71	3.64	$41,168,722.31	
31-Dec-72	3.52	$42,587,714.05	
31-Dec-73	3.24	$46,323,793.56	
31-Dec-74	2.89	$51,981,798.59	$44,380,313.73
31-Dec-75	2.70	$55,628,068.49	
31-Dec-76	2.57	$58,304,394.68	
31-Dec-77	2.41	$62,256,017.24	
31-Dec-78	2.21	$67,860,136.51	
31-Dec-79	1.95	$76,894,982.64	$64,188,719.91
31-Dec-80	1.74	$86,432,762.54	
31-Dec-81	1.59	$94,156,388.46	
31-Dec-82	1.53	$97,802,658.36	
31-Dec-83	1.48	$101,520,775.95	
31-Dec-84	1.42	$105,526,284.28	$97,087,773.92
31-Dec-85	1.37	$109,513,830.68	
31-Dec-86	1.35	$110,753,203.21	
31-Dec-87	1.30	$115,638,845.65	
31-Dec-88	1.24	$120,740,031.13	
31-Dec-89	1.19	$126,344,150.40	$116,598,012.21
31-Dec-90	1.12	$134,067,776.31	
31-Dec-91	1.09	$138,181,056.16	
31-Dec-92	1.05	$142,186,564.48	
31-Dec-93	1.03	$146,084,301.28	
31-Dec-94	1.00	$150,000,000.00	$150,000,000.00
31-Dec-95	1.00	$150,000,000.00	
31-Dec-96*	1.00	$150,000,000.00	

*Inflation adjustment will move up in 1998.

Table 3-2. Large Stocks as a Percentage of Compustat, 1952–1996

Year ending	Number of stocks with market capitalization above database mean	Number of stocks in database	Percent
31-Dec-52	110	560	20%
31-Dec-53	137	581	24%
31-Dec-54	153	629	24%
31-Dec-55	147	657	22%
31-Dec-56	136	682	20%
31-Dec-57	141	692	20%
31-Dec-58	148	797	19%
31-Dec-59	160	860	19%
31-Dec-60	177	1447	12%
31-Dec-61	220	1622	14%
31-Dec-62	300	1792	17%
31-Dec-63	272	1986	14%
31-Dec-64	342	2136	16%
31-Dec-65	377	2351	16%
31-Dec-66	402	2487	16%
31-Dec-67	430	2698	16%
31-Dec-68	479	2969	16%
31-Dec-69	525	3132	17%
31-Dec-70	539	3155	17%
31-Dec-71	541	3414	16%
31-Dec-72	580	3684	16%
31-Dec-73	589	3639	16%
31-Dec-74	584	3644	16%
31-Dec-75	544	3695	15%
31-Dec-76	599	3832	16%
31-Dec-77	635	3852	16%
31-Dec-78	667	3980	17%
31-Dec-79	670	4262	16%
31-Dec-80	739	4478	17%
31-Dec-81	712	4917	14%
31-Dec-82	814	5030	16%
31-Dec-83	830	5531	15%
31-Dec-84	868	5476	16%
31-Dec-85	833	5537	15%
31-Dec-86	860	5992	14%
31-Dec-87	842	6130	14%
31-Dec-88	830	6009	14%
31-Dec-89	842	5877	14%
31-Dec-90	833	5457	15%
31-Dec-91	806	5891	14%
31-Dec-92	845	6554	13%
31-Dec-93	947	7312	13%
31-Dec-94	1008	7919	13%
31-Dec-95	1158	8718	13%
31-Dec-96	1214	9326	13%
Average	540	3566	16%

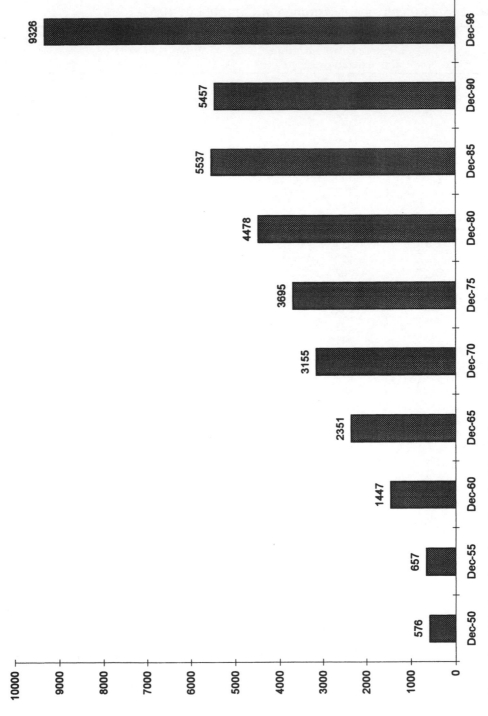

Figure 3-1. Number of stocks in Standard Poor's Compustat Universe, 1950–1996.

Annual Rebalance with Risk-Adjusted Figures.   I construct and rebalance portfolios annually. Stocks are equally weighted with no adjustments for beta, industry, or other variables. Foreign stocks included in the Compustat Universe are allowed. Because of data limitations, I was forced to add dividend returns to capital appreciation to arrive at a total return for the year. This results in a slight understatement of the compounding effect of dividend reinvestment. From 1994 on, real-time results are used and the results reflect total returns, with full dividend reinvestment.

The assumption that no trades are made throughout the year may bias my results slightly, since it rewards trade-averse strategies, but I believe many excellent strategies that require numerous trades turn mediocre once trading costs are included. I also examined annual returns and removed stocks with extreme returns or data that were inconsistent with outside information.

I also compare absolute and risk-adjusted returns. Risk-adjusted returns take the volatility of a portfolio—as measured by the standard deviation of return—into account when considering absolute returns. Generally, investors prefer a portfolio earning 15 percent a year with a standard deviation of 20 percent to one earning 16 percent a year with a standard deviation of 30 percent. A 1 percent absolute advantage doesn't compensate for the terror of the wild ride. I use the well-known Sharpe ratio of reward to risk for my calculations, with higher numbers indicating better risk-adjusted returns. To arrive at the Sharpe ratio, simply take the average return from a strategy, subtract the risk-free rate of interest, and then divide that number by the standard deviation of return. The ratio is important because it reflects risk. The strategy in Table 3-3, for example, had a higher *absolute* return than the S&P 500 but a *lower* risk-adjusted return because it was much more volatile.

Minimum and Maximum Expected Returns.   Also, in all summary information about a strategy, I provide the maximum and minimum projected returns, as well as the actual maximum and minimum over the past 45 years. This is *extremely* useful information, since investors can glance at the worst loss and decide if they can stomach the volatility of any particular strategy.

50 Stock Portfolios.   Except for Chapter 4, which reviews returns by market capitalization, all portfolios contain 50 stocks. A cursory review of private and institutional money managers reveals that 50 stocks are a common portfolio minimum. Many of the popular averages, such as the S&P 500, use more, yet many, such as the Dow Jones Industrial Average and Barron's 50 stock average, use the same or less. Next, I considered

Table 3-3. Determining a Strategy's Risk-adjusted Return

Year ending	S&P 500	Strategy	T-bills	S&P 500 T-bills	Strategy T-bills
31-Dec-86	18.47%	27.00%	5.98%	12.49%	21.02%
31-Dec-87	5.23%	10.50%	5.78%	−0.55%	4.73%
31-Dec-88	16.81%	7.00%	6.67%	10.14%	0.33%
31-Dec-89	31.49%	36.50%	8.11%	23.38%	28.39%
31-Dec-90	−3.17%	−10.90%	7.49%	−10.66%	−18.39%
31-Dec-91	30.55%	63.90%	5.38%	25.18%	58.53%
31-Dec-92	7.67%	0.70%	3.43%	4.24%	−2.73%
31-Dec-93	9.99%	44.10%	3.00%	6.99%	41.10%
31-Dec-94	1.31%	−4.20%	4.25%	−2.94%	−8.45%
31-Dec-95	37.43%	25.00%	5.49%	31.94%	19.51%
31-Dec-96	23.07%	18.60%	5.21%	17.86%	13.39%
Average	16.26%	19.84%	5.53%	10.73%	14.31%
Standard deviation	12.69%	21.38%	1.50%	12.43%	21.55%

Risk-adjusted return for the S&P 500 equals 10.73% divided by 12.69%, or 84.55.
Risk-adjusted return for the strategy equals 14.31% divided by 21.38%, or 66.93.

the benefits of diversification. Researchers Gerald Newbould and Percy Poon, professors of finance at the University of Nevada, studied the effect that the number of stocks held in a portfolio has on overall volatility and total return. They found that holding between 8 and 20 stocks—a common recommendation—wasn't nearly enough to diversify a portfolio adequately. Rather, they found that to be within 20 percent of the commonly quoted risk-and-reward figures, you have to expand the number of stocks you own to at least 25. And if your portfolio contains smaller capitalization stocks, you should hold 50 or more names.

With this edition, we'll also include information on the returns to various ratios by decile.

Discipline. I test investment disciplines, not trading strategies. My results show that U.S. equity markets are not perfectly efficient. Investors *can* outperform the market by sticking with superior strategies over long periods. Simple, disciplined strategies—such as buying the top 10-yielding stocks in the Dow Jones Industrial Average—have worked over the last 69 years because they are immune to the emotions of the market and *force* investors to buy industrial stocks when the companies are under distress. No one *wants* to buy Union Carbide after Bhopal or Exxon after the Valdez oil spill, yet it is precisely these times that offer the best buys.

Costs. Transaction costs are not included. Each reader faces different transaction costs. Institutional investors making million-dollar trades face substantially different costs than individual, odd-lot traders. Thus, each group will be able to review raw data and remove whatever costs fit its situation.

Since the first edition of this book was published, however, on-line brokers have seriously reduced the transaction costs that individual investors pay for trading stocks. In many instances, an individual can now trade any number of shares for a flat $12 commission. The change makes buying a large number of stocks a far more realistic idea for individual investors, since they now face costs similar to those of large institutional investors.

Now let's look at the tests. We'll start with a review of returns by market capitalization and then look at returns by single and multifactor combinations.

4

Ranking Stocks by Market Capitalization: Size Matters

*Order and simplification are the first steps
toward the mastery of a subject.*
—THOMAS MANN

First, we'll look at the returns from our two universes of stocks based on market capitalization to establish a base rate for comparison with all other strategies. All Stocks are those with market capitalizations in excess of a deflated $150 million. Large Stocks are those with a market capitalization greater than the Compustat database average (usually the top 16 percent of the database by market capitalization). In each case, we start with a $10,000 investment on December 31, 1951 and rebalance the portfolio annually. As with all our tests, the stocks are equally weighted, all dividends are reinvested, and all variables such as common shares outstanding are time-lagged to avoid look-ahead bias. Figure 4-1 shows the results. As mentioned in Chapter 1, there is virtually no difference between stocks with market capitalizations above the Compustat mean (Large Stocks) and the S&P 500. Remember that $10,000 invested in the S&P 500 on December 31, 1951 was worth

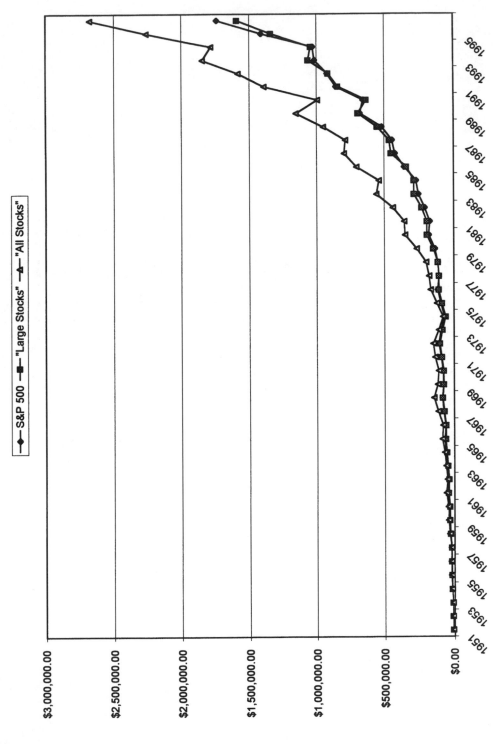

Figure 4-1. Total return by universe, 1951–1996. Year-end 1951 = $10,000.

$1,738,417 on December 31, 1996 and $1,590,667 if invested in the Large Stocks group. The result is not surprising, since investing in the S&P 500 is nothing more than a bet on big, well-known stocks. Table 4-1 shows the annual returns for each universe.

An investment in the All Stocks group did considerably better: $10,000 grew to $2,677,557. The performance was not without bumps, however, as Table 4-2 shows. There were several times when All Stocks significantly outperformed Large Stocks and other times where the reverse was true. Large Stocks did quite a bit worse than All Stocks between December 31, 1975 and December 31, 1983, only to turn around and do somewhat better between December 31, 1984 and December 31, 1990. The All Stocks universe also had a higher standard deviation of return than the Large Stocks universe.

Looking at returns for rolling 5- and 10-year periods to establish a base rate, we see that All Stocks outperformed Large Stocks in 30 of the 41 rolling 5-year periods, or 73 percent of the time. All Stocks also outperformed Large Stocks in 27 of the 36 rolling 10-year periods, or 75 percent of the time. The returns show that you're better off fishing in the larger pond of All Stocks than exclusively buying large, well-known stocks. Table 4-3 summarizes the results and Table 4-4 shows returns by decade.

How Much Better?

Most academic studies of market capitalization sort stocks by deciles (10 percent) and review how an investment in each fares over time. The studies are nearly unanimous in their findings that small stocks (those in the lowest four deciles) do significantly better than large ones. We too have found tremendous returns from tiny stocks.

The glaring problem with this method is that it's virtually impossible to *buy* the stocks that account for the performance advantage of small capitalization strategies. Table 4-5 illustrates the problem. On December 31, 1996, there were approximately 7260 stocks in the active Compustat database that had both year-end prices and a number for common shares outstanding. If we sorted the database by decile, each decile would be made up of 726 stocks. As Table 4-5 shows, market capitalization doesn't get past $150 million until decile 6! The top market capitalization in the fourth decile is $57 million, a number far too small to allow widespread buying of those stocks. This presents an interesting paradox: Small cap mutual funds justify their investments with academic research showing small stocks outperforming large ones, yet the funds themselves cannot buy the stocks that provide the lion's share of performance because of a lack of trading liquidity.

Table 4-1. Annual Returns for Stocks with Market Capitalizations Above the Compustat Mean (Large Stocks) and Those with Capitalizations Above a Deflated $150 Million (All Stocks)

Year ending	S&P 500	Capitalization > mean Large Stocks	Capitalization > deflated $150m All Stocks
31-Dec-52	18.37%	9.30%	7.90%
31-Dec-53	−0.99%	2.30%	2.90%
31-Dec-54	52.62%	44.90%	47.00%
31-Dec-55	31.56%	21.20%	20.70%
31-Dec-56	6.56%	9.60%	17.00%
31-Dec-57	−10.78%	−6.90%	−7.10%
31-Dec-58	43.36%	42.10%	55.00%
31-Dec-59	11.96%	9.90%	23.00%
31-Dec-60	0.47%	4.80%	6.10%
31-Dec-61	26.89%	27.50%	31.20%
31-Dec-62	−8.73%	−8.90%	−12.00%
31-Dec-63	22.80%	19.50%	18.00%
31-Dec-64	16.48%	15.30%	16.30%
31-Dec-65	12.45%	16.20%	22.60%
31-Dec-66	−10.06%	−4.90%	−5.20%
31-Dec-67	23.98%	21.30%	41.10%
31-Dec-68	11.06%	16.80%	27.40%
31-Dec-69	−8.50%	−9.90%	−18.50%
31-Dec-70	4.01%	−0.20%	−5.80%
31-Dec-71	14.31%	17.30%	21.30%
31-Dec-72	18.98%	14.90%	11.00%
31-Dec-73	−14.66%	−18.90%	−27.20%
31-Dec-74	−26.47%	−26.70%	−27.90%
31-Dec-75	37.20%	43.10%	55.90%
31-Dec-76	23.84%	28.00%	35.60%
31-Dec-77	−7.18%	−2.50%	6.90%
31-Dec-78	6.56%	8.10%	12.20%
31-Dec-79	18.44%	27.30%	34.30%
31-Dec-80	32.42%	30.80%	31.50%
31-Dec-81	−4.91%	0.60%	1.70%
31-Dec-82	21.41%	19.90%	22.50%
31-Dec-83	22.51%	23.80%	28.10%
31-Dec-84	6.27%	−0.40%	−3.40%
31-Dec-85	32.16%	19.50%	30.80%
31-Dec-86	18.47%	32.20%	13.10%
31-Dec-87	5.23%	3.30%	−1.30%
31-Dec-88	16.81%	19.00%	21.20%
31-Dec-89	31.49%	26.00%	21.40%
31-Dec-90	−3.17%	−8.70%	−13.80%
31-Dec-91	30.55%	33.00%	39.80%
31-Dec-92	7.67%	8.70%	13.80%
31-Dec-93	9.99%	16.30%	16.60%
31-Dec-94	1.31%	−1.90%	−3.40%
31-Dec-95	37.43%	28.50%	27.00%
31-Dec-96	22.20%	18.70%	18.30%
Arithmetic average	13.39%	13.11%	14.97%
Standard deviation	16.65%	16.01%	19.51%

Table 4-2. Annual Performance of All Stocks Versus Large Stocks

Year ending	Large Stocks cap > mean	All Stocks cap > deflated $150m	All Stocks relative performance
31-Dec-52	9.30%	7.90%	−1.40%
31-Dec-53	2.30%	2.90%	0.60%
31-Dec-54	44.90%	47.00%	2.10%
31-Dec-55	21.20%	20.70%	−0.50%
31-Dec-56	9.60%	17.00%	7.40%
31-Dec-57	−6.90%	−7.10%	−0.20%
31-Dec-58	42.10%	55.00%	12.90%
31-Dec-59	9.90%	23.00%	13.10%
31-Dec-60	4.80%	6.10%	1.30%
31-Dec-61	27.50%	31.20%	3.70%
31-Dec-62	−8.90%	−12.00%	−3.10%
31-Dec-63	19.50%	18.00%	−1.50%
31-Dec-64	15.30%	16.30%	1.00%
31-Dec-65	16.20%	22.60%	6.40%
31-Dec-66	−4.90%	−5.20%	−0.30%
31-Dec-67	21.30%	41.10%	19.80%
31-Dec-68	16.80%	27.40%	10.60%
31-Dec-69	−9.90%	−18.50%	−8.60%
31-Dec-70	−0.20%	−5.80%	−5.60%
31-Dec-71	17.30%	21.30%	4.00%
31-Dec-72	14.90%	11.00%	−3.90%
31-Dec-73	−18.90%	−27.20%	−8.30%
31-Dec-74	−26.70%	−27.90%	−1.20%
31-Dec-75	43.10%	55.90%	12.80%
31-Dec-76	28.00%	35.60%	7.60%
31-Dec-77	−2.50%	6.90%	9.40%
31-Dec-78	8.10%	12.20%	4.10%
31-Dec-79	27.30%	34.30%	7.00%
31-Dec-80	30.80%	31.50%	0.70%
31-Dec-81	0.60%	1.70%	1.10%
31-Dec-82	19.90%	22.50%	2.60%
31-Dec-83	23.80%	28.10%	4.30%
31-Dec-84	−0.40%	−3.40%	−3.00%
31-Dec-85	19.50%	30.80%	11.30%
31-Dec-86	32.20%	13.10%	−19.10%
31-Dec-87	3.30%	−1.30%	−4.60%
31 Dcc 88	19.00%	21.20%	2.20%
31-Dec-89	26.00%	21.40%	−4.60%
31-Dec-90	−8.70%	−13.80%	−5.10%
31-Dec-91	33.00%	39.80%	6.80%
31-Dec-92	8.70%	13.80%	5.10%
31-Dec-93	16.30%	16.60%	0.30%
31-Dec-94	−1.90%	−3.40%	−1.50%
31-Dec-95	28.50%	27.00%	−1.50%
31-Dec-96	18.70%	18.30%	−0.40%
Arithmetic average	13.11%	14.97%	1.99%
Standard deviation	16.01%	19.51%	3.50%

Table 4-3. Summary Return Results, Large Stocks, All Stocks, and Standard
and Poor's 500, December 31, 1951–December 31, 1996

	S&P 500	Large Stocks Capitalization > mean	All Stocks Capitalization > deflated $150m
Arithmetic average	13.39%	13.11%	14.97%
Standard deviation of return	16.65%	16.01%	19.51%
Sharpe risk-adjusted ratio	48.00	48.00	49.00
3-yr compounded	19.38%	14.38%	13.22%
5-yr compounded	15.04%	13.60%	14.00%
10-yr compounded	15.20%	13.53%	12.92%
15-yr compounded	16.74%	15.16%	14.44%
20-yr compounded	14.51%	14.37%	14.97%
25-yr compounded	12.51%	12.34%	12.74%
30-yr compounded	11.82%	11.67%	12.43%
35-yr compounded	10.93%	10.96%	11.64%
40-yr compounded	11.16%	11.36%	12.62%
Compound annual return	12.15%	11.92%	13.23%
$10,000 becomes:	$1,726,128.00	$1,590,667.00	$2,677,557.00
Maximum return	52.62%	44.90%	55.90%
Minimum return	−26.47%	−26.70%	−27.90%
Maximum expected return*	46.69%	45.12%	53.98%
Minimum expected return**	−19.92%	−18.91%	−24.04%

*Maximum expected return is average return plus 2 times the standard deviation.
**Minimum expected return is average return minus 2 times the standard deviation.

Table 4-4. Compound Annual Rates of Return by Decade

Universe	1950s*	1960s	1970s	1980s	1990s**
S&P 500	17.33%	7.81%	5.86%	17.55%	14.41%
Large Stocks	15.33%	8.99%	6.99%	16.89%	12.61%
All Stocks	19.22%	11.09%	8.53%	15.85%	12.78%

*Returns for 1952–1959.
**Returns for 1990–1996.

Table 4-5. Compustat Database Sorted by Market
Capitalization Decile on December 31, 1996

Decile	Largest market capitalization of top stock
1	$5 million
2	$15 million
3	$31 million
4	$57 million
5	$94 million
6	$162 million
7	$296 million
8	$585 million
9	$1.7 billion
10	$163 billion

A review of the Morningstar Mutual Fund database proves this. On September 30, 1997, the median market capitalization of the 514 mutual funds in Morningstar's all-equity, small cap category was $860 million! That's right between decile 8 and 9 from the Compustat universe—hardly small. Only seven had median market capitalizations below $100 million dollars, and of these, only two managed more than $100 million.

Reviewing Stocks by Size

Rather than review stocks by decile, it's illuminating to review performance by grouping stocks in absolute size categories. This conforms to the way active managers look at stocks. They don't think about a stock being in the sixth decile; they think of it as a midcap stock.

Thus, I split up the universe by absolute market cap, adjusted for inflation:

- Capitalization less than $25 million
- Capitalization between $25 million and $100 million
- Capitalization between $100 million and $250 million
- Capitalization between $250 million and $500 million
- Capitalization between $500 million and $1 billion
- Capitalization above $1 billion

I also looked at two additional distinct groups of stocks: Small Stocks, or stocks that have market capitalizations greater than a deflated $150 million but less than the database average, and Market Leaders. Market Leaders are like Large Stocks on steroids. They come from the Large Stocks universe but also possess characteristics beyond mere size. To be a Market Leader, a company must be a nonutility stock with a market capitalization greater than the average, shares outstanding greater than the average, cashflow greater than the average, and finally sales 50 percent greater than the average stock. Applying these factors to the overall Compustat database leaves just 6 percent of the database qualifying as Market Leaders. The returns, shown in Figures 4-2 and 4-3, are stunning. Almost all the superior returns offered by small stocks come from microcap stocks with market capitalizations below $25 million. An investment of $10,000 in that group on December 31, 1951 soared to over $806 million in value, achieving a compound growth rate of over 28 percent for the 45 years reviewed! The microcap returns absolutely dwarf their nearest competitor, the $25 million to $100 million group. They even manage to overcome their breathtaking risk—an annual standard deviation of return of 47.53 percent—and land at the top of the risk-adjusted return index featured in Figure 4-4.

But the microcap stock's returns are a chimera. The only way to achieve these stellar returns is to invest a few million dollars in over 2000 stocks. Precious few investors can do that. The stocks are far too small for a mutual fund to buy and far too numerous for an individual to tackle. So there they sit, tantalizingly out of reach of nearly everyone. We commissioned Lehman Brothers to do a study of microcap liquidity in 1997. We gave them a list of the 1990 stocks from Compustat that had market capitalizations less than $25 million as of December 31, 1996. We asked them to do an analysis on trading patterns, bid and ask spreads, and other relevant information on how easy the stocks would be to trade. The results confirmed that these stocks are virtually untradable. In many instances, the difference between the bid, or what someone was willing to pay for a stock, and the ask, or what someone was willing to sell the stock for, was over 100 percent! More, the majority of the stocks in this category had virtually no trading volume, so even if you wanted to buy the shares, there would be no one to sell them to you.

Small Stocks Are the Winners, But Not by Much

Figure 4-5 shows returns by market capitalization with the microcap stocks removed. These results show that investors who pay no heed to risk are best off concentrating on smaller stocks from the Compustat database. As we'll see later, this is appropriate only for investors who

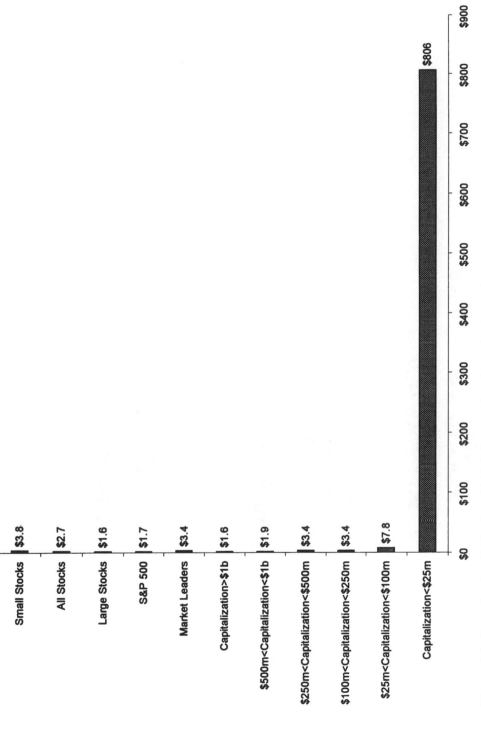

Figure 4-2. December 31, 1996 value of $10,000 invested on December 31, 1951 and annually rebalanced by market capitalization (in millions).

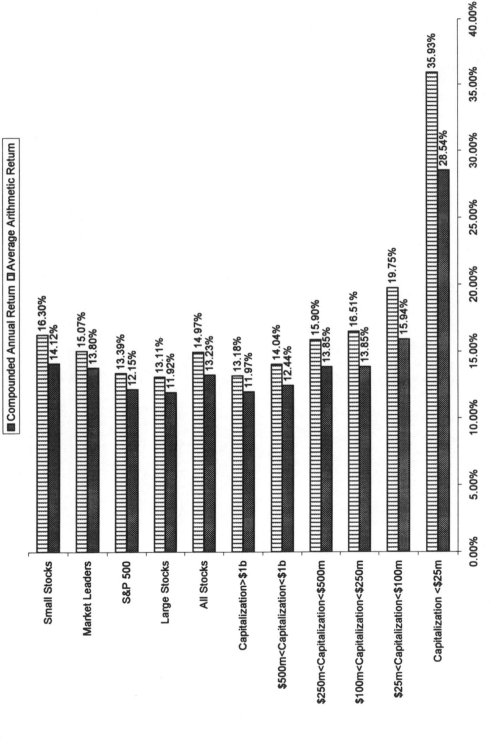

Figure 4-3. Market returns by capitalization, 1951–1996.

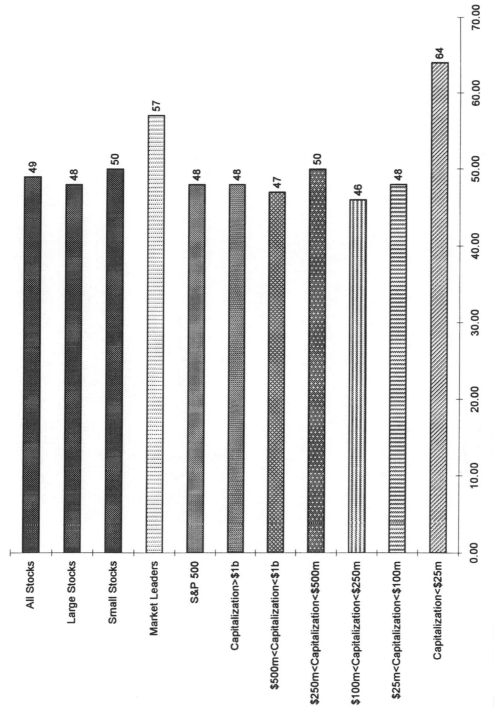

Figure 4-4. Sharpe risk-adjusted return index by market capitalization, 1951–1996. (Higher is better.)

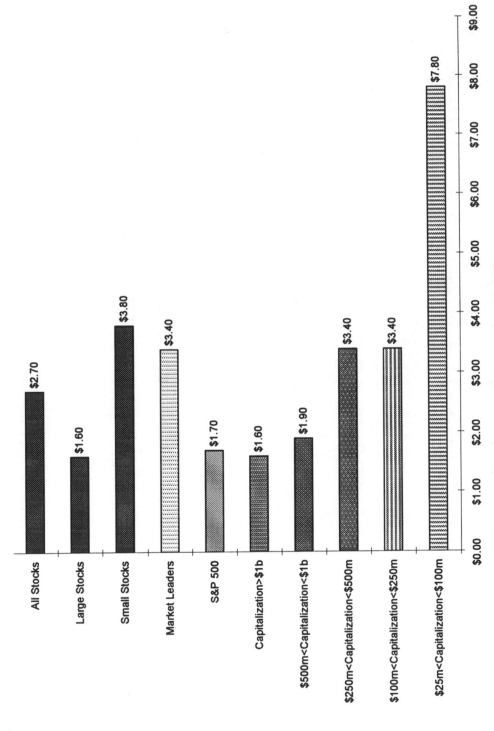

Figure 4-5. December 31, 1996, value of $10,000 invested on December 31, 1951, and annually rebalanced; excludes microcap stocks (in millions).

want to make market capitalization the sole criterion for stock selection. These results confirm the academic studies showing smaller stocks beating large stocks, but once microcaps are removed, not by nearly the large margins that other studies found. What's really fascinating is the performance of the midcap stocks, with capitalizations between $500 million and $1 billion. They perform *nearly the same* as Large Stocks and considerably worse than All Stocks, Small Stocks, and Market Leaders. The results contradict the belief that midcap stocks offer the greatest potential to investors.

Finally, a comparison of Market Leaders with Small Stocks shows the powerful ability of market-leading companies to return almost as much to investors as Small Stocks, but with a vastly lower risk level. Tables 4-6 through 4-9 summarize the findings for each market capitalization group.

Implications for Investors

Investors should be wary of small stock strategies that promise high returns *simply* because they invest in smaller issues. The numbers show the smallest stocks—those with market capitalizations below $25 million—account for the lion's share of the difference between small and large stock returns. They're virtually impossible to buy and are therefore shunned by mutual funds and individual investors alike.

Stocks with market capitalizations between $25 million and $100 million, as well as those with market capitalizations between $100 million and $250 million, *do* outperform large stocks on an absolute basis but fail when risk is taken into account. The Sharpe ratio for each is 48 and 46 respectively, compared with ratios of 49 for All Stocks and 48 for Large Stocks. (Remember that higher Sharpe ratios are better.)

The big surprise is the performance of Market Leaders. These large, well-known stocks outperformed All Stocks, Large Stocks, and the S&P 500 and did nearly as well as Small Stocks, while taking considerably less risk. They had the highest Sharpe ratio of all stocks that you can actually invest in and proved to be excellent performers over a variety of market cycles. Investors who invest in so-called small cap funds just because they like smaller stocks should actually analyze the results of the $500 million to $1 billion category. As previously noted, on September 30, 1997 the median market capitalization of the 514 mutual funds in Morningstar's all-equity, small capitalization category was $860 million.

We'll see later on that investors who want to beat the S&P 500 and are willing to take more risk should concentrate on all reasonably sized

Table 4-6. Annual Returns for Stocks by Deflated Market Capitalization: Portfolios Rebalanced Annually

Year ending	Capitalization < $25m	$25m < capitalization < $100m	$100m < capitalization < $250m
31-Dec-52	8.60%	11.57%	10.85%
31-Dec-53	9.87%	4.68%	2.47%
31-Dec-54	53.02%	59.24%	50.51%
31-Dec-55	40.76%	28.97%	21.83%
31-Dec-56	10.77%	15.16%	13.07%
31-Dec-57	−7.99%	−5.87%	−9.77%
31-Dec-58	97.70%	68.67%	62.06%
31-Dec-59	92.79%	41.76%	32.04%
31-Dec-60	17.66%	4.42%	9.18%
31-Dec-61	67.15%	46.47%	43.31%
31-Dec-62	−16.91%	−18.32%	−14.91%
31-Dec-63	20.07%	16.48%	20.44%
31-Dec-64	34.99%	21.53%	17.83%
31-Dec-65	95.47%	42.74%	31.88%
31-Dec-66	5.48%	−3.05%	−7.40%
31-Dec-67	190.94%	113.42%	71.22%
31-Dec-68	119.29%	69.24%	39.31%
31-Dec-69	−33.08%	−31.48%	−28.48%
31-Dec-70	−20.88%	−18.24%	−15.37%
31-Dec-71	39.17%	32.19%	23.25%
31-Dec-72	17.67%	5.92%	6.44%
31-Dec-73	−33.22%	−37.00%	−35.80%
31-Dec-74	−18.34%	−23.72%	−26.32%
31-Dec-75	87.18%	60.72%	49.12%
31-Dec-76	53.44%	49.43%	47.11%
31-Dec-77	38.29%	24.83%	18.55%
31-Dec-78	41.32%	24.05%	15.95%
31-Dec-79	47.03%	44.48%	45.14%
31-Dec-80	51.64%	36.97%	37.15%
31-Dec-81	3.95%	0.58%	1.26%
31-Dec-82	35.29%	24.88%	26.41%
31-Dec-83	63.43%	34.67%	32.55%
31-Dec-84	−9.57%	−16.59%	−9.86%
31-Dec-85	18.92%	26.62%	30.03%
31-Dec-86	8.51%	1.52%	6.13%
31-Dec-87	−5.45%	−14.42%	−8.30%
31-Dec-88	20.36%	18.09%	20.89%
31-Dec-89	13.13%	9.50%	13.91%
31-Dec-90	−21.81%	−27.18%	−18.81%
31-Dec-91	167.60%	49.55%	42.18%
31-Dec-92	57.83%	22.32%	15.27%
31-Dec-93	64.30%	26.77%	16.97%
31-Dec-94	−0.49%	−4.85%	−5.28%
31-Dec-95	33.64%	34.66%	30.30%
31-Dec-96	57.28%	17.30%	18.85%
Arithmetic average	35.93%	19.75%	16.51%
Standard deviation	48.51%	30.71%	24.65%

Table 4-7. Annual Returns for Stocks by Deflated Market Capitalization: Portfolios Rebalanced Annually

Year ending	$250m < capitalization < $500m	$500m < capitalization < $1b	Capitalization > $1b
31-Dec-52	6.06%	6.80%	9.91%
31-Dec-53	2.71%	6.29%	1.03%
31-Dec-54	53.91%	39.69%	47.91%
31-Dec-55	19.98%	15.22%	20.72%
31-Dec-56	10.93%	3.85%	10.91%
31-Dec-57	−7.75%	−5.15%	−5.34%
31-Dec-58	54.94%	49.91%	43.28%
31-Dec-59	20.04%	17.22%	11.68%
31-Dec-60	4.46%	9.99%	5.75%
31-Dec-61	31.50%	33.92%	29.81%
31-Dec-62	6.10%	−13.70%	−11.25%
31-Dec-63	23.73%	17.73%	18.14%
31-Dec-64	15.26%	15.25%	15.18%
31-Dec-65	27.64%	19.03%	15.76%
31-Dec-66	−6.87%	−6.67%	−5.55%
31-Dec-67	44.75%	37.66%	20.68%
31-Dec-68	33.11%	29.07%	17.88%
31-Dec-69	−22.80%	−15.15%	−11.43%
31-Dec-70	−7.45%	−3.56%	0.13%
31-Dec-71	23.10%	24.64%	17.50%
31-Dec-72	10.71%	10.78%	15.27%
31-Dec-73	−31.99%	−26.55%	−19.68%
31-Dec-74	−29.36%	−29.75%	−26.46%
31-Dec-75	56.53%	48.16%	37.07%
31-Dec-76	42.92%	40.19%	27.23%
31-Dec-77	12.46%	5.46%	−3.51%
31-Dec-78	16.61%	9.98%	7.88%
31-Dec-79	42.22%	32.63%	26.74%
31-Dec-80	32.49%	28.54%	30.95%
31-Dec-81	2.99%	3.71%	−0.10%
31-Dec-82	23.10%	23.84%	18.73%
31-Dec-83	29.18%	28.35%	23.33%
31-Dec-84	−2.64%	−1.63%	−0.39%
31-Dec-85	29.46%	30.17%	33.35%
31-Dec-86	7.76%	13.09%	20.74%
31-Dec-87	−5.05%	−2.19%	4.53%
31-Dec-88	24.98%	19.02%	18.90%
31-Dec-89	17.60%	20.74%	27.61%
31-Dec-90	−17.63%	−15.40%	−8.50%
31-Dec-91	45.64%	40.02%	33.26%
31-Dec-92	16.32%	16.15%	8.74%
31-Dec-93	18.20%	16.67%	16.56%
31-Dec-94	−4.85%	−2.47%	−1.28%
31-Dec-95	27.82%	23.50%	30.71%
31-Dec-96	16.71%	16.81%	18.75%
Arithmetic average	15.90%	14.04%	13.18%
Standard deviation	21.13%	18.55%	16.21%

Table 4-8. Summary Return Results Based on Deflated Market Capitalization, December 31, 1951–December 31, 1996

	Capitalization < $25m	$25m < capitalization < $100m	$100m < capitalization < $250m
Arithmetic average	35.93%	19.75%	16.51%
Standard deviation of return	47.53%	30.11%	24.19%
Sharpe risk-adjusted ratio	64.00	48.00	46.00
3-yr compounded	27.89%	14.55%	13.62%
5-yr compounded	40.24%	18.44%	14.61%
10-yr compounded	30.76%	10.88%	11.17%
15-yr compounded	27.38%	11.42%	12.70%
20-yr compounded	29.30%	14.73%	15.10%
25-yr compounded	25.87%	12.52%	12.35%
30-yr compounded	27.55%	14.01%	12.33%
35-yr compounded	26.84%	13.40%	11.71%
40-yr compounded	29.21%	15.14%	13.26%
Compound annual return	28.54%	15.94%	13.85%
$10,000 becomes:	$806,444,130.00	$7,767,454.00	$3,432,526.00
Maximum return	190.94%	113.42%	71.22%
Minimum return	−33.22%	−37.00%	−35.80%
Maximum expected return*	130.99%	79.97%	64.89%
Minimum expected return**	−59.13%	−40.47%	−31.87%

*Maximum expected return is average return plus 2 times the standard deviation.

**Minimum expected return is average return minus 2 times the standard deviation.

Table 4-9. Summary Return Results Based on Deflated Market Capitalization, December 31, 1951–December 31, 1996

	$250m < capitalization < $500m	$500m < capitalization < $1b	Capitalization > $1b
Arithmetic average	15.90%	14.04%	13.18%
Standard deviation of return	21.13%	18.55%	16.21%
Sharpe risk-adjusted ratio	50.00	47.00	48.00
3-yr compounded	12.38%	12.05%	15.29%
5-yr compounded	14.31%	13.78%	14.20%
10-yr compounded	12.57%	12.24%	14.15%
15-yr compounded	13.91%	14.18%	15.62%
20-yr compounded	15.54%	14.49%	14.58%
25-yr compounded	13.03%	12.20%	12.28%
30-yr compounded	12.71%	12.27%	11.58%
35-yr compounded	12.67%	11.26%	10.73%
40-yr compounded	13.41%	12.28%	11.34%
Compound annual return	13.85%	12.44%	11.97%
$10,000 becomes:	$3,425,430	$1,953,056	$1,618,012
Maximum return	56.53%	49.91%	47.91%
Minimum return	−31.99%	−29.46%	−26.46%
Maximum expected return*	58.16%	51.14%	45.60%
Minimum expected return**	−26.36%	−23.06%	−19.24%

*Maximum expected return is average return plus 2 times the standard deviation.
**Minimum expected return is average return minus 2 times the standard deviation.

Table 4-10. Base Rates for All Stocks Universe and Large Stocks Universe, 1951–1996

Item	All Stocks beat Large Stocks	Percent
Single-year return	26 out of 45	58%
Rolling 5-year compound return	30 out of 41	73%
Rolling 10-year compound return	27 out of 36	75%

stocks—those in the All Stocks group with market capitalizations above $150 million—instead of focusing exclusively on tiny or huge stocks. As of December 31, 1996, the All Stocks group included 2908 stocks, ranging from General Electric at the top to ABT Building Products at the bottom. Their average market capitalization of $2.6 billion was considerably smaller than that of the Large Stocks universe, with an average market capitalization of $6.7 billion. (See Tables 4-10 through 4-15.)

Our Two Benchmarks

In each chapter to follow, we'll use the All Stocks and Large Stocks groups as benchmarks for all the strategies we study. Each provides an excellent indication of what can be achieved in each capitalization class.

Table 4-11. Annual Performance of Large Stocks Versus Market Leaders

Year ending	Large Stocks	Market Leaders	Market Leaders relative performance
31-Dec-52	9.30%	15.30%	6.00%
31-Dec-53	2.30%	0.80%	−1.50%
31-Dec-54	44.90%	50.60%	5.70%
31-Dec-55	21.20%	27.00%	5.80%
31-Dec-56	9.60%	14.40%	4.80%
31-Dec-57	−6.90%	−10.10%	−3.20%
31-Dec-58	42.10%	36.10%	−6.00%
31-Dec-59	9.90%	12.20%	2.30%
31-Dec-60	4.80%	−0.90%	−5.70%
31-Dec-61	27.50%	23.00%	−4.50%
31-Dec-62	−8.90%	−9.50%	−0.60%
31-Dec-63	19.50%	21.80%	2.30%
31-Dec-64	15.30%	18.90%	3.60%
31-Dec-65	16.20%	19.50%	3.30%
31-Dec-66	−4.90%	−5.10%	−0.20%
31-Dec-67	21.30%	27.90%	6.60%
31-Dec-68	16.80%	18.70%	1.90%
31-Dec-69	−9.90%	−9.90%	0.00%
31-Dec-70	−0.20%	1.80%	2.00%
31-Dec-71	17.30%	18.40%	1.10%
31-Dec-72	14.90%	18.30%	3.40%
31-Dec-73	−18.90%	−11.60%	7.30%
31-Dec-74	−26.70%	−21.40%	5.30%
31-Dec-75	43.10%	66.00%	22.90%
31-Dec-76	28.00%	28.00%	0.00%
31-Dec-77	−2.50%	−5.00%	−2.50%
31-Dec-78	8.10%	10.40%	2.30%
31-Dec-79	27.30%	24.80%	−2.50%
31-Dec-80	30.80%	30.20%	−0.60%
31-Dec-81	0.60%	1.20%	0.60%
31-Dec-82	19.90%	24.70%	4.80%
31-Dec-83	23.80%	29.00%	5.20%
31-Dec-84	−0.40%	2.60%	3.00%
31-Dec-85	19.50%	33.70%	14.20%
31-Dec-86	32.20%	22.90%	−9.30%
31-Dec-87	3.30%	8.90%	5.60%
31-Dec-88	19.00%	21.20%	2.20%
31-Dec-89	26.00%	25.50%	−0.50%
31-Dec-90	−8.70%	−7.40%	1.30%
31-Dec-91	33.00%	29.60%	−3.40%
31-Dec-92	8.70%	7.30%	−1.40%
31-Dec-93	16.30%	14.80%	−1.50%
31-Dec-94	−1.90%	2.70%	4.60%
31-Dec-95	28.50%	28.70%	0.20%
31-Dec-96	18.70%	22.00%	3.30%
Arithmetic average	13.11%	15.07%	1.97%
Standard deviation	16.01%	17.02%	1.02%

Table 4-12. Compound Annual Rates of Return by Decade

Universe	1950s*	1960s	1970s	1980s	1990s**
S&P 500	17.33%	7.81%	5.86%	17.55%	14.41%
Large Stocks	15.33%	8.99%	6.99%	16.89%	12.61%
Market Leaders	16.91%	9.50%	10.67%	19.46%	13.21%
All Stocks	19.22%	11.09%	8.53%	15.85%	12.78%
Small Stocks	20.04%	12.37%	9.69%	15.00%	15.26%

*Returns for 1952–1959.
**Returns for 1990–1996.

Table 4-13. Summary Return Results for Large Stocks and Market Leaders, December 31, 1951–December 31, 1996

	Large Stocks	Market Leaders
Arithmetic average	13.11%	15.07%
Standard deviation of return	16.01%	17.02%
Sharpe risk-adjusted ratio	48.00	57.00
3-yr compounded	14.38%	17.27%
5-yr compounded	13.60%	14.71%
10-yr compounded	13.53%	14.72%
15-yr compounded	15.16%	17.12%
20-yr compounded	14.37%	15.70%
25-yr compounded	12.34%	14.91%
30-yr compounded	11.67%	14.16%
35-yr compounded	10.96%	13.30%
40-yr compounded	11.36%	12.99%
Compound annual return	11.92%	13.80%
$10,000 becomes:	$1,590,667	$3,363,529
Maximum return	44.90%	66.00%
Minimum return	−26.70%	−21.40%
Maximum expected return*	45.12%	49.11%
Minimum expected return**	−18.91%	−18.98%

*Maximum expected return is average return plus 2 times the standard deviation.

**Minimum expected return is average return minus 2 times the standard deviation.

Table 4-14. Annual Performance of All Stocks Versus Small Stocks

Year ending	All Stocks	Small Stocks	Small Stocks relative performance
31-Dec-52	7.90%	7.00%	−0.90%
31-Dec-53	2.90%	3.90%	1.00%
31-Dec-54	47.00%	47.60%	0.60%
31-Dec-55	20.70%	20.00%	−0.70%
31-Dec-56	17.00%	20.60%	3.60%
31-Dec-57	−7.10%	−6.60%	0.50%
31-Dec-58	55.00%	61.00%	6.00%
31-Dec-59	23.00%	20.77%	−2.23%
31-Dec-60	6.10%	7.30%	1.20%
31-Dec-61	31.20%	32.60%	1.40%
31-Dec-62	−12.00%	−13.79%	−1.79%
31-Dec-63	18.00%	19.20%	1.20%
31-Dec-64	16.30%	16.90%	0.60%
31-Dec-65	22.60%	26.60%	4.00%
31-Dec-66	−5.20%	−5.60%	−0.40%
31-Dec-67	41.10%	51.80%	10.70%
31-Dec-68	27.40%	32.20%	4.80%
31-Dec-69	−18.50%	−21.70%	−3.20%
31-Dec-70	−5.80%	−8.50%	−2.70%
31-Dec-71	21.30%	23.50%	2.20%
31-Dec-72	11.00%	9.60%	−1.40%
31-Dec-73	−27.20%	−31.20%	−4.00%
31-Dec-74	−27.90%	−28.50%	−0.60%
31-Dec-75	55.90%	61.00%	5.10%
31-Dec-76	35.60%	42.00%	6.40%
31-Dec-77	6.90%	13.20%	6.30%
31-Dec-78	12.20%	15.00%	2.80%
31-Dec-79	34.30%	39.10%	4.80%
31-Dec-80	31.50%	32.10%	0.60%
31-Dec-81	1.70%	2.50%	0.80%
31-Dec-82	22.50%	24.60%	2.10%
31-Dec-83	28.10%	31.40%	3.30%
31-Dec-84	−3.40%	−5.40%	−2.00%
31-Dec-85	30.80%	29.60%	−1.20%
31-Dec-86	13.10%	7.80%	−5.30%
31-Dec-87	−1.30%	−4.90%	−3.60%
31-Dec-88	21.20%	22.90%	1.70%
31-Dec-89	21.40%	18.10%	−3.30%
31-Dec-90	−13.80%	−17.60%	−3.80%
31-Dec-91	39.80%	44.70%	4.90%
31-Dec-92	13.80%	16.50%	2.70%
31-Dec-93	16.60%	17.40%	0.80%
31-Dec-94	−3.40%	−4.20%	−0.80%
31-Dec-95	27.00%	27.40%	0.40%
31-Dec-96	18.30%	35.80%	17.50%
Arithmetic average	14.97%	16.30%	0.98%
Standard deviation	19.51%	21.91%	2.40%

Table 4-15. Summary Return Results for All Stocks and Small Stocks, December 31, 1951–December 31, 1996

	All Stocks	Small Stocks
Arithmetic average	14.97%	15.91%
Standard deviation of return	19.51%	21.71%
Sharpe risk-adjusted ratio	49.00	49.00
3-yr compounded	13.22%	12.96%
5-yr compounded	14.00%	14.54%
10-yr compounded	12.92%	12.49%
15-yr compounded	14.44%	13.87%
20-yr compounded	14.97%	15.29%
25-yr compounded	12.74%	13.00%
30-yr compounded	12.43%	12.86%
35-yr compounded	11.64%	12.08%
40-yr compounded	12.62%	13.15%
Compound annual return	13.23%	13.77%
$10,000 becomes:	$2,677,557	$3,319,218
Maximum return	55.90%	61.00%
Minimum return	−27.90%	−31.20%
Maximum expected return*	53.98%	59.33%
Minimum expected return**	−24.04%	−27.51%

*Maximum expected return is average return plus 2 times the standard deviation.

**Minimum expected return is average return minus 2 times the standard deviation.

5

Price-to-Earnings Ratios: Separating the Winners and Losers

*When it comes to making money, everyone
is of the same religion.*
                    —VOLTAIRE

For many on Wall Street, buying stocks with low price-to-earnings ratios (PE ratios) is the one true faith. You find a stock's current PE ratio by dividing the price by the current earnings per share. The higher the PE, the more investors are paying for earnings, and the larger the implied expectations for future earnings growth. A stock's PE ratio is the most common measurement of how cheap or expensive it is relative to other stocks.

Investors who buy stocks with low PE ratios think they're getting a bargain. Generally, they believe that when a stock's PE ratio is high, investors have unrealistic expectations for the earnings growth of that stock. Low PE investors reason that high hopes are usually dashed along with the price of the stock. Conversely, they believe the prices of low PE stocks are unduly discounted and when earnings recover, the price of the stock will follow.

The Results

Remember that we look at two distinct groups—those with high and low PE ratios drawn from the All Stocks universe (all stocks with market capitalizations greater than a deflated $150 million) and those with high and low PE ratios drawn from the Large Stocks universe (those with market capitalizations greater than the Compustat mean, usually the upper 16 percent of the database). We'll also be looking at the All Stocks and Large Stocks universes ranked by PE decile.

Let's look at low PE stocks first. We start with $10,000 on December 31, 1951 and buy the 50 stocks with the highest earnings-to-price ratios from the All Stocks and Large Stocks universes. Because of Compustat's internal math, we must rank stocks by the 50 *highest* earnings-to-price ratios, which is the reciprocal of the PE ratio. Remember that stocks with high earnings-to-price ratios are low PE stocks. We rebalance the portfolios annually to hold the 50 stocks with the lowest PE ratios in any given year. As with all the tests, the stocks are equally weighted and the earnings variable is time-lagged to avoid look-ahead bias.

Figure 5-1 shows the growth of $10,000 invested on December 31, 1951 and Tables 5-1 through 5-6 summarize the results for low PE investing.

Our 45 years of data show that low PE ratios are not nearly as important for smaller stocks as they are for larger stocks. The 50 lowest PE stocks from the All Stock universe turned $10,000 into $2,125,935, a compound rate of return of 12.65 percent a year. While that beat the return for the Large Stocks universe, it failed to beat the All Stocks return of 13.23 percent a year. It also did worse than All Stocks on a risk-adjusted basis: the Sharpe ratio for the 50 low PE stocks was 40, nine points behind the All Stock group's score of 49. Analyzing the base rate information in Table 5-5, we see little more than chance at work in the number of years the strategy beats the universe.

Large Stocks Are Different

Large Stocks are entirely different. Here, an investment in the 50 stocks with the lowest PE ratios turned $10,000 into $3,787,460, more than double the Large Stocks return of $1,590,667. The compound return of the 50 low PE stocks was 14.1 percent, 2.18 percent better than the Large Stocks return of 11.92 percent a year. More, the 50 low PE stocks from Large Stocks had a better risk-adjusted return—sporting a Sharpe ratio of 50, compared with 48 for the Large Stocks group. Here, as Table 5-6 shows, base rates are not random. When looking at rolling 10-year rates of return of the 50 low PE stocks, we see that they beat the Large Stocks group 86 percent of the time.

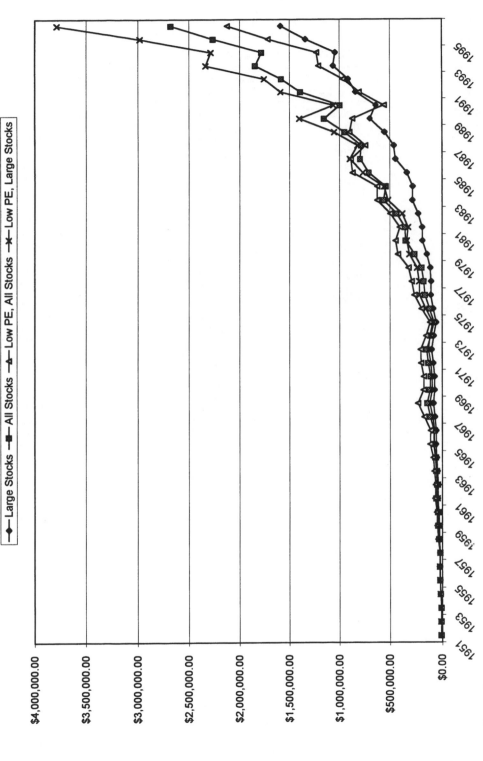

Figure 5-1. Returns on low PE stocks versus All Stocks and Large Stocks, 1951–1996.
Year-end 1951 = $10,000.

Table 5-1. Annual Performance of All Stocks Versus 50 Stocks with High
Earnings-to-Price (Low PE) Ratios from All Stocks Universe

Year ending	All Stocks	Universe = All Stocks Top 50, EPS/price	Top 50 EPS/price relative performance
31-Dec-52	7.90%	11.10%	3.20%
31-Dec-53	2.90%	−5.60%	−8.50%
31-Dec-54	47.00%	69.20%	22.20%
31-Dec-55	20.70%	29.50%	8.80%
31-Dec-56	17.00%	18.90%	1.90%
31-Dec-57	−7.10%	−16.80%	−9.70%
31-Dec-58	55.00%	75.30%	20.30%
31-Dec-59	23.00%	21.90%	−1.10%
31-Dec-60	6.10%	6.70%	0.60%
31-Dec-61	31.20%	28.90%	−2.30%
31-Dec-62	−12.00%	−5.30%	6.70%
31-Dec-63	18.00%	19.90%	1.90%
31-Dec-64	16.30%	14.00%	−2.30%
31-Dec-65	22.60%	34.90%	12.30%
31-Dec-66	−5.20%	−4.10%	1.10%
31-Dec-67	41.10%	52.80%	11.70%
31-Dec-68	27.40%	36.30%	8.90%
31-Dec-69	−18.50%	−23.00%	−4.50%
31-Dec-70	−5.80%	−1.80%	4.00%
31-Dec-71	21.30%	14.10%	−7.20%
31-Dec-72	11.00%	2.50%	−8.50%
31-Dec-73	−27.20%	−25.50%	1.70%
31-Dec-74	−27.90%	−25.10%	2.80%
31-Dec-75	55.90%	71.60%	15.70%
31-Dec-76	35.60%	34.60%	−1.00%
31-Dec-77	6.90%	9.40%	2.50%
31-Dec-78	12.20%	10.10%	−2.10%
31-Dec-79	34.30%	31.50%	−2.80%
31-Dec-80	31.50%	5.30%	−26.20%
31-Dec-81	1.70%	−8.70%	−10.40%
31-Dec-82	22.50%	22.10%	−0.40%
31-Dec-83	28.10%	25.00%	−3.10%
31-Dec-84	−3.40%	−0.10%	3.30%
31-Dec-85	30.80%	41.10%	10.30%
31-Dec-86	13.10%	2.00%	−11.10%
31-Dec-87	−1.30%	−16.70%	−15.40%
31-Dec-88	21.20%	21.80%	0.60%
31-Dec-89	21.40%	−3.20%	−24.60%
31-Dec-90	−13.80%	−36.30%	−22.50%
31-Dec-91	39.80%	44.60%	4.80%
31-Dec-92	13.80%	20.40%	6.60%
31-Dec-93	16.60%	25.10%	8.50%
31-Dec-94	−3.40%	1.80%	5.20%
31-Dec-95	27.00%	39.50%	12.50%
31-Dec-96	18.30%	23.80%	5.50%
Arithmetic average	14.97%	15.41%	0.44%
Standard deviation	19.51%	25.14%	5.63%

Table 5-2. Annual Performance of Large Stocks Versus 50 Stocks with High Earnings-to-Price (Low PE) Ratios from Large Stocks Universe

Year ending	Large Stocks	Universe = Large Stocks Top 50, EPS/price	Top 50 EPS/price relative performance
31-Dec-52	9.30%	14.60%	5.30%
31-Dec-53	2.30%	−5.10%	−7.40%
31-Dec-54	44.90%	64.10%	19.20%
31-Dec-55	21.20%	23.20%	2.00%
31-Dec-56	9.60%	11.10%	1.50%
31-Dec-57	−6.90%	−13.80%	−6.90%
31-Dec-58	42.10%	48.70%	6.60%
31-Dec-59	9.90%	5.60%	−4.30%
31-Dec-60	4.80%	5.30%	0.50%
31-Dec-61	27.50%	28.10%	0.60%
31-Dec-62	−8.90%	−2.90%	6.00%
31-Dec-63	19.50%	19.50%	0.00%
31-Dec-64	15.30%	20.50%	5.20%
31-Dec-65	16.20%	23.60%	7.40%
31-Dec-66	−4.90%	−6.60%	−1.70%
31-Dec-67	21.30%	25.90%	4.60%
31-Dec-68	16.80%	30.30%	13.50%
31-Dec-69	−9.90%	−19.50%	−9.60%
31-Dec-70	−0.20%	3.70%	3.90%
31-Dec-71	17.30%	10.30%	−7.00%
31-Dec-72	14.90%	19.40%	4.50%
31-Dec-73	−18.90%	−11.10%	7.80%
31-Dec-74	−26.70%	−22.20%	4.50%
31-Dec-75	43.10%	72.90%	29.80%
31-Dec-76	28.00%	39.80%	11.80%
31-Dec-77	−2.50%	1.50%	4.00%
31-Dec-78	8.10%	8.60%	0.50%
31-Dec-79	27.30%	30.70%	3.40%
31-Dec-80	30.80%	7.90%	−22.90%
31-Dec-81	0.60%	−4.00%	−4.60%
31-Dec-82	19.90%	17.60%	−2.30%
31-Dec-83	23.80%	35.50%	11.70%
31-Dec-84	−0.40%	6.90%	7.30%
31-Dec-85	19.50%	38.70%	19.20%
31-Dec-86	32.20%	17.20%	−15.00%
31-Dec-87	3.30%	−8.30%	−11.60%
31-Dec-88	19.00%	28.10%	9.10%
31-Dec-89	26.00%	33.10%	7.10%
31-Dec-90	−8.70%	−24.40%	−15.70%
31-Dec-91	33.00%	49.90%	16.90%
31-Dec-92	8.70%	10.60%	1.90%
31-Dec-93	16.30%	32.90%	16.60%
31-Dec-94	−1.90%	−2.10%	−0.20%
31-Dec-95	28.50%	30.40%	1.90%
31-Dec-96	18.70%	27.00%	8.30%
Arithmetic average	13.11%	16.07%	2.96%
Standard deviation	16.01%	21.39%	5.38%

Table 5-3. Summary Return Results for All Stocks and 50
Highest Earnings-to-Price (Low PE) Stocks from All Stocks
Universe, December 31, 1951–December 31, 1996

	All Stocks	Universe = All Stocks top 50 earnings/price (low PE)
Arithmetic average	14.97%	15.41%
Standard deviation of return	19.51%	25.14%
Sharpe risk-adjusted ratio	49.00	40.00
3-yr compounded	13.22%	20.69%
5-yr compounded	14.00%	21.50%
10-yr compounded	12.92%	9.13%
15-yr compounded	14.44%	11.70%
20-yr compounded	14.97%	10.96%
25-yr compounded	12.74%	9.89%
30-yr compounded	12.43%	10.31%
35-yr compounded	11.64%	10.39%
40-yr compounded	12.62%	11.50%
Compound annual return	13.23%	12.65%
$10,000 becomes:	$2,677,556.77	$2,125,934.84
Maximum return	55.90%	75.30%
Minimum return	−27.90%	−36.30%
Maximum expected return*	53.98%	65.69%
Minimum expected return**	−24.04%	−34.87%

*Maximum expected return is average return plus 2 times the standard deviation.

**Minimum expected return is average return minus 2 times the standard deviation.

While both the Large Stocks and All Stocks versions of the strategy had higher standard deviations of return than their universes, only the Large Stocks with low PE ratios compensated for the higher risk. The difference in returns for the large and small stock sections of the database is striking, but it makes sense. Small companies can have a string of spectacular earnings gains on their way to becoming large companies. It's sensible for investors to award them higher PE ratios. Indeed, while you would not want to buy small stocks with very high PE ratios, you might not want them too low either. Since low PE ratios indicate

Table 5-4. Summary Return Results for Large Stocks and 50 Highest Earnings-to-Price (Low PE) Stocks from All Stocks Universe, December 31, 1951–December 31, 1996

	Large Stocks	Universe = Large Stocks top 50 earnings/price (low PE)
Arithmetic average	13.11%	16.07%
Standard deviation of return	16.01%	21.39%
Sharpe risk-adjusted ratio	48.00	50.00
3-yr compounded	14.38%	17.48%
5-yr compounded	13.60%	18.97%
10-yr compounded	13.53%	15.49%
15-yr compounded	15.16%	17.81%
20-yr compounded	14.37%	15.37%
25-yr compounded	12.34%	15.26%
30-yr compounded	11.67%	14.12%
35-yr compounded	10.96%	13.53%
40-yr compounded	11.36%	13.44%
Compound annual return	11.92%	14.10%
$10,000 becomes:	$1,590,667.04	$3,787,460.34
Maximum return	44.90%	72.90%
Minimum return	−26.70%	−24.40%
Maximum expected return*	45.12%	58.85%
Minimum expected return**	−18.91%	−26.71%

*Maximum expected return is average return plus 2 times the standard deviation.

**Minimum expected return is average return minus 2 times the standard deviation.

lower investor expectations for earnings growth, a small company with a low PE might have very limited prospects. As companies grow, their ability to produce dazzling earnings gains decreases, and so too should the expectations of investors. On the other hand, investors consistently reward large stocks with lower PE ratios, possibly because their prices are more realistic in relation to their prospective growth rates.

We'll see that low PE ratios become even more important when multifactor models are used to select stocks, but their importance now for larger stocks is obvious from the data.

Table 5-5. Base Rates for All Stocks and 50 Highest Earnings-to-Price (Low PE) Stocks from All Stocks Universe, 1951–1996

Item	50 low PE beat All Stocks	Percent
Single-year return	26 out of 45	58%
Rolling 5-year compound return	22 out of 41	54%
Rolling 10-year compound return	18 out of 36	50%

Table 5-6. Base Rates for Large Stocks and 50 Highest Earnings-to-Price (Low PE) Stocks from Large Stocks Universe, 1951–1996

Item	50 low PE beat Large Stocks	Percent
Single-year return	32 out of 45	71%
Rolling 5-year compound return	30 out of 41	73%
Rolling 10-year compound return	31 out of 36	86%

High PE Ratios Are Dangerous

Buying high PE stocks, regardless of their market capitalization, is a dangerous endeavor. You shouldn't let the flash of the latest glamour stock draw you in to paying ridiculous prices for earnings. Yet many investors do exactly that. Witness investors pushing Polaroid's PE to 164 in 1961 and Best Buy's to 712 in 1997. Figure 5-2 and Tables 5-7 through 5-12 catalog the damage.

Let's start with the All Stocks universe: $10,000 invested in 1951 in the 50 stocks with the highest PE ratios and rebalanced annually grew to $558,065 by the end of 1996, $2,119,492 less than if we bought the All Stocks universe itself! The compound return of 9.35 percent was well behind All Stocks' 13.23 percent annual return. When we adjust for risk, the news gets even grimmer. The 50 high PE stocks' Sharpe ratio of 27 was nearly half that of the All Stocks universe. The high PE stocks beat the All Stock group just 11 percent of the time in all rolling 10-year periods.

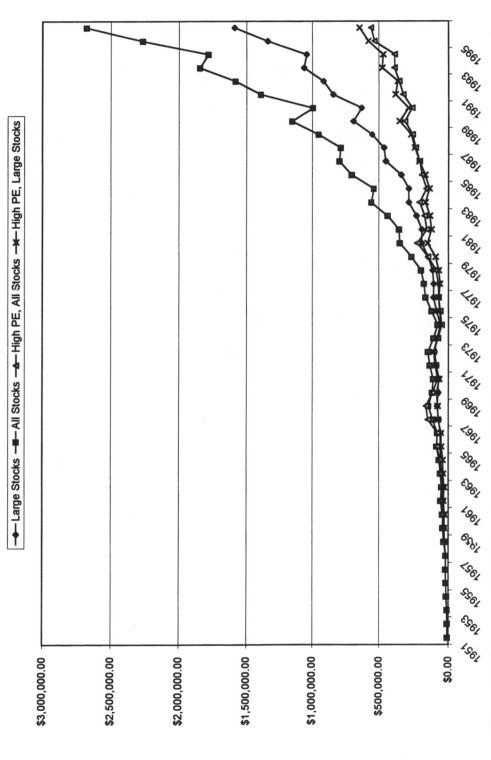

Figure 5-2. Returns on high PE stocks versus All Stocks and Large Stocks, 1951–1996. Year-end 1951 = $10,000.

Table 5-7. Annual Performance of All Stocks Versus 50 Stocks with High PE Ratios from All Stocks Universe

Year ending	All Stocks	Universe = All Stocks top 50 high PE	Top 50 PE relative performance
31-Dec-52	7.90%	0.30%	−7.60%
31-Dec-53	2.90%	5.60%	2.70%
31-Dec-54	47.00%	43.10%	−3.90%
31-Dec-55	20.70%	24.30%	3.60%
31-Dec-56	17.00%	10.10%	−6.90%
31-Dec-57	−7.10%	−2.00%	5.10%
31-Dec-58	55.00%	57.50%	2.50%
31-Dec-59	23.00%	27.90%	4.90%
31-Dec-60	6.10%	4.00%	−2.10%
31-Dec-61	31.20%	15.30%	−15.90%
31-Dec-62	−12.00%	−27.10%	−15.10%
31-Dec-63	18.00%	53.20%	35.20%
31-Dec-64	16.30%	6.80%	−9.50%
31-Dec-65	22.60%	42.00%	19.40%
31-Dec-66	−5.20%	−4.60%	0.60%
31-Dec-67	41.10%	84.80%	43.70%
31-Dec-68	27.40%	9.90%	−17.50%
31-Dec-69	−18.50%	−28.10%	−9.60%
31-Dec-70	−5.80%	−33.20%	−27.40%
31-Dec-71	21.30%	23.50%	2.20%
31-Dec-72	11.00%	9.80%	−1.20%
31-Dec-73	−27.20%	−27.50%	−0.30%
31-Dec-74	−27.90%	−36.10%	−8.20%
31-Dec-75	55.90%	22.20%	−33.70%
31-Dec-76	35.60%	21.10%	−14.50%
31-Dec-77	6.90%	0.06%	−6.84%
31-Dec-78	12.20%	24.30%	12.10%
31-Dec-79	34.30%	61.90%	27.60%
31-Dec-80	31.50%	53.90%	22.40%
31-Dec-81	1.70%	−30.30%	−32.00%
31-Dec-82	22.50%	9.70%	−12.80%
31-Dec-83	28.10%	20.60%	−7.50%
31-Dec-84	−3.40%	−23.60%	−20.20%
31-Dec-85	30.80%	20.80%	−10.00%
31-Dec-86	13.10%	8.80%	−4.30%
31-Dec-87	−1.30%	13.60%	14.90%
31-Dec-88	21.20%	9.80%	−11.40%
31-Dec-89	21.40%	21.40%	0.00%
31-Dec-90	−13.80%	−16.80%	−3.00%
31-Dec-91	39.80%	24.70%	−15.10%
31-Dec-92	13.80%	9.00%	−4.80%
31-Dec-93	16.60%	9.70%	−6.90%
31-Dec-94	−3.40%	−0.50%	2.90%
31-Dec-95	27.00%	37.60%	10.60%
31-Dec-96	18.30%	5.10%	−13.20%
Arithmetic average	14.97%	12.50%	−2.52%
Standard deviation	19.51%	26.33%	6.82%

Table 5-8. Annual Performance of Large Stocks Versus 50 Stocks with High PE Ratios from Large Stocks Universe

Year ending	Large Stocks	Universe = Large Stocks top 50 high PE	Top 50 PE relative performance
31-Dec-52	9.30%	3.50%	−5.80%
31-Dec-53	2.30%	5.40%	3.10%
31-Dec-54	44.90%	38.00%	−6.90%
31-Dec-55	21.20%	23.60%	2.40%
31-Dec-56	9.60%	8.40%	−1.20%
31-Dec-57	−6.90%	−7.30%	−0.40%
31-Dec-58	42.10%	37.70%	−4.40%
31-Dec-59	9.90%	16.90%	7.00%
31-Dec-60	4.80%	−4.30%	−9.10%
31-Dec-61	27.50%	20.70%	−6.80%
31-Dec-62	−8.90%	−15.30%	−6.40%
31-Dec-63	19.50%	25.80%	6.30%
31-Dec-64	15.30%	7.80%	−7.50%
31-Dec-65	16.20%	27.00%	10.80%
31-Dec-66	−4.90%	3.00%	7.90%
31-Dec-67	21.30%	41.60%	20.30%
31-Dec-68	16.80%	4.20%	−12.60%
31-Dec-69	−9.90%	10.30%	20.20%
31-Dec-70	−0.20%	−22.20%	−22.00%
31-Dec-71	17.30%	33.40%	16.10%
31-Dec-72	14.90%	21.70%	6.80%
31-Dec-73	−18.90%	−25.30%	−6.40%
31-Dec-74	−26.70%	−33.40%	−6.70%
31-Dec-75	43.10%	19.20%	−23.90%
31-Dec-76	28.00%	9.90%	−18.10%
31-Dec-77	−2.50%	−12.70%	−10.20%
31-Dec-78	8.10%	13.60%	5.50%
31-Dec-79	27.30%	34.40%	7.10%
31-Dec-80	30.80%	60.90%	30.10%
31-Dec-81	0.60%	−20.00%	−20.60%
31-Dec-82	19.90%	9.90%	−10.00%
31-Dec-83	23.80%	24.90%	1.10%
31-Dec-84	−0.40%	17.70%	−17.30%
31-Dec-85	19.50%	22.10%	2.60%
31-Dec-86	32.20%	25.40%	−6.80%
31-Dec-87	3.30%	15.80%	12.50%
31-Dec-88	19.00%	11.20%	−7.80%
31-Dec-89	26.00%	30.60%	4.60%
31-Dec-90	−8.70%	−18.00%	−9.30%
31-Dec-91	33.00%	32.60%	−0.40%
31-Dec-92	8.70%	−4.50%	−13.20%
31-Dec-93	16.30%	30.60%	14.30%
31-Dec-94	−1.90%	−1.40%	0.50%
31-Dec-95	28.50%	23.80%	−4.70%
31-Dec-96	18.70%	11.90%	−6.80%
Arithmetic average	13.11%	11.64%	−1.47%
Standard deviation	16.01%	20.14%	4.13%

Table 5-9. Summary Return Results for All Stocks and 50
Highest PE Stocks from All Stocks Universe,
December 31, 1951–December 31, 1996

	All Stocks	Universe = All Stocks top 50 price/earnings (high PE)
Arithmetic average	14.97%	12.50%
Standard deviation of return	19.51%	26.33%
Sharpe risk-adjusted ratio	49.00	27.00
3-yr compounded	13.22%	12.90%
5-yr compounded	14.00%	11.46%
10-yr compounded	12.92%	10.46%
15-yr compounded	14.44%	8.90%
20-yr compounded	14.97%	10.79%
25-yr compounded	12.74%	7.31%
30-yr compounded	12.43%	6.72%
35-yr compounded	11.64%	7.19%
40-yr compounded	12.62%	8.58%
Compound annual return	13.23%	9.35%
$10,000 becomes:	$2,677,556.77	$558,065.32
Maximum return	55.90%	84.80%
Minimum return	−27.90%	−36.10%
Maximum expected return*	53.98%	65.15%
Minimum expected return**	−24.04%	−40.15%

*Maximum expected return is average return plus 2 times the standard deviation.

**Minimum expected return is average return minus 2 times the standard deviation.

Large Stocks Fare No Better

The high PE damage is similar in the Large Stocks group. Here $10,000 invested in the 50 Large Stocks with the highest PE ratios grows to $646,963 at the end of 1996, less than half what we'd earn with an investment in Large Stocks. Compound returns for all the high PE stocks, from the most recent to the long term, fall short of the Large Stocks universe, with a Sharpe ratio of 31.17 points lower than the Large Stocks universe.

Adding insult to injury, the 50 Large Stocks with the highest PE ratios beat the Large Stocks universe just 22 percent of the time over all rolling 10-year periods.

Table 5-10. Summary Return Results for Large Stocks and 50
Highest PE Stocks from Large Stocks Universe,
December 31, 1951–December 31, 1996

	Large Stocks	Universe = Large Stocks top 50 price/earnings (high PE)
Arithmetic average	13.11%	11.64%
Standard deviation of return	16.01%	20.14%
Sharpe risk-adjusted ratio	48.00	31.00
3-yr compounded	14.38%	10.95%
5-yr compounded	13.60%	11.24%
10-yr compounded	13.53%	12.03%
15-yr compounded	15.16%	11.88%
20-yr compounded	14.37%	11.76%
25-yr compounded	12.34%	8.30%
30-yr compounded	11.67%	8.75%
35-yr compounded	10.96%	8.71%
40-yr compounded	11.36%	9.06%
Compound annual return	11.92%	9.71%
$10,000 becomes:	$1,590,667.04	$646,962.87
Maximum return	44.90%	60.90%
Minimum return	−26.70%	−33.40%
Maximum expected return*	45.12%	51.91%
Minimum expected return**	−18.91%	−28.64%

*Maximum expected return is average return plus 2 times the standard deviation.

**Minimum expected return is average return minus 2 times the standard deviation.

Deciles

Sorting the All Stocks and Large Stocks paints a different picture, particularly in the All Stocks universe. Here we see that the lowest four deciles by PE all outperformed an investment in All Stocks, whereas deciles 5 through 10 (with decile 10 being the 10 percent of stocks with the highest PE ratios) all underperformed. Perhaps the 50 lowest PE stocks from All Stocks underperform the universe because they have problems that are more serious than those of other low PE stocks. Indeed, an investor would have been better off focusing on the second decile by low PE rather than the lowest.

Table 5-11. Base Rates for All Stocks and 50 Highest PE Stocks from All Stocks Universe, 1951–1996

Item	50 high PE beat All Stocks	Percent
Single-year return	16 out of 45	36%
Rolling 5-year compound return	11 out of 41	27%
Rolling 10-year compound return	4 out of 36	11%

Table 5-12. Base Rates for Large Stocks and 50 Highest PE Stocks from Large Stocks Universe, 1951–1996

Item	50 high PE beat Large Stocks	Percent
Single-year return	19 out of 45	42%
Rolling 5-year compound return	11 out of 41	27%
Rolling 10-year compound return	8 out of 36	22%

The Large Stocks universe paints a similar picture, with the lowest deciles by PE outperforming Large Stocks and the highest all underperforming the universe.

Implications

Figures 5-3 and 5-4, as well as Table 5-13, summarize what you can expect when buying stocks with the 50 lowest and highest PE ratios. Figures 5-5 and 5-6 and Tables 5-14 and 5-15 summarize the results by decile. The results are striking. Both Large Stocks and All Stocks with high PE ratios do substantially worse than the market. This is true for the 50 highest PE stocks as well as the highest PE stocks by decile. Companies with the 50 lowest PE ratios from the Large Stocks universe do much better than the universe, and the three lowest deciles by PE substantially outperform Large Stocks. The decile results from All Stocks show that investors using the All Stocks universe would be bet-

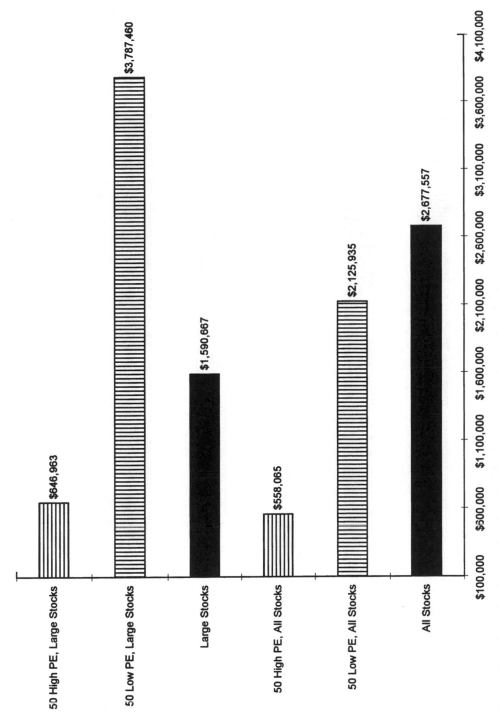

Figure 5-3. December 31, 1996, value of $10,000 invested on December 31, 1951, and annually rebalanced.

71

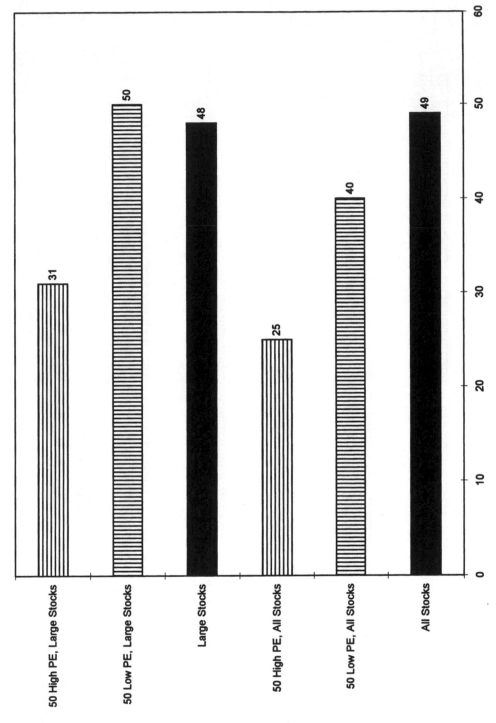

Figure 5-4. Sharpe risk-adjusted return ratio, 1951–1996. (Higher is better.)

Table 5-13. Compound Annual Rates of Return by Decade

Portfolio	1950s*	1960s	1970s	1980s	1990s**
Large Stocks	15.33%	8.99%	6.99%	16.89%	12.61%
50 high PE from Large Stocks	14.77%	10.94%	0.93%	14.11%	9.21%
50 low PE from Large Stocks	16.12%	11.14%	12.64%	16.19%	15.25%
All Stocks	19.22%	11.09%	8.53%	15.85%	12.78%
50 high PE from All Stocks	19.27%	10.96%	2.26%	7.99%	8.63%
50 low PE from All Stocks	21.84%	13.96%	8.89%	7.56%	13.58%

*Returns for 1952–1959.
**Returns for 1990–1996.

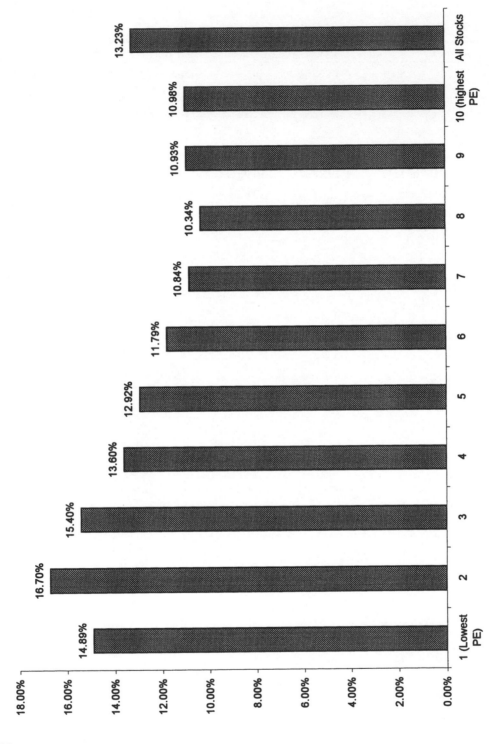

Figure 5-5. Compound return by PE decile, All Stocks universe, 1951–1996.

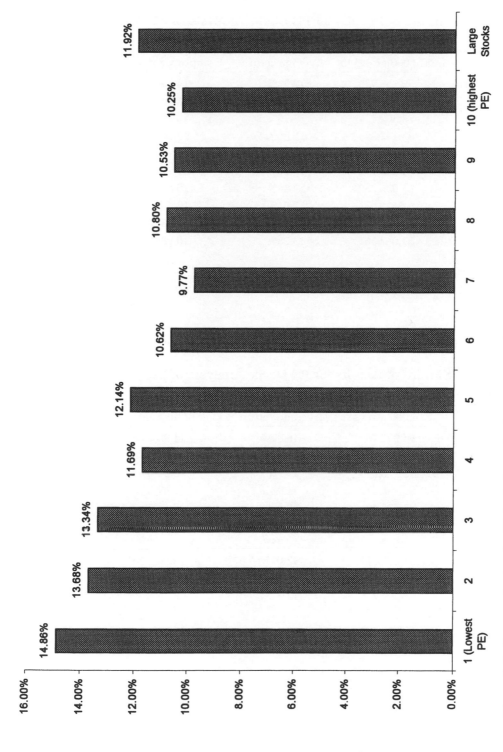

Figure 5-6. Compound return by P/E decile, Large Stocks universe, 1951–1996.

Table 5-14. Summary Results for PE Decile Analysis of All Stocks Universe, 1951–1996

Decile	$10,000 grows to	Average return	Compound return	Standard deviation
1 (lowest PE)	$5,159,955	17.33%	14.89%	23.66%
2	$10,427,991	18.78%	16.70%	22.03%
3	$6,307,424	17.13%	15.40%	19.97%
4	$3,102,398	15.35%	13.60%	20.17%
5	$2,365,448	14.50%	12.92%	18.48%
6	$1,504,992	13.39%	11.79%	18.44%
7	$1,026,280	12.44%	10.84%	18.02%
8	$838,031	12.03%	10.34%	18.84%
9	$1,065,155	12.93%	10.93%	20.39%
10 (highest PE)	$1,087,361	13.78%	10.98%	24.65%
All Stocks	$2,677,557	14.97%	13.23%	19.51%

Table 5-15. Summary Results for PE Decile Analysis of Large Stocks Universe, 1951–1996

Decile	$10,000 grows to	Average return	Compound return	Standard deviation
1 (lowest PE)	$5,092,753	16.87%	14.86%	21.89%
2	$3,204,878	15.40%	13.68%	19.86%
3	$2,796,638	14.78%	13.34%	18.36%
4	$1,446,427	12.93%	11.69%	16.67%
5	$1,735,401	13.42%	12.14%	16.75%
6	$940,571	11.73%	10.62%	15.35%
7	$662,102	10.98%	9.77%	15.96%
8	$1,009,014	12.07%	10.80%	16.26%
9	$906,383	12.08%	10.53%	17.78%
10 (highest PE)	$807,266	12.34%	10.25%	21.02%
Large Stocks	$1,590,667	13.11%	11.92%	16.01%

ter off avoiding the 50 lowest PE stocks in favor of selecting more generally from the four deciles with the lowest PE ratios. In both groups, *stocks with low PE ratios do much better than stocks with high PE ratios, both at the 50-stock extreme and at the larger deciles.* More, there's not much difference in risk. In the All Stocks universe, the standard deviation of return on the 50 low PE stocks was 25.14 percent, whereas the 50 highest PE stocks had a standard deviation of 26.33 percent. In the Large Stocks universe, the low PE strategy had a standard deviation of 21.39 percent, whereas the high PE strategy's standard deviation was 20.14 percent.

Ben Graham and David Dodd were absolutely right in their 1940 book *Security Analysis: Principles and Technique.* They said: "People who habitually purchase common stocks at more than about 20 times their average earnings are likely to lose considerable money in the long run."

6

Price-to-Book Ratios:
A Better Gauge
of Value

*Life can only be understood backwards; but
it must be lived forwards.*
—SØREN KIERKEGAARD

In this chapter, we'll review price-to-book ratios. Many investors believe this is a more important ratio when looking for bargain stocks. They argue that earnings can be easily manipulated by a clever chief financial officer, using an old joke as an example. A company wants to hire a new chief financial officer. Each candidate is asked just one question: "What does 2 plus 2 equal?" Each candidate answers 4, with the exception of the one who is hired. Her answer is: "What number did you have in mind?"

The price-to-book ratio is found by dividing the current price of the stock by the book value per share. Here, we use the common equity liquidating value per share as a proxy for book value per share. Essentially, investors who buy stocks with low price-to-book ratios believe they are getting stocks at a price close to their liquidating value, and that they will be rewarded for not paying high prices for assets.

We'll look at both the high and low price-to-book ratio stocks from All Stocks and Large Stocks. We'll start on December 31, 1951 and buy the 50 stocks with the highest book-to-price ratios from the All Stocks universe. (Again, because of Compustat's ranking function, we must rank stocks by the 50 *highest* book-to-price ratios, the inverse of the price-to-book ratio.) We'll also look at All Stocks and Large Stocks segregated by decile.

The Results

Over the long term, the market rewards stocks with low price-to-book ratios and punishes those with high ones. An investment of $10,000 on December 31, 1951 in the 50 stocks with the lowest price-to-book ratios from the All Stocks universe grew to $5,490,122 by December 31, 1996, a compound return of 15.05 percent a year. That's much better than the $2,677,557 you'd earn from an investment in All Stocks. Risk was fairly high. The standard deviation for the 50 low price-to-book stocks was 25.45 percent, considerably higher than the 19.51 percent for the All Stocks universe. But because of the higher returns, the Sharpe ratio for both the 50 low price-to-book stocks and the All Stocks universe was 49.

Large Stocks Are Less Volatile

The 50 low price-to-book stocks from the Large Stocks universe did much better on a risk-adjusted basis. Here $10,000 invested in 1951 grew to $5,025,656 by the end of 1996, a compound return of 14.82 percent a year. That's more than three times the $1,590,667 you'd earn from $10,000 invested in the Large Stocks universe, but with a standard deviation of 19.96 percent. While higher than the Large Stocks' 16.01 percent, it's much less volatile than the low price-to-book stocks from All Stocks. The Sharpe ratio here was 56, a strong showing from a single variable.

Base rates here are mixed. While the 50 low price-to-book stocks from All Stocks beat the universe 60 percent of the time on a year-by-year basis and 69 percent of the time over all rolling 10-year periods, they beat the All Stocks group just 51 percent of the time on a rolling 5-year basis. The results suggest that the low price-to-book group saw some wild rides on the way to beating the All Stocks universe. Indeed, when you look at the annual performance comparisons in Table 6-1, you see four years where the low price-to-book group did 20 percent better than All Stocks. But there was also some rough sledding. The low price-to-book strategy underperformed the All Stocks universe four years in a

Table 6-1. Annual Performance of All Stocks Versus 50 Stocks with High Book-to-Price (Low Price-to-Book) Ratios from All Stocks Universe

Year ending	All Stocks	Universe = All Stocks top 50 book/price	Top 50 book/price relative performance
31-Dec-52	7.90%	5.40%	−2.50%
31-Dec-53	2.90%	−2.60%	−5.50%
31-Dec-54	47.00%	62.20%	15.20%
31-Dec-55	20.70%	19.30%	−1.40%
31-Dec-56	17.00%	8.20%	−8.80%
31-Dec-57	−7.10%	−14.50%	−7.40%
31-Dec-58	55.00%	77.49%	22.49%
31-Dec-59	23.00%	22.10%	−0.90%
31-Dec-60	6.10%	−8.50%	−14.60%
31-Dec-61	31.20%	32.60%	1.40%
31-Dec-62	−12.00%	−4.10%	7.90%
31-Dec-63	18.00%	23.50%	5.50%
31-Dec-64	16.30%	16.80%	0.50%
31-Dec-65	22.60%	39.20%	16.60%
31-Dec-66	−5.20%	−12.80%	−7.60%
31-Dec-67	41.10%	43.60%	2.50%
31-Dec-68	27.40%	37.40%	10.00%
31-Dec-69	−18.50%	−26.20%	−7.70%
31-Dec-70	−5.80%	0.07%	5.87%
31-Dec-71	21.30%	23.30%	2.00%
31-Dec-72	11.00%	13.80%	2.80%
31-Dec-73	−27.20%	−10.30%	16.90%
31-Dec-74	−27.90%	−8.50%	19.40%
31-Dec-75	55.90%	69.80%	13.90%
31-Dec-76	35.60%	62.40%	26.80%
31-Dec-77	6.90%	6.30%	−0.60%
31-Dec-78	12.20%	10.10%	−2.10%
31-Dec-79	34.30%	29.90%	−4.40%
31-Dec-80	31.50%	13.50%	−18.00%
31-Dec-81	1.70%	2.70%	1.00%
31-Dec-82	22.50%	36.70%	14.20%
31-Dec-83	28.10%	41.90%	13.80%
31-Dec-84	−3.40%	−19.40%	−16.00%
31-Dec-85	30.80%	33.60%	2.80%
31-Dec-86	13.10%	−5.80%	−18.90%
31-Dec-87	−1.30%	9.70%	11.00%
31-Dec-88	21.20%	34.40%	13.20%
31-Dec-89	21.40%	1.70%	−19.70%
31-Dec-90	−13.80%	−34.50%	−20.70%
31-Dec-91	39.80%	48.20%	8.40%
31-Dec-92	13.80%	40.40%	26.60%
31-Dec-93	16.60%	36.70%	20.10%
31-Dec-94	−3.40%	−1.80%	1.60%
31-Dec-95	27.00%	35.40%	8.40%
31-Dec-96	18.30%	12.90%	−5.40%
Arithmetic average	14.97%	17.83%	2.86%
Standard deviation	19.51%	25.45%	5.95%

row between 1976 and 1980, and had a devastating period between 1988 and 1990. These periods are important to keep in mind when considering any strategy, since many investors would jettison the strategy after such a poor showing. For a strategy to be valuable, it must be consistent enough for investors to stick with it through rough patches.

Base Rates More Consistent for Large Stocks

Base rates for the low price-to-book stocks from the Large Stocks universe are more consistent. Here the low price-to-book stocks beat the Large Stocks universe a minimum of 62 percent of the time, with rolling 10-year returns showing the highest probability of beating the Large Stocks universe. Figure 6-1 and Tables 6-2 through 6-6 summarize the results.

High Price-to-Book Stocks Do Poorly

Like high price-to-earnings stocks, stocks with high price-to-book ratios are generally bad investments. Figure 6-2 and Tables 6-7 through 6-12 summarize the results. Here $10,000 invested in the 50 stocks with the highest price-to-book ratios drawn from the All Stocks universe grew to just $380,440 at the end of 1996, more than $2 million dollars behind an investment in All Stocks and several million behind an investment in the 50 stocks with the lowest price-to-book ratios. The standard deviation of 28.43 percent signifies a wild ride, verified by the year-by-year returns. In 1973 through 1976 and 1981 through 1985, the group did 20 percent *worse* than the All Stocks universe annually. The years 1981 and 1984 are worthy of special mention. In 1981 the All Stocks universe had a gain of 1.7 percent. The 50 stocks with the highest price-to-book ratios *lost* over 31 percent. In 1984 the results were more terrifying, with the All Stocks group losing 3.4 percent while high price-to-book stocks lost almost 40 percent.

The 50 stocks with high price-to-book ratios from the Large Stocks group didn't fare much better: $10,000 invested on December 31, 1951 grew to $893,583 by the end of 1996, a compound return of 10.50 percent, or about half the return of the Large Stocks group. The standard deviation was a bit lower—22.84 percent—but the Sharpe ratio of 33 was still dismal. Figures 6-3 and 6-4 summarize the results.

The base rates for the high price-to-book stocks are unusual. While the longer-term numbers are overwhelmingly negative, high price-to-

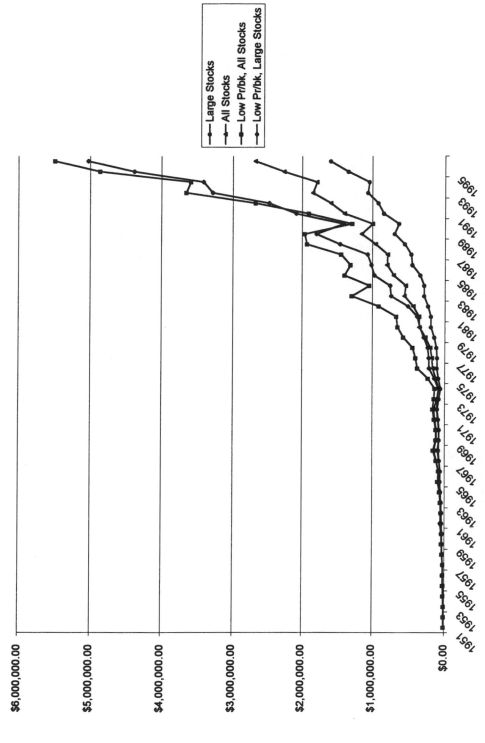

Figure 6-1. Returns on low price-to-book strategies versus All Stocks and Large Stocks, 1951–1996. Year-end 1951 = $10,000.

Table 6-2. Annual Performance of Large Stocks Versus 50 Stocks with High Book-to-Price (Low Price-to-Book) Ratios from Large Stocks Universe

Year ending	Large Stocks	Universe = Large Stocks top 50 book/price	Top 50 book/price relative performance
31-Dec-52	9.30%	11.90%	2.60%
31-Dec-53	2.30%	1.40%	−0.90%
31-Dec-54	44.90%	59.60%	14.70%
31-Dec-55	21.20%	17.20%	−4.00%
31-Dec-56	9.60%	10.90%	1.30%
31-Dec-57	−6.90%	−10.70%	−3.80%
31-Dec-58	42.10%	41.70%	−0.40%
31-Dec-59	9.90%	5.70%	−4.20%
31-Dec-60	4.80%	−1.10%	−5.90%
31-Dec-61	27.50%	28.20%	0.70%
31-Dec-62	−8.90%	−3.20%	5.70%
31-Dec-63	19.50%	24.60%	5.10%
31-Dec-64	15.30%	19.30%	4.00%
31-Dec-65	16.20%	17.90%	1.70%
31-Dec-66	−4.90%	−10.10%	−5.20%
31-Dec-67	21.30%	22.50%	1.20%
31-Dec-68	16.80%	30.80%	14.00%
31-Dec-69	−9.90%	−19.50%	−9.60%
31-Dec-70	−0.20%	1.80%	2.00%
31-Dec-71	17.30%	19.00%	1.70%
31-Dec-72	14.90%	12.00%	−2.90%
31-Dec-73	−18.90%	−2.90%	16.00%
31-Dec-74	−26.70%	−16.90%	9.80%
31-Dec-75	43.10%	66.60%	23.50%
31-Dec-76	28.00%	50.10%	22.10%
31-Dec-77	−2.50%	2.50%	5.00%
31-Dec-78	8.10%	5.50%	−2.60%
31-Dec-79	27.30%	24.70%	−2.60%
31-Dec-80	30.80%	18.50%	−12.30%
31-Dec-81	0.60%	10.20%	9.60%
31-Dec-82	19.90%	33.00%	13.10%
31-Dec-83	23.80%	46.60%	22.80%
31-Dec-84	−0.40%	1.80%	2.20%
31-Dec-85	19.50%	29.10%	9.60%
31-Dec-86	32.20%	4.40%	−27.80%
31-Dec-87	3.30%	5.50%	2.20%
31-Dec-88	19.00%	36.30%	17.30%
31-Dec-89	26.00%	23.20%	−2.80%
31-Dec-90	−8.70%	−21.90%	−13.20%
31-Dec-91	33.00%	49.00%	16.00%
31-Dec-92	8.70%	18.80%	10.10%
31-Dec-93	16.30%	32.50%	16.20%
31-Dec-94	−1.90%	4.00%	5.90%
31-Dec-95	28.50%	28.20%	−0.30%
31-Dec-96	18.70%	14.70%	−4.00%
Arithmetic average	13.11%	16.52%	3.41%
Standard deviation	16.01%	19.96%	3.96%

Table 6-3. Summary Return Results for All Stocks and 50 Highest Book-to-Price (Low Price-to-Book) Stocks from All Stocks Universe, December 31, 1951–December 31, 1996

	All Stocks	Universe = All Stocks top 50 book/price (low price/book)
Arithmetic average	14.97%	17.83%
Standard deviation of return	19.51%	25.45%
Sharpe risk-adjusted ratio	49.00	49.00
3-yr compounded	13.22%	14.50%
5-yr compounded	14.00%	23.57%
10-yr compounded	12.92%	15.41%
15-yr compounded	14.44%	15.11%
20-yr compounded	14.97%	14.35%
25-yr compounded	12.74%	15.62%
30-yr compounded	12.43%	15.08%
35-yr compounded	11.64%	14.48%
40-yr compounded	12.62%	14.86%
Compound annual return	13.23%	15.05%
$10,000 becomes:	$2,677,556.77	$5,490,121.79
Maximum return	55.90%	77.49%
Minimum return	−27.90%	−34.50%
Maximum expected return*	53.98%	68.74%
Minimum expected return**	−24.04%	−33.08%

*Maximum expected return is average return plus 2 times the standard deviation.

**Minimum expected return is average return minus 2 times the standard deviation.

Table 6-4. Summary Return Results for Large Stocks and 50 Highest Book-to-Price (Low Price-to-Book) Stocks from Large Stocks Universe, December 31, 1951–December 31, 1996

	Large Stocks	Universe = Large Stocks top 50 book/price (low price/book)
Arithmetic average	13.11%	16.52%
Standard deviation of return	16.01%	19.96%
Sharpe risk-adjusted ratio	48.00	56.00
3-yr compounded	14.38%	15.21%
5-yr compounded	13.60%	19.21%
10-yr compounded	13.53%	17.37%
15-yr compounded	15.16%	18.82%
20-yr compounded	14.37%	17.07%
25-yr compounded	12.34%	17.20%
30-yr compounded	11.67%	15.85%
35-yr compounded	10.96%	14.82%
40-yr compounded	11.36%	14.35%
Compound annual return	11.92%	14.82%
$10,000 becomes:	$1,590,667.04	$5,025,655.77
Maximum return	44.90%	66.60%
Minimum return	−26.70%	−21.90%
Maximum expected return*	45.12%	56.44%
Minimum expected return**	−18.91%	−23.40%

  *Maximum expected return is average return plus 2 times the standard deviation.
  **Minimum expected return is average return minus 2 times the standard deviation.

Table 6-5. Base Rates for All Stocks and 50 Highest Book-to-Price (Low Price-to-Book) Stocks from All Stocks Universe, 1951–1996

Item	50 low price-to-book beat All Stocks	Percent
Single-year return	27 out of 45	60%
Rolling 5-year compound return	21 out of 41	51%
Rolling 10-year compound return	25 out of 36	69%

Table 6-6. Base Rates for Large Stocks and 50 Highest Book-to-Price (Low Price-to-Book) Stocks from Large Stocks Universe, 1951–1996

Item	50 low price-to-book beat Large Stocks	Percent
Single-year return	28 out of 45	62%
Rolling 5-year compound return	32 out of 41	78%
Rolling 10-year compound return	32 out of 36	89%

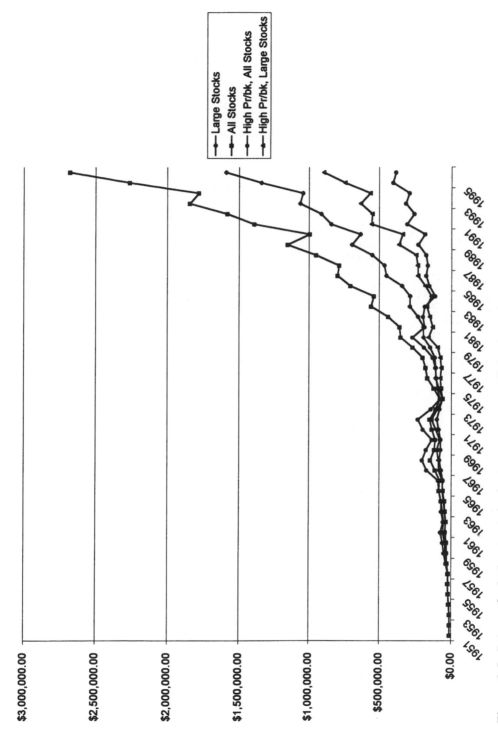

Figure 6-2. Returns for high price-to-book strategies versus All Stocks and Large Stocks, 1951–1996. Year-end 1951 = $10,000.

Table 6-7. Annual Performance of All Stocks Versus 50 Stocks with High
Price-to-Book Ratios from All Stocks Universe

Year ending	All Stocks	Universe = All Stocks top 50 price/book	Top 50 price/book relative performance
31-Dec-52	7.90%	3.90%	−4.00%
31-Dec-53	2.90%	3.40%	0.50%
31-Dec-54	47.00%	49.60%	2.60%
31-Dec-55	20.70%	19.00%	−1.70%
31-Dec-56	17.00%	21.50%	4.50%
31-Dec-57	−7.10%	−5.40%	1.70%
31-Dec-58	55.00%	61.80%	6.80%
31-Dec-59	23.00%	40.90%	17.90%
31-Dec-60	6.10%	19.20%	13.10%
31-Dec-61	31.20%	23.00%	−8.20%
31-Dec-62	−12.00%	−23.30%	−11.30%
31-Dec-63	18.00%	21.82%	3.82%
31-Dec-64	16.30%	3.20%	−13.10%
31-Dec-65	22.60%	20.20%	−2.40%
31-Dec-66	−5.20%	5.90%	11.10%
31-Dec-67	41.10%	87.60%	46.50%
31-Dec-68	27.40%	18.00%	−9.40%
31-Dec-69	−18.50%	−13.80%	4.70%
31-Dec-70	−5.80%	−22.20%	−16.40%
31-Dec-71	21.30%	45.10%	23.80%
31-Dec-72	11.00%	17.60%	6.60%
31-Dec-73	−27.20%	−38.10%	−10.90%
31-Dec-74	−27.90%	−44.80%	−16.90%
31-Dec-75	55.90%	21.90%	−34.00%
31-Dec-76	35.60%	7.30%	−28.30%
31-Dec-77	6.90%	7.90%	1.00%
31-Dec-78	12.20%	16.30%	4.10%
31-Dec-79	34.30%	45.70%	11.40%
31-Dec-80	31.50%	43.00%	11.50%
31-Dec-81	1.70%	−31.20%	−32.90%
31-Dec-82	22.50%	5.90%	−16.60%
31-Dec-83	28.10%	−6.30%	−34.40%
31-Dec-84	−3.40%	−38.60%	−35.20%
31-Dec-85	30.80%	34.60%	3.80%
31-Dec-86	13.10%	15.40%	2.30%
31-Dec-87	−1.30%	−7.10%	−5.80%
31-Dec-88	21.20%	7.60%	−13.60%
31-Dec-89	21.40%	30.60%	9.20%
31-Dec-90	−13.80%	−20.90%	−7.10%
31-Dec-91	39.80%	68.30%	28.50%
31-Dec-92	13.80%	−15.80%	−29.60%
31-Dec-93	16.60%	22.50%	5.90%
31-Dec-94	−3.40%	−8.10%	−4.70%
31-Dec-95	27.00%	40.00%	13.00%
31-Dec-96	18.30%	−5.10%	−23.40%
Arithmetic average	14.97%	12.18%	−2.68%
Standard deviation	19.51%	28.43%	8.92%

Table 6-8. Annual Performance of Large Stocks Versus 50 Stocks with High Price-to-Book Ratios from Large Stocks Universe

Year ending	Large Stocks	Universe = Large Stocks top 50 price/book	Top 50 price/book relative performance
31-Dec-52	9.30%	6.00%	−3.30%
31-Dec-53	2.30%	0.60%	−1.70%
31-Dec-54	44.90%	43.50%	−1.40%
31-Dec-55	21.20%	31.90%	10.70%
31-Dec-56	9.60%	9.50%	−0.10%
31-Dec-57	−6.90%	−11.00%	−4.10%
31-Dec-58	42.10%	44.60%	2.50%
31-Dec-59	9.90%	19.70%	9.80%
31-Dec-60	4.80%	2.80%	−2.00%
31-Dec-61	27.50%	24.20%	−3.30%
31-Dec-62	−8.90%	−17.20%	−8.30%
31-Dec-63	19.50%	21.80%	2.30%
31-Dec-64	15.30%	8.40%	−6.90%
31-Dec-65	16.20%	20.00%	3.80%
31-Dec-66	−4.90%	8.40%	13.30%
31-Dec-67	21.30%	40.20%	18.90%
31-Dec-68	16.80%	2.30%	−14.50%
31-Dec-69	−9.90%	12.00%	21.90%
31-Dec-70	−0.20%	−19.90%	−19.70%
31-Dec-71	17.30%	34.60%	17.30%
31-Dec-72	14.90%	26.10%	11.20%
31-Dec-73	−18.90%	−28.80%	−9.90%
31-Dec-74	−26.70%	−38.70%	−12.00%
31-Dec-75	43.10%	18.60%	−24.50%
31-Dec-76	28.00%	9.20%	−18.80%
31-Dec-77	−2.50%	−10.40%	−7.90%
31-Dec-78	8.10%	10.40%	2.30%
31-Dec-79	27.30%	23.90%	−3.40%
31-Dec-80	30.80%	67.80%	37.00%
31-Dec-81	0.60%	−18.80%	−19.40%
31-Dec-82	19.90%	15.80%	−4.10%
31-Dec-83	23.80%	13.80%	−10.00%
31-Dec-84	−0.40%	−18.40%	−18.00%
31-Dec-85	19.50%	29.80%	10.30%
31-Dec-86	32.20%	28.40%	−3.80%
31-Dec-87	3.30%	1.00%	−2.30%
31-Dec-88	19.00%	4.80%	−14.20%
31-Dec-89	26.00%	48.50%	22.50%
31-Dec-90	−8.70%	−7.00%	1.70%
31-Dec-91	33.00%	65.60%	32.60%
31-Dec-92	8.70%	−0.90%	−9.60%
31-Dec-93	16.30%	15.20%	−1.10%
31-Dec-94	−1.90%	−10.80%	−8.90%
31-Dec-95	28.50%	31.50%	3.00%
31-Dec-96	18.70%	20.70%	2.00%
Arithmetic average	13.11%	12.88%	−0.22%
Standard deviation	16.01%	22.84%	6.84%

Table 6-9. Summary Return Results for All Stocks and 50 Highest
Price-to-Book Stocks from All Stocks Universe,
December 31, 1951–December 31, 1996

	All Stocks	Universe = All Stocks top 50 price/book
Arithmetic average	14.97%	12.18%
Standard deviation of return	19.51%	28.43%
Sharpe risk-adjusted ratio	49.00	24.00
3-yr compounded	13.22%	6.88%
5-yr compounded	14.00%	4.72%
10-yr compounded	12.92%	8.15%
15-yr compounded	14.44%	4.97%
20-yr compounded	14.97%	6.80%
25-yr compounded	12.74%	2.72%
30-yr compounded	12.43%	4.92%
35-yr compounded	11.64%	4.81%
40-yr compounded	12.62%	7.24%
Compound annual return	13.23%	8.42%
$10,000 becomes:	$2,677,556.77	$380,440.10
Maximum return	55.90%	87.60%
Minimum return	−27.90%	−44.80%
Maximum expected return*	53.98%	69.04%
Minimum expected return**	−24.04%	−44.68%

*Maximum expected return is average return plus 2 times the standard deviation.

**Minimum expected return is average return minus 2 times the standard deviation.

Table 6-10. Summary Return Results for Large Stocks and 50 Highest Price-to-Book Stocks from Large Stocks Universe, December 31, 1951–December 31, 1996

	Large Stocks	Universe = Large Stocks top 50 price/book
Arithmetic average	13.11%	12.88%
Standard deviation of return	16.01%	22.84%
Sharpe risk-adjusted ratio	48.00	33.00
3-yr compounded	14.38%	12.29%
5-yr compounded	13.60%	10.08%
10-yr compounded	13.53%	14.62%
15-yr compounded	15.16%	13.87%
20-yr compounded	14.37%	13.09%
25-yr compounded	12.34%	8.86%
30-yr compounded	11.67%	9.31%
35-yr compounded	10.96%	9.02%
40-yr compounded	11.36%	9.69%
Compound annual return	11.92%	10.50%
$10,000 becomes:	$1,590,667.04	$893,582.92
Maximum return	44.90%	67.80%
Minimum return	−26.70%	−38.70%
Maximum expected return*	45.12%	58.57%
Minimum expected return**	−18.91%	−32.80%

*Maximum expected return is average return plus 2 times the standard deviation.

**Minimum expected return is average return minus 2 times the standard deviation.

Table 6-11. Base Rates for All Stocks and 50 Highest Price-to-Book Stocks from All Stocks Universe, 1951–1996

Item	50 high price-to-book beat All Stocks	Percent
Single-year return	23 out of 45	51%
Rolling 5-year compound return	14 out of 41	34%
Rolling 10-year compound return	12 out of 36	33%

Table 6-12. Base Rates for Large Stocks and 50 Highest Price-to-Book Stocks from Large Stocks Universe, 1951–1996

Item	50 high price-to-book beat Large Stocks	Percent
Single-year return	18 out of 45	40%
Rolling 5-year compound return	22 out of 41	54%
Rolling 10-year compound return	15 out of 36	42%

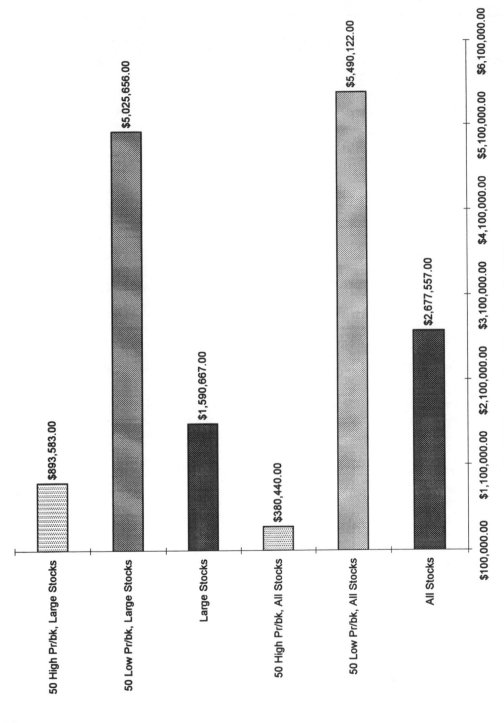

Figure 6-3. December 31, 1996, value of $10,000 invested on December 31, 1951, and annually rebalanced.

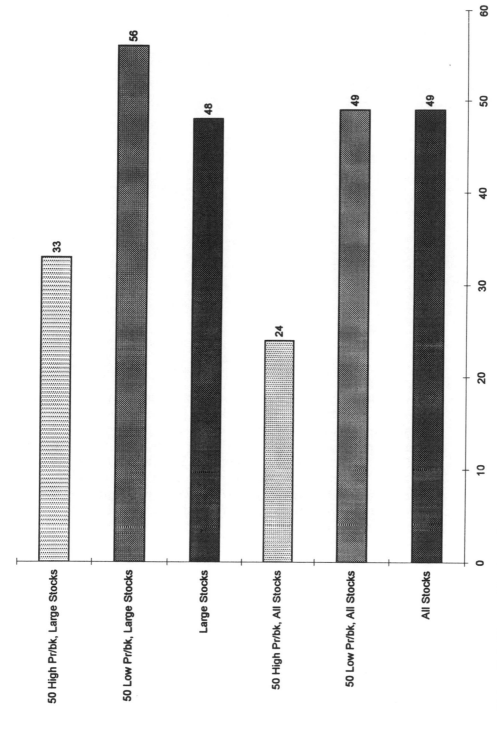

Figure 6-4. Sharpe risk-adjusted return ratio, 1951–1996. (Higher is better.)

Table 6-13. Compound Annual Rates of Return by Decade

Portfolio	1950s*	1960s	1970s	1980s	1990s**
Large Stocks	15.33%	8.99%	6.99%	16.89%	12.61%
50 high price-to-book from Large Stocks	16.55%	11.30%	−0.60%	14.40%	13.92%
50 low price-to-book from Large Stocks	15.41%	9.57%	13.95%	19.99%	15.85%
All Stocks	19.22%	11.09%	8.53%	15.85%	12.78%
50 high price-to-book from All Stocks	22.32%	13.13%	0.82%	1.97%	7.66%
50 low price-to-book from All Stocks	21.84%	13.96%	8.89%	7.56%	15.83%

*Returns for 1952–1959.
**Returns for 1990–1996.

book stocks from the Large Stocks universe actually beat the group 54 percent of the time over rolling 5-year periods. What's more, the compound returns in Table 6-13 show that the 50 Large Stocks with the highest price-to-book ratios did better than Large Stocks in both the 1950s and 1960s! In contrast, large stocks with high PE ratios failed to beat the universe in any of the decades from the 1950s to the 1990s. Clearly you need to be careful when reviewing returns by decade. As Table 6-14 shows, you're better off looking at rolling 10-year returns on a continuous basis.

Deciles

The decile results confirm our 50-stock findings. In both the All Stocks and Large Stocks groups, the low price-to-book deciles do better than both their benchmark and the high price-to-book deciles. Indeed, in the All Stocks universe, the lowest decile did eight times as well as the highest! Tables 6-15 and 6-16 as well as Figures 6-5 and 6-6 summarize the results.

Table 6-14. Rolling Compound 10-Year Returns for All Stocks and 50 Highest Price-to-Book Stocks from All Stocks Universe, December 31, 1961–December 31, 1996

For the 10 years ending	All Stocks	Universe = All Stocks top 50 price/book	Top 50 price-book relative performance
31-Dec-61	18.97%	22.07%	3.10%
31-Dec-62	16.57%	18.42%	1.85%
31-Dec-63	18.18%	20.38%	2.20%
31-Dec-64	15.44%	15.99%	0.55%
31-Dec-65	15.63%	16.11%	0.48%
31-Dec-66	13.22%	14.52%	1.31%
31-Dec-67	18.05%	22.64%	4.59%
31-Dec-68	15.76%	18.83%	3.07%
31-Dec-69	11.09%	13.13%	2.04%
31-Dec-70	9.78%	8.41%	−1.37%
31-Dec-71	8.92%	10.21%	1.29%
31-Dec-72	11.48%	15.02%	3.55%
31-Dec-73	6.22%	7.49%	1.27%
31-Dec-74	1.26%	0.97%	−0.29%
31-Dec-75	3.72%	1.12%	−2.61%
31-Dec-76	7.50%	1.25%	−6.26%
31-Dec-77	4.56%	−4.20%	−8.76%
31-Dec-78	3.24%	−4.34%	−7.58%
31-Dec-79	8.53%	0.82%	−7.71%
31-Dec-80	12.21%	7.14%	−5.07%
31-Dec-81	10.25%	−0.56%	−10.81%
31-Dec-82	11.34%	−1.60%	−12.94%
31-Dec-83	17.82%	2.57%	−15.25%
31-Dec-84	21.31%	3.67%	−17.65%
31-Dec-85	19.20%	4.70%	−14.50%
31-Dec-86	17.06%	5.46%	−11.59%
31-Dec-87	16.13%	3.90%	−12.23%
31-Dec-88	17.03%	3.09%	−13.93%
31-Dec-89	15.85%	1.97%	−13.88%
31-Dec-90	11.06%	−3.89%	−14.95%
31-Dec-91	14.65%	5.10%	−9.55%
31-Dec-92	13.81%	2.72%	−11.09%
31-Dec-93	12.74%	5.51%	−7.24%
31-Dec-94	12.74%	9.85%	−2.89%
31-Dec-95	12.41%	10.28%	−2.13%
31-Dec-96	12.92%	8.15%	−4.77%
Arithmetic average	12.69%	7.41%	−5.27%

Table 6-15. Summary Results for Price-to-Book Decile Analysis of All Stocks Universe, 1951–1996

Decile	$10,000 grows to	Average return	Compound return	Standard deviation
1 (lowest price/book)	$8,670,540	18.86%	16.22%	25.06%
2	$6,625,560	17.47%	15.53%	21.21%
3	$5,591,529	16.86%	15.09%	19.98%
4	$4,210,648	16.29%	14.37%	20.87%
5	$2,234,283	14.75%	12.77%	20.64%
6	$1,481,636	13.71%	11.75%	20.45%
7	$1,512,844	13.61%	11.80%	19.46%
8	$1,810,470	14.72%	12.25%	23.34%
9	$2,076,414	15.09%	12.59%	23.42%
10 (highest price/book)	$1,002,074	13.91%	10.78%	26.61%
All Stocks	$2,677,557	14.97%	13.23%	19.51%

Table 6-16. Summary Results for Price-to-Book Decile Analysis of Large Stocks Universe, 1951–1996

Decile	$10,000 grows to	Average return	Compound return	Standard deviation
1 (lowest price/book)	$6,475,018	17.15%	15.47%	20.01%
2	$2,451,539	14.50%	13.01%	18.38%
3	$1,995,238	13.79%	12.49%	17.03%
4	$1,434,077	12.92%	11.67%	16.60%
5	$1,455,251	12.98%	11.70%	16.85%
6	$1,065,948	12.39%	10.93%	17.46%
7	$877,525	11.88%	10.45%	17.30%
8	$1,299,473	12.88%	11.42%	17.58%
9	$1,182,866	12.99%	11.19%	19.49%
10 (highest price/book)	$1,127,200	13.42%	11.07%	22.54%
Large Stocks	$1,590,667	13.11%	11.92%	16.01%

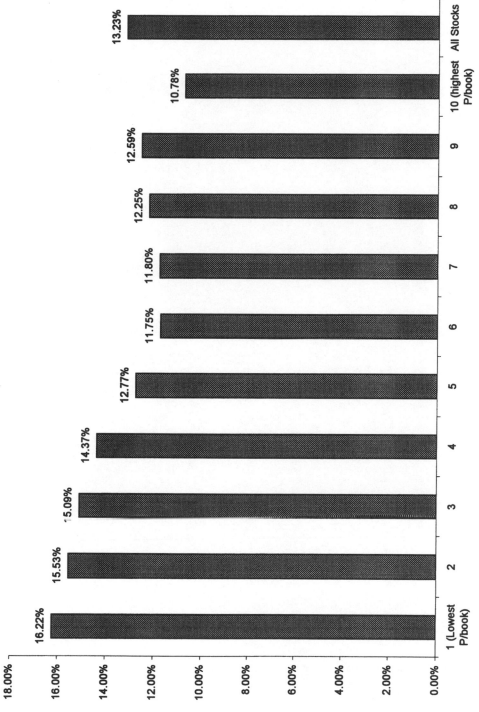

Figure 6-5. Compound return by P/book decile, All Stocks universe, 1951–1996.

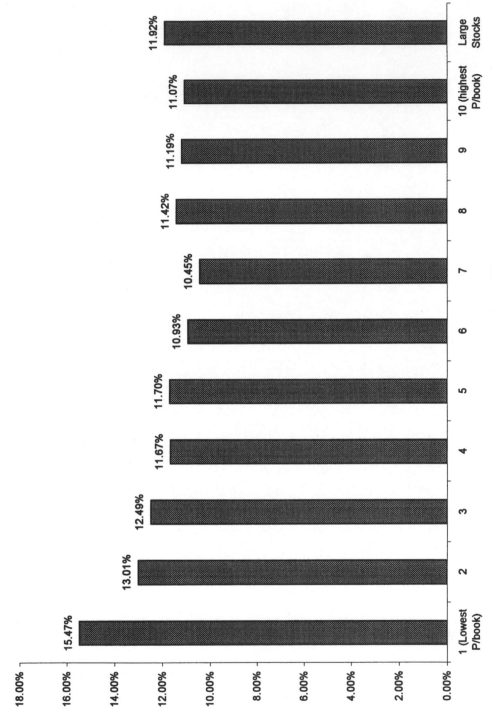

Figure 6-6. Compound return by P/book decile, Large Stocks universe, 1951–1996.

Implications

Over the long term, the market clearly rewards low price-to-book ratios and punishes high ones. Yet the data show why investors are willing to overlook high price-to-book ratios: For 20 years, the 50 Large Stocks with high price-to-book ratios did *better* than the Large Stocks universe. A high price-to-book ratio is one of the hallmarks of a growth stock, so high price-to-book ratios alone shouldn't keep you from buying a stock. But the long-term results should caution you against the highest price-to-book ratio stocks.

7

Price-to-Cashflow Ratios: Using Cash to Determine Value

Losing an illusion makes you wiser than finding a truth. —LUDWIG BORNE

The price-to-cashflow ratio is yet another measure of whether a stock is cheap or not. You find cashflow by adding income (before extraordinary items) to depreciation and amortization. The price-to-cashflow ratio is the market value of the stock divided by total cashflow. We'll look at it on a per share basis.

Some value investors prefer using price-to-cashflow ratios to find bargain-priced stocks because cashflow is more difficult to manipulate than earnings. We exclude utility stocks here, since utilities show up frequently and we want to avoid bias to one industry.

As usual, we look at both the low and high price-to-cashflow ratio stocks from our All Stocks and Large Stocks universes. We start with $10,000 on December 31, 1951, and buy the 50 stocks with the highest cashflow-to-price ratios from the All Stocks universe. (Again, because of Compustat's ranking function, we must rank stocks by the 50 *highest* cashflow-to-price ratios, the inverse of the price-to-cashflow ratio.) We'll also rank both All Stocks and Large stocks by price-to-cashflow decile. We'll rebalance the portfolio annually. The stocks are equally weighted, and all variables except price are time-lagged to avoid look-ahead bias.

The Results

As with the other value criteria, investors reward stocks with low price-to-cashflow ratios and punish those with high ones. Figure 7-1 summarizes the results. Let's look at the returns of low price-to-cashflow ratio stocks first. Here $10,000 invested on December 31, 1951 in the 50 stocks with the lowest price-to-cashflow ratios from the All Stocks universe was worth $4,483,126 on December 31,1996, a compound return of 14.53 percent a year—better than the $2,677,557 you'd earn from the same investment in the All Stocks universe. Risk was fairly high. The standard deviation of return for the 50 lowest price-to-cashflow stocks was 25.71 percent, considerably higher than the 19.51 percent for the All Stocks universe. Indeed, because of the higher risk, the Sharpe ratio for the low price-to-cashflow stocks was lower than that for the All Stocks universe, indicating that risk was not being fully rewarded. Tables 7-1 through 7-5 summarize the returns for the All Stocks group.

Large Stocks Are Less Volatile

As we've seen with the other value factors, the 50 low price-to-cashflow stocks from the Large Stocks universe did much better on both an absolute and a risk-adjusted basis. The original $10,000 invested in 1951 grew to $5,773,333 at the end of 1996, a compound return of 15.18 percent a year. That's more than three times the $1,590,667 you'd earn from $10,000 invested in the Large Stocks universe. The standard deviation of return of 20.56 percent is higher than the Large Stocks' 16.01 percent, but considerably lower than that for the low price-to-cashflow stocks from the All Stocks category. The Sharpe ratio for the low price-to-cashflow stocks from Large Stocks was 56. Reviewing Table 7-2, you see that the low price-to-cashflow stocks from the Large Stocks universe had five years where they did at least 15 percent better than the Large Stocks universe and only one year where they did more than 15 percent worse.

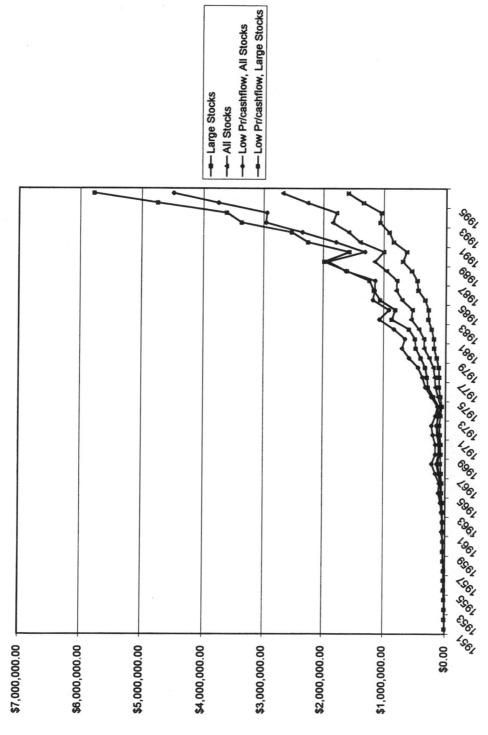

Figure 7-1. Returns on low price-to-cashflow strategies versus All Stocks and Large Stocks, 1951–1996. Year-end 1951 = $10,000.

Table 7-1. Annual Performance of All Stocks Versus 50 Stocks with High Cashflow-to-Price (Low Price-to-Cashflow) Ratios from All Stocks Universe

Year ending	All Stocks	Universe = All Stocks top 50 cashflow/price	Top 50 cashflow/price relative performance
31-Dec-52	7.90%	8.80%	0.90%
31-Dec-53	2.90%	−3.50%	−6.40%
31-Dec-54	47.00%	72.40%	25.40%
31-Dec-55	20.70%	26.70%	6.00%
31-Dec-56	17.00%	7.88%	−9.12%
31-Dec-57	−7.10%	−17.50%	−10.40%
31-Dec-58	55.00%	70.40%	15.40%
31-Dec-59	23.00%	13.40%	−9.60%
31-Dec-60	6.10%	−8.60%	−14.70%
31-Dec-61	31.20%	32.20%	1.00%
31-Dec-62	−12.00%	0.90%	12.90%
31-Dec-63	18.00%	31.30%	13.30%
31-Dec-64	16.30%	26.00%	9.70%
31-Dec-65	22.60%	40.60%	18.00%
31-Dec-66	−5.20%	−8.80%	−3.60%
31-Dec-67	41.10%	60.70%	19.60%
31-Dec-68	27.40%	36.50%	9.10%
31-Dec-69	−18.50%	−26.10%	−7.60%
31-Dec-70	−5.80%	−2.10%	3.70%
31-Dec-71	21.30%	28.30%	7.00%
31-Dec-72	11.00%	9.10%	−1.90%
31-Dec-73	−27.20%	−27.70%	−0.50%
31-Dec-74	−27.90%	−20.40%	7.50%
31-Dec-75	55.90%	77.70%	21.80%
31-Dec-76	35.60%	41.00%	5.40%
31-Dec-77	6.90%	15.10%	8.20%
31-Dec-78	12.20%	18.70%	6.50%
31-Dec-79	34.30%	32.20%	−2.10%
31-Dec-80	31.50%	18.90%	−12.60%
31-Dec-81	1.70%	−6.40%	−8.10%
31-Dec-82	22.50%	26.60%	4.10%
31-Dec-83	28.10%	28.70%	0.60%
31-Dec-84	−3.40%	−14.70%	−11.30%
31-Dec-85	30.80%	29.40%	−1.40%
31-Dec-86	13.10%	−2.60%	−15.70%
31-Dec-87	−1.30%	−0.60%	0.70%
31-Dec-88	21.20%	42.30%	21.10%
31-Dec-89	21.40%	18.10%	−3.30%
31-Dec-90	−13.80%	−31.60%	−17.80%
31-Dec-91	39.80%	36.30%	−3.50%
31-Dec-92	13.80%	31.20%	17.40%
31-Dec-93	16.60%	26.00%	9.40%
31-Dec-94	−3.40%	−0.50%	2.90%
31-Dec-95	27.00%	27.40%	0.40%
31-Dec-96	18.30%	19.40%	1.10%
Arithmetic average	14.97%	17.40%	2.43%
Standard deviation	19.51%	25.71%	6.20%

Table 7-2. Annual Performance of Large Stocks Versus 50 Stocks with High Cashflow-to-Price (Low Price-to-Cashflow) Ratios from Large Stocks Universe

Year ending	Large Stocks	Universe = Large Stocks top 50 cashflow/price	Top 50 cashflow/price relative performance
31-Dec-52	9.30%	14.10%	4.80%
31-Dec-53	2.30%	−0.09%	−2.39%
31-Dec-54	44.90%	64.60%	19.70%
31-Dec-55	21.20%	27.20%	6.00%
31-Dec-56	9.60%	16.50%	6.90%
31-Dec-57	−6.90%	−16.30%	−9.40%
31-Dec-58	42.10%	46.20%	4.10%
31-Dec-59	9.90%	5.20%	−4.70%
31-Dec-60	4.80%	−2.10%	−6.90%
31-Dec-61	27.50%	22.20%	−5.30%
31-Dec-62	−8.90%	0.01%	8.91%
31-Dec-63	19.50%	22.50%	3.00%
31-Dec-64	15.30%	22.90%	7.60%
31-Dec-65	16.20%	27.70%	11.50%
31-Dec-66	−4.90%	−7.30%	−2.40%
31-Dec-67	21.30%	25.70%	4.40%
31-Dec-68	16.80%	29.90%	13.10%
31-Dec-69	−9.90%	−23.00%	−13.10%
31-Dec-70	−0.20%	−0.30%	−0.10%
31-Dec-71	17.30%	18.20%	0.90%
31-Dec-72	14.90%	20.80%	5.90%
31-Dec-73	−18.90%	−5.60%	13.30%
31-Dec-74	−26.70%	−12.40%	14.30%
31-Dec-75	43.10%	75.70%	32.60%
31-Dec-76	28.00%	44.30%	16.30%
31-Dec-77	−2.50%	5.00%	7.50%
31-Dec-78	8.10%	10.90%	2.80%
31-Dec-79	27.30%	20.50%	−6.80%
31-Dec-80	30.80%	20.80%	−10.00%
31-Dec-81	0.60%	2.60%	2.00%
31-Dec-82	19.90%	19.40%	−0.50%
31-Dec-83	23.80%	45.80%	22.00%
31-Dec-84	−0.40%	−6.20%	−5.80%
31-Dec-85	19.50%	30.00%	10.50%
31-Dec-86	32.20%	10.00%	−22.20%
31-Dec-87	3.30%	6.70%	3.40%
31-Dec-88	19.00%	29.70%	10.70%
31-Dec-89	26.00%	23.20%	−2.80%
31-Dec-90	−8.70%	−21.00%	−12.30%
31-Dec-91	33.00%	43.80%	10.80%
31-Dec-92	8.70%	12.20%	3.50%
31-Dec-93	16.30%	33.40%	17.10%
31-Dec-94	−1.90%	7.30%	9.20%
31-Dec-95	28.50%	30.90%	2.40%
31-Dec-96	18.70%	21.90%	3.20%
Arithmetic average	13.11%	16.97%	3.86%
Standard deviation	16.01%	20.56%	4.55%

Table 7-3. Summary Return Results for All Stocks and 50 Highest Cashflow-to-Price (Low Price-to-Cashflow) Stocks from All Stocks Universe, December 31, 1951–December 31, 1996

	All Stocks	Universe = All Stocks top 50 cashflow/price (low price/cashflow)
Arithmetic average	14.97%	17.40%
Standard deviation of return	19.51%	25.71%
Sharpe risk-adjusted ratio	49.00	47.00
3-yr compounded	13.22%	14.82%
5-yr compounded	14.00%	20.13%
10-yr compounded	12.92%	14.57%
15-yr compounded	14.44%	13.66%
20-yr compounded	14.97%	13.99%
25-yr compounded	12.74%	13.07%
30-yr compounded	12.43%	13.44%
35-yr compounded	11.64%	13.86%
40-yr compounded	12.62%	13.88%
Compound annual return	13.23%	14.53%
$10,000 becomes:	$2,677,556.77	$4,483,125.62
Maximum return	55.90%	77.70%
Minimum return	−27.90%	−31.60%
Maximum expected return*	53.98%	68.82%
Minimum expected return**	−24.04%	−34.02%

*Maximum expected return is average return plus 2 times the standard deviation.

**Minimum expected return is average return minus 2 times the standard deviation.

Table 7-4. Summary Return Results for Large Stocks and 50 Highest Cashflow-to-Price (Low Price-to-Cashflow) Stocks from Large Stocks Universe, December 31, 1951–December 31, 1996

	Large Stocks	Universe = Large Stocks top 50 cashflow/price (Low price/cashflow)
Arithmetic average	13.11%	16.97%
Standard deviation of return	16.01%	20.56%
Sharpe risk-adjusted ratio	48.00	56.00
3-yr compounded	14.38%	19.63%
5-yr compounded	13.60%	20.71%
10-yr compounded	13.53%	17.38%
15-yr compounded	15.16%	17.74%
20-yr compounded	14.37%	16.20%
25-yr compounded	12.34%	17.04%
30-yr compounded	11.67%	15.51%
35-yr compounded	10.96%	15.04%
40-yr compounded	11.36%	14.27%
Compound annual return	11.92%	15.18%
$10,000 becomes:	$1,590,667.04	$5,773,333.43
Maximum return	44.90%	75.70%
Minimum return	−26.70%	−23.00%
Maximum expected return*	45.12%	58.09%
Minimum expected return**	−18.91%	−24.15%

*Maximum expected return is average return plus 2 times the standard deviation.
**Minimum expected return is average return minus 2 times the standard deviation.

Table 7-5. Base Rates for All Stocks and 50 Highest Cashflow-to-Price (Low Price-to-Cashflow) Stocks from All Stocks Universe, 1951–1996

Item	50 low price-to-cashflow beat All Stocks	Percent
Single-year return	27 out of 45	60.00%
Rolling 5-year compound return	23 out of 41	56.00%
Rolling 10-year compound return	23 out of 36	64.00%

Table 7-6. Base Rates for Large Stocks and 50 Highest Cashflow-to-Price
(Low Price-to-Cashflow) Stocks from Large Stocks Universe, 1951–1996

Item	50 low price-to-cashflow beat Large Stocks	Percent
Single-year return	30 out of 45	67.00%
Rolling 5-year compound return	28 out of 41	68.00%
Rolling 10-year compound return	33 out of 36	92.00%

Table 7-6 summarizes the Large Stocks base rates. The base rates for
the low price-to-cashflow stocks from the Large Stocks universe are
uniformly high. Over all rolling 10-year periods, the 50 lowest price-to-
cashflow stocks from the Large Stocks group beat the universe 92 percent of the time.

High Price-to-Cashflow Ratios
Are Dangerous

As with the other value factors, we see stocks with high price-to-cashflow ratios are usually bad investments. Figure 7-2 and Tables 7-7
through 7-10 summarize the data. The 50 stocks with the highest price-
to-cashflow ratios from All Stocks had eight years where they underperformed the All Stocks group by more than 15 percent, but only four
years where they beat it by 15 percent or more. Some of the periods are
horrific. For example, $10,000 invested in the All Stocks universe on
December 31, 1972 was worth $13,167 at the end of 1977. The same
$10,000 invested in the 50 highest price-to-cashflow stocks from the All
Stocks universe was worth just $5249, a loss of almost 50 percent.

The same is true over the long-term. Here $10,000 invested on
December 31, 1951 in the 50 stocks with the highest price-to-cashflow
ratios from All Stocks grew to just $334,876 by the end of 1996. That
return is dwarfed by a simple investment in the All Stocks universe.
The Sharpe ratio is a dismal 23.

Large Stocks Hit Too

Large stocks with high price-to-cashflows fared little better. Here
$10,000 invested on December 31, 1951 grew to $718,758 by the end of
1996, less than half what you'd earn from an investment in the Large
Stocks universe. The Sharpe ratio was a paltry 31.

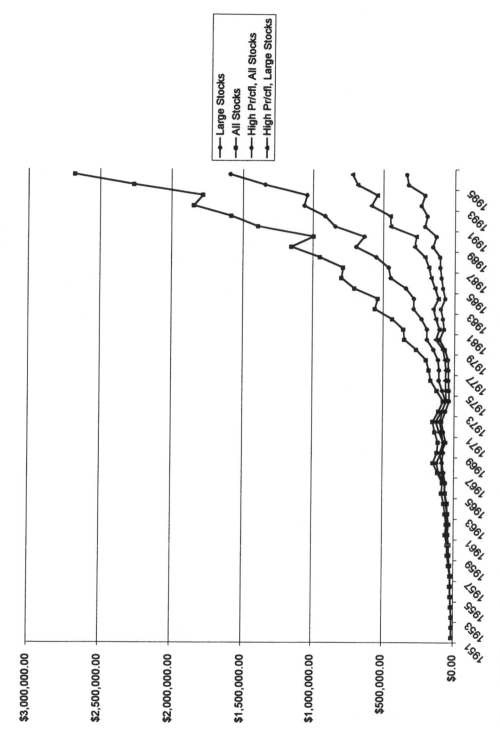

Figure 7-2. Returns for high price-to-cashflow strategies versus All Stocks and Large Stocks, 1951–1996. Year-end 1951 = $10,000.

Table 7-7. Annual Performance of All Stocks Versus 50 Stocks with High Price-to-Cashflow Ratios from All Stocks Universe

Year ending	All Stocks	Universe = All Stocks top 50 price/cashflow	Top 50 price/cashflow relative performance
31-Dec-52	7.90%	1.80%	−6.10%
31-Dec-53	2.90%	4.70%	1.80%
31-Dec-54	47.00%	39.80%	−7.20%
31-Dec-55	20.70%	26.30%	5.60%
31-Dec-56	17.00%	5.00%	−12.00%
31-Dec-57	−7.10%	−2.10%	5.00%
31-Dec-58	55.00%	59.70%	4.70%
31-Dec-59	23.00%	32.80%	9.80%
31-Dec-60	6.10%	11.60%	5.50%
31-Dec-61	31.20%	14.50%	−16.70%
31-Dec-62	−12.00%	−25.80%	−13.80%
31-Dec-63	18.00%	21.09%	3.09%
31-Dec-64	16.30%	5.10%	−11.20%
31-Dec-65	22.60%	28.20%	5.60%
31-Dec-66	−5.20%	−1.30%	3.90%
31-Dec-67	41.10%	67.20%	26.10%
31-Dec-68	27.40%	14.30%	−13.10%
31-Dec-69	−18.50%	−25.90%	−7.40%
31-Dec-70	−5.80%	−37.90%	−32.10%
31-Dec-71	21.30%	34.90%	13.60%
31-Dec-72	11.00%	17.10%	6.10%
31-Dec-73	−27.20%	−32.50%	−5.30%
31-Dec-74	−27.90%	−41.80%	−13.90%
31-Dec-75	55.90%	7.73%	−48.17%
31-Dec-76	35.60%	7.10%	−28.50%
31-Dec-77	6.90%	−1.10%	−8.00%
31-Dec-78	12.20%	13.00%	0.80%
31-Dec-79	34.30%	48.00%	13.70%
31-Dec-80	31.50%	60.30%	28.80%
31-Dec-81	1.70%	−30.70%	−32.40%
31-Dec-82	22.50%	12.50%	−10.00%
31-Dec-83	28.10%	16.10%	−12.00%
31-Dec-84	−3.40%	−31.40%	−28.00%
31-Dec-85	30.80%	24.00%	−6.80%
31-Dec-86	13.10%	13.90%	0.80%
31-Dec-87	−1.30%	9.10%	10.40%
31-Dec-88	21.20%	3.40%	−17.80%
31-Dec-89	21.40%	46.10%	24.70%
31-Dec-90	−13.80%	−15.70%	−1.90%
31-Dec-91	39.80%	63.30%	23.50%
31-Dec-92	13.80%	−8.10%	−21.90%
31-Dec-93	16.60%	21.10%	4.50%
31-Dec-94	−3.40%	−10.70%	−7.30%
31-Dec-95	27.00%	55.70%	28.70%
31-Dec-96	18.30%	4.00%	−14.30%
Arithmetic average	14.97%	11.65%	−3.80%
Standard deviation	19.51%	27.42%	7.91%

Table 7-8. Annual Performance of Large Stocks Versus 50 Stocks with High
Price-to-Cashflow Ratios from Large Stocks Universe

Year ending	Large Stocks	Universe = Large Stocks top 50 price/cashflow	Top 50 price/cashflow relative performance
31-Dec-52	9.30%	4.60%	−4.70%
31-Dec-53	2.30%	0.09%	−2.21%
31-Dec-54	44.90%	40.40%	−4.50%
31-Dec-55	21.20%	23.50%	2.30%
31-Dec-56	9.60%	6.70%	−2.90%
31-Dec-57	−6.90%	−6.20%	0.70%
31-Dec-58	42.10%	39.60%	−2.50%
31-Dec-59	9.90%	18.40%	8.50%
31-Dec-60	4.80%	4.00%	−0.80%
31-Dec-61	27.50%	25.20%	−2.30%
31-Dec-62	−8.90%	−16.10%	−7.20%
31-Dec-63	19.50%	26.70%	7.20%
31-Dec-64	15.30%	8.10%	−7.20%
31-Dec-65	16.20%	32.80%	16.60%
31-Dec-66	−4.90%	3.10%	8.00%
31-Dec-67	21.30%	38.80%	17.50%
31-Dec-68	16.80%	0.70%	−16.10%
31-Dec-69	−9.90%	11.90%	21.80%
31-Dec-70	−0.20%	−21.10%	−20.90%
31-Dec-71	17.30%	34.40%	17.10%
31-Dec-72	14.90%	23.80%	8.90%
31-Dec-73	−18.90%	−31.20%	−12.30%
31-Dec-74	−26.70%	−36.80%	−10.10%
31-Dec-75	43.10%	9.59%	−33.51%
31-Dec-76	28.00%	3.00%	−25.00%
31-Dec-77	−2.50%	−7.70%	−5.20%
31-Dec-78	8.10%	12.80%	4.70%
31-Dec-79	27.30%	23.70%	−3.60%
31-Dec-80	30.80%	60.50%	29.70%
31-Dec-81	0.60%	−18.50%	−19.10%
31-Dec-82	19.90%	22.80%	2.90%
31-Dec-83	23.80%	13.50%	−10.30%
31-Dec-84	−0.40%	−23.70%	23.30%
31-Dec-85	19.50%	21.60%	2.10%
31-Dec-86	32.20%	20.40%	−11.80%
31-Dec-87	3.30%	10.20%	6.90%
31-Dec-88	19.00%	14.40%	−4.60%
31-Dec-89	26.00%	35.60%	9.60%
31-Dec-90	−8.70%	−4.30%	4.40%
31-Dec-91	33.00%	68.00%	35.00%
31-Dec-92	8.70%	0.80%	−7.90%
31-Dec-93	16.30%	29.60%	13.30%
31-Dec-94	−1.90%	−7.10%	−5.20%
31-Dec-95	28.50%	25.60%	−2.90%
31-Dec-96	18.70%	5.50%	−13.20%
Arithmetic average	13.11%	12.17%	−0.94%
Standard deviation	16.01%	21.78%	5.77%

Table 7-9. Summary Return Results for All Stocks and 50 Highest
Price-to-Cashflow Stocks from All Stocks Universe,
December 31, 1951–December 31, 1996

	All Stocks	Universe = All Stocks top 50 price/cashflow
Arithmetic average	14.97%	11.65%
Standard deviation of return	19.51%	27.42%
Sharpe risk-adjusted ratio	49.00	23.00
3-yr compounded	13.22%	13.08%
5-yr compounded	14.00%	9.98%
10-yr compounded	12.92%	13.83%
15-yr compounded	14.44%	10.74%
20-yr compounded	14.97%	11.29%
25-yr compounded	12.74%	6.21%
30-yr compounded	12.43%	5.75%
35-yr compounded	11.64%	5.44%
40-yr compounded	12.62%	7.33%
Compound annual return	13.23%	8.12%
$10,000 becomes:	$2,677,556.77	$334,875.65
Maximum return	55.90%	67.20%
Minimum return	−27.90%	−41.80%
Maximum expected return*	53.98%	66.49%
Minimum expected return**	−24.04%	−43.18%

*Maximum expected return is average return plus 2 times the standard deviation.
**Minimum expected return is average return minus 2 times the standard deviation.

Looking at the data in Table 7-10, you see why scrutinizing long-term results is the only way to understand the value of a strategy. If you saw only the data for the 10 years ending December 31, 1996, you'd be dangerously misled. The 50 Large Stocks with the highest price-to-cashflow ratios handily *beat* the Large Stocks universe by a little less than 3 percent, with a compound return of 16.02 percent. But when we review the base rates for high price-to-cashflow stocks found in Tables 7-11 and 7-12, we see that those 10 years were an anomaly. The 50 high price-to-cashflow stocks from the All Stocks universe had only *three* 10-year peri-

Table 7-10. Summary Return Results for Large Stocks and 50 Highest Price-to-Cashflow Stocks from Large Stocks Universe, December 31, 1951–December 31, 1996

	Large Stocks	Universe = Large Stocks top 50 price/cashflow
Arithmetic average	13.11%	12.17%
Standard deviation of return	16.01%	21.78%
Sharpe risk-adjusted ratio	48.00	31.00
3-yr compounded	14.38%	7.17%
5-yr compounded	13.60%	9.97%
10-yr compounded	13.53%	16.02%
15-yr compounded	15.16%	13.72%
20-yr compounded	14.37%	13.03%
25-yr compounded	12.34%	8.12%
30-yr compounded	11.67%	8.54%
35-yr compounded	10.96%	8.67%
40-yr compounded	11.36%	9.46%
Compound annual return	11.92%	9.97%
$10,000 becomes:	$1,590,667.04	$718,758.43
Maximum return	44.90%	68.00%
Minimum return	−26.70%	−36.80%
Maximum expected return*	45.12%	55.73%
Minimum expected return**	−18.91%	−31.39%

*Maximum expected return is average return plus 2 times the standard deviation.
**Minimum expected return is average return minus 2 times the standard deviation.

Table 7-11. Base Rates for All Stocks and 50 Highest Price-to-Cashflow Stocks from All Stocks Universe, 1951–1996

Item	50 high price-to-cashflow beat All Stocks	Percent
Single-year return	21 out of 45	47.00%
Rolling 5-year compound return	11 out of 41	27.00%
Rolling 10-year compound return	3 out of 36	8.00%

Table 7-12. Base Rates for Large Stocks and 50 Highest Price-to-Cashflow Stocks from Large Stocks Universe, 1951–1996

Item	50 high price-to-cashflow beat Large Stocks	Percent
Single-year return	19 out of 45	42.00%
Rolling 5-year compound return	21 out of 41	51.00%
Rolling 10-year compound return	14 out of 36	39.00%

ods where they beat the All Stocks universe! Tables 7-13 and 7-14 catalog the woe. The 50 high price-to-cashflow stocks from the Large Stocks group didn't do as poorly, but the failure rate for all rolling 10-year periods was 61 percent.

Deciles

The decile analysis of All Stocks by price-to-cashflow ratios shows the same theme as we've found with our other ratios: Stocks in the lowest deciles have much higher returns than stocks in the highest deciles. As we move from the lowest decile to the highest, risk skyrockets and returns plummet. The decile with the stocks with the lowest price-to-cashflow ratios turned $10,000 invested in 1951 into $7,142,991 at the end of 1996, whereas the highest grew to just $480,155. What's more, the highest decile *took a greater risk than the lowest.*

The lowest decile from the Large Stocks universe earned even more. There the decile made up of the stocks from Large Stocks with the lowest price-to-cashflow ratios turned the $10,000 investment into

Table 7-13. Compound Annual Rates of Return by Decade

Portfolio	1950s*	1960s	1970s	1980s	1990s**
Large Stocks	15.33%	8.99%	6.99%	16.89%	12.61%
50 high price-to-cashflow from Large Stocks	14.85%	12.35%	−1.85%	13.29%	14.53%
50 low price-to-cashflow from Large Stocks	17.28%	10.36%	15.40%	17.31%	16.49%
All Stocks	19.22%	11.09%	8.53%	15.85%	12.78%
50 high price-to-cashflow from All Stocks	19.30%	8.02%	−3.03%	8.77%	12.03%
50 low price-to-cashflow from All Stocks	18.71%	15.41%	13.57%	12.53%	12.86%

**Returns for 1952–1959.
**Returns for 1990–1996.

Table 7-14. Rolling Compound 10-Year Returns for All Stocks and 50 Highest Price-to-Cashflow Stocks from All Stocks Universe, December 31, 1961–December 31, 1996

For the 10 years ending	All Stocks	Universe = All Stocks top 50 price/cashflow	Top 50 price/cashflow relative performance
31-Dec-61	18.97%	18.02%	−0.95%
31-Dec-62	16.57%	14.35%	−2.23%
31-Dec-63	18.18%	16.02%	−2.16%
31-Dec-64	15.44%	12.76%	−2.69%
31-Dec-65	15.63%	12.93%	−2.70%
31-Dec-66	13.22%	12.23%	−0.99%
31-Dec-67	18.05%	18.40%	0.35%
31-Dec-68	15.76%	14.51%	−1.25%
31-Dec-69	11.09%	8.02%	−3.07%
31-Dec-70	9.78%	1.87%	−7.91%
31-Dec-71	8.92%	3.55%	−5.37%
31-Dec-72	11.48%	8.38%	−3.09%
31-Dec-73	6.22%	2.23%	−3.99%
31-Dec-74	1.26%	−3.64%	−4.90%
31-Dec-75	3.72%	−5.30%	−9.02%
31-Dec-76	7.50%	−4.52%	−12.02%
31-Dec-77	4.56%	−9.40%	−13.97%
31-Dec-78	3.24%	−9.51%	−12.75%
31-Dec-79	8.53%	−3.03%	−11.55%
31-Dec-80	12.21%	6.62%	−5.59%
31-Dec-81	10.25%	−0.25%	−10.50%
31-Dec-82	11.34%	−0.65%	−11.99%
31-Dec-83	17.82%	4.89%	−12.93%
31-Dec-84	21.31%	6.63%	−14.69%
31-Dec-85	19.20%	8.14%	−11.07%
31-Dec-86	17.06%	8.80%	−8.25%
31-Dec-87	16.13%	9.88%	−6.25%
31-Dec-88	17.03%	8.91%	−8.12%
31-Dec-89	15.85%	8.77%	−7.09%
31-Dec-90	11.06%	2.00%	−9.07%
31-Dec-91	14.65%	11.12%	−3.53%
31-Dec-92	13.81%	8.90%	−4.91%
31-Dec-93	12.74%	9.36%	−3.39%
31-Dec-94	12.74%	12.28%	−0.46%
31-Dec-95	12.41%	14.87%	2.45%
31-Dec-96	12.92%	13.83%	0.91%
Arithmetic average	12.69%	6.72%	−5.96%

Table 7-15. Summary Results for Price-to-Cashflow Decile Analysis of All
Stocks Universe, 1951–1996

Decile	$10,000 grows to	Average return	Compound return	Standard deviation
1 (lowest price/cashflow)	$7,142,991	18.08%	15.72%	23.51%
2	$7,857,275	17.79%	15.97%	20.77%
3	$3,925,764	15.91%	14.19%	19.66%
4	$1,521,773	13.06%	11.81%	16.64%
5	$1,817,115	13.74%	12.26%	17.87%
6	$2,306,919	14.44%	12.85%	18.33%
7	$1,139,450	12.33%	11.10%	16.17%
8	$624,573	11.66%	9.62%	20.45%
9	$929,454	12.60%	10.60%	20.36%
10 (highest price/cashflow)	$480,155	12.08%	8.98%	25.95%
All Stocks	$2,677,557	14.97%	13.23%	19.51%

$8,546,977 by the end of 1996, almost $8 million more than an investment
in Large Stocks. Tables 7-15 and 7-16, as well as Figures 7-5 and 7-6, summarize the results.

Implications

As Figures 7-3 and 7-4 show, the odds strongly favor stocks with low price-
to-cashflow ratios. Both the 50-stock and the decile analysis prove this.
Unless there are additional compelling factors (e.g., the stock is selected by
a successful growth model's criteria to absorb some high price-to-cashflow
risk), you should avoid stocks with the highest price-to-cashflow ratios.

Table 7-16. Summary Results for Price-to-Cashflow Decile Analysis of Large
Stocks Universe, 1951–1996

Decile	$10,000 grows to	Average return	Compound return	Standard deviation
1 (lowest price/cashflow)	$8,546,977	18.00%	16.16%	21.03%
2	$3,388,215	15.25%	13.82%	17.99%
3	$1,924,875	13.59%	12.40%	16.22%
4	$1,628,285	13.24%	11.98%	16.75%
5	$1,662,363	13.09%	12.03%	15.25%
6	$822,499	11.50%	10.30%	16.00%
7	$1,137,045	12.32%	11.09%	16.19%
8	$873,890	11.87%	10.44%	17.31%
9	$659,556	11.27%	9.76%	17.72%
10 (highest price/cashflow)	$941,401	12.90%	10.63%	21.87%
Large Stocks	$1,590,667	13.11%	11.92%	16.01%

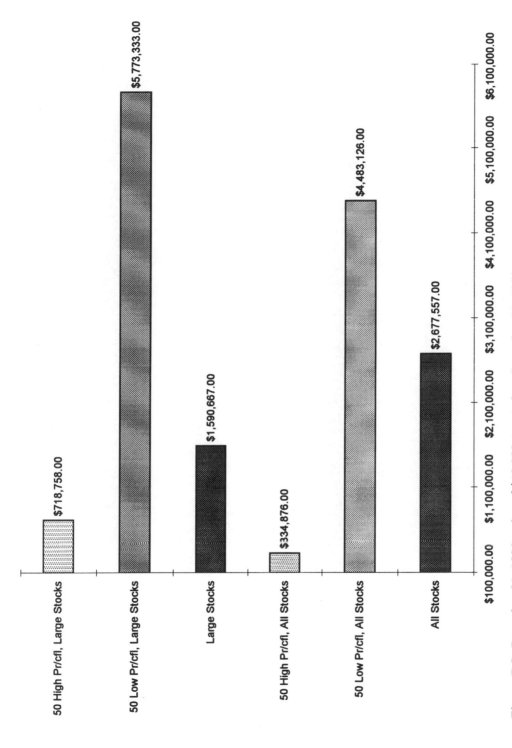

Figure 7-3. December 31, 1996, value of $10,000 invested on December 31, 1951, and annually rebalanced.

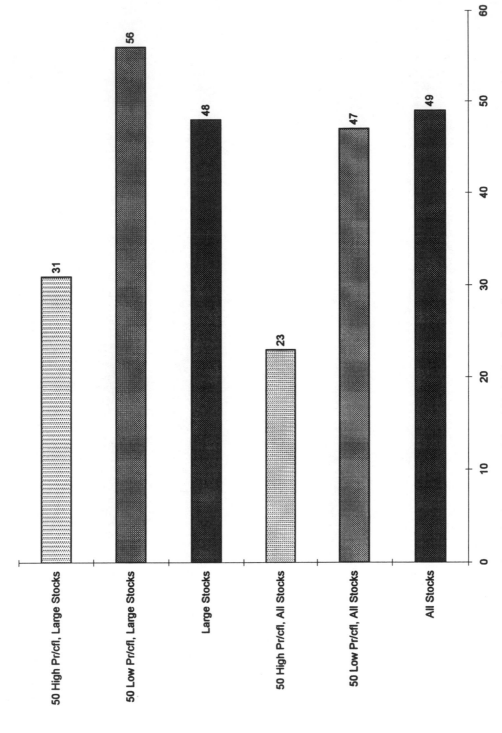

Figure 7-4. Sharpe risk-adjusted return ratio, 1951–1996. (Higher is better.)

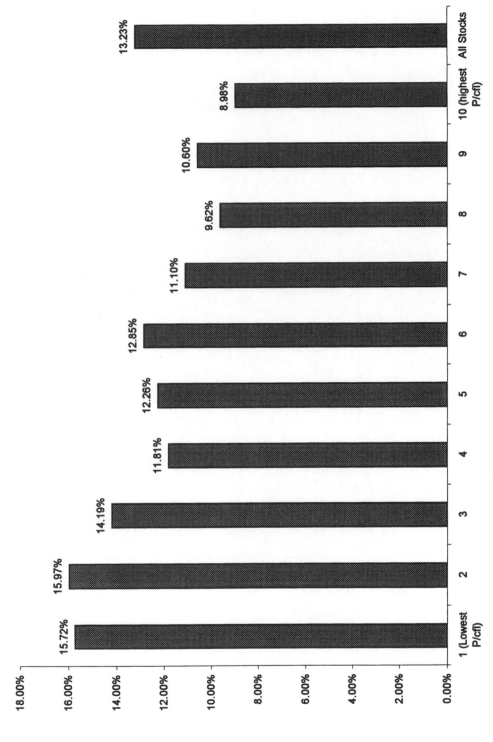

Figure 7-5. Compound return by Price/cashflow decile, All Stocks universe, 1951–1996.

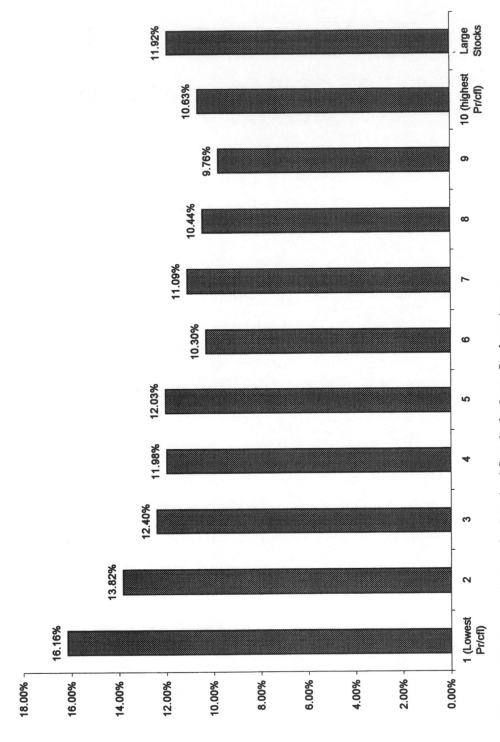

Figure 7-6. Compound return by Price/cashflow decile, Large Stocks universe, 1951–1996.

8

Price-to-Sales Ratios: The King of the Value Factors

*For me the greatest beauty always lay in the
greatest clarity.* —GOTTHOLD LESSING

The last individual value ratio we'll review is also the best. A stock's price-to-sales ratio (PSR) is similar to its price-to-earnings ratio, but measures the price of the company against annual sales instead of earnings. Like investors who favor low PE stocks, investors who buy low PSR stocks believe they're getting a bargain. In his 1984 book *Super Stocks*, Ken Fisher says that a stock's PSR is "an almost perfect measure of popularity," warning that only hope and hype will increase the price of a stock with a high PSR.

As usual, we'll look at both the 50 lowest PSR stocks and the 50 highest PSR stocks from both universes. And as with the other ratios, we'll also look at how the two universes stack up when ranked by price-to-sales decile. All accounting data are time-lagged to avoid look-ahead bias, and the portfolios are rebalanced annually.

Starting December 31, 1951, we'll buy the 50 stocks from All Stocks with the lowest PSRs. Again, because of Compustat's ranking function, we must rank stocks by the 50 *highest* sales-to-price ratios, the inverse of the price-to-sales ratio. They will be referred to, however, as high and low PSR stocks throughout the chapter.

The Results

An investment of $10,000 on December 31, 1951 in the 50 lowest PSR stocks from the All Stocks universe grew to $8,252,734 by December 31, 1996, a compound return of 16.09 percent. This dwarfs the $2,677,557 earned from the $10,000 invested in the All Stocks universe and beats the returns of all the 50-stock value ratios we've examined. The strategy also performs well over time. With the exception of 1989 through 1991, the annual returns found in Table 8-1 show that low PSR stocks consistently beat the All Stocks universe. The low PSR stocks also do well on a risk-adjusted basis, with a Sharpe ratio of 53. Tables 8-2 through 8-4 summarize the returns of low PSR stocks from the All Stocks universe and Table 8-5 compares the base rates for the strategy with All Stocks.

Large Stocks with Low Price-to-Sales Ratios Do Well

Large stocks with low PSRs also beat the Large Stocks universe, but not by as much as the smaller stocks from All Stocks. Here $10,000 invested on December 31, 1951 was worth $3,853,418 at the end of 1996, a compound return of 14.15 percent. The return was considerably better than the $1,590,667 you'd earn if you invested $10,000 in the Large Stocks universe itself. We also see consistency here and a fairly high Sharpe ratio of 52.

The rolling 5- and 10-year base rates for both groups of low PSR stocks are outstanding—the best of all the value ratios. For all rolling 10-year periods, both the large and smaller stock versions of the strategy beat their universes 90 percent of the time. That consistency is rare. Rolling 10-year returns for both the large and small low PSR stocks are reviewed in Tables 8-13 and 8-14. Table 8-15 gives compound returns by decades.

High PSR Stocks Are Toxic

An investment in the 50 stocks with the highest PSRs from the All Stocks universe turns in the worst performance to date: $10,000 invested on December 31, 1951 was worth just $91,520 at the end of 1996. You'd be better off with T-bills! The Sharpe ratio is 12, the bottom of the barrel.

It's painful to catalog the carnage. The All Stocks universe beat the 50 highest PSR stocks 67 percent of the time. December 31, 1980 through December 31, 1984 is particularly gruesome. Here $10,000 invested in the All Stocks universe grew by more than 50 percent to $15,416, but an investment in the 50 stocks with the highest PSRs fell by 70 percent, turning $10,000 into $3079.

Table 8-1. Annual Performance of All Stocks Versus 50 Stocks with High Sales-to-Price (Low Price-to-Sales) Ratios from All Stocks Universe

Year ending	All Stocks	Universe = All Stocks top 50 sales/price	Top 50 sales/price relative performance
31-Dec-52	7.90%	13.40%	5.50%
31-Dec-53	2.90%	5.90%	3.00%
31-Dec-54	47.00%	59.40%	12.40%
31-Dec-55	20.70%	19.80%	−0.90%
31-Dec-56	17.00%	4.60%	−12.40%
31-Dec-57	−7.10%	−1.90%	5.20%
31-Dec-58	55.00%	73.90%	18.90%
31-Dec-59	23.00%	11.20%	−11.80%
31-Dec-60	6.10%	4.00%	−2.10%
31-Dec-61	31.20%	31.70%	0.50%
31-Dec-62	−12.00%	−12.10%	−0.10%
31-Dec-63	18.00%	14.40%	−3.60%
31-Dec-64	16.30%	27.40%	11.10%
31-Dec-65	22.60%	34.70%	12.10%
31-Dec-66	−5.20%	−17.60%	−12.40%
31-Dec-67	41.10%	48.30%	7.20%
31-Dec-68	27.40%	39.90%	12.50%
31-Dec-69	−18.50%	−28.80%	−10.30%
31-Dec-70	−5.80%	−4.50%	1.30%
31-Dec-71	21.30%	29.50%	8.20%
31-Dec-72	11.00%	−1.80%	−12.80%
31-Dec-73	−27.20%	−22.30%	4.90%
31-Dec-74	−27.90%	−12.60%	15.30%
31-Dec-75	55.90%	76.90%	21.00%
31-Dec-76	35.60%	48.40%	12.80%
31-Dec-77	6.90%	3.50%	−3.40%
31-Dec-78	12.20%	16.90%	4.70%
31-Dec-79	34.30%	51.80%	17.50%
31-Dec-80	31.50%	13.70%	−17.80%
31-Dec-81	1.70%	3.10%	1.40%
31-Dec-82	22.50%	63.30%	40.80%
31-Dec-83	28.10%	37.70%	9.60%
31-Dec-84	3.40%	−2.60%	0.80%
31-Dec-85	30.80%	46.70%	15.90%
31-Dec-86	13.10%	9.30%	−3.80%
31-Dec-87	−1.30%	2.20%	3.50%
31-Dec-88	21.20%	42.90%	21.70%
31-Dec-89	21.40%	6.70%	−14.70%
31-Dec-90	−13.80%	−27.50%	−13.70%
31-Dec-91	39.80%	37.10%	−2.70%
31-Dec-92	13.80%	32.60%	18.80%
31-Dec-93	16.60%	24.80%	8.20%
31-Dec-94	−3.40%	8.00%	11.40%
31-Dec-95	27.00%	29.40%	2.40%
31-Dec-96	18.30%	7.50%	−10.80%
Arithmetic average	14.97%	18.86%	3.90%
Standard deviation	19.51%	25.60%	6.10%

Table 8-2. Annual Performance of Large Stocks Versus 50 Stocks with High Sales-to-Price (Low Price-to-Sales) Ratios from Large Stocks Universe

Year ending	Large Stocks	Universe = Large Stocks top 50 sales/price	Top 50 sales/price relative performance
31-Dec-52	9.30%	14.30%	5.00%
31-Dec-53	2.30%	2.00%	−0.30%
31-Dec-54	44.90%	51.90%	7.00%
31-Dec-55	21.20%	21.90%	0.70%
31-Dec-56	9.60%	10.00%	0.40%
31-Dec-57	−6.90%	−12.40%	−5.50%
31-Dec-58	42.10%	47.80%	5.70%
31-Dec-59	9.90%	9.50%	−0.40%
31-Dec-60	4.80%	−1.80%	−6.60%
31-Dec-61	27.50%	29.30%	1.80%
31-Dec-62	−8.90%	−7.40%	1.50%
31-Dec-63	19.50%	21.00%	1.50%
31-Dec-64	15.30%	22.00%	6.70%
31-Dec-65	16.20%	27.00%	10.80%
31-Dec-66	−4.90%	−10.30%	−5.40%
31-Dec-67	21.30%	33.00%	11.70%
31-Dec-68	16.80%	23.30%	6.50%
31-Dec-69	−9.90%	−23.70%	−13.80%
31-Dec-70	−0.20%	−3.00%	−2.80%
31-Dec-71	17.30%	20.60%	3.30%
31-Dec-72	14.90%	11.40%	−3.50%
31-Dec-73	−18.90%	−25.40%	−6.50%
31-Dec-74	−26.70%	−14.20%	12.50%
31-Dec-75	43.10%	64.50%	21.40%
31-Dec-76	28.00%	47.30%	19.30%
31-Dec-77	−2.50%	0.80%	3.30%
31-Dec-78	8.10%	13.60%	5.50%
31-Dec-79	27.30%	21.60%	−5.70%
31-Dec-80	30.80%	15.10%	−15.70%
31-Dec-81	0.60%	9.40%	8.80%
31-Dec-82	19.90%	34.30%	14.40%
31-Dec-83	23.80%	36.40%	12.60%
31-Dec-84	−0.40%	3.20%	3.60%
31-Dec-85	19.50%	40.90%	21.40%
31-Dec-86	32.20%	11.10%	−21.10%
31-Dec-87	3.30%	3.70%	0.40%
31-Dec-88	19.00%	39.10%	20.10%
31-Dec-89	26.00%	16.10%	−9.90%
31-Dec-90	−8.70%	−22.60%	−13.90%
31-Dec-91	33.00%	41.80%	8.80%
31-Dec-92	8.70%	22.30%	13.60%
31-Dec-93	16.30%	29.60%	13.30%
31-Dec-94	−1.90%	0.02%	1.92%
31-Dec-95	28.50%	21.80%	−6.70%
31-Dec-96	18.70%	24.30%	5.60%
Arithmetic average	13.11%	16.02%	2.92%
Standard deviation	16.01%	20.50%	4.49%

Table 8-3. Summary Return Results for All Stocks and 50 Highest
Sales-to-Price (Low Price-to-Sales) Stocks from All Stocks Universe,
December 31, 1951–December 31, 1996

	All Stocks	Universe = All Stocks top 50 sales/price (low price-to-sales)
Arithmetic average	14.97%	18.86%
Standard deviation of return	19.51%	25.60%
Sharpe risk-adjusted ratio	49.00	53.00
3-yr compounded	13.22%	14.53%
5-yr compounded	14.00%	19.98%
10-yr compounded	12.92%	14.43%
15-yr compounded	14.44%	18.96%
20-yr compounded	14.97%	18.36%
25-yr compounded	12.74%	17.03%
30-yr compounded	12.43%	16.31%
35-yr compounded	11.64%	14.98%
40-yr compounded	12.62%	15.72%
Compound annual return	13.23%	16.09%
$10,000 becomes:	$2,677,556.77	$8,252,734.31
Maximum return	55.90%	76.90%
Minimum return	−27.90%	−28.80%
Maximum expected return*	53.98%	70.07%
Minimum expected return**	−24.04%	−32.34%

*Maximum expected return is average return plus 2 times the standard deviation.

**Minimum expected return is average return minus 2 times the standard deviation.

Table 8-4. Summary Return Results for Large Stocks and 50 Highest Sales-to-Price (Low Price-to-Sales) Stocks from Large Stocks Universe, December 31, 1951–December 31, 1996

	Large Stocks	Universe = Large Stocks top 50 sales/price (low price-to-sales)
Arithmetic average	13.11%	16.02%
Standard deviation of return	16.01%	20.50%
Sharpe risk-adjusted ratio	48.00	52.00
3-yr compounded	14.38%	14.83%
5-yr compounded	13.60%	19.14%
10-yr compounded	13.53%	16.00%
15-yr compounded	15.16%	18.68%
20-yr compounded	14.37%	16.95%
25-yr compounded	12.34%	15.85%
30-yr compounded	11.67%	14.49%
35-yr compounded	10.96%	13.72%
40-yr compounded	11.36%	13.57%
Compound annual return	11.92%	14.15%
$10,000 becomes:	$1,590,667.04	$3,853,417.66
Maximum return	44.90%	64.50%
Minimum return	−26.70%	−25.40%
Maximum expected return*	45.12%	57.02%
Minimum expected return**	−18.91%	−24.97%

*Maximum expected return is average return plus 2 times the standard deviation.

**Minimum expected return is average return minus 2 times the standard deviation.

Table 8-5. Base Rates for All Stocks and 50 Lowest PSR Stocks from All Stocks Universe, 1951–1996

Item	50 low price-to-sales beat All Stocks	Percent
Single-year return	29 out of 45	64.00%
Rolling 5-year compound return	28 out of 41	68.00%
Rolling 10-year compound return	33 out of 36	92.00%

Table 8-6. Base Rates for Large Stocks and 50 Lowest PSR Stocks from Large Stocks Universe, 1951–1996

Item	50 low price-to-sales beat Large Stocks	Percent
Single-year return	30 out of 45	67.00%
Rolling 5-year compound return	29 out of 41	71.00%
Rolling 10-year compound return	33 out of 36	92.00%

Table 8-7. Annual Performance of All Stocks Versus 50 Stocks with High Price-to-Sales Ratios from All Stocks Universe

Year ending	All Stocks	Universe = All Stocks top 50 price/sales	Top 50 price/sales relative performance
31-Dec-52	7.90%	5.30%	−2.60%
31-Dec-53	2.90%	1.30%	−1.60%
31-Dec-54	47.00%	33.60%	−13.40%
31-Dec-55	20.70%	14.10%	−6.60%
31-Dec-56	17.00%	10.00%	−7.00%
31-Dec-57	−7.10%	−1.00%	6.10%
31-Dec-58	55.00%	53.80%	−1.20%
31-Dec-59	23.00%	12.00%	−11.00%
31-Dec-60	6.10%	11.50%	5.40%
31-Dec-61	31.20%	23.10%	−8.10%
31-Dec-62	−12.00%	−12.70%	−0.70%
31-Dec-63	18.00%	20.90%	2.90%
31-Dec-64	16.30%	8.80%	−7.50%
31-Dec-65	22.60%	18.80%	−3.80%
31-Dec-66	−5.20%	1.90%	7.10%
31-Dec-67	41.10%	69.10%	28.00%
31-Dec-68	27.40%	26.90%	−0.50%
31-Dec-69	−18.50%	−24.20%	−5.70%
31-Dec-70	−5.80%	−25.30%	−19.50%
31-Dec-71	21.30%	29.10%	7.80%
31-Dec-72	11.00%	24.60%	13.60%
31-Dec-73	−27.20%	−13.30%	13.90%
31-Dec-74	−27.90%	−38.70%	−10.80%
31-Dec-75	55.90%	7.90%	−48.00%
31-Dec-76	35.60%	30.90%	−4.70%
31-Dec-77	6.90%	8.90%	2.00%
31-Dec-78	12.20%	6.40%	−5.80%
31-Dec-79	34.30%	68.50%	34.20%
31-Dec-80	31.50%	43.90%	12.40%
31-Dec-81	1.70%	−47.60%	−49.30%
31-Dec-82	22.50%	−11.30%	−33.80%
31-Dec-83	28.10%	1.90%	−26.20%
31-Dec-84	−3.40%	35.00%	−31.60%
31-Dec-85	30.80%	22.20%	−8.60%
31-Dec-86	13.10%	16.00%	2.90%
31-Dec-87	−1.30%	−7.90%	−6.60%
31-Dec-88	21.20%	1.70%	−19.50%
31-Dec-89	21.40%	38.60%	17.20%
31-Dec-90	−13.80%	−18.00%	−4.20%
31-Dec-91	39.80%	47.50%	7.70%
31-Dec-92	13.80%	−25.20%	−39.00%
31-Dec-93	16.60%	−13.10%	−29.70%
31-Dec-94	−3.40%	−32.10%	−28.70%
31-Dec-95	27.00%	46.00%	19.00%
31-Dec-96	18.30%	−13.60%	−31.90%
Arithmetic average	14.97%	8.58%	−6.38%
Standard deviation	19.51%	27.13%	7.63%

Table 8-8. Annual Performance of Large Stocks Versus 50 Stocks with High Price-to-Sales Ratios from Large Stocks Universe

Year ending	Large Stocks	Universe = Large Stocks top 50 price/sales	Top 50 price/sales relative performance
31-Dec-52	9.30%	4.80%	−4.50%
31-Dec-53	2.30%	1.30%	−1.00%
31-Dec-54	44.90%	32.00%	−12.90%
31-Dec-55	21.20%	17.20%	−4.00%
31-Dec-56	9.60%	8.10%	−1.50%
31-Dec-57	−6.90%	−3.50%	3.40%
31-Dec-58	42.10%	40.60%	−1.50%
31-Dec-59	9.90%	12.00%	2.10%
31-Dec-60	4.80%	9.80%	5.00%
31-Dec-61	27.50%	23.90%	−3.60%
31-Dec-62	−8.90%	−8.30%	0.60%
31-Dec-63	19.50%	20.20%	0.70%
31-Dec-64	15.30%	14.20%	−1.10%
31-Dec-65	16.20%	17.70%	1.50%
31-Dec-66	−4.90%	1.90%	6.80%
31-Dec-67	21.30%	23.20%	1.90%
31-Dec-68	16.80%	7.90%	−8.90%
31-Dec-69	−9.90%	11.00%	20.90%
31-Dec-70	−0.20%	−17.80%	−17.60%
31-Dec-71	17.30%	25.60%	8.30%
31-Dec-72	14.90%	24.30%	9.40%
31-Dec-73	−18.90%	−20.80%	−1.90%
31-Dec-74	−26.70%	−36.80%	−10.10%
31-Dec-75	43.10%	14.50%	−28.60%
31-Dec-76	28.00%	13.50%	−14.50%
31-Dec-77	−2.50%	−2.90%	−0.40%
31-Dec-78	8.10%	15.00%	6.90%
31-Dec-79	27.30%	47.40%	20.10%
31-Dec-80	30.80%	67.52%	36.72%
31-Dec-81	0.60%	−20.60%	−21.20%
31-Dec-82	19.90%	−3.90%	−23.80%
31-Dec-83	23.80%	11.80%	−12.00%
31-Dec-84	−0.40%	−23.90%	−23.50%
31-Dec-85	19.50%	23.70%	4.20%
31-Dec-86	32.20%	19.50%	−12.70%
31-Dec-87	3.30%	10.10%	6.80%
31-Dec-88	19.00%	3.00%	−16.00%
31-Dec-89	26.00%	36.43%	10.43%
31-Dec-90	−8.70%	−6.30%	2.40%
31-Dec-91	33.00%	53.70%	20.70%
31-Dec-92	8.70%	−9.40%	−18.10%
31-Dec-93	16.30%	26.70%	10.40%
31-Dec-94	−1.90%	−9.90%	−8.00%
31-Dec-95	28.50%	35.30%	6.80%
31-Dec-96	18.70%	13.20%	−5.50%
Arithmetic average	13.11%	11.62%	−1.49%
Standard deviation	16.01%	20.59%	4.58%

Table 8-9. Summary Return Results for All Stocks and 50 Highest
Price-to-Sales Stocks from All Stocks Universe,
December 31, 1951–December 31, 1996

	All Stocks	Universe = All Stocks top 50 price/sales
Arithmetic average	14.97%	8.58%
Standard deviation of return	19.51%	27.13%
Sharpe risk-adjusted ratio	49.00	12.00
3-yr compounded	13.22%	−5.03%
5-yr compounded	14.00%	−11.05%
10-yr compounded	12.92%	−1.34%
15-yr compounded	14.44%	−2.09%
20-yr compounded	14.97%	0.35%
25-yr compounded	12.74%	0.01%
30-yr compounded	12.43%	1.52%
35-yr compounded	11.64%	2.26%
40-yr compounded	12.62%	4.17%
Compound annual return	13.23%	5.04%
$10,000 becomes:	$2,677,556.77	$91,519.66
Maximum return	55.90%	69.10%
Minimum return	−27.90%	−47.60%
Maximum expected return*	53.98%	62.85%
Minimum expected return**	−24.04%	−45.69%

*Maximum expected return is average return plus 2 times the standard deviation.

**Minimum expected return is average return minus 2 times the standard deviation.

Table 8-10. Summary Return Results for Large Stocks and 50 Highest Price-to-Sales Stocks from Large Stocks Universe, December 31, 1951–December 31, 1996

	Large Stocks	Universe = Large Stocks top 50 price/sales
Arithmetic average	13.11%	11.62%
Standard deviation of return	16.01%	20.59%
Sharpe risk-adjusted ratio	48.00	30.00
3-yr compounded	14.38%	11.33%
5-yr compounded	13.60%	9.64%
10-yr compounded	13.53%	13.44%
15-yr compounded	15.16%	10.15%
20-yr compounded	14.37%	11.82%
25-yr compounded	12.34%	8.42%
30-yr compounded	11.67%	8.48%
35-yr compounded	10.96%	8.50%
40-yr compounded	11.36%	9.37%
Compound annual return	11.92%	9.67%
$10,000 becomes:	$1,590,667.04	$637,433.71
Maximum return	44.90%	67.52%
Minimum return	−26.70%	−36.80%
Maximum expected return*	45.12%	52.80%
Minimum expected return**	−18.91%	−29.56%

*Maximum expected return is average return plus 2 times the standard deviation.
**Minimum expected return is average return minus 2 times the standard deviation.

Table 8-11. Base Rates for All Stocks and 50 Highest PSR Stocks from All Stocks Universe, 1951–1996

Item	50 high price-to-sales beat All Stocks	Percent
Single-year return	15 out of 45	33.00%
Rolling 5-year compound return	5 out of 41	12.00%
Rolling 10-year compound return	7 out of 36	19.00%

Table 8-12. Base Rates for Large Stocks and 50 Highest PSR Stocks from Large Stocks Universe, 1951–1996

Item	50 high price-to-sales beat Large Stocks	Percent
Single-year return	21 out of 45	47.00%
Rolling 5-year compound return	18 out of 41	44.00%
Rolling 10-year compound return	12 out of 36	33.00%

Table 8-13. Rolling 10-Year Compound Returns for Low PSR Stocks from the All Stocks Universe

For the 10 years ending	All Stocks	Universe = All Stocks 50 low PSR stocks	50 low PSR relative performance
31-Dec-61	18.97%	20.08%	1.10%
31-Dec-62	16.57%	17.06%	0.49%
31-Dec-63	18.18%	17.97%	−0.21%
31-Dec-64	15.44%	15.35%	−0.09%
31-Dec-65	15.63%	16.71%	1.09%
31-Dec-66	13.22%	13.96%	0.74%
31-Dec-67	18.05%	18.77%	0.72%
31-Dec-68	15.76%	16.21%	0.46%
31-Dec-69	11.09%	11.15%	0.06%
31-Dec-70	9.78%	10.20%	0.43%
31-Dec-71	8.92%	10.02%	1.10%
31-Dec-72	11.48%	11.24%	−0.23%
31-Dec-73	6.22%	7.02%	0.80%
31-Dec-74	1.26%	3.06%	1.80%
31-Dec-75	3.72%	5.91%	2.19%
31-Dec-76	7.50%	12.33%	4.82%
31-Dec-77	4.56%	8.36%	3.80%
31-Dec-78	3.24%	6.43%	3.19%
31-Dec-79	8.53%	14.80%	6.27%
31-Dec-80	12.21%	16.82%	4.61%
31-Dec-81	10.25%	14.19%	3.94%
31-Dec-82	11.34%	20.15%	8.80%
31-Dec-83	17.82%	27.22%	9.41%
31-Dec-84	21.31%	28.61%	7.30%
31-Dec-85	19.20%	26.22%	7.02%
31-Dec-86	17.06%	22.42%	5.36%
31-Dec-87	16.13%	22.27%	6.14%
31-Dec-88	17.03%	24.75%	7.72%
31-Dec-89	15.85%	20.43%	4.57%
31-Dec-90	11.06%	15.13%	4.07%
31-Dec-91	14.65%	18.46%	3.80%
31-Dec-92	13.81%	16.01%	2.20%
31-Dec-93	12.74%	14.88%	2.13%
31-Dec-94	12.74%	16.07%	3.33%
31-Dec-95	12.41%	14.62%	2.21%
31-Dec-96	12.92%	14.43%	1.52%

Table 8-14. Rolling 10-Year Compound Returns for Low PSR Stocks from the Large Stocks Universe

For the 10 years ending	Large Stocks	Universe = Large Stocks 50 low PSR stocks	50 low PSR relative performance
31-Dec-61	15.38%	15.64%	0.26%
31-Dec-62	13.30%	13.23%	−0.07%
31-Dec-63	15.07%	15.18%	0.11%
31-Dec-64	12.47%	12.68%	0.21%
31-Dec-65	12.00%	13.14%	1.14%
31-Dec-66	10.42%	10.86%	0.44%
31-Dec-67	13.38%	15.58%	2.20%
31-Dec-68	11.18%	13.51%	2.33%
31-Dec-69	8.99%	9.48%	0.49%
31-Dec-70	8.46%	9.35%	0.88%
31-Dec-71	7.56%	8.59%	1.03%
31-Dec-72	10.09%	10.61%	0.53%
31-Dec-73	5.90%	5.39%	−0.51%
31-Dec-74	1.21%	1.75%	0.53%
31-Dec-75	3.34%	4.41%	1.07%
31-Dec-76	6.46%	9.72%	3.26%
31-Dec-77	4.16%	6.72%	2.56%
31-Dec-78	3.35%	5.85%	2.50%
31-Dec-79	6.99%	10.90%	3.91%
31-Dec-80	9.92%	12.82%	2.89%
31-Dec-81	8.25%	11.72%	3.47%
31-Dec-82	8.71%	13.83%	5.12%
31-Dec-83	13.41%	20.91%	7.50%
31-Dec-84	16.94%	23.16%	6.23%
31-Dec-85	14.85%	21.27%	6.42%
31-Dec-86	15.22%	17.90%	2.68%
31-Dec-87	15.89%	18.23%	2.35%
31-Dec-88	17.01%	20.65%	3.65%
31-Dec-89	16.89%	20.09%	3.21%
31-Dec-90	12.76%	15.42%	2.66%
31-Dec-91	15.95%	18.46%	2.50%
31-Dec-92	14.82%	17.35%	2.53%
31-Dec-93	14.10%	16.75%	2.65%
31-Dec-94	13.93%	16.39%	2.46%
31-Dec-95	14.76%	14.71%	−0.06%
31-Dec-96	13.53%	16.00%	2.47%

Table 8-15. Compound Annual Rates of Return by Decade

Portfolio	1950s*	1960s	1970s	1980s	1990s**
Large Stocks	15.33%	8.99%	6.99%	16.89%	12.61%
50 high price-to-sales from Large Stocks	13.21%	11.73%	3.23%	9.54%	12.50%
50 low price-to-sales from Large Stocks	16.39%	9.48%	10.90%	20.09%	14.84%
All Stocks	19.22%	11.09%	8.53%	15.85%	12.78%
50 high price-to-sales from All Stocks	14.96%	11.99%	5.82%	−2.02%	−5.49%
50 low price-to-sales from All Stocks	20.85%	11.15%	14.80%	20.43%	13.80%

*Returns for 1952–1959.
**Returns for 1990–1996.

For 5-year rolling returns, the All Stocks universe beat the high PSR stocks 88 percent of the time. On a rolling 10-year basis the All Stocks universe beat high PSR stocks 83 percent of the time. Yet look at 1995, a year when the overhyped stocks that typically dominate the highest PSR group from All Stocks soared some 46 percent, swamping All Stocks' gain of 27 percent. Imagine how you would feel looking at the one-year performance of these sexy-story stocks. The urge to jump on board would be great, but the fullness of time reveals what a disastrous decision that would be. Indeed, 1996 shows the group reverting to its base rate by *losing* over 13.6 percent in a bull market year.

Large Stocks Do a Little Better

The picture is only slightly brighter for Large Stocks. Here $10,000 invested in the 50 stocks with the highest PSRs on December 31, 1951 grew to $637,434, a compound return of 9.67 percent. That's less than half what you'd earn from Large Stocks, but much better than the 50 high PSR stocks from All Stocks. The Sharpe ratio is 30, considerably below Large Stocks' 48. All base rates are negative, with the 50 highest price-to-sales ratio stocks from Large Stocks underperforming the Large Stocks universe 67 percent of the time over all 10-year periods. Tables 8-6 through 8-12 summarize the damage.

Deciles

The decile results for price-to-sales ratios are stunning. Look at Table 8-16 and Figure 8-1. The total returns march downhill, from a compound return of 17.63 percent for the decile made up of the stocks with the low-

Table 8-16. Summary Results for Price-to-Sales Decile Analysis of All Stocks Universe, 1951–1996

Decile	$10,000 grows to	Average return	Compound return	Standard deviation
1 (lowest PSR)	$14,910,164	19.32%	17.63%	19.79%
2	$9,737,147	18.16%	16.52%	19.36%
3	$9,646,689	18.25%	16.50%	20.01%
4	$6,924,259	17.35%	15.64%	19.56%
5	$3,505,492	15.81%	13.91%	20.40%
6	$2,629,117	15.04%	13.18%	19.95%
7	$1,406,604	13.40%	11.62%	19.23%
8	$709,086	11.54%	9.93%	18.19%
9	$291,074	9.70%	7.78%	19.81%
10 (highest PSR)	$94,437	7.69%	5.12%	22.73%
All Stocks	$2,677,557	14.97%	13.23%	19.51%

est price-to-sales ratios to an abysmal 5.12 percent for the decile with the stocks with the highest PSRs. An investment of $10,000 in 1951 in the 10 percent of stocks from the All Stocks universe, annually rebalanced, was worth $14.9 million. Compare that with the $94,437 total from investing in the decile made up of the highest price-to-sales ratios! And PSR also emerges as the most consistent in decile performance, with each decile returning less than the previous as you move from low to high. More, risk was *highest* when returns were lowest—in the tenth decile, populated by the stocks from All Stocks with the highest PSRs.

Large stocks had similar, though more muted findings. There, the six deciles made up of low PSR stocks did better than the Large Stocks universe, whereas deciles 7 through 10, populated with the high PSR stocks, did significantly worse. Table 8-17 and Figure 8-2 summarize the findings for Large Stocks.

Implications

Low price-to-sales ratios beat the market more than any other value ratio and did so more consistently, in terms of both the 50-stock portfolios and the decile analysis. Low PSR stocks from both the All Stocks and Large Stocks groups beat the universes in every decade. The only time high PSR stocks beat the benchmarks was in the 1960s, an era dominated by performance-obsessed managers who would pay any price for a stock with a good story. Indeed, 1967 was the second-best year for

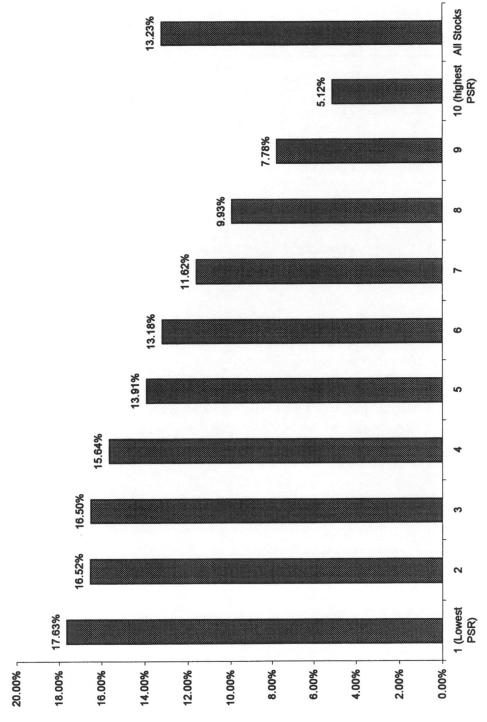

Figure 8-1. Compound return by PSR decile, All Stocks Universe, 1951–1996.

Table 8-17. Summary Results for PSR Decile Analysis of Large Stocks
Universe, 1951–1996

Decile	$10,000 grows to	Average return	Compound return	Standard deviation
1 (lowest PSR)	$4,043,295	16.06%	14.27%	20.16%
2	$3,603,757	15.71%	13.98%	20.18%
3	$2,029,206	13.89%	12.53%	17.25%
4	$1,826,745	13.48%	12.27%	16.28%
5	$1,881,358	13.64%	12.34%	16.78%
6	$2,058,352	13.75%	12.57%	16.11%
7	$866,428	11.47%	10.42%	14.92%
8	$800,749	11.25%	10.23%	14.55%
9	$596,203	10.70%	9.51%	15.61%
10 (highest PSR)	$875,010	12.31%	10.45%	20.12%
Large Stocks	$1,590,667	13.11%	11.92%	16.01%

high PSR stocks drawn from All Stocks. In his book *101 Years on Wall Street*, John Dennis Brown calls 1967 "a vintage year for speculators. About 45 percent of all issues listed at the NYSE would gain 50 percent or more." Thus, high PSR stocks perform best in frothy, speculative markets but do poorly in all other years. Amazingly, during this speculative time, low PSR stocks still did well. The results are depicted graphically in Figures 8-3 through 8-6.

The decile analysis confirms that of all the value ratios, PSR is the most consistent and best guide for future performance.

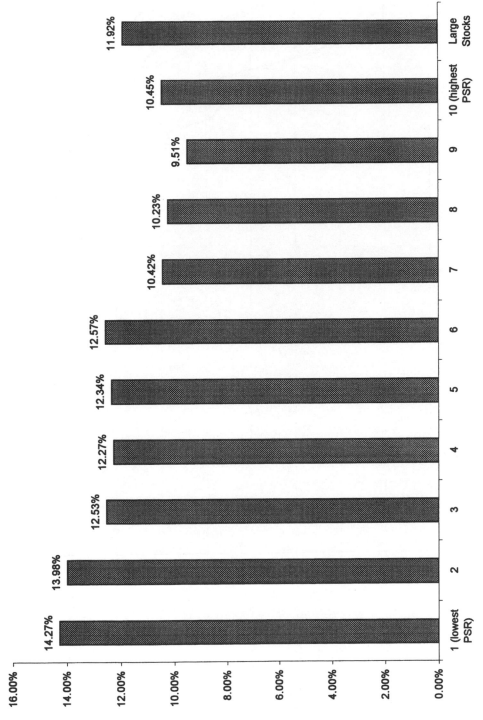

Figure 8-2. Compound return by PSR decile, Large Stocks Universe, 1951–1996.

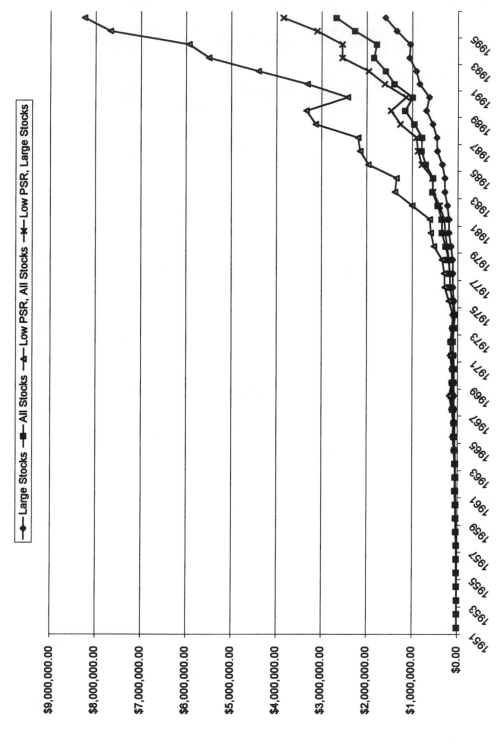

Figure 8-3. Returns on low price-to-sales strategies versus All Stocks and Large Stocks, 1951–1996. Year-end 1951 = $10,000.

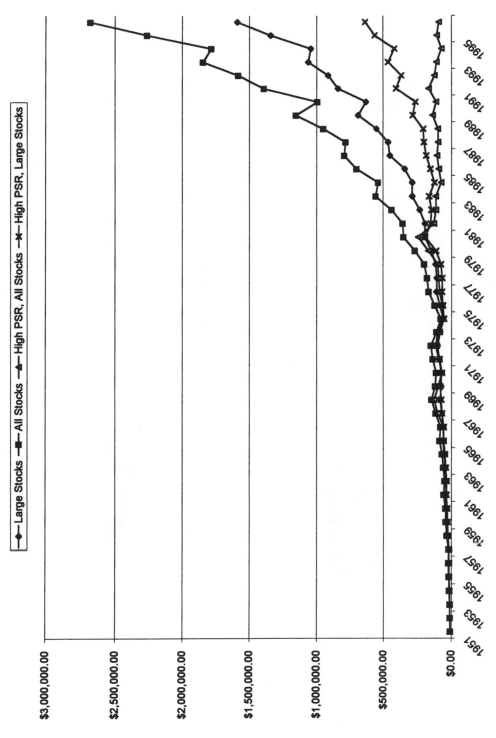

Figure 8-4. Returns on high price-to-sales strategies versus All Stocks and Large Stocks, 1951–1996. Year-end 1951 = $10,000.

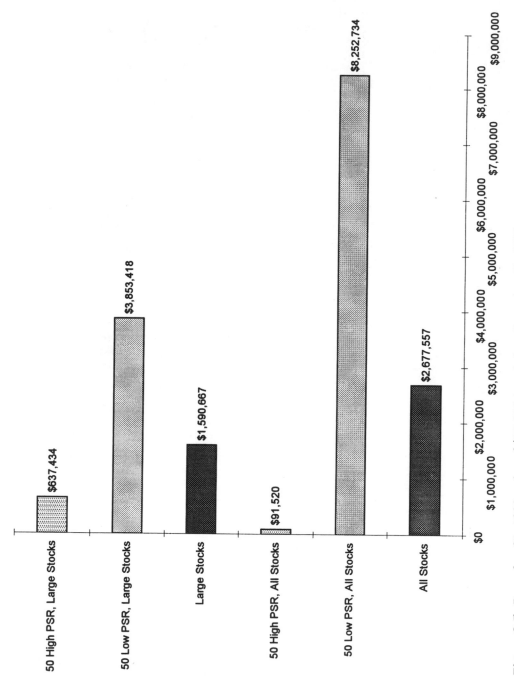

Figure 8-5. December 31, 1996, value of $10,000 invested on December 31, 1951, and annually rebalanced.

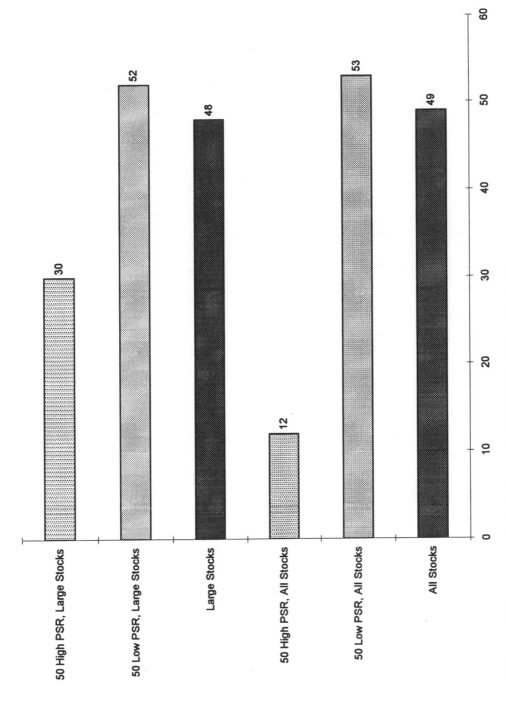

Figure 8-6. Sharpe risk-adjusted return ratio, 1951–1996. (Higher is better.)

9

Dividend Yields: Buying an Income

October. This is one of the peculiarly dangerous months to speculate in stocks. The others are July, January, September, April, November, May, March, June, December, August, and February.
—MARK TWAIN

Investors who find all months "peculiarly dangerous" often seek redemption in stocks with high dividend yields. Since dividends often account for more than half a stock's total return, they think it wise to concentrate on stocks paying high dividends. What's more, it's impossible to monkey with a dividend yield, since a company must either pay or defer it, or cancel it.

You find a stock's dividend yield by dividing the indicated annual dividend rate by the current price of the stock. The result is then multiplied by 100 to make it a percentage. Thus, if a company pays an annual dividend of $1 and the current price of the stock is $10, the dividend yield is 10 percent.

We'll look at buying the 50 highest-yielding stocks from All Stocks and Large Stocks. We're going to *exclude* utility stocks, since they would dominate the list if included.

The Results

As Tables 9-1 through 9-7 show, the effectiveness of high dividend yields depends almost entirely on the size of the companies you buy. Reviewing Tables 9-1 and 9-3, we see that the 50 high-yielding stocks drawn from All Stocks fail to beat the universe. Here $10,000 invested in the 50 highest-yielding stocks from the All Stocks universe on December 31, 1951 was worth $1,634,900 at the end of 1996, more than $1 million less than an investment in the All Stocks universe. The strategy also has a lower risk-adjusted return, since it took more risk. The base rate of positive returns for high-yielding stocks from the All Stocks universe shown in Table 9-5 is negative, with the strategy beating its universe just 17 percent of the time over all rolling 10-year periods.

Large Stocks Entirely Different

The returns of the 50 high-yielding Large Stocks are entirely different. Here, we see the 50 highest-yielding stocks doing almost twice as well as their universe with virtually the same risk: $10,000 invested in the 50 highest-yielding stocks from the Large Stocks universe on December 31, 1951 grew to $2,898,099 by the end of 1996. That's a compound return of 13.43 percent, some 1.51 percent better than the return of 11.92 percent for the Large Stocks universe. The 50 highest-yielding stocks from the Large Stocks universe had a standard deviation of return of 17.52 percent, 1.51 percent higher than the Large Stocks universe. This, coupled with the higher absolute return, accounts for the high Sharpe ratio of 54. In absolute terms, the strategy is less risky than Large Stocks. The largest loss was 16.5 percent in 1969, much better than the 26.7 percent drop that the Large Stocks universe suffered in 1974.

The high-yield strategy is also far more consistent when used on Large Stocks. Here the 50 highest-yielding stocks beat the universe 89 percent of the time over all rolling 10-year periods.

Figures 9-1 through 9-4 chart these trends.

Deciles

The decile analysis paints a different picture from the more extreme 50-stock portfolios. Here we see the top six deciles by dividend yield doing better than the All Stocks universe itself, while deciles 7 through 10, those with lower dividend yields, fail to beat the benchmark.

Table 9-1. Annual Performance of All Stocks Versus 50 Stocks with Highest Dividend Yields from All Stocks Universe

Year ending	All Stocks	Universe = All Stocks top 50 dividend yield	Top 50 dividend yield relative performance
31-Dec-52	7.90%	14.50%	6.60%
31-Dec-53	2.90%	7.70%	4.80%
31-Dec-54	47.00%	57.80%	10.80%
31-Dec-55	20.70%	24.40%	3.70%
31-Dec-56	17.00%	10.60%	−6.40%
31-Dec-57	−7.10%	−16.60%	−9.50%
31-Dec-58	55.00%	61.00%	6.00%
31-Dec-59	23.00%	21.90%	−1.10%
31-Dec-60	6.10%	−4.40%	−10.50%
31-Dec-61	31.20%	26.50%	−4.70%
31-Dec-62	−12.00%	−8.94%	3.06%
31-Dec-63	18.00%	19.70%	1.70%
31-Dec-64	16.30%	20.70%	4.40%
31-Dec-65	22.60%	23.10%	0.50%
31-Dec-66	−5.20%	−10.60%	−5.40%
31-Dec-67	41.10%	32.40%	−8.70%
31-Dec-68	27.40%	43.10%	15.70%
31-Dec-69	−18.50%	−17.90%	0.60%
31-Dec-70	−5.80%	3.40%	9.20%
31-Dec-71	21.30%	10.10%	−11.20%
31-Dec-72	11.00%	13.10%	2.10%
31-Dec-73	−27.20%	−18.50%	8.70%
31-Dec-74	−27.90%	−40.50%	−12.60%
31-Dec-75	55.90%	51.70%	−4.20%
31-Dec-76	35.60%	42.60%	7.00%
31-Dec-77	6.90%	6.80%	−0.10%
31-Dec-78	12.20%	4.70%	−7.50%
31-Dec-79	34.30%	24.90%	−9.40%
31-Dec-80	31.50%	14.00%	−17.50%
31-Dec-81	1.70%	8.60%	6.90%
31-Dec-82	22.50%	29.50%	7.00%
31-Dec-83	28.10%	28.50%	0.40%
31-Dec-84	−3.40%	5.40%	8.80%
31-Dec-85	30.80%	19.30%	−11.50%
31-Dec-86	13.10%	7.00%	−6.10%
31-Dec-87	−1.30%	−13.80%	−12.50%
31-Dec-88	21.20%	17.00%	−4.20%
31-Dec-89	21.40%	3.40%	−18.00%
31-Dec-90	−13.80%	−15.90%	−2.10%
31-Dec-91	39.80%	47.50%	7.70%
31-Dec-92	13.80%	12.90%	−0.90%
31-Dec-93	16.60%	31.90%	15.30%
31-Dec-94	−3.40%	−7.50%	−4.10%
31-Dec-95	27.00%	21.40%	−5.60%
31-Dec-96	18.30%	21.10%	2.80%
Arithmetic average	14.97%	14.08%	−0.89%
Standard deviation	19.51%	21.27%	1.76%

Table 9-2. Annual Performance of Large Stocks Versus 50 Stocks with Highest Dividend Yields from Large Stocks Universe

Year ending	Large Stocks	Universe = Large Stocks top 50 dividend yield	Top 50 dividend yield relative performance
31-Dec-52	9.30%	12.60%	3.30%
31-Dec-53	2.30%	−5.30%	−7.60%
31-Dec-54	44.90%	56.90%	12.00%
31-Dec-55	21.20%	20.00%	−1.20%
31-Dec-56	9.60%	11.30%	1.70%
31-Dec-57	−6.90%	−11.90%	−5.00%
31-Dec-58	42.10%	44.00%	1.90%
31-Dec-59	9.90%	9.40%	−0.50%
31-Dec-60	4.80%	1.70%	−3.10%
31-Dec-61	27.50%	29.40%	1.90%
31-Dec-62	−8.90%	−3.70%	5.20%
31-Dec-63	19.50%	20.60%	1.10%
31-Dec-64	15.30%	17.70%	2.40%
31-Dec-65	16.20%	18.80%	2.60%
31-Dec-66	−4.90%	−11.10%	−6.20%
31-Dec-67	21.30%	21.30%	0.00%
31-Dec-68	16.80%	32.60%	15.80%
31-Dec-69	−9.90%	−16.50%	−6.60%
31-Dec-70	−0.20%	8.00%	8.20%
31-Dec-71	17.30%	12.70%	−4.60%
31-Dec-72	14.90%	12.10%	−2.80%
31-Dec-73	−18.90%	−10.10%	8.80%
31-Dec-74	−26.70%	−13.30%	13.40%
31-Dec-75	43.10%	51.70%	8.60%
31-Dec-76	28.00%	41.80%	13.80%
31-Dec-77	−2.50%	4.50%	7.00%
31-Dec-78	8.10%	2.80%	−5.30%
31-Dec-79	27.30%	20.20%	−7.10%
31-Dec-80	30.80%	14.90%	−15.90%
31-Dec-81	0.60%	12.70%	12.10%
31-Dec-82	19.90%	26.00%	6.10%
31-Dec-83	23.80%	33.60%	9.80%
31-Dec-84	−0.40%	2.10%	2.50%
31-Dec-85	19.50%	32.80%	13.30%
31-Dec-86	32.20%	17.80%	−14.40%
31-Dec-87	3.30%	−3.00%	−6.30%
31-Dec-88	19.00%	22.40%	3.40%
31-Dec-89	26.00%	17.80%	−8.20%
31-Dec-90	−8.70%	−10.80%	−2.10%
31-Dec-91	33.00%	44.80%	11.80%
31-Dec-92	8.70%	8.30%	−0.40%
31-Dec-93	16.30%	26.30%	10.00%
31-Dec-94	−1.90%	0.09%	1.99%
31-Dec-95	28.50%	18.60%	−9.90%
31-Dec-96	18.70%	21.40%	2.70%
Arithmetic average	13.11%	14.76%	1.65%
Standard deviation	16.01%	17.52%	1.51%

Table 9-3. Summary Return Results for All Stocks and 50 Highest Dividend Yield Stocks from All Stocks Universe, December 31, 1951–December 31, 1996

	All Stocks	Universe = All Stocks Top 50 dividend yield
Arithmetic average	14.97%	14.08%
Standard deviation of return	19.51%	21.27%
Sharpe risk-adjusted ratio	49.00	41.00
3-yr compounded	13.22%	10.79%
5-yr compounded	14.00%	15.16%
10-yr compounded	12.92%	10.11%
15-yr compounded	14.44%	12.52%
20-yr compounded	14.97%	12.28%
25-yr compounded	12.74%	10.46%
30-yr compounded	12.43%	10.73%
35-yr compounded	11.64%	10.29%
40-yr compounded	12.62%	10.83%
Compound annual return	13.23%	11.99%
$10,000 becomes:	$2,677,556.77	$1,634,899.51
Maximum return	55.90%	61.00%
Minimum return	−27.90%	−40.50%
Maximum expected return*	53.98%	56.62%
Minimum expected return**	−24.04%	−28.46%

*Maximum expected return is average return plus 2 times the standard deviation.

**Minimum expected return is average return minus 2 times the standard deviation.

Table 9-4. Summary Return Results for Large Stocks and 50 Highest Dividend Yield Stocks from Large Stocks Universe, December 31, 1951–December 31, 1996

	Large Stocks	Universe = Large Stocks Top 50 dividend yield
Arithmetic average	13.11%	14.76%
Standard deviation of return	16.01%	17.52%
Sharpe risk-adjusted ratio	48.00	54.00
3-yr compounded	14.38%	12.95%
5-yr compounded	13.60%	14.54%
10-yr compounded	13.53%	13.54%
15-yr compounded	15.16%	16.25%
20-yr compounded	14.37%	14.87%
25-yr compounded	12.34%	14.59%
30-yr compounded	11.67%	13.87%
35-yr compounded	10.96%	12.95%
40-yr compounded	11.36%	12.93%
Compound annual return	11.92%	13.43%
$10,000 becomes:	$1,590,667.04	$2,898,099.42
Maximum return	44.90%	56.90%
Minimum return	−26.70%	−16.50%
Maximum expected return*	45.12%	49.80%
Minimum expected return**	−18.91%	−20.28%

*Maximum expected return is average return plus 2 times the standard deviation.

**Minimum expected return is average return minus 2 times the standard deviation.

Table 9-5. Base Rates for All Stocks and 50 Highest Dividend Yield Stocks from All Stocks Universe, 1951–1996

Item	50 highest dividend yield stocks beat All Stocks	Percent
Single-year return	22 out of 45	49.00%
Rolling 5-year compound return	14 out of 41	34.00%
Rolling 10-year compound return	6 out of 36	17.00%

Table 9-6. Base Rates for Large Stocks and 50 Highest Dividend Yield Stocks from Large Stocks Universe, 1951–1996

Item	50 highest dividend yield stocks beat Large Stocks	Percent
Single-year return	26 out of 45	58.00%
Rolling 5-year compound return	29 out of 41	71.00%
Rolling 10-year compound return	32 out of 36	89.00%

Table 9-7. Compound Annual Rates of Return by Decade

Portfolio	1950s*	1960s	1970s	1980s	1990s**
Large Stocks	15.33%	8.99%	6.99%	16.89%	12.61%
50 highest dividend yield from Large Stocks	15.20%	9.82%	11.44%	17.15%	13.65%
All Stocks	19.22%	11.09%	8.53%	15.85%	12.78%
50 highest dividend yield from All Stocks	20.29%	10.54%	6.55%	11.20%	14.06%

*Returns for 1952–1959.
**Returns for 1990–1996.

Contrasting this with the 50-stock portfolios, we see that perhaps we're better off simply selecting *broadly* from higher-yielding stocks from All Stocks rather than focusing in on the stocks with the *absolute* highest yields.

The Large Stocks decile analysis shows that we're still better off focusing on the highest-yielding stocks from the Large Stocks universe. Tables 9-8 and 9-9 and Figure 9-5 summarize the results.

Implications

The differences among the returns for the 50 stocks from All Stocks with the highest yields based on market capitalization are huge. Investors who want to use yield as a sole determinant should stick to large, better-known companies, because they usually have the stronger balance sheets and longer operating histories that make higher dividends possible. Indeed, in the multifactor section we'll see that when other criteria are included—such as strong cashflows, large sales, and large numbers of shares outstanding—large stocks with high dividend yields offer the best risk-adjusted returns available.

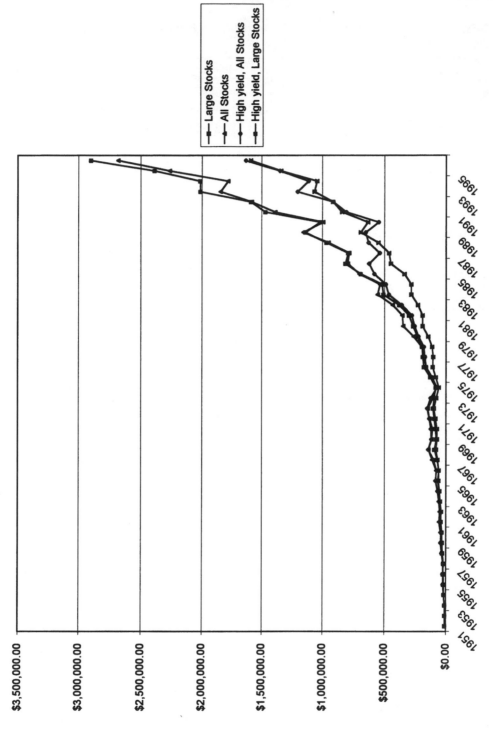

Figure 9-1. Returns on high-yield strategies versus All Stocks and Large Stocks, 1951–1996. Year-end 1951 = $10,000.

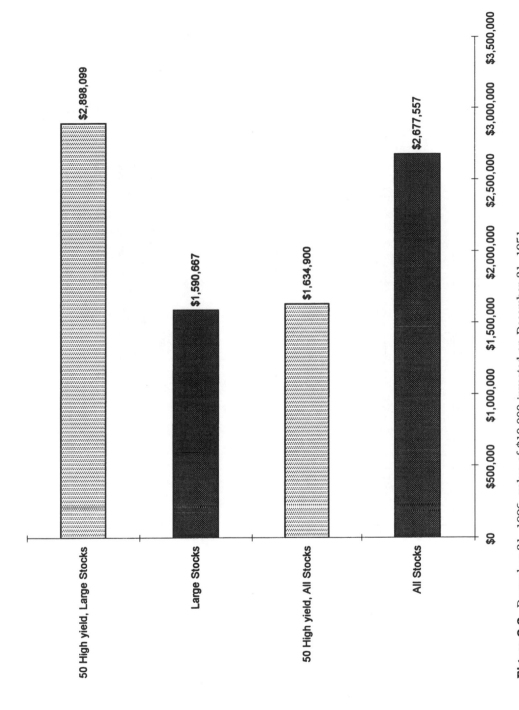

Figure 9-2. December 31, 1996, value of $10,000 invested on December 31, 1951, and annually rebalanced.

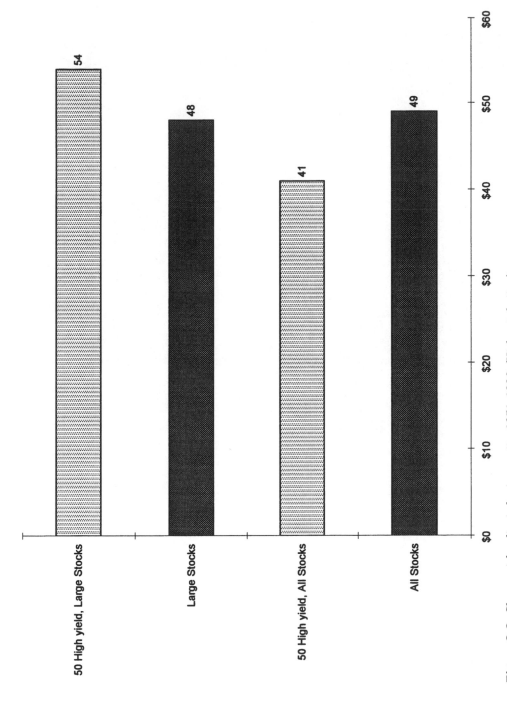

Figure 9-3. Sharpe risk-adjusted return ratio, 1951–1996. (Higher is better.)

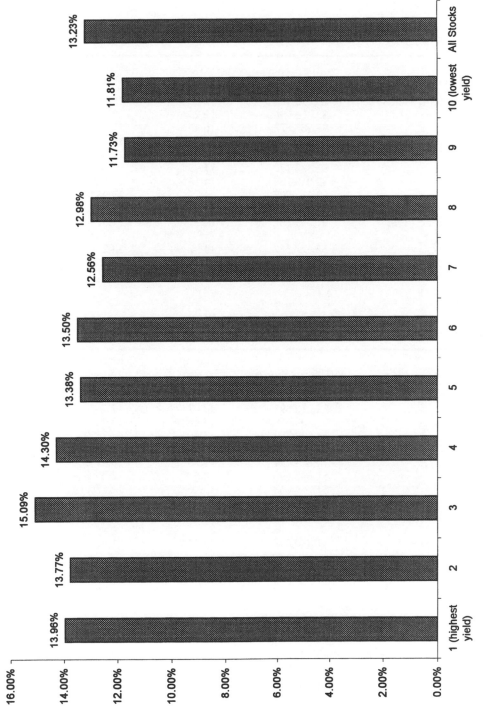

Figure 9-4. Compound return by dividend yield decile, All Stocks universe, 1951–1996.

Table 9-8. Summary Results for Dividend Yield Decile Analysis of All Stocks Universe, 1951–1996

Decile	$10,000 grows to	Average return	Compound return	Standard deviation
1 (highest dividend yield)	$3,573,468	15.63%	13.96%	19.43%
2	$3,324,096	15.25%	13.77%	18.48%
3	$5,585,878	16.45%	15.09%	17.72%
4	$4,090,087	15.62%	14.30%	17.31%
5	$2,848,919	14.73%	13.38%	17.19%
6	$2,983,170	14.99%	13.50%	17.81%
7	$2,049,286	14.16%	12.56%	18.42%
8	$2,422,707	14.73%	12.98%	19.39%
9	$1,473,512	13.64%	11.73%	19.91%
10 (lowest dividend yield)	$1,521,652	14.37%	11.81%	23.15%
All Stocks	$2,677,557	14.97%	13.23%	19.51%

Table 9-9. Summary Results for Dividend Yield Decile Analysis of Large Stocks Universe, 1951–1996

Decile	$10,000 grows to	Average return	Compound return	Standard deviation
1 (highest dividend yield)	$2,012,446	14.14%	12.51%	19.82%
2	$2,218,892	14.07%	12.76%	17.32%
3	$2,896,639	14.56%	13.42%	16.15%
4	$1,839,799	13.30%	12.29%	14.87%
5	$1,550,418	12.97%	11.86%	15.52%
6	$884,614	11.73%	10.47%	16.28%
7	$1,845,490	13.59%	12.29%	16.67%
8	$1,754,063	13.46%	12.17%	16.44%
9	$691,205	11.34%	9.87%	17.59%
10 (lowest dividend yield)	$1,066,255	13.14%	10.93%	21.68%
Large Stocks	$1,590,667	13.11%	11.92%	16.01%

With the smaller stocks from All Stocks, you're better off focusing on the larger decile group of high yield and should avoid buying the 50 stocks from All Stocks with the absolutely highest dividend yield. With these smaller stocks, such a huge yield may be a sign of problems to come.

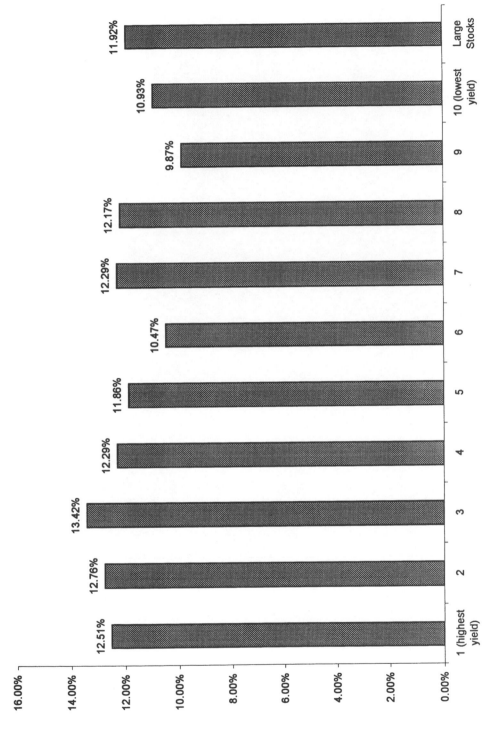

Figure 9-5. Compound return by dividend yield decile, Large Stocks universe, 1951–1996.

10

The Value of Value Factors

Discovery consists in seeing what everybody has
seen and thinking what nobody has thought.
— ALBERT SZENT-GYORGYI

The past 45 years show that rather than careening about like a drunken monkey, the stock market methodically rewards certain types of stocks while punishing others. There's nothing random about Figure 10-1. Stocks with low price-to-book, price-to-cashflow and price-to-sales ratios dramatically outperform the All Stocks universe. Just as important, those with *high* price-to-book, price-to-cashflow, and price-to-sales ratios do dramatically worse. The symmetry is striking. What's more, the new decile results confirm our 50-stock portfolio findings. Investors putting money into the lowest deciles by price-to-earnings, price-to-book, price-to-cashflow, and price-to-sales ratios did much better than those who invested in the market and *vastly* better than investors who continually put money into high-ratio stocks. Indeed, with the decile studies—particularly PSR—we see a continuum in which returns fall and risk rises as we move from low- to high-ratio deciles.

The 50-stock portfolios with low price-to-earnings ratios and those with high dividend yields fail to beat All Stocks, but the decile analysis shows that we're better off in the deciles with low PE ratios and in those with higher dividend yields. Even with the 50-stock portfolios, the symmetry exists, with the 50 highest price-to-earnings ratio stocks from All Stocks returning far less than the All Stocks universe and the 50 lowest price-to-earnings stocks. (See Figures 10-2 and 10-3.)

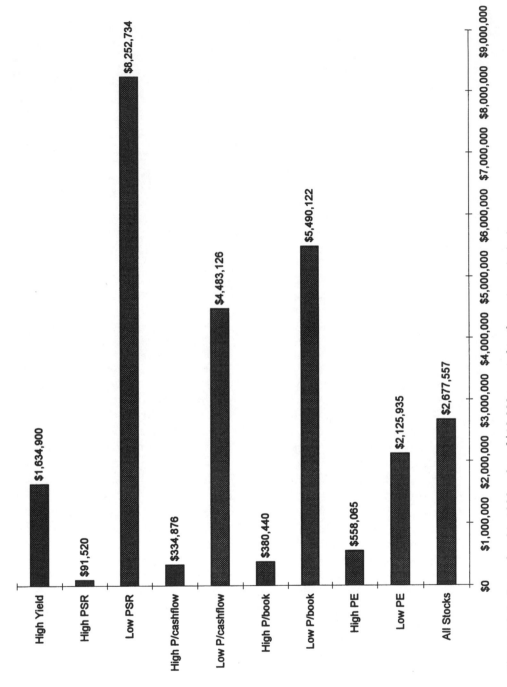

Figure 10-1. December 31, 1996, value of $10,000 invested in the various strategies using the All Stocks universe. Initial investment made December 31, 1951. 1951 = $10,000.

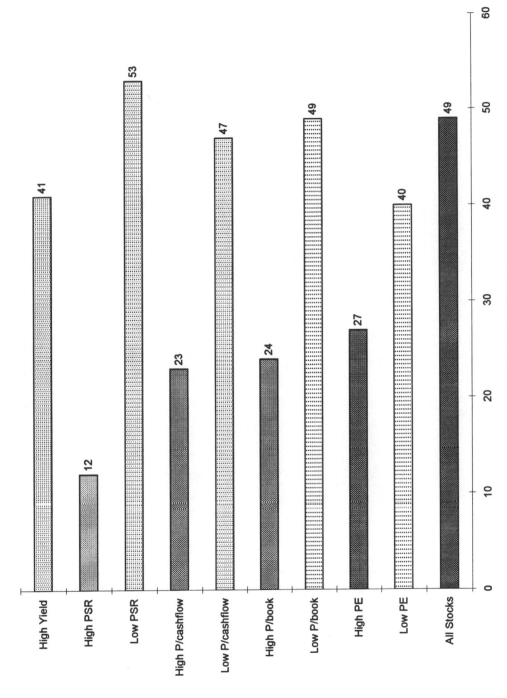

Figure 10-2. Sharpe ratios for the various strategies applied to the All Stocks universe, 1951–1996. (Higher is better.)

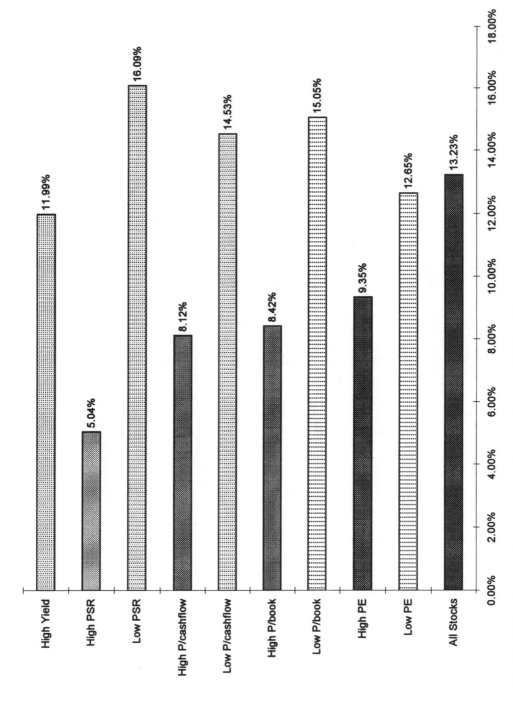

Figure 10-3. Compound average annual rates of return for the 45 years ending December 31, 1996. Results of applying strategies on the All Stocks universe.

Risk Doesn't Always Equal Reward

An important principle of the Capital Asset Pricing Model is that risk is compensated. It steers investors seeking higher returns to stocks with higher standard deviations. All the winning strategies thus far have higher standard deviations of return than the All Stocks universe. But the principle that higher risk equals higher rewards is not always true. As Figure 10-4 shows, the higher risk of the *high* price-to-earnings, price-to-book, price-to-cashflow, and price-to-sales ratios was uncompensated. Indeed, each of the strategies significantly underperformed the All Stocks universe. Buying the 50 *lowest* price-to-sales ratio stocks turns $10,000 into $8,252,734 with a standard deviation of return of 25.6 percent, but buying the 50 stocks with the *highest* price-to-sales ratios turns $10,000 into $91,520 with a higher standard deviation of return of 27.13 percent. The same is true with the decile analysis: A $10,000 investment in the lowest price-to-sales decile grows to $14,910,164 with a standard deviation of 19.79 percent, and the same $10,000 invested in the highest PSR decile grows to $94,437 with a higher standard deviation of 22.73 percent.

Is It Worth the Risk?

Risk acts like a powerful predator, culling the weak strategies from the herd. Buying the 50 stocks with the lowest price-to-sales ratios is the only strategy that beat the All Stocks universe on a risk-adjusted basis. The other value strategies come close, with the low price-to-book group matching All Stocks' Sharpe ratio of 49, and the low price-to-cashflow group close behind with a Sharpe ratio of 47. The Sharpe ratios on the deciles for these ratios show that sticking with the lowest decile generally offers a higher Sharpe ratio than the 50-stock portfolio versions. For example, the Sharpe ratio for decile 1 (lowest) for both price-to-book and price-to-cashflow ratios is 54, five points ahead of All Stocks.

Strategies that buy stocks with high price-to-earnings, price-to-book, price-to-cashflow, or price-to-sales ratios have abysmal risk-adjusted returns. This is true for both the 50-stock portfolios and the decile analysis. It's as if you must endure a night at sea on a rickety ship being tossed to and fro by a powerful hurricane only to have the ship dashed upon the rocks before reaching shore.

You must *always* consider risk before investing in strategies that buy stocks significantly different from the market. High risk does not

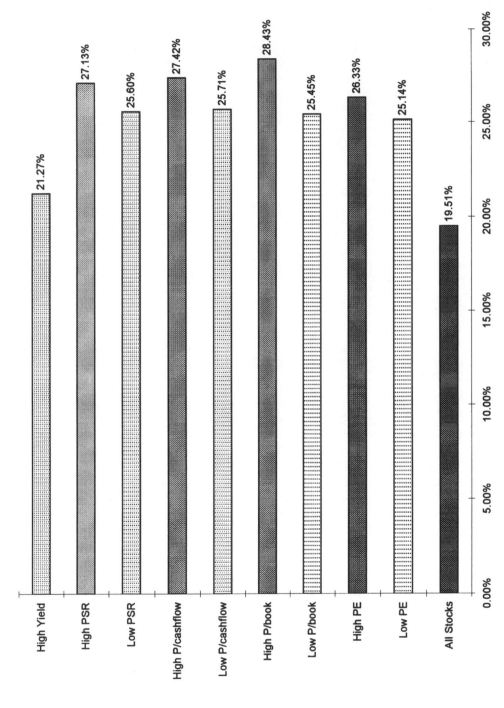

Figure 10-4. Standard deviation of return for strategies from the All Stocks universe, 1951–1996. (Higher is riskier.)

always mean high reward. Indeed, all the higher-risk strategies are eventually dashed on the rocks.

Embrace Consistency

A strategy won't help if you can't stick with it, so you must look for consistency over time. Here all the value strategies beat the All Stocks universe more than 50 percent of the time over all rolling 10-year periods, but the records are mixed. If you bought the 50 lowest price-to-book stocks annually, you'd underperform the All Stocks universe during a *majority* of 5-year periods. Only the low price-to-sales strategy shows consistency worth betting on. All the high-ratio strategies have horrible batting averages and should be avoided. Table 10-1 shows the compound rates of return by decade.

Table 10-1. Compound Annual Rates of Return by Decade: All Stocks Universe

Portfolio	1950s*	1960s	1970s	1980s	1990s**
All Stocks	19.22%	11.09%	8.53%	15.85%	12.78%
50 low PE	21.84%	13.96%	8.89%	7.56%	13.58%
50 high PE	19.27%	10.96%	2.26%	7.99%	8.63%
50 low price-to-book ratios	18.86%	11.49%	17.06%	13.15%	15.83%
50 high price-to-book ratios	22.32%	13.13%	0.82%	1.97%	7.66%
50 low price-to-cashflow ratios	18.71%	15.41%	13.57%	12.53%	12.86%
50 high price-to-cashflow ratios	19.30%	8.02%	−3.03%	8.77%	12.03%
50 low price-to-sales ratios	20.85%	11.15%	14.80%	20.43%	13.80%
50 high price-to-sales ratios	14.96%	11.99%	5.82%	−2.02%	−5.49%
50 highest-yielding stocks	20.29%	10.54%	6.55%	11.20%	14.06%

*Returns for 1952–1959.
**Returns for 1990–1996.

Large Stocks Are Different

When looking at the Large Stocks universe, we see the same results as for All Stocks. Figures 10-5 through 10-8 summarize the results. All the value strategies with low ratios beat the market and all the strategies with high ratios do considerably worse. All the high ratio strategies— save high PE—had higher standard deviations of return and did significantly worse than their low ratio counterparts. But the absolute amounts are more modest. With Large Stocks, the best-performing strategy is to buy the 50 stocks with the lowest price-to-cashflow ratios, with a $10,000 investment on December 31, 1951 growing to $5,773,333 by the end of 1996. We also see stocks with high dividend yields and low PE ratios beating the Large Stocks universe by wide margins. Figure 10-5 shows the returns of $10,000 invested on December 31, 1951 in the various value strategies.

The base rates for the Large Stocks value strategies are far more consistent than for the All Stocks universe. All the Large Stocks value strategies beat the universe *at least* 86 percent of the time over the 36 rolling 10-year periods. All the high ratio strategies fail to beat the universe a majority of the time over all rolling 10-year periods, with the most successful beating the Large Stocks universe just 42 percent of the time. Table 10-2 shows the compound rates of return by decade.

Implications

Value strategies work, rewarding patient investors who stick with them through hill and valley. All the Large Stocks value strategies beat the Large Stocks universe on an absolute and risk-adjusted basis, and they did so at least 88 percent of the time over all rolling 10-year periods. That's an extraordinary track record. The decile analysis confirms our 50-stock findings, and in the case of the All Stocks universe extends the win ratio of value strategies to PE ratios and high-yielding stocks.

High ratio strategies (e.g., high PE, high price-to-book) consistently underperform their universes over the long term. They take more risk and give lower rewards. This is true for both the 50-stock portfolios and the high ratio deciles. They have some spectacular runs that encourage investors to pay unwarranted prices for the stocks with the best story or most sizzle. But they consistently disappoint and should be avoided unless there are *extremely compelling* strategic reasons for buying the stock.

Now let's turn to growth variables and look for any extremely compelling strategies that might overcome the horrendous returns from high ratio stocks.

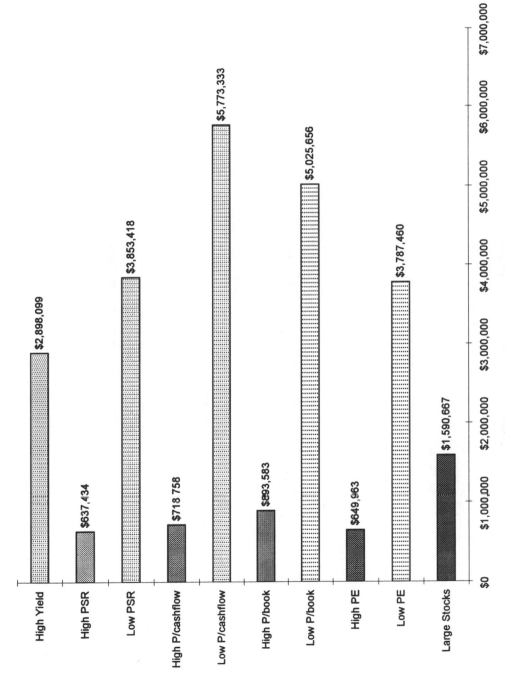

Figure 10-5. December 31, 1996, value of $10,000 invested in the various strategies using the Large Stocks universe. Initial investment made December 31, 1951. 1951 = $10,000.

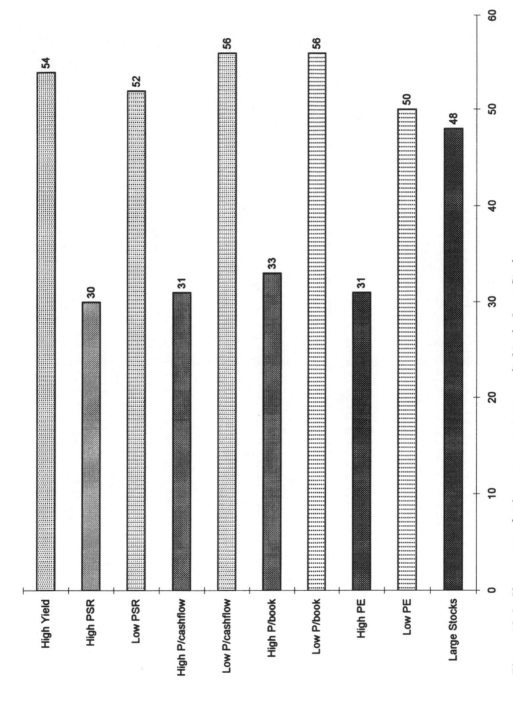

Figure 10-6. Sharpe ratios for the various strategies applied to the Large Stocks universe, 1951–1996. (Higher is better.)

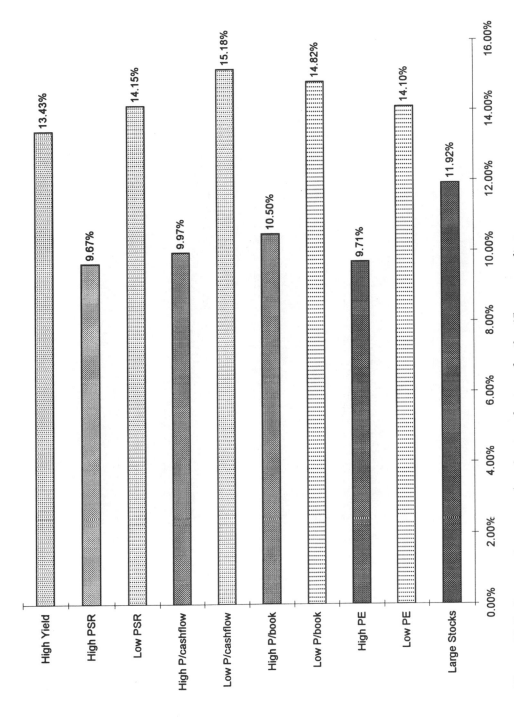

Figure 10-7. Compound average annual rates of return for the 45 years ending December 31, 1996. Results of applying strategies on the Large Stocks universe.

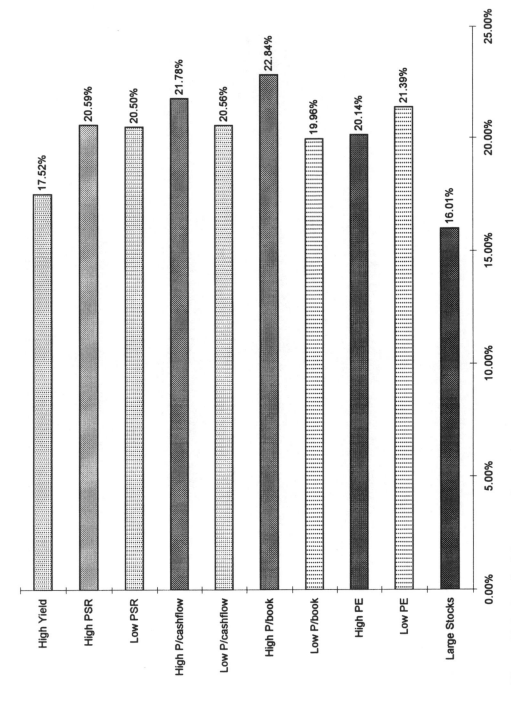

Figure 10-8. Standard deviation of return for strategies from the Large Stocks universe, 1951–1996. (Higher is riskier.)

Table 10-2. Compound Annual Rates of Return by Decade: Large Stocks Universe

Portfolio	1950s*	1960s	1970s	1980s	1990s**
Large Stocks	15.33%	8.99%	6.99%	16.89%	12.61%
50 low PE	16.12%	11.14%	12.64%	16.19%	15.25%
50 high PE	14.77%	10.94%	0.93%	14.11%	9.21%
50 low price-to-book ratios	15.41%	9.57%	13.95%	19.99%	15.85%
50 high price-to-book ratios	16.55%	11.30%	−0.60%	14.40%	13.92%
50 low price-to-cashflow ratios	17.28%	10.36%	15.40%	17.31%	16.49%
50 high price-to-cashflow ratios	14.85%	12.35%	−1.85%	13.29%	14.53%
50 low price-to-sales ratios	16.39%	9.48%	10.90%	20.09%	14.84%
50 high price-to-sales ratios	13.21%	11.73%	3.23%	9.54%	12.50%
50 highest-yielding stocks	15.20%	9.82%	11.44%	17.15%	13.65%

*Returns for 1952–1959.
**Returns for 1990–1996.

11

One-Year Earnings-Per-Share Percentage Changes: Do High Earnings Gains Mean High Performance?

It ain't so much what people know that hurts as what they know that ain't so.
—ARTEMUS WARD

Now let's look at factors commonly associated with growth investing. Generally, growth investors like *high* while value investors like *low*. Growth investors want high earnings and sales growth with prospects for more of the same. They usually don't care if a stock has a high PE ratio, reasoning that a company can grow its way out of short-term overvaluations. Growth investors often award high prices to stocks with rapidly increasing earnings.

Unfortunately, Compustat lacks long-term data on earnings forecasts. Many growth investors make substantial use of earnings forecasts when constructing their portfolios, so our inability to do a long-term test is somewhat limiting. However, some studies have found that forecasts are remarkably undependable. In the October 11, 1993 issue of *Forbes* magazine, David Dreman recounts a study that used a sample of 67,375 analysts' quarterly estimates for companies listed on the New York and American stock exchanges between 1973 and 1990. It found that analysts' average forecast error was 40 percent and that estimates were misleading (i.e., missed their mark by more than 10 percent) two-thirds of the time. Here, we'll look at *actual* earnings changes, not earnings forecasts.

Examining Annual Earnings Changes

First, we'll look at buying the 50 stocks with the best and the worst one-year earnings per share percentage changes from the All Stocks and Large Stocks universes. For the rankings to work smoothly, we eliminate stocks whose annual earnings went from positive to negative. Also, because of time-lag constraints, we must start the test on December 31, 1952. When comparing these returns with those of other strategies, keep in mind that 1952 isn't included. We'll do the same for the decile tests, with decile 1 being the 10 percent of stocks from each universe that had the highest earnings gains and decile 10 being the 10 percent that had the worst.

First, let's look at the returns from buying the 50 stocks from All Stocks with the best one-year earnings per share percentage gains. As usual, we start with $10,000 and rebalance the portfolio annually. As Tables 11-1 and 11-2 show, buying stocks with the best one-year earnings gains is like closing the barn door after the horse has left: $10,000 invested on December 31, 1952 in the top 50 one-year earnings gainers from All Stocks grew to $1,292,138 by the end of 1996. That's $1,189,379 shy of the $2,481,517 you'd earn with a similar investment in All Stocks. The 50 highest one-year earnings gainers also took considerably more risk—their standard deviation was 27 percent compared with All Stocks' 19.7 percent. The strategy *has* had some magnificent runs, however. Between December 31, 1962 and December 31, 1967, the strategy almost doubled the performance of the All Stocks universe, turning $10,000 into $38,546. It had another terrific streak between 1976 and 1980, but it lacks long-term consistency. Right after these great runs, it went on to do significantly worse than All Stocks. The base rates in Table 11-3 show that the strategy underperforms the All Stocks universe in each period.

Table 11-1. Annual Performance of All Stocks Versus 50 Stocks with Highest One-Year Earnings Gains from All Stocks Universe

Year ending	All Stocks	Universe = All Stocks Top 50 1-yr earnings gains	Top 50 1-yr earnings gains relative performance
31-Dec-53	2.90%	−3.80%	−6.70%
31-Dec-54	47.00%	65.70%	18.70%
31-Dec-55	20.70%	20.00%	−0.70%
31-Dec-56	17.00%	17.50%	0.50%
31-Dec-57	−7.10%	−20.80%	−13.70%
31-Dec-58	55.00%	69.60%	14.60%
31-Dec-59	23.00%	28.20%	5.20%
31-Dec-60	6.10%	3.10%	−3.00%
31-Dec-61	31.20%	21.30%	−9.90%
31-Dec-62	−12.00%	−17.80%	−5.80%
31-Dec-63	18.00%	31.19%	13.19%
31-Dec-64	16.30%	23.40%	7.10%
31-Dec-65	22.60%	35.20%	12.60%
31-Dec-66	−5.20%	−2.70%	2.50%
31-Dec-67	41.10%	81.00%	39.90%
31-Dec-68	27.40%	18.80%	−8.60%
31-Dec-69	−18.50%	−30.90%	−12.40%
31-Dec-70	−5.80%	−28.00%	−22.20%
31-Dec-71	21.30%	30.00%	8.70%
31-Dec-72	11.00%	13.20%	2.20%
31-Dec-73	−27.20%	−32.00%	−4.80%
31-Dec-74	−27.90%	−28.90%	−1.00%
31-Dec-75	55.90%	53.40%	−2.50%
31-Dec-76	35.60%	39.70%	4.10%
31-Dec-77	6.90%	17.70%	10.80%
31-Dec-78	12.20%	15.30%	3.10%
31-Dec-79	34.30%	50.70%	16.40%
31-Dec-80	31.50%	53.80%	22.30%
31-Dec-81	1.70%	−23.20%	−24.90%
31-Dec-82	22.50%	3.40%	−19.10%
31-Dec-83	28.10%	22.00%	−6.10%
31-Dec-84	−3.40%	−7.40%	−4.00%
31-Dec-85	30.80%	13.80%	−17.00%
31-Dec-86	13.10%	7.70%	−5.40%
31-Dec-87	−1.30%	−1.10%	0.20%
31-Dec-88	21.20%	17.50%	−3.70%
31-Dec-89	21.40%	16.90%	−4.50%
31-Dec-90	−13.80%	−17.40%	−3.60%
31-Dec-91	39.80%	37.20%	−2.60%
31-Dec-92	13.80%	12.50%	−1.30%
31-Dec-93	16.60%	19.30%	2.70%
31-Dec-94	−3.40%	−7.70%	−4.30%
31-Dec-95	27.00%	29.80%	2.80%
31-Dec-96	18.30%	9.20%	−9.10%
Arithmetic average	15.13%	14.92%	−0.21%
Standard deviation	19.70%	27.00%	7.30%

Table 11-2. Summary Return Results for All Stocks and 50 Stocks with Highest One-Year Earnings Gains from All Stocks Universe, December 31, 1952–December 31, 1996

	All Stocks	Universe = All Stocks Top 50 highest 1-year earnings gains
Arithmetic average	15.13%	14.92%
Standard deviation of return	19.70%	27.00%
Sharpe risk-adjusted ratio	47.00	34.00
3-yr compounded	13.22%	9.37%
5-yr compounded	14.00%	11.92%
10-yr compounded	12.92%	10.46%
15-yr compounded	14.44%	9.44%
20-yr compounded	14.97%	11.82%
25-yr compounded	12.74%	10.05%
30-yr compounded	12.43%	9.51%
35-yr compounded	11.64%	9.84%
40-yr compounded	12.62%	10.66%
Compound annual return	13.35%	11.68%
$10,000 becomes:	$2,481,516.93	$1,292,137.70
Maximum return	55.90%	81.00%
Minimum return	−27.90%	−32.00%
Maximum expected return*	54.52%	68.91%
Minimum expected return**	−24.27%	−39.08%

*Maximum expected return is average return plus 2 times the standard deviation.

**Minimum expected return is average return minus 2 times the standard deviation.

Table 11-3. Base Rates for All Stocks and 50 Stocks with Highest One-Year Earnings Gains from All Stocks Universe, 1952–1996

Item	50 high 1-yr earnings gains beat All Stocks	Percent
Single-year return	19 out of 44	43.00%
Rolling 5-year compound return	11 out of 40	28.00%
Rolling 10-year compound return	10 out of 35	29.00%

Large Stocks Do Worse

The 50 stocks with the highest one-year earnings gains from the Large Stocks universe did worse. Here $10,000 invested on December 31, 1952 grew to $567,407 by the end of 1996, a compound return of 9.61 percent. That's less than half the $1,455,322 you'd earn investing $10,000 in the Large Stocks universe, which had a return of 11.98 percent a year. The Sharpe ratio is a sorry 28 compared with Large Stocks' 45. Tables 11-4, 11-5, and 11-6 summarize the results. All base rates are negative, with the 50 highest one-year earnings gainers beating Large Stocks just 11 percent of the time over all rolling 10-year periods.

The record shows that buying stocks with the highest one-year earnings gains rarely beats the market. This probably occurs because high expectations are hard to meet. Seduced by stellar earnings gains, investors bid the stocks to unsustainable levels. When earnings growth fails to continue, they become disenchanted and sell their shares in disgust.

Buying Stocks with the Worst Earnings Changes

Perhaps you'd be better off buying the 50 stocks with the *worst* annual earnings changes. At least expectations for these stocks are modest. Remember that we require stocks to have positive earnings, so although these stocks aren't losing money, they will have experienced substantial declines in earnings.

An investment of $10,000 on December 31, 1952 in the 50 stocks from All Stocks with the worst one-year earnings changes grew to $1,486,429 by the end of 1996. That's better than the return from buying the *best* 50 earnings gainers, but it still falls short of the $2,481,517 you'd make investing the $10,000 in All Stocks. Risk was lower at 24.12 percent, but again still higher than the 19.07 percent for the All Stocks universe. Table 11-7 summarizes the results.

Large Stocks Do Better

An investment of $10,000 in the 50 stocks from Large Stocks with the worst one-year earnings changes actually beat the Large Stocks universe, growing to $1,398,514 on December 31, 1996, a compound return of 11.88 percent. A $10,000 investment in Large Stocks on December 31, 1952 grew to $1,455,322, a return of 11.98 percent a year. The Sharpe ratio for each was virtually identical—45 for Large Stocks and 43 for the 50 stocks with the worst one-year earnings change. Tables 11-8, 11-9, 11-10, 11-11, and 11-12 summarize the results.

Table 11-4. Annual Performance of Large Stocks Versus 50 Stocks with Highest One-Year Earnings Gains from Large Stocks Universe

Year ending	Large Stocks	Universe = Large Stocks Top 50 1-yr earnings gains	Top 50 1-yr earnings gains relative performance
31-Dec-53	2.30%	−4.40%	−6.70%
31-Dec-54	44.90%	48.10%	3.20%
31-Dec-55	21.20%	28.40%	7.20%
31-Dec-56	9.60%	8.50%	−1.10%
31-Dec-57	−6.90%	−13.90%	−7.00%
31-Dec-58	42.10%	41.40%	−0.70%
31-Dec-59	9.90%	11.10%	1.20%
31-Dec-60	4.80%	15.10%	10.30%
31-Dec-61	27.50%	16.50%	−11.00%
31-Dec-62	−8.90%	−14.60%	−5.70%
31-Dec-63	19.50%	22.70%	3.20%
31-Dec-64	15.30%	15.30%	0.00%
31-Dec-65	16.20%	26.70%	10.50%
31-Dec-66	−4.90%	−5.00%	−0.10%
31-Dec-67	21.30%	29.60%	8.30%
31-Dec-68	16.80%	9.00%	−7.80%
31-Dec-69	−9.90%	−5.60%	4.30%
31-Dec-70	−0.20%	−12.10%	−11.90%
31-Dec-71	17.30%	20.50%	3.20%
31-Dec-72	14.90%	11.00%	−3.90%
31-Dec-73	−18.90%	−31.60%	−12.70%
31-Dec-74	−26.70%	−31.80%	−5.10%
31-Dec-75	43.10%	37.80%	−5.30%
31-Dec-76	28.00%	32.30%	4.30%
31-Dec-77	−2.50%	−7.50%	−5.00%
31-Dec-78	8.10%	18.20%	10.10%
31-Dec-79	27.30%	37.10%	9.80%
31-Dec-80	30.80%	42.00%	11.20%
31-Dec-81	0.60%	−18.20%	−18.80%
31-Dec-82	19.90%	1.70%	−18.20%
31-Dec-83	23.80%	21.60%	−2.20%
31-Dec-84	−0.40%	−11.80%	−11.40%
31-Dec-85	19.50%	27.00%	−7.50%
31-Dec-86	32.20%	12.20%	−20.00%
31-Dec-87	3.30%	−5.40%	−8.70%
31-Dec-88	19.00%	17.60%	−1.40%
31-Dec-89	26.00%	21.50%	−4.50%
31-Dec-90	−8.70%	−9.20%	−0.50%
31-Dec-91	33.00%	32.10%	−0.90%
31-Dec-92	8.70%	9.30%	0.60%
31-Dec-93	16.30%	19.80%	3.50%
31-Dec-94	−1.90%	−1.50%	0.40%
31-Dec-95	28.50%	25.80%	−2.70%
31-Dec-96	18.70%	14.90%	−3.80%
Arithmetic average	13.19%	11.41%	−1.78%
Standard deviation	16.18%	19.36%	3.19%

Table 11-5. Summary Return Results for Large Stocks and 50 Stocks with Highest One-Year Earnings Gains from Large Stocks Universe, December 31, 1952–December 31, 1996

	Large Stocks	Universe = Large Stocks Top 50 highest 1-year earnings gains
Arithmetic average	13.19%	10.99%
Standard deviation of return	16.18%	19.68%
Sharpe risk-adjusted ratio	45.00	28.00
3-yr compounded	14.38%	12.50%
5-yr compounded	13.60%	13.27%
10-yr compounded	13.53%	11.70%
15-yr compounded	15.16%	10.86%
20-yr compounded	14.37%	11.08%
25-yr compounded	12.34%	8.52%
30-yr compounded	11.67%	8.29%
35-yr compounded	10.96%	8.22%
40-yr compounded	11.36%	8.76%
Compound annual return	11.98%	9.61%
$10,000 becomes:	$1,455,322.08	$567,407.09
Maximum return	44.90%	48.10%
Minimum return	−26.70%	−31.80%
Maximum expected return*	45.55%	50.36%
Minimum expected return**	−19.16%	−28.38%

*Maximum expected return is average return plus 2 times the standard deviation.

**Minimum expected return is average return minus 2 times the standard deviation.

Table 11-6. Base Rates for Large Stocks and 50 Stocks with Highest One-Year Earnings Gains from Large Stocks Universe, 1952–1996

Item	50 high 1-yr earnings gains beat Large Stocks	Percent
Single-year return	18 out of 44	41.00%
Rolling 5-year compound return	9 out of 40	23.00%
Rolling 10-year compound return	4 out of 35	11.00%

Table 11-7. Annual Performance of All Stocks Versus 50 Stocks with Worst One-Year Earnings Gains from All Stocks Universe

Year ending	All Stocks	Universe = All Stocks Worst 50 1-yr earnings gains	Worst 50 1-yr earnings gains relative performance
31-Dec-53	2.90%	−2.80%	−5.70%
31-Dec-54	47.00%	47.90%	0.90%
31-Dec-55	20.70%	26.40%	5.70%
31-Dec-56	17.00%	14.50%	−2.50%
31-Dec-57	−7.10%	−12.40%	−5.30%
31-Dec-58	55.00%	60.10%	5.10%
31-Dec-59	23.00%	16.20%	−6.80%
31-Dec-60	6.10%	−16.00%	−22.10%
31-Dec-61	31.20%	25.00%	−6.20%
31-Dec-62	−12.00%	−9.90%	2.10%
31-Dec-63	18.00%	23.90%	5.90%
31-Dec-64	16.30%	22.60%	6.30%
31-Dec-65	22.60%	45.00%	22.40%
31-Dec-66	−5.20%	−9.10%	−3.90%
31-Dec-67	41.10%	39.10%	−2.00%
31-Dec-68	27.40%	37.30%	9.90%
31-Dec-69	−18.50%	−32.00%	−13.50%
31-Dec-70	−5.80%	−16.00%	−10.20%
31-Dec-71	21.30%	26.20%	4.90%
31-Dec-72	11.00%	0.60%	−10.40%
31-Dec-73	−27.20%	−15.70%	11.50%
31-Dec-74	−27.90%	−26.50%	1.40%
31-Dec-75	55.90%	58.90%	3.00%
31-Dec-76	35.60%	47.10%	11.50%
31-Dec-77	6.90%	4.10%	−2.80%
31-Dec-78	12.20%	9.90%	−2.30%
31-Dec-79	34.30%	52.80%	18.50%
31-Dec-80	31.50%	45.40%	13.90%
31-Dec-81	1.70%	−10.50%	−12.20%
31-Dec-82	22.50%	19.40%	−3.10%
31-Dec-83	28.10%	30.90%	2.80%
31-Dec-84	−3.40%	−9.40%	−6.00%
31-Dec-85	30.80%	18.60%	−12.20%
31-Dec-86	13.10%	11.70%	−1.40%
31-Dec-87	−1.30%	0.90%	2.20%
31-Dec-88	21.20%	23.30%	2.10%
31-Dec-89	21.40%	15.10%	−6.30%
31-Dec-90	−13.80%	−29.70%	−15.90%
31-Dec-91	39.80%	26.60%	−13.20%
31-Dec-92	13.80%	22.60%	8.80%
31-Dec-93	16.60%	23.20%	6.60%
31-Dec-94	−3.40%	7.20%	10.60%
31-Dec-95	27.00%	17.20%	−9.80%
31-Dec-96	18.30%	11.80%	−6.50%
Arithmetic average	15.13%	14.58%	−0.55%
Standard deviation	19.70%	23.57%	3.88%

Table 11-8. Annual Performance of Large Stocks Versus 50 Stocks with Worst One-Year Earnings Gains from Large Stocks Universe

Year ending	Large Stocks	Universe = Large Stocks Worst 50 1-yr earnings gains	Worst 50 1-yr earnings gains relative performance
31-Dec-53	2.30%	0.0260	0.30%
31-Dec-54	44.90%	0.5320	8.30%
31-Dec-55	21.20%	0.2020	−1.00%
31-Dec-56	9.60%	0.1310	3.50%
31-Dec-57	−6.90%	−0.0740	−0.50%
31-Dec-58	42.10%	0.4490	2.80%
31-Dec-59	9.90%	0.1400	4.10%
31-Dec-60	4.80%	−0.1110	−15.90%
31-Dec-61	27.50%	0.2770	0.20%
31-Dec-62	−8.90%	−0.1240	−3.50%
31-Dec-63	19.50%	0.2420	4.70%
31-Dec-64	15.30%	0.1590	0.60%
31-Dec-65	16.20%	0.2180	5.60%
31-Dec-66	−4.90%	−0.0700	−2.10%
31-Dec-67	21.30%	0.2000	−1.30%
31-Dec-68	16.80%	0.1740	0.60%
31-Dec-69	−9.90%	−0.1810	−8.20%
31-Dec-70	−0.20%	−0.0030	−0.10%
31-Dec-71	17.30%	0.1660	−0.70%
31-Dec-72	14.90%	0.0450	−10.40%
31-Dec-73	−18.90%	−0.0010	18.80%
31-Dec-74	−26.70%	−0.2330	3.40%
31-Dec-75	43.10%	0.5740	14.30%
31-Dec-76	28.00%	0.3460	6.60%
31-Dec-77	−2.50%	−0.0710	−4.60%
31-Dec-78	8.10%	0.0620	−1.90%
31-Dec-79	27.30%	0.3060	3.30%
31-Dec-80	30.80%	0.4720	16.40%
31-Dec-81	0.60%	0.0760	7.00%
31-Dec-82	19.90%	0.2430	4.40%
31-Dec-83	23.80%	0.2650	2.70%
31-Dec-84	−0.40%	−0.0960	−9.20%
31-Dec-85	19.50%	0.2200	2.50%
31-Dec-86	32.20%	0.2150	−10.70%
31-Dec-87	3.30%	0.1190	8.60%
31-Dec-88	19.00%	0.2280	3.80%
31-Dec-89	26.00%	0.1800	−8.00%
31-Dec-90	−8.70%	−0.1720	−8.50%
31-Dec-91	33.00%	0.1680	−16.20%
31-Dec-92	8.70%	0.0950	0.80%
31-Dec-93	16.30%	0.2210	5.80%
31-Dec-94	−1.90%	0.0340	5.30%
31-Dec-95	28.50%	0.1340	−15.10%
31-Dec-96	18.70%	0.0970	−9.00%
Arithmetic average	13.19%	13.36%	0.17%
Standard deviation	16.18%	18.26%	2.08%

Table 11-9. Summary Return Results for All Stocks and 50 Stocks with Worst One-Year Earnings Gains from All Stocks Universe, December 31, 1952–December 31, 1996

	All Stocks	Universe = All Stocks Worst 50 1-year earnings gains
Arithmetic average	15.13%	14.58%
Standard deviation of return	19.70%	24.12%
Sharpe risk-adjusted ratio	47.00	38.00
3-yr compounded	13.22%	11.99%
5-yr compounded	14.00%	16.23%
10-yr compounded	12.92%	10.46%
15-yr compounded	14.44%	11.43%
20-yr compounded	14.97%	13.01%
25-yr compounded	12.74%	11.95%
30-yr compounded	12.43%	11.04%
35-yr compounded	11.64%	11.25%
40-yr compounded	12.62%	11.26%
Compound annual return	13.35%	12.04%
$10,000 becomes:	$2,481,516.93	$1,486,429.21
Maximum return	55.90%	60.10%
Minimum return	−27.90%	−32.00%
Maximum expected return*	54.52%	62.82%
Minimum expected return**	−24.27%	−33.66%

*Maximum expected return is average return plus 2 times the standard deviation.

**Minimum expected return is average return minus 2 times the standard deviation.

Table 11-10. Summary Return Results for Large Stocks and 50 Stocks with Worst One-Year Earnings Gains from Large Stocks Universe, December 31, 1952–December 31, 1996

	Large Stocks	Universe = Large Stocks Top 50 Worst 1-year earnings gains
Arithmetic average	13.19%	13.45%
Standard deviation of return	16.18%	18.68%
Sharpe risk-adjusted ratio	45.00	43.00
3-yr compounded	14.38%	8.75%
5-yr compounded	13.60%	11.45%
10-yr compounded	13.53%	10.43%
15-yr compounded	15.16%	12.28%
20-yr compounded	14.37%	13.04%
25-yr compounded	12.34%	12.66%
30-yr compounded	11.67%	11.53%
35-yr compounded	10.96%	10.93%
40-yr compounded	11.36%	11.02%
Compound annual return	11.98%	11.88%
$10,000 becomes:	$1,455,322.08	$1,398,513.51
Maximum return	44.90%	57.40%
Minimum return	−26.70%	−23.30%
Maximum expected return*	45.55%	50.80%
Minimum expected return**	−19.16%	−23.90%

*Maximum expected return is average return plus 2 times the standard deviation.

**Minimum expected return is average return minus 2 times the standard deviation.

Table 11-11. Base Rates for All Stocks and 50 Stocks with Worst One-Year Earnings Gains from All Stocks Universe, 1952–1996

Item	50 worst 1-year earnings gains beat All Stocks	Percent
Single-year return	21 out of 44	48.00%
Rolling 5-year compound return	17 out of 40	43.00%
Rolling 10-year compound return	8 out of 35	23.00%

Table 11-12. Base Rates for Large Stocks and 50 Stocks with Worst One-Year Earnings Changes from Large Stocks Universe, 1952–1996

Item	50 worst 1-year earnings changes beat Large Stocks	Percent
Single-year return	25 out of 44	57.00%
Rolling 5-year compound return	20 out of 40	50.00%
Rolling 10-year compound return	17 out of 35	49.00%

Table 11-13 shows the compound annual rates of return by decade for the Large Stocks and All Stocks universes. Figures 11-1 through 11-4 depict the results graphically for both groups.

Deciles

The decile analysis shows that earnings gains aren't a very good variable to use when selecting stocks. Tables 11-14 and 11-15 present the results. As we found in the 50-stock portfolios, concentrating on the stocks with the best earnings per share gains is a losing proposition, probably because investors have unrealistic expectations for such stocks and have pushed up their price-to-earnings and price-to-sales ratios.

All in all, the decile analysis confirms the 50-stock findings that one-year earnings changes are an unreliable tool for making security selections. Figures 11-5 and 11-6 summarize the results.

Table 11-13. Compound Annual Rates of Return by Decade

Portfolio	1950s*	1960s	1970s	1980s	1990s**
Large stocks	16.21%	8.99%	6.99%	16.89%	12.61%
50 highest 1-yr earnings gains from Large Stocks	15.05%	7.10%	9.25%	4.55%	12.18%
50 worst 1-yr earnings gains from Large Stocks	18.43%	7.69%	14.14%	11.77%	7.54%
All Stocks	20.94%	11.09%	8.53%	15.85%	12.78%
50 highest 1-yr earnings gains from All Stocks	21.33%	8.55%	16.97%	2.12%	10.33%
50 worst 1-yr earnings gains from All Stocks	19.06%	9.40%	16.67%	5.39%	9.51%

*Returns for 1953–1959.

**Returns for 1990–1996.

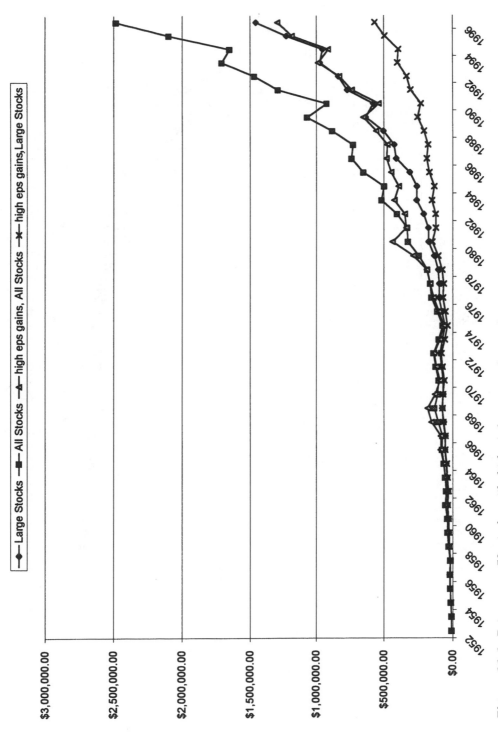

— Large Stocks — ■ — All Stocks — ▲ — high eps gains, All Stocks — ✳ — high eps gains, Large Stocks

Figure 11-1. Returns on 50 stocks with highest 1-year earnings gains versus
All Stocks and Large Stocks, 1952–1996. Year-end 1952 = $10,000.

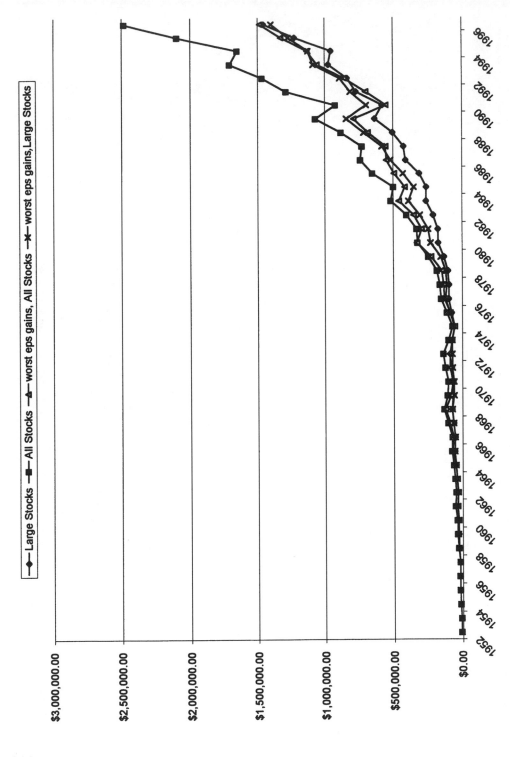

Figure 11-2. Returns on 50 stocks with worst 1-year earnings gains versus All Stocks and Large Stocks, 1952–1996. Year-end 1952 = $10,000.

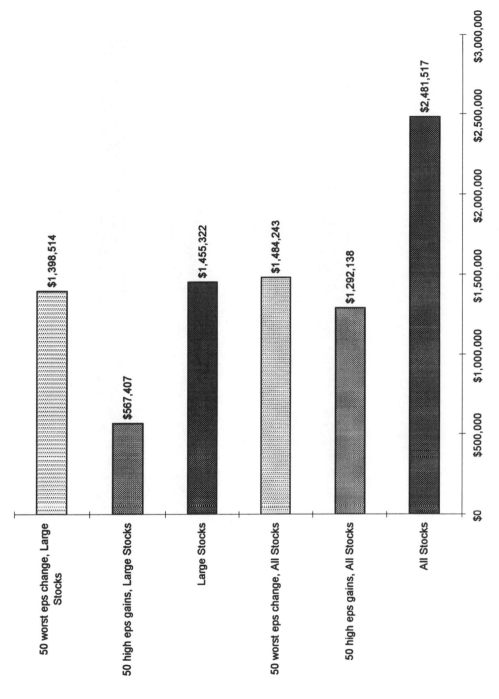

Figure 11-3. December 31, 1996, value of $10,000 invested on December 31, 1952, and annually rebalanced.

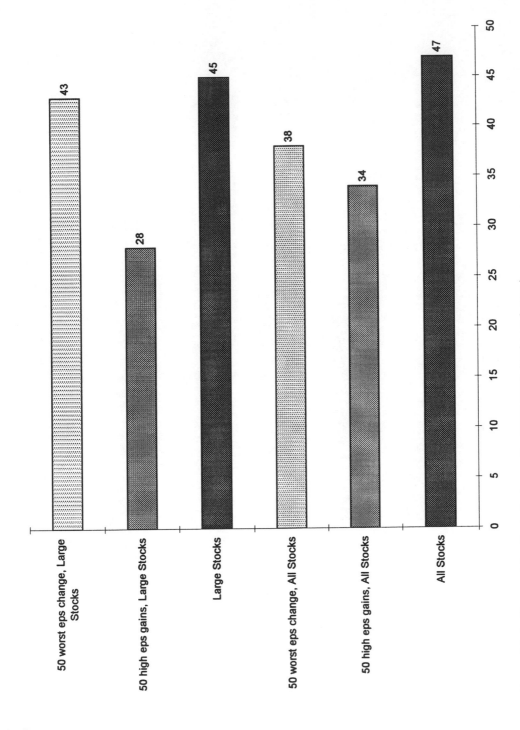

Figure 11-4. Sharpe risk-adjusted return ratio, 1952–1996. (Higher is better.)

Table 11-14. Summary Results for Earnings Gains Decile Analysis of All Stocks Universe, 1952–1996

Decile	$10,000 grows to	Average return	Compound return	Standard deviation
1 (highest earnings gains)	$1,421,161	14.73%	11.92%	24.92%
2	$2,214,524	15.59%	13.06%	23.44%
3	$2,645,321	15.61%	13.52%	21.20%
4	$3,472,637	15.95%	14.22%	19.30%
5	$3,320,691	15.67%	14.10%	18.68%
6	$2,125,633	14.55%	12.95%	18.57%
7	$4,109,005	16.26%	14.66%	18.99%
8	$1,483,682	13.54%	12.03%	18.02%
9	$2,284,575	14.82%	13.14%	19.24%
10 (worst earnings gains)	$1,476,875	14.23%	12.02%	22.02%
All Stocks	$2,481,517	15.13%	13.35%	19.70%

Table 11-15. Summary Results for Earnings per Share Change Decile Analysis of Large Stocks Universe, 1952–1996

Decile	$10,000 grows to	Average return	Compound return	Standard deviation
1 (highest earnings gains)	$739,604	12.16%	10.28%	19.80%
2	$1,171,160	13.32%	11.43%	20.27%
3	$1,175,709	12.89%	11.44%	17.87%
4	$1,935,792	13.87%	12.71%	15.69%
5	$1,943,967	14.23%	12.72%	18.34%
6	$1,256,093	12.88%	11.61%	16.48%
7	$1,204,035	12.87%	11.50%	17.45%
8	$1,376,905	12.97%	11.84%	15.69%
9	$1,866,949	14.19%	12.62%	18.80%
10 (worst earnings gains)	$1,260,875	13.08%	11.62%	17.96%
Large Stocks	$1,455,322	13.19%	11.98%	16.18%

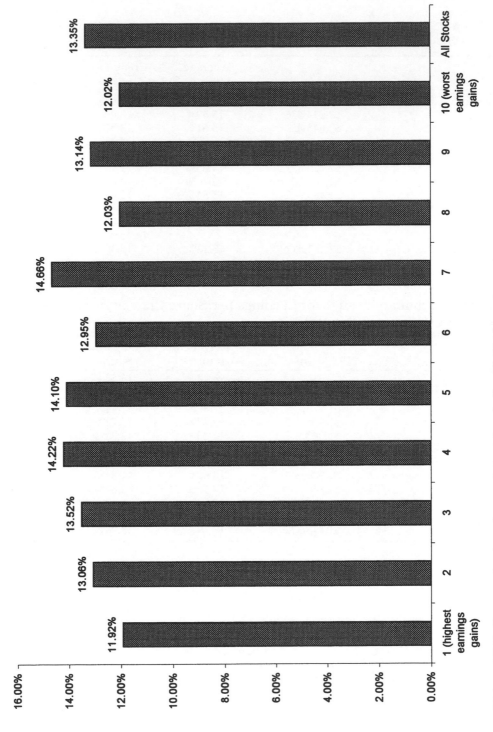

Figure 11-5. Compound return by earnings gains decile, All Stocks universe, 1952–1996.

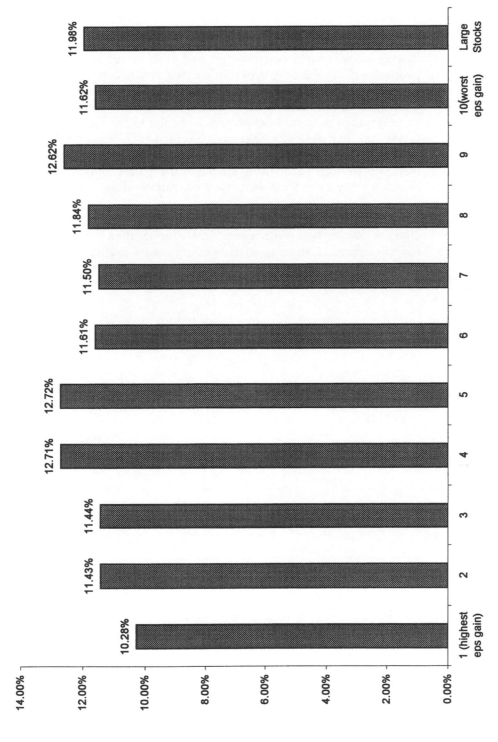

Figure 11-6. Compound return by earnings gain decile, Large Stocks universe, 1952–1996.

Implications

Buying stocks simply because they had great earnings gains is a losing proposition. Investors get overly excited about companies with dramatic earnings gains, projecting these earnings assumptions too far into the future. It's interesting to note that the stocks with the highest one-year earnings gains almost always have the highest price-to-earnings ratios, another indicator that poor performance lies ahead. We'll see later that *good* earnings gains coupled with strong price momentum will lead you to high-performing stocks, but for now remember that you shouldn't buy a stock just because it has outstanding one-year earnings gains.

You're not much better off buying stocks with the worst earnings changes. While their returns are slightly higher than those with the best earnings changes, there is no compelling theory to justify buying them. History suggests that you should not make investment decisions on either one of these variables.

12

Five-Year Earnings-Per-Share Percentage Changes

The same thing happened today that happened yesterday, only to different people.
—Walter Winchell

Some analysts believe that a one-year change in earnings is meaningless and that we should focus on five-year growth rates. This, they argue, is enough time to separate the one-trick pony from the true thoroughbred.

The Results

Unfortunately, five years of big earnings gains doesn't help us pick thoroughbreds. Starting on December 31, 1954 (we need five years of data to compute the compound five-year earnings growth rate), $10,000 invested in the 50 stocks from All Stocks with the highest five-year compound earnings-per-share growth rates grew to just $534,963 by the end of 1996, a compound return of 9.94 percent. A $10,000 investment in the All Stocks universe on December 31, 1954 was worth $1,640,531 on December 31, 1996, a return of 12.91 percent a year.

As with the 50 stocks with the highest one-year earnings gains, investors get dazzled by high five-year earnings growth rates and bid prices to unsustainable levels. When the future earnings are lower than expected, investors punish their former darlings and prices swoon.

The 50 stocks from All Stocks with the highest compound five-year earnings growth rates were also risky—their standard deviation of return was 26.57 percent, well ahead of All Stocks' 19.46 percent. High risk coupled with poor return accounts for the Sharpe ratio of 27. Over the same period, the Sharpe ratio for All Stocks was 44.

All the base rates for the strategy are horrible, with the 50 stocks with the highest five-year compound earnings growth rates beating All Stocks just 3 percent of the time over all rolling 10-year periods. Tables 12-1, 12-2, and 12-3 summarize the results.

Large Stocks Are Similar

The news is just as bad for large stocks with outstanding five-year earnings gains. They perform about half as well as an investment in the Large Stocks universe. Starting on December 31, 1954, $10,000 invested in the 50 stocks from Large Stocks with the highest five-year compound earnings growth rates grew to $613,441 at the end of 1996, a compound annual return of 10.3 percent. A $10,000 investment in the Large Stocks universe grew to $981,782, an annual return of 11.54 percent. The stocks with high earnings gains were also riskier than Large Stocks, having a standard deviation of return of 21.59 percent, well ahead of Large Stocks' 15.72 percent.

The base rates are only marginally better than for All Stocks, with the strategy beating the Large Stocks universe 21 percent of the time over all rolling ten-year periods. Tables 12-4, 12-5, and 12-6 summarize the returns for Large Stocks. Table 12-7 shows returns by decades. The results for both groups are shown graphically in Figures 12-1 through 12-3.

Deciles

The decile analysis for All Stocks suggests that you could be somewhat better off focusing not on the upper 10 percent of the database by five-year earnings gains, but on deciles 2 through 6. But no such consistency is apparent in the Large Stocks universe, where returns simply show you're best off *avoiding* the 10 percent of the database with the highest five-year earnings-per-share gains. The results are presented in Tables 12-8 and 12-9, and in Figures 12-4 and 12-5.

Table 12-1. Annual Performance of All Stocks Versus 50 Stocks with Highest Compound 5-Year EPS Growth from All Stocks Universe

Year ending	All Stocks	Universe = All Stocks Top 50 5-yr compound EPS growth	Top 50 5-yr compound EPS growth relative performance
31-Dec-55	20.70%	28.40%	7.70%
31-Dec-56	17.00%	19.40%	2.40%
31-Dec-57	−7.10%	−15.90%	−8.80%
31-Dec-58	55.00%	78.90%	23.90%
31-Dec-59	23.00%	37.80%	14.80%
31-Dec-60	6.10%	5.30%	−0.80%
31-Dec-61	31.20%	21.80%	−9.40%
31-Dec-62	−12.00%	−19.00%	−7.00%
31-Dec-63	18.00%	21.40%	3.40%
31-Dec-64	16.30%	3.90%	−12.40%
31-Dec-65	22.60%	22.00%	−0.60%
31-Dec-66	−5.20%	−1.90%	3.30%
31-Dec-67	41.10%	56.60%	15.50%
31-Dec-68	27.40%	20.10%	−7.30%
31-Dec-69	−18.50%	−21.40%	−2.90%
31-Dec-70	−5.80%	−34.50%	−28.70%
31-Dec-71	21.30%	35.80%	14.50%
31-Dec-72	11.00%	4.90%	−6.10%
31-Dec-73	−27.20%	−45.90%	−18.70%
31-Dec-74	−27.90%	−34.80%	−6.90%
31-Dec-75	55.90%	38.10%	−17.80%
31-Dec-76	35.60%	39.00%	3.40%
31-Dec-77	6.90%	5.90%	−1.00%
31-Dec-78	12.20%	7.30%	−4.90%
31-Dec-79	34.30%	52.50%	18.20%
31-Dec-80	31.50%	44.80%	13.30%
31-Dec-81	1.70%	−7.50%	−9.20%
31-Dec-82	22.50%	27.20%	4.70%
31-Dec-83	28.10%	20.90%	−7.20%
31-Dec-84	−3.40%	−19.40%	−16.00%
31-Dec-85	30.80%	28.40%	−2.40%
31-Dec-86	13.10%	6.60%	−6.50%
31-Dec-87	−1.30%	−16.80%	−15.50%
31-Dec-88	21.20%	21.10%	−0.10%
31-Dec-89	21.40%	30.90%	9.50%
31-Dec-90	−13.80%	−14.20%	−0.40%
31-Dec-91	39.80%	51.50%	11.70%
31-Dec-92	13.80%	5.50%	−8.30%
31-Dec-93	16.60%	13.40%	−3.20%
31-Dec-94	−3.40%	−6.00%	−2.60%
31-Dec-95	27.00%	31.50%	4.50%
31-Dec-96	18.30%	15.10%	−3.20%
Arithmetic average	14.66%	13.30%	−1.36%
Standard deviation	19.46%	26.57%	7.11%

Table 12-2. Summary Return Results for All Stocks and 50 Stocks with Highest 5-Year EPS Compound Growth Rates from All Stocks Universe, December 31, 1954–December 31, 1996

| | | Universe = Large Stocks |
	Large Stocks	Top 50 5-yr EPS compound growth rates
Arithmetic average	12.70%	12.47%
Standard deviation of return	15.72%	21.59%
Sharpe risk-adjusted ratio	41.00	28.00
3-yr compounded	14.38%	16.35%
5-yr compounded	13.60%	11.32%
10-yr compounded	13.53%	12.75%
15-yr compounded	15.16%	12.26%
20-yr compounded	14.37%	13.83%
25-yr compounded	12.34%	10.56%
30-yr compounded	11.67%	9.52%
35-yr compounded	10.96%	9.42%
40-yr compounded	11.36%	9.83%
Compound annual return	11.54%	10.30%
$10,000 becomes:	$981,782.08	$613,440.50
Maximum return	43.10%	51.90%
Minimum return	−26.70%	−31.90%
Maximum expected return*	44.14%	55.65%
Minimum expected return**	−18.74%	−30.70%

*Maximum expected return is average return plus 2 times the standard deviation.

**Minimum expected return is average return minus 2 times the standard deviation.

Table 12-3. Base Rates for All Stocks and 50 Stocks with Highest 5-Year EPS Compound Growth Rates from All Stocks Universe, 1954–1996

Item	50 highest 5-yr EPS growth stocks beat All Stocks	Percent
Single-year return	15 out of 42	36.00%
Rolling 5-year compound return	11 out of 38	29.00%
Rolling 10-year compound return	1 out of 33	3.00%

Table 12-4. Annual Performance of Large Stocks Versus 50 Stocks with Highest 5-Year Compound EPS Growth Rates from Large Stocks Universe

Year ending	Large Stocks	Universe = Large Stocks Top 50 5-yr compound EPS growth	Top 50 5-yr compound EPS growth relative performance
31-Dec-55	21.20%	28.10%	6.90%
31-Dec-56	9.60%	12.40%	2.80%
31-Dec-57	−6.90%	−14.70%	−7.80%
31-Dec-58	42.10%	49.00%	6.90%
31-Dec-59	9.90%	16.70%	6.80%
31-Dec-60	4.80%	5.50%	0.70%
31-Dec-61	27.50%	16.50%	−11.00%
31-Dec-62	−8.90%	−16.90%	−8.00%
31-Dec-63	19.50%	23.70%	4.20%
31-Dec-64	15.30%	10.30%	−5.00%
31-Dec-65	16.20%	30.90%	14.70%
31-Dec-66	−4.90%	3.00%	7.90%
31-Dec-67	21.30%	23.30%	2.00%
31-Dec-68	16.80%	12.50%	−4.30%
31-Dec-69	−9.90%	−15.30%	−5.40%
31-Dec-70	−0.20%	−21.60%	−21.40%
31-Dec-71	17.30%	34.80%	17.50%
31-Dec-72	14.90%	12.50%	−2.40%
31-Dec-73	−18.90%	−29.10%	−10.20%
31-Dec-74	−26.70%	−31.90%	−5.20%
31-Dec-75	43.10%	42.70%	−0.40%
31-Dec-76	28.00%	19.00%	−9.00%
31-Dec-77	−2.50%	−0.09%	2.41%
31-Dec-78	8.10%	13.20%	5.10%
31-Dec-79	27.30%	51.80%	24.50%
31-Dec-80	30.80%	51.90%	21.10%
31-Dec-81	0.60%	−9.70%	−10.30%
31-Dec-82	19.90%	26.40%	6.50%
31-Dec-83	23.80%	10.50%	−13.30%
31-Dec-84	−0.40%	−20.00%	−19.60%
31-Dec-85	19.50%	31.20%	11.70%
31-Dec-86	32.20%	16.50%	−15.70%
31-Dec-87	3.30%	−7.20%	−10.50%
31-Dec-88	19.00%	16.60%	−2.40%
31-Dec-89	26.00%	26.30%	0.30%
31-Dec-90	−8.70%	−3.60%	5.10%
31-Dec-91	33.00%	47.40%	14.40%
31-Dec-92	8.70%	6.80%	−1.90%
31-Dec-93	16.30%	1.60%	−14.70%
31-Dec-94	−1.90%	−4.50%	−2.60%
31-Dec-95	28.50%	37.10%	8.60%
31-Dec-96	18.70%	20.30%	1.60%
Arithmetic average	12.70%	12.47%	−0.22%
Standard deviation of return	15.72%	21.59%	5.87%

Table 12-5. Summary Return Results for Large Stocks and 50 stocks with highest 5-year EPS compound growth rates from Large Stocks universe, December 31, 1954–December 31, 1996.

	Large Stocks	Universe = Large Stocks Top 50, 5-yr EPS compound growth rates
Arithmetic average	12.70%	12.47%
Standard deviation of return	15.72%	21.59%
Sharpe risk-adjusted ratio	41.00	28.00
3-yr compounded	14.38%	16.35%
5-yr compounded	13.60%	11.32%
10-yr compounded	13.53%	12.75%
15-yr compounded	15.18%	12.26%
20-yr compounded	14.37%	13.83%
25-yr compounded	12.34%	10.56%
30-yr compounded	11.67%	9.52%
35-yr compounded	10.96%	9.42%
40-yr compounded	11.36%	9.83%
Compound annual return	11.54%	10.30%
$10,000 becomes:	$981,782.08	$613,440.50
Maximum return	43.10%	51.90%
Minimum return	−26.70%	−31.90%
Maximum expected return (1)	44.14%	55.65%
Minimum expected return (2)	−18.74%	−30.70%

(1) Maximum expected return is average return plus 2 times the standard deviation.

(2) Minimum expected return is average return minus 2 times the standard deviation.

Table 12-6. Base Rates for Large Stocks and 50 Stocks with Highest 5-Year EPS Compound Growth Rates from Large Stocks Universe, 1954–1996

Item	50 highest 5-yr EPS growth stocks beat Large Stocks	Percent
Single-year return	21 out of 42	50.00%
Rolling 5-year compound return	14 out of 38	37.00%
Rolling 10-year compound return	7 out of 33	21.00%

Table 12-7. Compound Annual Rates of Return by Decade

Portfolio	1950s*	1960s	1970s	1980s	1990s**
Large Stocks	14.07%	8.99%	6.99%	16.89%	12.61%
50 highest 5-yr EPS growth rates from Large Stocks	16.39%	8.24%	5.28%	12.34%	13.51%
All Stocks	20.12%	11.09%	8.53%	15.85%	12.78%
50 highest 5-yr EPS growth rates from All Stocks	26.02%	8.77%	0.91%	11.60%	12.01%

*Returns for 1955–1959.

**Returns for 1990–1996.

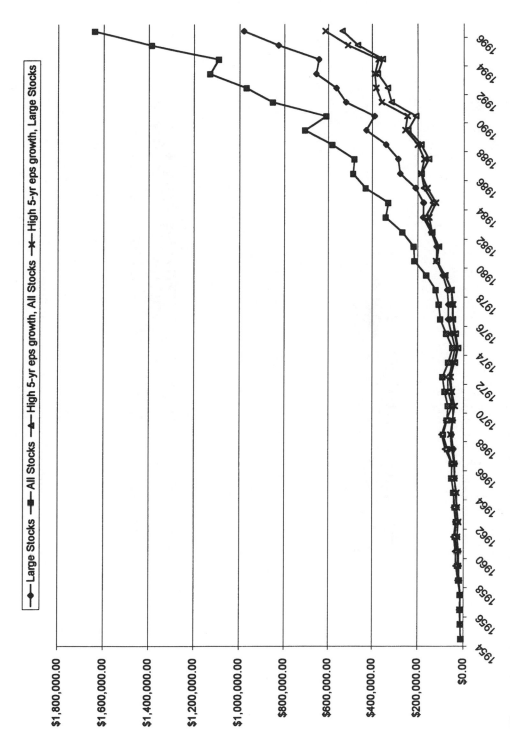

Figure 12-1. Returns on high five-year compound earnings growth stocks versus All Stocks and Large Stocks, 1954–1996. Year-end 1954 = $10,000.

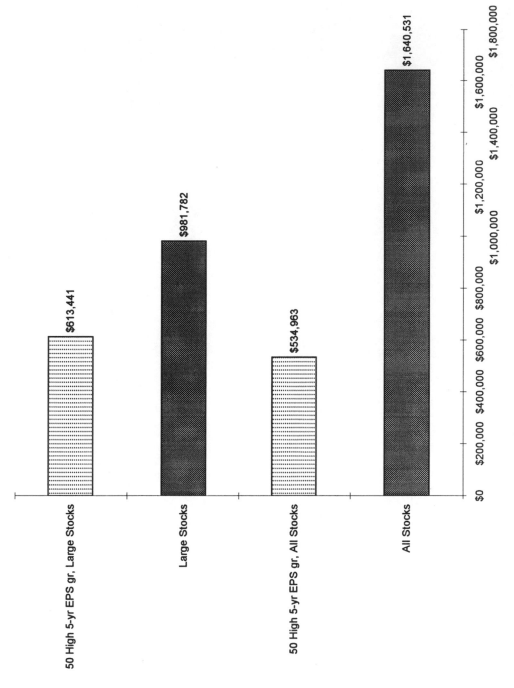

Figure 12-2. December 31, 1996, value of $10,000 invested on December 31, 1954, and annually rebalanced.

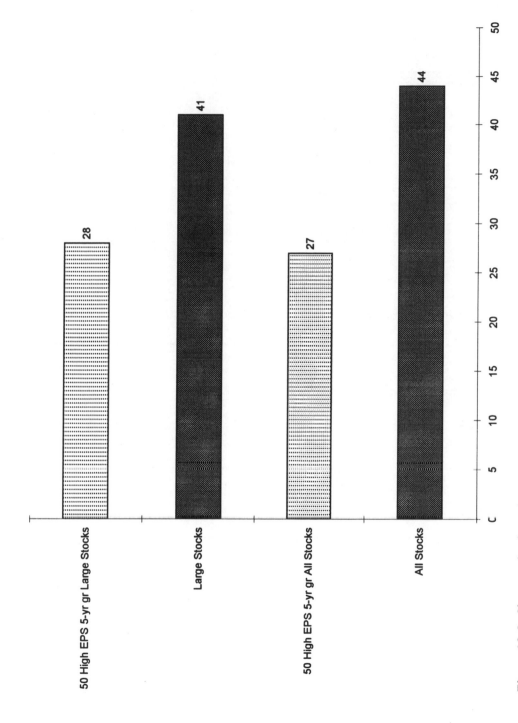

Figure 12-3. Sharpe risk-adjusted return ratio, 1954–1996. (Higher is better.)

Table 12-8. Summary Results for 5-Year Earnings Gains Decile Analysis of All Stocks Universe, 1954–1996

Decile	$10,000 grows to	Average return	Compound return	Standard deviation
1 (highest 5-year earnings gains)	$742,682	14.27%	10.80%	26.95%
2	$1,740,636	15.75%	13.07%	23.87%
3	$1,930,632	15.24%	13.35%	20.19%
4	$1,529,521	14.37%	12.72%	18.55%
5	$2,145,440	15.06%	13.64%	17.60%
6	$2,850,670	15.98%	14.41%	18.90%
7	$1,107,607	13.12%	11.86%	16.53%
8	$1,687,350	14.30%	12.99%	16.93%
9	$1,300,356	13.67%	12.29%	17.18%
10 (worst 5-year earnings gains)	$1,362,278	14.41%	12.41%	20.86%
All Stocks	$1,640,531	14.66%	12.91%	19.46%

Table 12-9. Summary Results for 5-Year Earnings-Per-Share Change Decile Analysis of Large Stocks Universe, 1954–1996

Decile	$10,000 grows to	Average return	Compound return	Standard deviation
1 (highest 5-year earnings gains)	$546,699	12.27%	10.00%	21.74%
2	$1,529,661	14.80%	12.72%	21.32%
3	$726,102	12.09%	10.74%	16.83%
4	$779,049	12.39%	10.93%	17.60%
5	$1,360,083	13.64%	12.41%	16.39%
6	$885,256	12.32%	11.27%	15.04%
7	$865,587	12.52%	11.21%	16.93%
8	$1,013,943	12.68%	11.63%	15.23%
9	$1,064,588	12.72%	11.75%	14.33%
10 (worst 5-year earnings gains)	$1,034,170	12.98%	11.68%	16.96%
Large Stocks	$981,782	12.70%	11.54%	15.72%

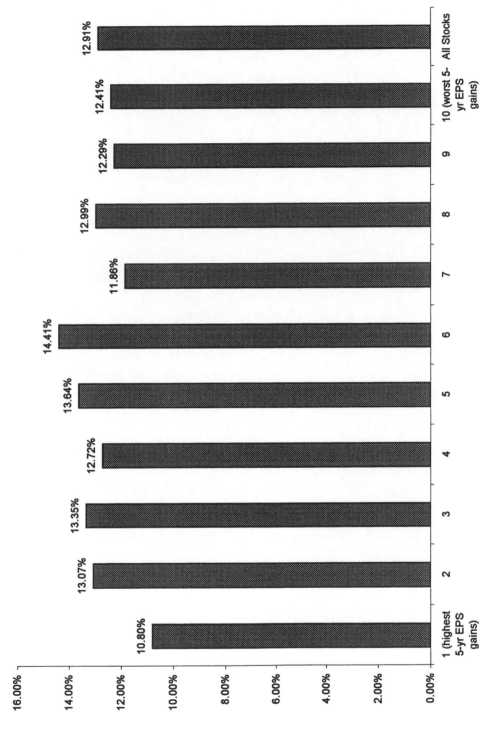

Figure 12-4. Compound return by five-year earnings gains decile, All Stocks universe, 1954–1996.

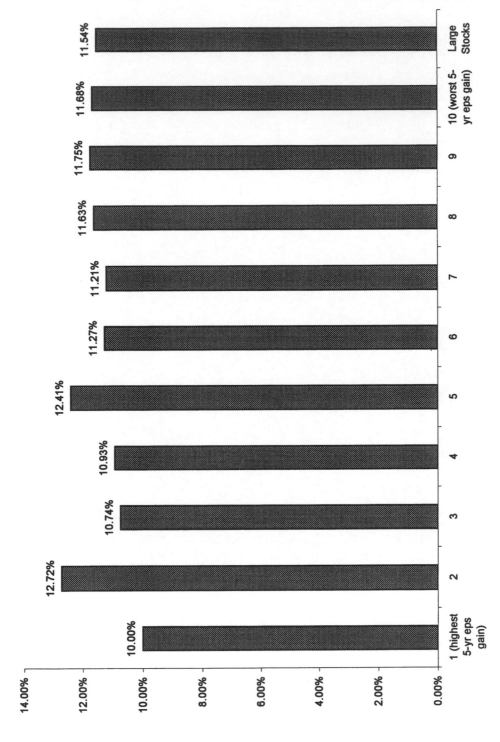

Figure 12-5. Compound return by five-year earnings gains decile, Large Stocks universe, 1954–1996.

Implications

As with the one-year earnings winners, investors consistently pay too much for stocks with outstanding five-year gains. While we were unable to look at the 50 worst five-year earnings changes because of the way Compustat calculates the compound returns, they are probably similar to the one-year tests. The evidence shows it's a mistake to get overly excited by big earners. Investors pay a premium for these stocks and would be better off indexing their portfolios to the Large Stocks universe.

13

Profit Margins: Do Investors Profit from Corporate Profits?

I am a strong believer that as you move toward the future, the strongest and clearest way to do it is if you have a good sense of your past. You cannot have a very tall tree without deep roots.
—CESAR PELLI

Net profit margins are an excellent gauge of a company's operating efficiency and ability to compete successfully with other firms in its field. Thus many believe that firms with high profit margins are better investments, since they are the leaders in their industries. Net profit margins are found by dividing income before extraordinary items (a company's income after all expenses but before provisions for dividends) by net sales. The result is then multiplied by 100 to get a percentage.

The Results

We'll test this strategy by buying the 50 stocks from All Stocks and Large Stocks with the highest profit margins. Here we're able to start the test on December 31, 1951, so we're again looking at the full 45 years of data. As usual, we'll time-lag all the accounting data to avoid look-ahead bias and rebalance the portfolio annually.

A $10,000 investment on December 31, 1951 in the 50 stocks from the All Stocks universe with the highest profit margins grew to $1,075,959 by the end of 1996, a compound return of 10.96 percent. That's a million and a half dollars less than you'd earn investing the money in the All Stocks universe. There $10,000 grew to $2,677,557, a return of 13.23 percent a year.

Risk for the 50 high stocks with profit margins was virtually the same as that for the All Stocks universe. The standard deviation of return of 20.48 percent was not even 1 percent higher than All Stocks' 19.51 percent. All the base rates for the 50 stocks with the highest profit margins were negative, with the strategy beating All Stocks just 11 percent of the time over all rolling 10-year periods. Tables 13-1, 13-2, and 13-3 summarize the returns for the All Stocks version of the strategy.

Large Stocks Do Slightly Better

The 50 stocks with the highest profit margins from the Large Stocks universe do slightly better. Here $10,000 invested on December 31, 1951 grew to $1,091,707 by the end of 1996. That's less than the $1,590,667 you'd earn investing the money in the Large Stocks universe, but better than the return from the high profit margin stocks in All Stocks. Here the 50 stocks with the highest profit margins were actually *less* risky than the Large Stocks universe—with a standard deviation of 15.91 percent compared with 16.01 percent for Large Stocks. This low standard deviation accounts for the strategy's fairly respectable Sharpe ratio of 43. All base rates are negative, with the 50 stocks with the highest profit margins beating the Large Stocks universe just 33 percent of the time over all rolling 10-year periods. Tables 13-4, 13-5, and 13-6 summarize the returns for the stocks with high profit margins from Large Stocks.

Table 13-7 shows compound rates of return by decade for the Large Stocks and All Stocks universes. The results are depicted graphically in Figures 13-1 through 13-3.

Deciles

The decile analysis of profit margins confirms the 50-stock results. It's not a good idea to buy a stock simply because it has a high profit margin. Indeed, the decile results show quite the opposite, with stocks in

Table 13-1. Annual Performance of All Stocks Versus 50 Stocks with Highest Profit Margins from All Stocks Universe

Year ending	All Stocks	Universe = All Stocks Top 50 profit margin	Top 50 profit margin relative performance
31-Dec-52	7.90%	11.30%	3.40%
31-Dec-53	2.90%	1.40%	−1.50%
31-Dec-54	47.00%	37.80%	−9.20%
31-Dec-55	20.70%	13.90%	−6.80%
31-Dec-56	17.00%	8.40%	−8.60%
31-Dec-57	−7.10%	−0.01%	7.09%
31-Dec-58	55.00%	46.10%	−8.90%
31-Dec-59	23.00%	9.20%	−13.80%
31-Dec-60	6.10%	22.40%	16.30%
31-Dec-61	31.20%	30.60%	−0.60%
31-Dec-62	−12.00%	−3.50%	8.50%
31-Dec-63	18.00%	17.70%	−0.30%
31-Dec-64	16.30%	17.00%	0.70%
31-Dec-65	22.60%	9.90%	−12.70%
31-Dec-66	−5.20%	1.70%	6.90%
31-Dec-67	41.10%	33.40%	−7.70%
31-Dec-68	27.40%	26.30%	−1.10%
31-Dec-69	−18.50%	−15.00%	3.50%
31-Dec-70	−5.80%	−3.80%	2.00%
31-Dec-71	21.30%	5.60%	−15.70%
31-Dec-72	11.00%	15.60%	4.60%
31-Dec-73	−27.20%	−20.90%	6.30%
31-Dec-74	−27.90%	−45.70%	−17.80%
31-Dec-75	55.90%	28.10%	−27.80%
31-Dec-76	35.60%	37.50%	1.90%
31-Dec-77	6.90%	16.00%	9.10%
31-Dec-78	12.20%	14.60%	2.40%
31-Dec-79	34.30%	85.10%	50.80%
31-Dec-80	31.50%	29.40%	−2.10%
31-Dec-81	1.70%	−11.70%	−13.40%
31-Dec-82	22.50%	4.70%	−17.80%
31-Dec-83	28.10%	17.70%	−10.40%
31-Dec-84	−3.40%	−6.70%	−3.30%
31-Dec-85	30.80%	10.80%	−20.00%
31-Dec-86	13.10%	11.60%	−1.50%
31-Dec-87	−1.30%	−1.70%	−0.40%
31-Dec-88	21.20%	9.40%	−11.80%
31-Dec-89	21.40%	25.40%	4.00%
31-Dec-90	−13.80%	−13.20%	0.60%
31-Dec-91	39.80%	32.40%	−7.40%
31-Dec-92	13.80%	4.90%	−8.90%
31-Dec-93	16.60%	29.50%	12.90%
31-Dec-94	−3.40%	−4.90%	−1.50%
31-Dec-95	27.00%	24.50%	−2.50%
31-Dec-96	18.30%	16.70%	−1.60%
Arithmetic average	14.97%	12.88%	−2.09%
Standard deviation	19.51%	20.48%	0.97%

Table 13-2. Summary Return Results for All Stocks and 50 Highest Profit Margin Stocks from All Stocks Universe, December 31, 1951–December 31, 1996

	All Stocks	Universe = All Stocks Top 50 profit margins
Arithmetic average	14.97%	12.88%
Standard deviation of return	19.51%	20.48%
Sharpe risk-adjusted ratio	49.00	37.00
3-yr compounded	13.22%	11.38%
5-yr compounded	14.00%	13.42%
10-yr compounded	12.92%	11.27%
15-yr compounded	14.44%	9.93%
20-yr compounded	14.97%	13.05%
25-yr compounded	12.74%	9.72%
30-yr compounded	12.43%	9.40%
35-yr compounded	11.64%	9.23%
40-yr compounded	12.62%	10.59%
Compounded annual return	13.23%	10.96%
$10,000 becomes:	$2,677,556.77	$1,075,958.53
Maximum return	55.90%	85.10%
Minimum return	−27.90%	−45.70%
Maximum expected return*	53.98%	53.83%
Minimum expected return**	−24.04%	−28.08%

*Maximum expected return is average return plus 2 times the standard deviation.

**Minimum expected return is average return minus 2 times the standard deviation.

Table 13-3. Base Rates for All Stocks and 50 Highest Profit Margin Stocks from All Stocks Universe, 1951–1996

Item	50 highest profit margin stocks beat All Stocks	Percent
Single-year return	17 out of 45	38.00%
Rolling 5-year compound return	12 out of 41	29.00%
Rolling 10-year compound return	4 out of 36	11.00%

Table 13-4. Annual Performance of Large Stocks Versus 50 Stocks with Highest Profit Margins from Large Stocks Universe

Year ending	Large Stocks	Universe = Large Stocks Top 50 profit margins	Top 50 profit margins relative performance
31-Dec-52	9.30%	7.80%	−1.50%
31-Dec-53	2.30%	1.30%	−1.00%
31-Dec-54	44.90%	39.60%	−5.30%
31-Dec-55	21.20%	16.20%	−5.00%
31-Dec-56	9.60%	5.40%	−4.20%
31-Dec-57	−6.90%	2.00%	8.90%
31-Dec-58	42.10%	42.20%	0.10%
31-Dec-59	9.90%	10.60%	0.70%
31-Dec-60	4.80%	17.20%	12.40%
31-Dec-61	27.50%	31.70%	4.20%
31-Dec-62	−8.90%	−0.06%	8.84%
31-Dec-63	19.50%	12.70%	−6.80%
31-Dec-64	15.30%	14.30%	−1.00%
31-Dec-65	16.20%	3.50%	−12.70%
31-Dec-66	−4.90%	−3.70%	1.20%
31-Dec-67	21.30%	2.40%	−18.90%
31-Dec-68	16.80%	8.80%	−8.00%
31-Dec-69	−9.90%	0.08%	9.98%
31-Dec-70	−0.20%	3.50%	3.70%
31-Dec-71	17.30%	9.70%	−7.60%
31-Dec-72	14.90%	17.60%	2.70%
31-Dec-73	−18.90%	−14.40%	4.50%
31-Dec-74	−26.70%	−31.70%	−5.00%
31-Dec-75	43.10%	27.90%	−15.20%
31-Dec-76	28.00%	23.20%	−4.80%
31-Dec-77	−2.50%	2.00%	4.50%
31-Dec-78	8.10%	9.00%	0.90%
31-Dec-79	27.30%	47.40%	20.10%
31-Dec-80	30.80%	38.20%	7.40%
31-Dec-81	0.60%	−11.80%	−12.40%
31-Dec-82	19.90%	2.80%	−17.10%
31-Dec-83	23.80%	16.70%	−7.10%
31 Dec 84	−0.40%	−1.80%	−1.40%
31-Dec-85	19.50%	24.70%	5.20%
31-Dec-86	32.20%	21.10%	−11.10%
31-Dec-87	3.30%	4.40%	1.10%
31-Dec-88	19.00%	11.20%	−7.80%
31-Dec-89	26.00%	30.80%	4.80%
31-Dec-90	−8.70%	−4.80%	3.90%
31-Dec-91	33.00%	40.70%	7.70%
31-Dec-92	8.70%	6.40%	−2.30%
31-Dec-93	16.30%	19.70%	3.40%
31-Dec-94	−1.90%	−0.02%	1.88%
31-Dec-95	28.50%	28.90%	0.40%
31-Dec-96	18.70%	13.10%	−5.60%
Arithmetic average	13.11%	12.14%	−0.96%
Standard deviation	16.01%	15.91%	−0.10%

Table 13-5. Summary Return Results for Large Stocks and 50 Highest Profit Margin Stocks from Large Stocks Universe, December 31, 1951–December 31, 1996

	Large Stocks	Universe = Large Stocks Top 50 profit margins
Arithmetic average	13.11%	12.14%
Standard deviation of return	16.01%	15.91%
Sharpe risk-adjusted ratio	48.00	43.00
3-yr compounded	14.38%	13.38%
5-yr compounded	13.60%	13.17%
10-yr compounded	13.53%	14.21%
15-yr compounded	15.16%	13.54%
20-yr compounded	14.37%	13.86%
25-yr compounded	12.34%	11.30%
30-yr compounded	11.67%	10.20%
35-yr compounded	10.96%	9.45%
40-yr compounded	11.36%	10.71%
Compounded annual return	11.92%	10.99%
$10,000 becomes:	$1,590,667.04	$1,091,707.48
Maximum return	44.90%	47.40%
Minimum return	−26.70%	−31.70%
Maximum expected return*	45.12%	43.96%
Minimum expected return**	−18.91%	−19.67%

*Maximum expected return is average return plus 2 times the standard deviation.

**Minimum expected return is average return minus 2 times the standard deviation.

Table 13-6. Base Rates for Large Stocks and 50 Highest Profit Margin Stocks from Large Stocks Universe, 1951–1996

Item	50 highest profit margin stocks beat Large Stocks	Percent
Single-year return	23 out of 45	51.00%
Rolling 5-year compound return	16 out of 41	39.00%
Rolling 10-year compound return	12 out of 36	33.00%

Table 13-7. Compound Annual Rates of Return by Decade

Portfolio	1950s*	1960s	1970s	1980s	1990s**
Large Stocks	15.33%	8.99%	6.99%	16.89%	12.61%
50 highest profit margins from Large Stocks	14.70%	8.24%	7.26%	12.66%	13.90%
All Stocks	19.22%	11.09%	8.53%	15.85%	12.78%
50 highest profit margins from All Stocks	15.02%	13.02%	8.14%	8.16%	11.61%

*Returns for 1952–1959.

**Returns for 1990–1996.

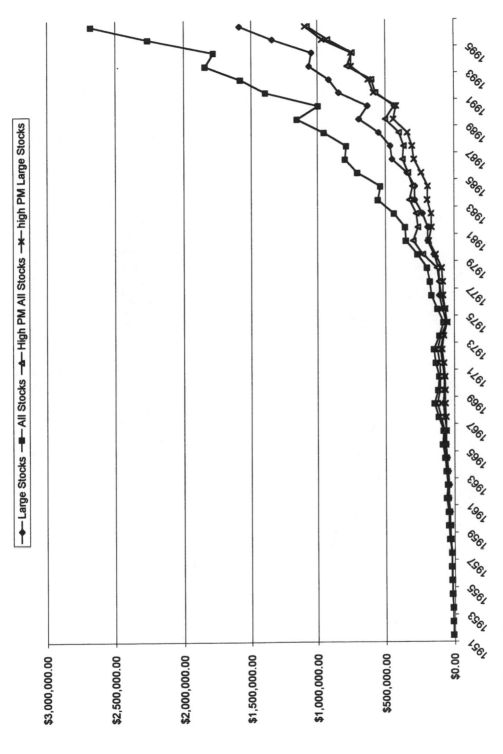

Figure 13-1. Returns on high profit margin strategy versus All Stocks and Large Stocks, 1951–1996. Year-end 1951 = $10,000.

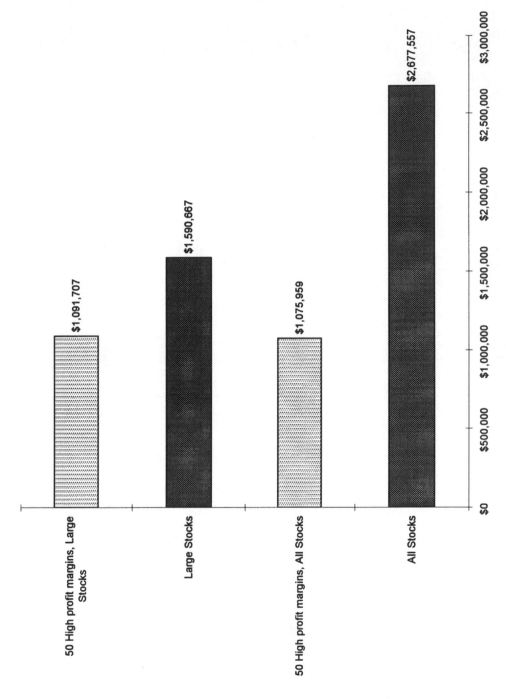

Figure 13-2. December 31, 1996, value of $10,000 invested on December 31, 1951, and annually rebalanced.

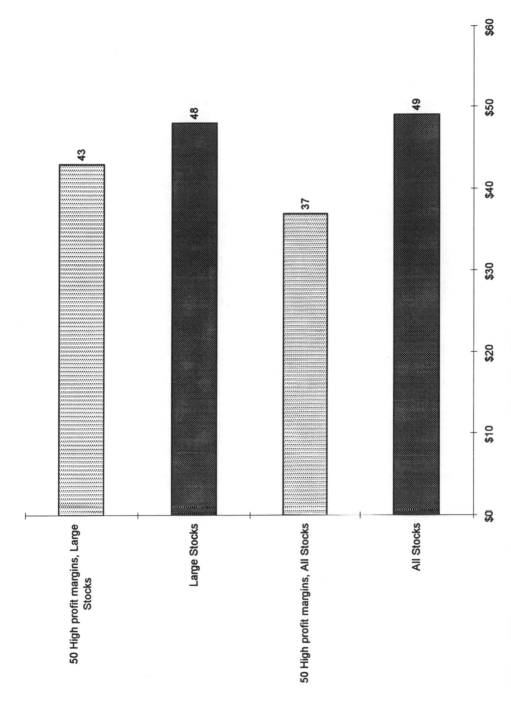

Figure 13-3. Sharpe risk-adjusted return ratios, 1951–1996. (Higher is better.)

some of the lowest deciles for profit margins outperforming those in the top (the exception is the tenth decile). For example, $10,000 invested in the 10 percent of stocks with the highest profit margins from All Stocks grew to $1,568,078, well behind All Stocks and *considerably* behind those in the ninth decile, one step removed from the bottom! The same holds true with Large Stocks, where lower margin deciles outperformed higher. Tables 13-8 and 13-9 and Figures 13-4 and 13-5 catalog the results.

Table 13-8. Summary Results for Profit Margin Decile Analysis of All Stocks Universe, 1951–1996

Decile	$10,000 grows to	Average return	Compound return	Standard deviation
1 (highest profit margins)	$1,568,078	13.36%	11.89%	17.77%
2	$1,907,174	13.55%	12.38%	15.90%
3	$2,153,167	13.99%	12.68%	16.81%
4	$1,512,735	13.05%	11.80%	16.74%
5	$1,894,891	14.17%	12.36%	19.40%
6	$2,699,742	15.26%	13.25%	20.82%
7	$2,529,680	15.17%	13.08%	21.10%
8	$3,305,809	15.88%	13.76%	21.62%
9	$3,454,324	16.03%	13.87%	21.83%
10 (lowest profit margins)	$1,604,494	14.86%	11.95%	25.57%
All Stocks	$2,677,557	14.97%	13.23%	19.51%

Table 13-9. Summary Results for Profit Margin Decile Analysis of Large Stocks Universe, 1951–1996

Decile	$10,000 grows to	Average return	Compound return	Standard deviation
1 (highest profit margins)	$1,011,172	12.01%	10.80%	16.26%
2	$1,484,857	12.81%	11.75%	15.14%
3	$2,017,522	13.57%	12.52%	14.92%
4	$1,771,464	13.42%	12.19%	16.55%
5	$2,170,358	14.01%	12.70%	16.77%
6	$1,790,421	13.54%	12.22%	16.92%
7	$2,014,218	14.06%	12.51%	18.44%
8	$2,341,631	14.38%	12.89%	17.95%
9	$2,108,530	14.12%	12.63%	18.18%
10 (lowest profit margins)	$2,100,283	14.17%	12.62%	18.50%
Large Stocks	$1,590,667	13.11%	11.92%	16.01%

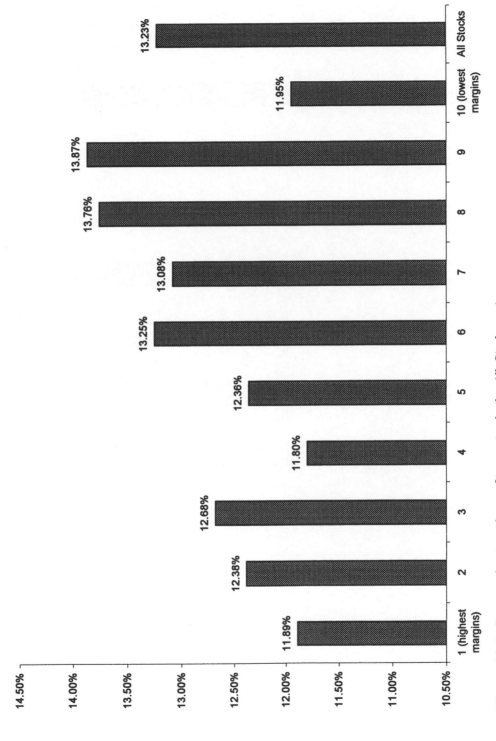

Figure 13-4. Compound return by profit margin decile, All Stocks universe, 1951–1996.

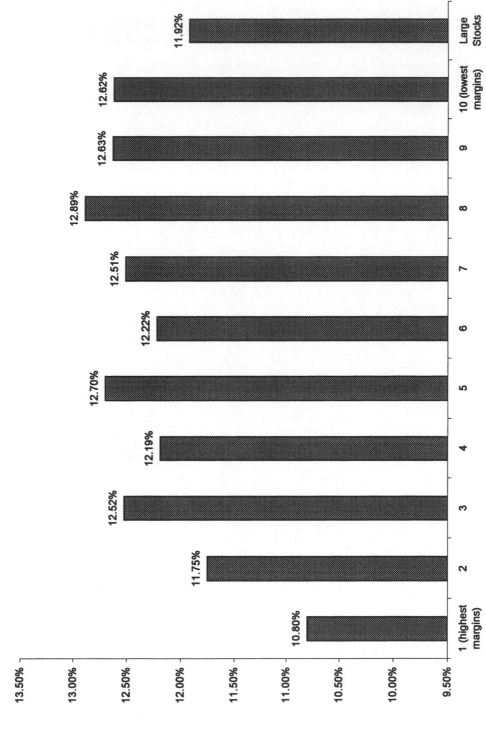

Figure 13-5. Compound return by profit margin decile, Large Stocks universe, 1951–1996.

Implications

History shows that using high profit margins as the only determinant in buying a stock will lead to disappointing results. Indeed, with the decile results, we see that if an investor were to use profit margin as a factor at all, it should simply be to avoid those stocks with the highest margins.

14

Return on Equity

*I'd rather see folks doubt what's true than accept
what isn't.* —FRANK A. CLARK

High return on equity is a hallmark of a growth stock. You find return
on equity by dividing common stock equity into income before extraordinary items (a company's income after all expenses but before provisions for dividends). The result is then multiplied by 100 to express
the term as a percentage. Here, we use common liquidating equity
(called CEQL in Compustat) as a proxy for common equity.

As with high profit margins, many believe that a high return on
equity (ROE) is an excellent gauge of how effectively a company invests
shareholders' money. The higher the ROE, the better the company's
ability to invest your money and, presumably, the better an investment
the stock will be.

The Results

We'll look at the results for high ROE stocks drawn from both the All
Stocks and Large Stocks universes. We start on December 31, 1951 with
a $10,000 investment in the 50 stocks from All Stocks with the highest
ROE. We'll also look at ROE by deciles for both All Stocks and Large
Stocks. As usual, we'll rebalance the portfolio annually and time-lag all
accounting data to avoid look-ahead bias.

As of December 31, 1996 $10,000 invested in the 50 stocks with the highest ROE was worth $2,507,363, a little less than the $2,677,557 you'd earn investing the money in All Stocks. But while earning a little less money, you'd take a lot more risk—the 50 stocks with the highest ROE had a standard deviation of return of 26.17 percent, considerably higher than All Stocks' 19.51 percent. This risk accounts for the 50 highest ROE stocks' Sharpe ratio of 41, eight points behind the All Stocks ratio of 49.

The base rates are almost dead even. The 50 highest ROE stocks beat the All Stocks universe 49 percent of the time over one year, 46 percent over 5-year rolling periods, and 42 percent of the time over 10-year rolling periods. You may as well flip a coin. Tables 14-1, 14-2, and 14-3 summarize the returns for the All Stocks group.

Large Stocks Do a Bit Worse

The 50 highest ROE stocks from the Large Stocks universe do a bit worse. Here, $10,000 grows to $1,138,300 at the end of 1996, a compound return of 11.10 percent a year. That's not as good as the $1,590,667 you'd make investing the money in the Large Stocks universe itself. The 50 highest ROE stocks from Large Stocks were also riskier: Their standard deviation of return was 19.45 percent, compared with 16.01 percent for the Large Stocks universe. The difference in risk and return accounts for the Sharpe ratio of the 50 highest ROE stocks of 39, nine points behind the 48 for the Large Stocks universe.

Base rates for the Large Stocks group are worse than those for All Stocks, with the 50 highest ROE stocks beating the Large Stocks universe 44 percent of the time in any one-year period, 39 percent of the time in 5-year rolling periods, and 36 percent of the time over all rolling 10-year periods. Tables 14-4, 14-5, and 14-6 summarize the returns for the Large Stocks group.

Table 14-7 shows compound annual returns for both groups by decade. The results are depicted graphically in Figures 14-1 through 14-3.

Deciles

The decile analysis of ROE paints a somewhat different picture. Here we see that an investor who concentrated on the higher ROE stocks that made up deciles 2 and 3 would have done nearly twice as well as someone who invested in the benchmark: $10,000 invested in the second decile by ROE from All Stocks (the second highest group by ROE)

Table 14-1. Annual Performance of All Stocks Versus 50 Stocks with Highest
Return on Equity from All Stocks Universe

Year ending	All Stocks	Universe = All Stocks top 50 ROE	Top 50 ROE relative performance
31-Dec-52	7.90%	9.80%	1.90%
31-Dec-53	2.90%	−2.30%	−5.20%
31-Dec-54	47.00%	64.90%	17.90%
31-Dec-55	20.70%	23.30%	2.60%
31-Dec-56	17.00%	25.20%	8.20%
31-Dec-57	−7.10%	−9.70%	−2.60%
31-Dec-58	55.00%	64.20%	9.20%
31-Dec-59	23.00%	41.30%	18.30%
31-Dec-60	6.10%	26.60%	20.50%
31-Dec-61	31.20%	24.30%	−6.90%
31-Dec-62	−12.00%	−15.50%	−3.50%
31-Dec-63	18.00%	12.30%	−5.70%
31-Dec-64	16.30%	14.70%	−1.60%
31-Dec-65	22.60%	25.90%	3.30%
31-Dec-66	−5.20%	0.02%	5.22%
31-Dec-67	41.10%	96.30%	55.20%
31-Dec-68	27.40%	18.40%	−9.00%
31-Dec-69	−18.50%	−19.60%	−1.10%
31-Dec-70	−5.80%	−3.40%	2.40%
31-Dec-71	21.30%	31.00%	9.70%
31-Dec-72	11.00%	3.80%	−7.20%
31-Dec-73	−27.20%	−44.00%	−16.80%
31-Dec-74	−27.90%	−26.50%	1.40%
31-Dec-75	55.90%	49.80%	−6.10%
31-Dec-76	35.60%	32.70%	−2.90%
31-Dec-77	6.90%	18.70%	11.80%
31-Dec-78	12.20%	10.70%	−1.50%
31-Dec-79	34.30%	39.00%	4.70%
31-Dec-80	31.50%	40.60%	9.10%
31-Dec-81	1.70%	−13.50%	−15.20%
31-Dec-82	22.50%	34.00%	11.50%
31-Dec-83	28.10%	13.20%	−14.90%
31-Dec-84	−3.40%	−27.10%	23.70%
31-Dec-85	30.80%	33.30%	2.50%
31-Dec-86	13.10%	18.70%	5.60%
31-Dec-87	−1.30%	−9.50%	−8.20%
31-Dec-88	21.20%	19.00%	−2.20%
31-Dec-89	21.40%	23.60%	2.20%
31-Dec-90	−13.80%	−18.10%	−4.30%
31-Dec-91	39.80%	31.30%	−8.50%
31-Dec-92	13.80%	8.50%	−5.30%
31-Dec-93	16.60%	23.60%	7.00%
31-Dec-94	−3.40%	−7.30%	−3.90%
31-Dec-95	27.00%	28.10%	1.10%
31-Dec-96	18.30%	14.20%	−4.10%
Arithmetic average	14.97%	16.10%	1.13%
Standard deviation	19.51%	26.17%	6.67%

Table 14-2. Summary Return Results for All Stocks and 50 Stocks with Highest Return on Equity from All Stocks Universe, December 31, 1951–December 31, 1996

	All Stocks	Universe = All Stocks top 50 ROE
Arithmetic average	14.97%	16.10%
Standard deviation of return	19.51%	26.17%
Sharpe risk-adjusted ratio	49.00	41.00
3-yr compounded	13.22%	10.69%
5-yr compounded	14.00%	12.71%
10-yr compounded	12.92%	10.04%
15-yr compounded	14.44%	10.64%
20-yr compounded	14.97%	12.27%
25-yr compounded	12.74%	8.98%
30-yr compounded	12.43%	10.56%
35-yr compounded	11.64%	9.97%
40-yr compounded	12.62%	11.96%
Compound annual return	13.23%	13.06%
$10,000 becomes:	$2,677,556.77	$2,507,363.29
Maximum return	55.90%	96.30%
Minimum return	−27.90%	−44.00%
Maximum expected return*	53.98%	68.44%
Minimum expected return**	−24.04%	−36.24%

*Maximum expected return is average return plus 2 times the standard deviation.

**Minimum expected return is average return minus 2 times the standard deviation.

Table 14-3. Base Rates for All Stocks and 50 Stocks with Highest Return on Equity from All Stocks Universe, 1951–1996

Item	50 highest ROE stocks beat All Stocks	Percent
Single-year return	22 out of 45	49.00%
Rolling 5-year compound return	19 out of 41	46.00%
Rolling 10-year compound return	15 out of 36	42.00%

Table 14-4. Annual Performance of Large Stocks Versus 50 Stocks with Highest Return on Equity from Large Stocks Universe

Year ending	Large Stocks	Universe = Large Stocks top 50 ROE	Top 50 ROE relative performance
31-Dec-52	9.30%	10.10%	0.80%
31-Dec-53	2.30%	−0.07%	−2.37%
31-Dec-54	44.90%	56.20%	11.30%
31-Dec-55	21.20%	30.40%	9.20%
31-Dec-56	9.60%	11.50%	1.90%
31-Dec-57	−6.90%	−13.30%	−6.40%
31-Dec-58	42.10%	46.50%	4.40%
31-Dec-59	9.90%	16.10%	6.20%
31-Dec-60	4.80%	9.40%	4.60%
31-Dec-61	27.50%	26.00%	−1.50%
31-Dec-62	−8.90%	−17.00%	−8.10%
31-Dec-63	19.50%	19.00%	−0.50%
31-Dec-64	15.30%	11.70%	−3.60%
31-Dec-65	16.20%	19.90%	3.70%
31-Dec-66	−4.90%	2.80%	7.70%
31-Dec-67	21.30%	27.60%	6.30%
31-Dec-68	16.80%	11.70%	−5.10%
31-Dec-69	−9.90%	−1.00%	8.90%
31-Dec-70	−0.20%	−1.80%	−1.60%
31-Dec-71	17.30%	25.70%	8.40%
31-Dec-72	14.90%	15.20%	0.30%
31-Dec-73	−18.90%	−31.40%	−12.50%
31-Dec-74	−26.70%	−32.40%	−5.70%
31-Dec-75	43.10%	39.80%	−3.30%
31-Dec-76	28.00%	31.50%	3.50%
31-Dec-77	−2.50%	−4.00%	−1.50%
31-Dec-78	8.10%	4.20%	−3.90%
31-Dec-79	27.30%	38.20%	10.90%
31-Dec-80	30.80%	42.60%	11.80%
31-Dec-81	0.60%	−9.60%	−10.20%
31-Dec-82	19.90%	14.70%	−5.20%
31-Dec-83	23.80%	13.00%	−10.80%
31-Dec-84	−0.40%	−6.90%	−6.50%
31-Dec-85	19.50%	39.20%	19.70%
31-Dec-86	32.20%	17.20%	−15.00%
31-Dec-87	3.30%	−5.40%	−8.70%
31-Dec-88	19.00%	15.10%	−3.90%
31-Dec-89	26.00%	26.00%	0.00%
31-Dec-90	−8.70%	−11.20%	−2.50%
31-Dec-91	33.00%	39.00%	6.00%
31-Dec-92	8.70%	2.00%	−6.70%
31-Dec-93	16.30%	10.70%	−5.60%
31-Dec-94	−1.90%	0.00%	1.90%
31-Dec-95	28.50%	23.60%	−4.90%
31-Dec-96	18.70%	16.20%	−2.50%
Arithmetic average	13.11%	12.86%	−0.25%
Standard deviation	16.01%	19.45%	3.44%

Table 14-5. Summary Return Results for Large Stocks and 50 Stocks with Highest Return on Equity from Large Stocks Universe, December 31, 1951–December 31, 1996

	Large Stocks	Universe = Large Stocks Top 50 ROE
Arithmetic average	13.11%	12.86%
Standard deviation of return	16.01%	19.45%
Sharpe risk-adjusted ratio	48.00	39.00
3-yr compounded	14.38%	12.83%
5-yr compounded	13.60%	10.15%
10-yr compounded	13.53%	10.63%
15-yr compounded	15.16%	11.91%
20-yr compounded	14.37%	11.99%
25-yr compounded	12.34%	9.41%
30-yr compounded	11.67%	9.79%
35-yr compounded	10.96%	9.29%
40-yr compounded	11.36%	10.02%
Compound annual return	11.92%	11.10%
$10,000 becomes:	$1,590,667.04	$1,138,299.52
Maximum return	44.90%	56.20%
Minimum return	−26.70%	−32.40%
Maximum expected return*	45.12%	51.75%
Minimum expected return**	−18.91%	−26.03%

*Maximum expected return is average return plus 2 times the standard deviation.

**Minimum expected return is average return minus 2 times the standard deviation.

Table 14-6. Base Rates for Large Stocks and 50 Stocks with Highest Return on Equity from Large Stocks Universe, 1951–1996

Item	50 highest ROE stocks beat Large Stocks	Percent
Single-year return	20 out of 45	44.00%
Rolling 5-year compound return	16 out of 41	39.00%
Rolling 10-year compound return	13 out of 36	36.00%

Table 14-7. Compound Annual Rates of Return by Decade

Portfolio	1950s*	1960s	1970s	1980s	1990s**
Large Stocks	15.33%	8.99%	6.99%	16.89%	12.61%
50 highest ROE from Large Stocks	17.71%	10.22%	5.30%	13.29%	10.42%
All Stocks	19.22%	11.09%	8.53%	15.85%	12.78%
50 highest ROE from All Stocks	24.36%	14.96%	6.98%	10.97%	10.06%

*Returns for 1952–1959.

**Returns for 1990–1996.

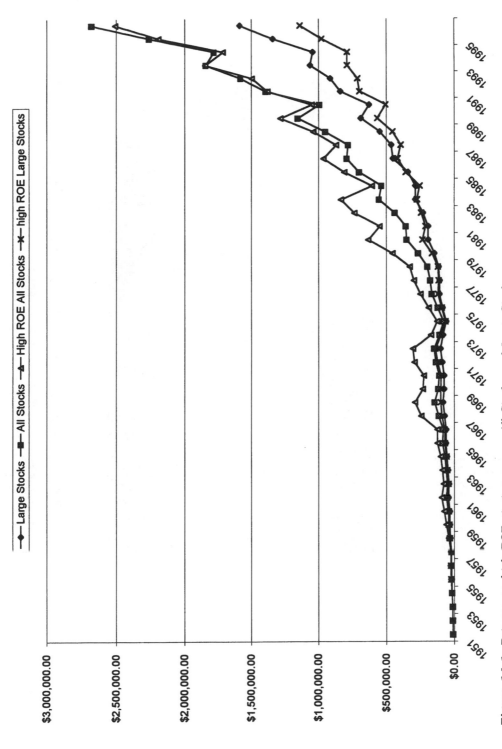

Figure 14-1. Returns on high ROE strategy versus All Stocks and Large Stocks, 1951–1996. Year-end 1951 = $10,000.

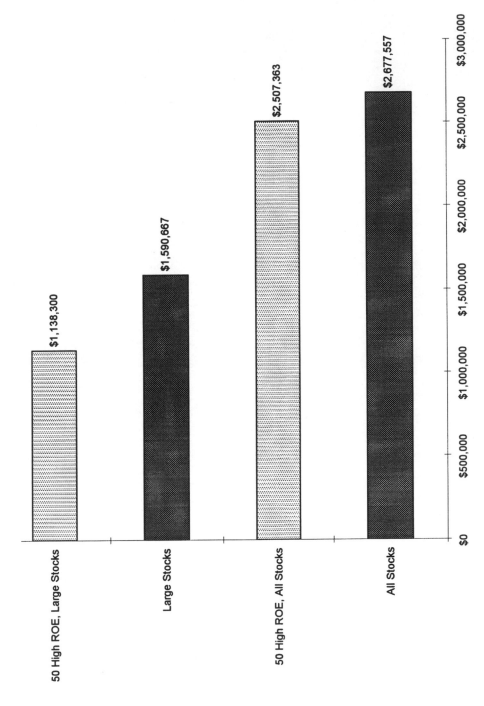

Figure 14-2. December 31, 1996, value of $10,000 invested on December 31, 1951, and annually rebalanced.

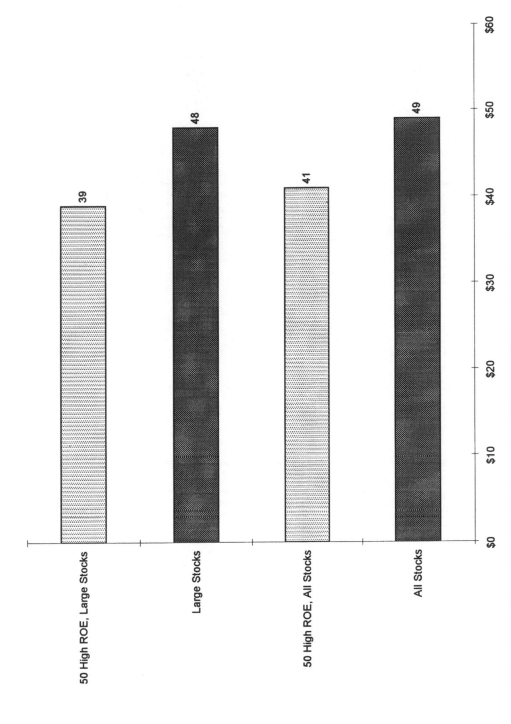

Figure 14-3. Sharpe risk-adjusted return ratios, 1951–1996. (Higher is better.)

would have grown to $5,761,996, a compound return of 15.17 percent. That's considerably better than All Stocks' 13.23 percent compound return. But the standard deviation of 26.27 percent pushed the Sharpe ratio to 48, one point below the All Stocks ratio of 49. Tables 14-8 and 14-9, as well as Figures 14-4 and 14-5, summarize the results.

Table 14-8. Summary Results for ROE Decile Analysis of All Stocks Universe, 1951–1996

Decile	$10,000 grows to	Average return	Compound return	Standard deviation
1 (highest ROE)	$2,805,327	16.05%	13.34%	24.72%
2	$5,761,996	17.91%	15.17%	26.27%
3	$3,566,269	16.27%	13.95%	22.55%
4	$2,004,480	14.22%	12.50%	19.21%
5	$2,948,707	15.44%	13.47%	20.61%
6	$2,692,199	15.22%	13.24%	20.73%
7	$2,653,724	14.93%	13.20%	19.27%
8	$4,144,374	16.16%	14.33%	20.15%
9	$2,059,215	14.49%	12.57%	20.50%
10 (lowest ROE)	$1,834,419	15.09%	12.28%	25.31%
All Stocks	$2,677,557	14.97%	13.23%	19.51%

Table 14-9. Summary Results for ROE Decile Analysis of Large Stocks Universe, 1951–1996

Decile	$10,000 grows to	Average return	Compound return	Standard deviation
1 (highest ROE)	$1,246,113	13.33%	11.32%	20.98%
2	$4,471,608	16.23%	14.52%	19.39%
3	$3,366,313	15.34%	13.80%	18.29%
4	$1,145,818	12.43%	11.11%	16.80%
5	$1,118,998	12.43%	11.05%	17.25%
6	$1,855,489	13.72%	12.31%	17.44%
7	$1,051,858	12.21%	10.90%	16.73%
8	$1,719,019	13.36%	12.12%	16.65%
9	$1,041,370	12.23%	10.88%	17.00%
10 (lowest ROE)	$1,830,812	13.69%	12.27%	17.57%
Large Stocks	$1,590,667	13.11%	11.92%	16.01%

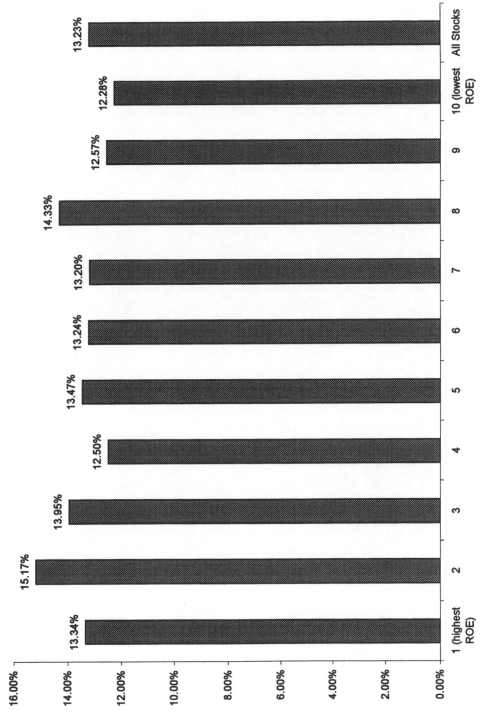

Figure 14-4. Compound return by ROE decile, All Stocks universe, 1951–1996.

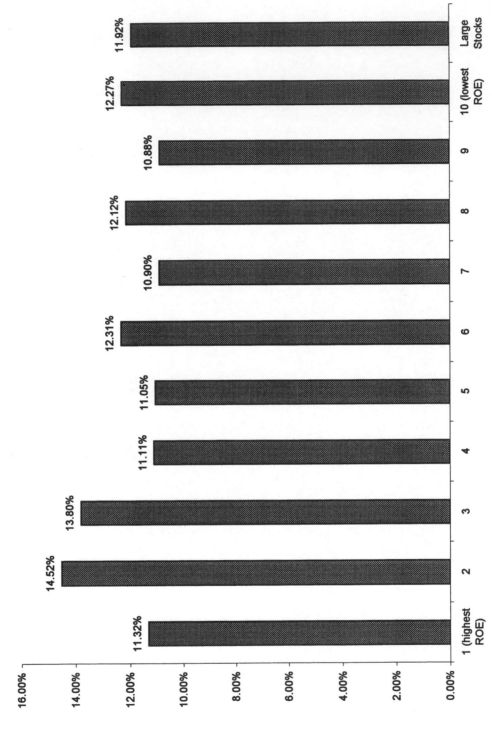

Figure 14-5. Compound return by ROE decile, Large Stocks universe, 1951–1996.

Implications

Return on equity is an excellent example of the importance of looking at the long term when judging a strategy's effectiveness. Imagine a young investor just out of college at the end of 1964. He lands a job on Wall Street and studies how stocks with high returns on equity perform. The evidence from the previous decade is very encouraging: Between December 31, 1951 and December 31, 1959, the 50 highest ROE stocks from both the All Stocks and Large Stocks universes outperformed their respective benchmarks, with the 50 from All Stocks returning 24.36 percent a year and the 50 from Large Stocks returning 17.71 percent a year.

Both the evidence and the story make sense. Buy companies that do a good job managing shareholders' money and let them manage yours. It's a simple and sensible thing to do. But our young investor is skeptical. He needs to see the evidence with his own eyes before he'll believe it.

And so, he watches. In 1965 the 50 highest ROE stocks from All Stocks return 26 percent, better than the 23 percent from All Stocks. Though the next year is a bear market for All Stocks, with the group losing 5 percent, the 50 stocks with the highest ROE eke out a gain of .02 percent. Our young investor is encouraged. Then comes 1967. The 50 stocks with the highest ROE from All Stocks soar, gaining 96 percent, 55 percent more than the All Stocks universe.

Our young investor is hooked. He has both the results of the last decade and the personal experience of the last three years to prove he's *really* on to something. He'll go on believing that high ROE stocks are great investments for many years, even though they manage to do a bit *worse* than the market year in and year out. With access to studies that looked at the 1930s and 1940s, our investor probably would have seen what we see: The 50 stocks with the highest ROE are a good investment only 50 percent of the time.

The decile analysis tells a somewhat different tale. It's really only the 10 percent of stocks with the highest ROE (decile 1) that are mediocre investments. Deciles 2 and 3 from both All Stocks and Large Stocks do considerably better than their benchmarks on an absolute basis, but only decile 2 from Large Stocks beats its benchmark on a risk-adjusted basis. In both instances, the decile performance lacks the consistency we found when looking at price-to-sales and other ratios.

15

Relative Price Strength: Winners Continue to Win

It may be that the race is not always to the swift, nor the battle to the strong—but that's the way to bet. —Damon Runyon

"Don't fight the tape."

"Make the trend your friend."

"Cut your losses and let your winners run."

All these Wall Street maxims mean the same thing—bet on price momentum. Of all the beliefs on Wall Street, price momentum makes efficient market theorists howl the loudest. The defining principle of their theory is that you cannot use past prices to predict future prices. A stock may triple in a year, but according to efficient market theory, that will not affect next year. Efficient market theorists also hate price momentum, because it is independent of all accounting variables. If buying winning stocks works, then stock prices have "memories" and carry useful information about the future direction of a stock.

Another school of thought says you should buy stocks that have been most battered by the market. This is the argument of Wall Street's bottom fishers, who use absolute price change as their guide, buying issues after they've done poorly. Let's see who is right.

The Results

We'll look at buying the 50 stocks with the *best* and the *worst* one-year price changes from both the All Stocks and Large Stocks universes. This will contrast the results of buying last year's biggest winners with last year's biggest losers. We'll also separate the stocks by decile for both the All Stocks and Large Stocks universes. Let's look at the winners first. (In this and future chapters, the terms *relative strength* and *price performers* will be used interchangeably. Stocks with the best relative strength are the biggest winners in terms of their previous year's price appreciation.) We'll start on December 31, 1951 and buy the 50 stocks with the largest price appreciation from the previous year. We arrive at this number by dividing this year's closing price by that from 12 months earlier. Thus, if XYZ closed this year at 10 and last year at 2, it would have a gain of 400 percent and a price index of 5 (10 ÷ 2).

A $10,000 investment on December 31, 1951 in the 50 stocks from All Stocks with the best one-year price appreciation was worth $4,113,706 at the end of 1996, a compound return of 14.31 percent a year. This is the first *big* performance advantage over All Stocks we've seen from a growth stock variable. (A $10,000 investment in All Stocks was worth $2,677,557 at the end of 1996.) The performance of the 50-stock portfolio comes with a huge caveat—risk was extraordinarily high. The standard deviation of return for the 50 best one-year price performers was 29.8 percent, the highest we've seen for an individual factor. The enormous risk pushed the Sharpe ratio to 43, below All Stocks' 49. We'll see in the discussion of deciles that performance is actually increased with reduced risk by focusing on the top 10 percent of stocks by price appreciation.

I cannot overstate how difficult it is to stick with volatile strategies such as this one. Investors are usually drawn to these strategies by outstanding relative performance, as when the 50 stocks with the best relative strength from All Stocks gained 101 percent in 1991. And while people *think* they can cope with volatility when a strategy is doing well, they have the wind knocked out of them when their volatile strategy is down 30 percent in a bull market. The emotional toll this takes is huge, and you must understand it before embracing a highly volatile strategy. As I make clear later in the book, you should have *some* exposure to volatile stocks, but they should never comprise the bulk of your portfolio. Few investors have the stomach for the roller-coaster ride.

The base rates for the 50 stocks with the best one-year relative strength are all positive, with the strategy beating the market 75 percent of the time over all rolling 10-year periods. Tables 15-1, 15-2, and 15-3 summarize the returns for the All Stocks group.

Large Stocks Do Better

The 50 stocks from the Large Stocks universe actually do better than those from All Stocks, more than doubling the return of an investment in the Large Stocks universe. Here $10,000 invested on December 31, 1951 in the 50 stocks from the Large Stocks universe with the best one-year price performance in the previous year grew to $4,429,185, almost three times the $1,590,667 you'd earn investing in the Large Stocks universe. Risk is more manageable here, with the 50 best price performers showing a standard deviation of return of 21.99 percent, 5.98 percent higher than the Large Stocks' 16.01 percent. Because the absolute return was so much higher, the Sharpe ratio for the 50 best one-year price performers from Large Stocks beat the universe, with a score of 51.

All the base rates are positive, with the 50 best relative strength stocks from Large Stocks beating the universe 89 percent of the time over all rolling 10-year periods. Tables 15-4, 15-5, and 15-6 summarize the results for Large Stocks.

Why Price Performance Works
While Other Measures Do Not

Price momentum conveys unique different information about the prospects of a stock and is a much better indicator than factors such as earnings growth rates. Many look at the disappointing results of buying stocks with the highest earnings gains and wonder why they differ from the best one-year price performers. First, price momentum is the market putting its money where its mouth is. Second, the common belief that stocks with strong relative strength also have the highest PE ratios or earnings growth rates is wrong. When you look at the top one-year performers over time, you find they usually have PE ratios 30 to 50 percent higher than the market, but *rarely* the highest in the market. The same is true for five-year earnings per share growth rates and one-year earnings per share growth rates. As a group, they are usually higher than the market, but not by extraordinary amounts.

Table 15-1. Annual Performance of All Stocks Versus 50 Stocks with Best One-Year Relative Strength (RS) from All Stocks Universe

Year ending	All Stocks	Universe = All Stocks top 50 1-year RS	Top 50 1-year RS relative performance
31-Dec-52	7.90%	3.10%	−4.80%
31-Dec-53	2.90%	3.80%	0.90%
31-Dec-54	47.00%	62.30%	15.30%
31-Dec-55	20.70%	32.00%	11.30%
31-Dec-56	17.00%	29.20%	12.20%
31-Dec-57	−7.10%	−16.50%	−9.40%
31-Dec-58	55.00%	68.10%	13.10%
31-Dec-59	23.00%	39.90%	16.90%
31-Dec-60	6.10%	9.40%	3.30%
31-Dec-61	31.20%	35.20%	4.00%
31-Dec-62	−12.00%	−22.60%	−10.60%
31-Dec-63	18.00%	33.60%	15.60%
31-Dec-64	16.30%	5.30%	−11.00%
31-Dec-65	22.60%	44.40%	21.80%
31-Dec-66	−5.20%	−3.90%	1.30%
31-Dec-67	41.10%	64.30%	23.20%
31-Dec-68	27.40%	18.40%	−9.00%
31-Dec-69	−18.50%	−21.90%	−3.40%
31-Dec-70	−5.80%	−26.30%	−20.50%
31-Dec-71	21.30%	39.90%	18.60%
31-Dec-72	11.00%	20.10%	9.10%
31-Dec-73	−27.20%	−32.10%	−4.90%
31-Dec-74	−27.90%	−27.10%	0.80%
31-Dec-75	55.90%	36.00%	−19.90%
31-Dec-76	35.60%	25.30%	−10.30%
31-Dec-77	6.90%	22.50%	15.60%
31-Dec-78	12.20%	25.80%	13.60%
31-Dec-79	34.30%	50.90%	16.60%
31-Dec-80	31.50%	66.00%	34.50%
31-Dec-81	1.70%	−13.50%	−15.20%
31-Dec-82	22.50%	27.10%	4.60%
31-Dec-83	28.10%	22.80%	−5.30%
31-Dec-84	−3.40%	−19.50%	−16.10%
31-Dec-85	30.80%	40.00%	9.20%
31-Dec-86	13.10%	14.30%	1.20%
31-Dec-87	−1.30%	−3.90%	−2.60%
31-Dec-88	21.20%	8.10%	−13.10%
31-Dec-89	21.40%	39.00%	17.60%
31-Dec-90	−13.80%	−11.90%	1.90%
31-Dec-91	39.80%	101.30%	61.50%
31-Dec-92	13.80%	−7.90%	−21.70%
31-Dec-93	16.60%	26.20%	9.60%
31-Dec-94	−3.40%	−19.70%	−16.30%
31-Dec-95	27.00%	34.00%	7.00%
31-Dec-96	18.30%	−7.26%	−25.56%
Arithmetic average	14.97%	18.09%	3.13%
Standard deviation	19.51%	29.80%	10.29%

Table 15-2. Summary Return Results for All Stocks and 50 Stocks with Best One-Year Relative Strength (RS) from All Stocks Universe, December 31, 1951–December 31, 1996

	All Stocks	Universe = All Stocks top 50 1-year RS
Arithmetic average	14.97%	18.09%
Standard deviation of return	19.51%	29.80%
Sharpe risk-adjusted ratio	49.00	43.00
3-yr compounded	13.22%	−0.07%
5-yr compounded	14.00%	3.01%
10-yr compounded	12.92%	11.50%
15-yr compounded	14.44%	12.65%
20-yr compounded	14.97%	16.14%
25-yr compounded	12.74%	12.78%
30-yr compounded	12.43%	12.20%
35-yr compounded	11.64%	11.68%
40-yr compounded	12.62%	13.13%
Compound annual return	13.23%	14.31%
$10,000 becomes:	$2,677,556.77	$4,113,706.26
Maximum return	55.90%	101.30%
Minimum return	−27.90%	−32.10%
Maximum expected return*	53.98%	77.70%
Minimum expected return**	−24.04%	−41.51%

*Maximum expected return is average return plus 2 times the standard deviation.
**Minimum expected return is average return minus 2 times the standard deviation.

Table 15-3. Base Rates for All Stocks and 50 Stocks with Best One-Year Relative Strength (RS) from All Stocks Universe, 1951–1996

Item	50 best 1-year RS beat All Stocks	Percent
Single-year return	27 out of 45	60.00%
Rolling 5-year compound return	27 out of 41	66.00%
Rolling 10-year compound return	27 out of 36	75.00%

Table 15-4. Annual Performance of Large Stocks Versus 50 Stocks with Best One-Year Relative Strength (RS) from Large Stocks Universe (Best Price Appreciation)

Year ending	Large Stocks	Universe = Large Stocks top 50 1-year RS	Top 50 1-year RS relative performance
31-Dec-52	9.30%	6.50%	−2.80%
31-Dec-53	2.30%	6.00%	3.70%
31-Dec-54	44.90%	44.40%	−0.50%
31-Dec-55	21.20%	31.60%	10.40%
31-Dec-56	9.60%	13.10%	3.50%
31-Dec-57	−6.90%	−11.50%	−4.60%
31-Dec-58	42.10%	42.40%	0.30%
31-Dec-59	9.90%	15.90%	6.00%
31-Dec-60	4.80%	1.00%	−3.80%
31-Dec-61	27.50%	32.20%	4.70%
31-Dec-62	−8.90%	−12.10%	−3.20%
31-Dec-63	19.50%	24.00%	4.50%
31-Dec-64	15.30%	20.90%	5.60%
31-Dec-65	16.20%	31.00%	14.80%
31-Dec-66	−4.90%	3.20%	8.10%
31-Dec-67	21.30%	40.60%	19.30%
31-Dec-68	16.80%	11.50%	−5.30%
31-Dec-69	−9.90%	−6.80%	3.10%
31-Dec-70	−0.20%	−13.90%	−13.70%
31-Dec-71	17.30%	21.50%	4.20%
31-Dec-72	14.90%	27.50%	12.60%
31-Dec-73	−18.90%	−16.40%	2.50%
31-Dec-74	−26.70%	−30.70%	−4.00%
31-Dec-75	43.10%	30.70%	−12.40%
31-Dec-76	28.00%	23.10%	−4.90%
31-Dec-77	−2.50%	0.03%	2.53%
31-Dec-78	8.10%	21.80%	13.70%
31-Dec-79	27.30%	28.60%	1.30%
31-Dec-80	30.80%	68.20%	37.40%
31-Dec-81	0.60%	−18.00%	−18.60%
31-Dec-82	19.90%	39.80%	19.90%
31-Dec-83	23.80%	18.90%	−4.90%
31-Dec-84	−0.40%	−10.10%	−9.70%
31-Dec-85	19.50%	45.20%	25.70%
31-Dec-86	32.20%	27.00%	−5.20%
31-Dec-87	3.30%	10.50%	7.20%
31-Dec-88	19.00%	7.00%	−12.00%
31-Dec-89	26.00%	36.50%	10.50%
31-Dec-90	−8.70%	−10.90%	−2.20%
31-Dec-91	33.00%	63.90%	30.90%
31-Dec-92	8.70%	0.70%	−8.00%
31-Dec-93	16.30%	44.10%	27.80%
31-Dec-94	−1.90%	−4.20%	−2.30%
31-Dec-95	28.50%	25.00%	−3.50%
31-Dec-96	18.70%	18.60%	−0.10%
Arithmetic average	13.11%	16.63%	3.52%
Standard deviation	16.01%	21.99%	5.99%

Table 15-5. Summary Return Results for Large Stocks and 50 Stocks with Best One-Year Relative Strength (RS) from Large Stocks Universe, December 31, 1951–December 31, 1996

	Large Stocks	Universe = Large Stocks top 50 1-year RS
Arithmetic average	13.11%	16.63%
Standard deviation of return	16.01%	21.99%
Sharpe risk-adjusted ratio	48.00	51.00
3-yr compounded	14.38%	12.41%
5-yr compounded	13.60%	15.56%
10-yr compounded	13.53%	17.12%
15-yr compounded	15.16%	18.88%
20-yr compounded	14.37%	18.32%
25-yr compounded	12.34%	15.20%
30-yr compounded	11.67%	14.12%
35-yr compounded	10.96%	13.85%
40-yr compounded	11.36%	13.90%
Compound annual return	11.92%	14.50%
$10,000 becomes:	$1,590,667.04	$4,429,185.39
Maximum return	44.90%	68.20%
Minimum return	−26.70%	−30.70%
Maximum expected return*	45.12%	60.61%
Minimum expected return**	−18.91%	−27.35%

*Maximum expected return is average return plus 2 times the standard deviation.
**Minimum expected return is average return minus 2 times the standard deviation.

Table 15-6. Base Rates for Large Stocks and 50 Stocks with Best One-Year Relative Strength (RS) from Large Stocks Universe, 1951–1996

Item	50 best 1-year RS best Large Stocks	Percent
Single-year return	25 out of 45	56.00%
Rolling 5-year compound return	34 out of 41	83.00%
Rolling 10-year compound return	32 out of 36	89.00%

Buying the Worst Performing Stocks

If you're looking for the perfect way to underperform the market, look no further. A $10,000 investment on December 31, 1951 in the 50 stocks from All Stocks with the worst one-year price performance was worth just $43,040 at the end of 1996, a compound return of 3.3 percent a year. Some *mattresses* pay better returns! The standard deviation of return for the 50 losers was 26.41 percent, considerably higher than All Stocks' 19.51 percent. With such abysmal returns, *any* risk will wreak havoc with the Sharpe ratio, and here it's a pathetic 5. Base rates are atrocious, with the 50 losers beating All Stocks in only 12 of the 45 years reviewed. The 5-year rolling returns are even worse. The 50 losers beat All Stocks only once in 42 of the rolling 5-year periods. But the booby prize goes to the 10-year returns, where the losers *never* beat the All Stocks universe. Tables 15-7, 15-8, and 15-9 detail the grim news.

Large Stocks Also Hit

Large Stocks also suffer, but the results aren't fatal. Here $10,000 invested in the 50 stocks with the worst one-year price performance from Large Stocks on December 31, 1951 grew to $605,645 by the end of 1996, a compound return of 9.55 percent a year. That's much worse than the $1,590,667 you'd earn from $10,000 invested in the Large Stocks universe, but not as damaging to your wealth as the biggest losers from All Stocks. The risk was 4 percent higher than for Large Stocks, with the standard deviation for the 50 losers at 20.41 percent. The Sharpe ratio was a fairly low 30.

The base rates are better here over the short term, but equally grim over the long term. The 50 biggest losers beat the Large Stocks universe 47 percent of the time over any single year, 34 percent over 5-year periods, and never over 10-year periods. Tables 15-10, 15-11, and 15-12 summarize the results for the 50 Large Stocks losers.

Table 15-13 shows compound annual returns by decade for the All Stocks and Large Stocks universes. The results are depicted graphically in Figures 15-1 through 15-4.

Deciles

The decile results confirm the 50-stock portfolio findings and actually show that you are better off focusing on the upper 10 percent (decile 1) than on just the 50 best performing stocks: $10,000 invested in the 10 percent of stocks with the best price appreciation over the previous year from the All Stocks universe grew to $11,063,109 by the end of 1996, a

Table 15-7. Annual Performance of All Stocks Versus 50 Stocks with Worst One-Year Relative Strength (RS) from All Stocks Universe (Worst Price Performance)

Year ending	All Stocks	Universe = All Stocks 50 Worst 1-year RS	50 worst 1-year RS relative performance
31-Dec-52	7.90%	8.10%	0.20%
31-Dec-53	2.90%	−11.00%	−13.90%
31-Dec-54	47.00%	50.80%	3.80%
31-Dec-55	20.70%	8.20%	−12.50%
31-Dec-56	17.00%	−1.90%	−18.90%
31-Dec-57	−7.10%	−9.00%	−1.90%
31-Dec-58	55.00%	63.60%	8.60%
31-Dec-59	23.00%	5.74%	−17.26%
31-Dec-60	6.10%	3.40%	−2.70%
31-Dec-61	31.20%	16.60%	−14.60%
31-Dec-62	−12.00%	−19.40%	−7.40%
31-Dec-63	18.00%	7.00%	−11.00%
31-Dec-64	16.30%	8.50%	−7.80%
31-Dec-65	22.60%	39.81%	17.21%
31-Dec-66	−5.20%	−14.30%	−9.10%
31-Dec-67	41.10%	46.80%	5.70%
31-Dec-68	27.40%	30.00%	2.60%
31-Dec-69	−18.50%	−40.90%	−22.40%
31-Dec-70	−5.80%	−18.40%	−12.60%
31-Dec-71	21.30%	0.01%	−21.29%
31-Dec-72	11.00%	−3.40%	−14.40%
31-Dec-73	−27.20%	−48.90%	−21.70%
31-Dec-74	−27.90%	−36.60%	−8.70%
31-Dec-75	55.90%	56.60%	0.70%
31-Dec-76	35.60%	27.00%	−8.60%
31-Dec-77	6.90%	−5.80%	−12.70%
31-Dec-78	12.20%	6.20%	−6.00%
31-Dec-79	34.30%	37.50%	3.20%
31-Dec-80	31.50%	8.50%	−23.00%
31-Dec-81	1.70%	−14.30%	−16.00%
31-Dec-82	22.50%	2.60%	−19.90%
31-Dec-83	28.10%	9.20%	−18.90%
31-Dec-84	−3.40%	−27.10%	−23.70%
31-Dec-85	30.80%	15.30%	−15.50%
31-Dec-86	13.10%	−21.20%	−34.30%
31-Dec-87	−1.30%	−4.20%	−2.90%
31-Dec-88	21.20%	33.90%	12.70%
31-Dec-89	21.40%	13.60%	−7.80%
31-Dec-90	−13.80%	−41.20%	−27.40%
31-Dec-91	39.80%	60.80%	21.00%
31-Dec-92	13.80%	12.70%	−1.10%
31-Dec-93	16.60%	2.00%	−14.60%
31-Dec-94	−3.40%	4.00%	7.40%
31-Dec-95	27.00%	22.30%	−4.70%
31-Dec-96	18.30%	19.90%	1.60%
Arithmetic average	14.97%	6.73%	−8.23%
Standard deviation	19.51%	26.41%	6.91%

Table 15-8. Summary Return Results for All Stocks and 50 Stocks with Worst One-Year Relative Strength (RS) from All Stocks Universe, December 31, 1951–December 31, 1996

	All Stocks	Universe = All Stocks 50 worst 1-year RS
Arithmetic average	14.97%	6.73%
Standard deviation of return	19.51%	26.41%
Sharpe risk-adjusted ratio	49.00	5.00
3-yr compounded	13.22%	15.10%
5-yr compounded	14.00%	11.88%
10-yr compounded	12.92%	9.22%
15-yr compounded	14.44%	3.97%
20-yr compounded	14.97%	4.24%
25-yr compounded	12.74%	1.43%
30-yr compounded	12.43%	0.91%
35-yr compounded	11.64%	1.11%
40-yr compounded	12.62%	2.60%
Compound annual return	13.23%	3.30%
$10,000 becomes:	$2,677,556.77	$43,039.76
Maximum return	55.90%	63.60%
Minimum return	−27.90%	−48.90%
Maximum expected return*	53.98%	59.56%
Minimum expected return**	−24.04%	−46.09%

*Maximum expected return is average return plus 2 times the standard deviation.

**Minimum expected return is average return minus 2 times the standard deviation.

Table 15-9. Base Rates for All Stocks and 50 Stocks with Worst One-Year Relative Strength (RS) from All Stocks Universe, 1951–1996

Item	50 worst 1-year RS beat All Stocks	Percent
Single-year return	12 out of 45	27.00%
Rolling 5-year compound return	2 out of 41	5.00%
Rolling 10-year compound return	0 out of 36	0.00%

Table 15-10. Annual Performance of Large Stocks Versus 50 Stocks with the Worst One-Year Relative Strength (RS) from Large Stocks Universe (Worst Price Performance)

Year ending	Large Stocks	Universe = Large Stocks 50 worst 1-year RS	50 worst 1-year RS relative performance
31-Dec-52	9.30%	12.00%	2.70%
31-Dec-53	2.30%	−3.90%	−6.20%
31-Dec-54	44.90%	53.00%	8.10%
31-Dec-55	21.20%	15.10%	−6.10%
31-Dec-56	9.60%	9.00%	−0.60%
31-Dec-57	−6.90%	−1.70%	5.20%
31-Dec-58	42.10%	47.00%	4.90%
31-Dec-59	9.90%	3.50%	−6.40%
31-Dec-60	4.80%	7.90%	3.10%
31-Dec-61	27.50%	18.80%	−8.70%
31-Dec-62	−8.90%	−13.80%	−4.90%
31-Dec-63	19.50%	20.20%	0.70%
31-Dec-64	15.30%	17.30%	2.00%
31-Dec-65	16.20%	19.20%	3.00%
31-Dec-66	−4.90%	−8.80%	−3.90%
31-Dec-67	21.30%	26.30%	5.00%
31-Dec-68	16.80%	19.50%	2.70%
31-Dec-69	−9.90%	−26.00%	−16.10%
31-Dec-70	−0.20%	−5.00%	−4.80%
31-Dec-71	17.30%	19.20%	1.90%
31-Dec-72	14.90%	8.90%	−6.00%
31-Dec-73	−18.90%	−18.60%	0.30%
31-Dec-74	−26.70%	−30.90%	−4.20%
31-Dec-75	43.10%	64.90%	21.80%
31-Dec-76	28.00%	25.40%	−2.60%
31-Dec-77	−2.50%	−2.30%	0.20%
31-Dec-78	8.10%	5.10%	−3.00%
31-Dec-79	27.30%	25.50%	−1.80%
31-Dec-80	30.80%	12.70%	−18.10%
31-Dec-81	0.60%	10.20%	9.60%
31-Dec-82	19.90%	2.90%	−17.00%
31-Dec-83	23.80%	16.70%	−7.10%
31-Dec-84	−0.40%	−15.60%	−15.20%
31-Dec-85	19.50%	25.70%	6.20%
31 Dec 86	32.20%	4.90%	−27.30%
31-Dec-87	3.30%	−1.70%	−5.00%
31-Dec-88	19.00%	38.40%	19.40%
31-Dec-89	26.00%	27.90%	1.90%
31-Dec-90	−8.70%	−25.50%	−16.80%
31-Dec-91	33.00%	55.00%	22.00%
31-Dec-92	8.70%	7.50%	−1.20%
31-Dec-93	16.30%	23.60%	7.30%
31-Dec-94	−1.90%	1.40%	3.30%
31-Dec-95	28.50%	11.40%	−17.10%
31-Dec-96	18.70%	12.00%	−6.70%
Arithmetic average	13.11%	11.43%	−1.68%
Standard deviation	16.01%	20.41%	4.40%

Table 15-11. Summary Return Results for Large Stocks and 50 Stocks with Worst One-Year Relative Strength (RS) from Large Stocks Universe, December 31, 1951–December 31, 1966

	Large Stocks	Universe = Large Stocks 50 worst 1-year RS
Arithmetic average	13.11%	11.43%
Standard deviation of return	16.01%	20.41%
Sharpe risk-adjusted ratio	48.00	30.00
3-yr compounded	14.38%	8.16%
5-yr compounded	13.60%	10.95%
10-yr compounded	13.53%	12.94%
15-yr compounded	15.16%	10.57%
20-yr compounded	14.37%	10.39%
25-yr compounded	12.34%	9.26%
30-yr compounded	11.67%	8.50%
35-yr compounded	10.96%	8.10%
40-yr compounded	11.36%	8.81%
Compound annual return	11.92%	9.55%
$10,000 becomes:	$1,590,667.04	$605,645.00
Maximum return	44.90%	64.90%
Minimum return	−26.70%	−30.90%
Maximum expected return*	45.12%	52.25%
Minimum expected return**	−18.91%	−29.39%

*Maximum expected return is average return plus 2 times the standard deviation.

**Minimum expected return is average return minus 2 times the standard deviation.

Table 15-12. Base Rates for Large Stocks and 50 Stocks with Worst One-Year Relative Strength (RS) from Large Stocks Universe, 1951–1996

Item	50 worst 1-year RS beat Large Stocks	Percent
Single-year return	21 out of 45	47.00%
Rolling 5-year compound return	14 out of 41	34.00%
Rolling 10-year compound return	0 out of 36	0.00%

Table 15-13. Compound Annual Rates of Return by Decade

Portfolio	1950s*	1960s	1970s	1980s	1990s**
Large Stocks	15.33%	8.99%	6.99%	16.89%	12.61%
50 best one-year RS from Large Stocks	17.13%	13.27%	6.90%	19.89%	17.05%
50 worst one-year RS from Large Stocks	15.14%	6.58%	6.34%	11.19%	9.94%
All Stocks	19.22%	11.09%	8.53%	15.85%	12.78%
50 best one-year RS from All Stocks	24.62%	13.00%	9.28%	15.35%	10.85%
50 worst one-year RS from All Stocks	11.70%	4.31%	−3.52%	0.06%	7.49%

*Returns for 1952–1959.

**Returns for 1990–1996.

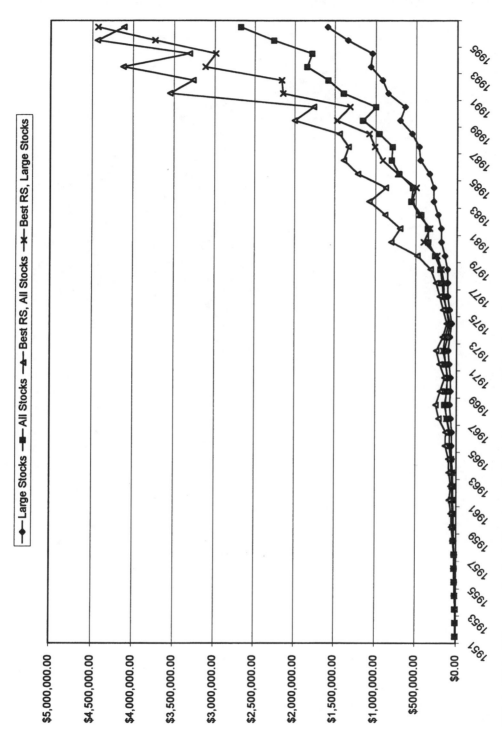

Figure 15-1. Returns on best relative strength strategies versus All Stocks and Large Stocks, 1951–1996. Year-end 1951 = $10,000.

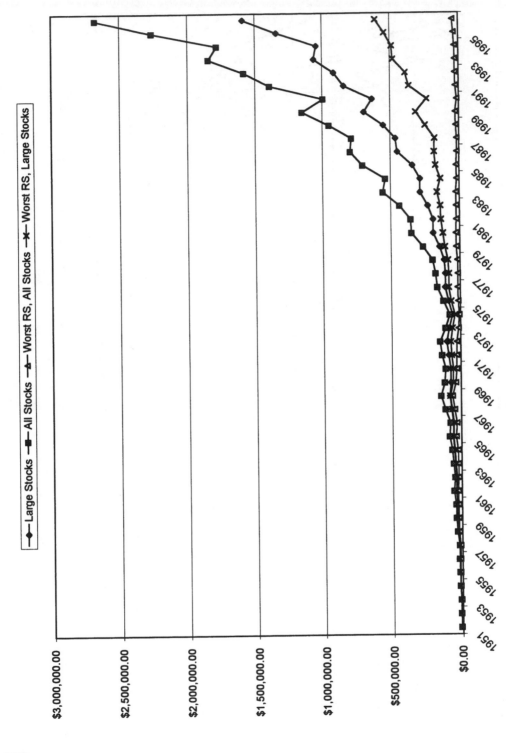

Figure 15-2. Returns on worst relative strength strategies versus All Stocks and Large Stocks, 1951–1996. Year-end 1951 = $10,000.

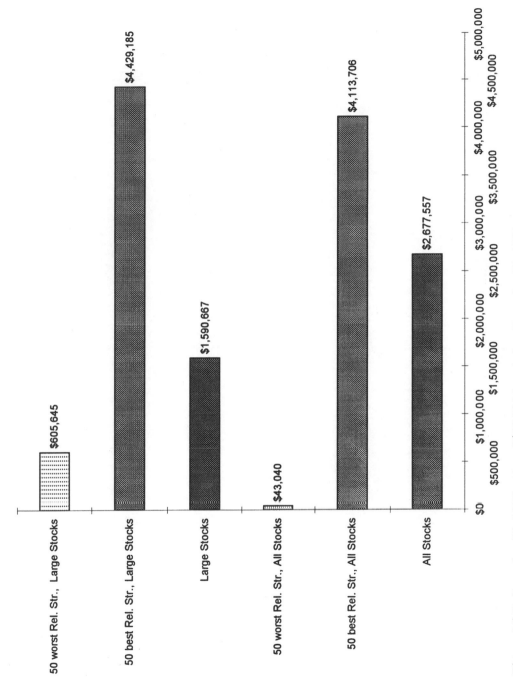

Figure 15-3. December 31, 1996, value of $10,000 invested on December 31, 1951, and annually rebalanced.

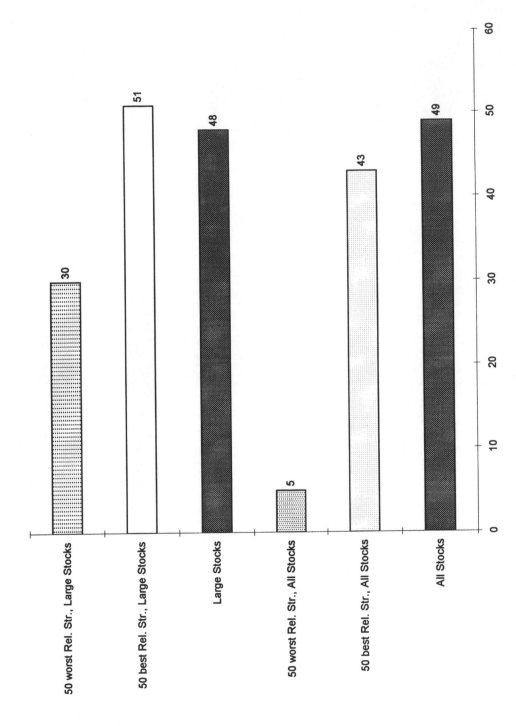

Figure 15-4. Sharpe risk-adjusted return ratio, 1951–1996. (Higher is better.)

compound return of 16.85 percent. The risk was less than the 50-stock portfolio, coming in at 26.37 percent. The higher absolute return coupled with the lower risk gave the group a fairly high Sharpe ratio of 55. We see a great symmetry to the decile analysis of stocks ranked by relative strength, with returns uniformly declining as we move from decile 1 to 10.

Large Stocks had similar results, with the best returns coming from decile 1 and the worst from decile 10. Here $10,000 invested in decile 1 grew to $5,878,229, whereas the same investment in decile 10 grew to $472,674. Tables 15-14 and 15-15, as well as Figures 15-5 and 15-6, summarize the results of the decile studies.

Table 15-14. Summary Results for Price Appreciation (Relative Strength) Decile Analysis of All Stocks Universe, 1951–1996

Decile	$10,000 grows to	Average return	Compound return	Standard deviation
1 (highest price appreciation)	$11,063,109	19.85%	16.85%	26.37%
2	$5,900,481	17.11%	15.23%	20.22%
3	$4,858,363	16.37%	14.74%	18.86%
4	$2,216,204	14.17%	12.75%	17.49%
5	$2,710,969	14.66%	13.26%	17.32%
6	$2,052,232	13.97%	12.56%	17.45%
7	$2,550,140	14.69%	13.10%	18.75%
8	$1,543,168	13.33%	11.85%	18.00%
9	$1,266,208	13.19%	11.36%	20.19%
10 (lowest price appreciation)	$142,400	8.66%	6.08%	23.20%
All Stocks	$2,677,557	14.97%	13.23%	19.51%

Table 15-15. Summary Results for Price Appreciation (Relative Strength) Decile Analysis of Large Stocks Universe, 1951–1996

Decile	$10,000 grows to	Average return	Compound return	Standard deviation
1 (highest price appreciation)	$5,878,229	17.47%	15.22%	22.57%
2	$2,703,044	14.78%	13.25%	18.39%
3	$1,906,525	13.69%	12.38%	16.84%
4	$1,589,726	13.00%	11.92%	15.32%
5	$1,172,642	12.36%	11.17%	16.01%
6	$1,108,322	12.16%	11.03%	15.45%
7	$1,348,381	12.63%	11.51%	15.42%
8	$1,847,414	13.43%	12.30%	16.01%
9	$883,666	11.72%	10.47%	16.48%
10 (lowest price appreciation)	$472,674	10.88%	8.95%	20.74%
Large Stocks	$1,590,667	13.11%	11.92%	16.01%

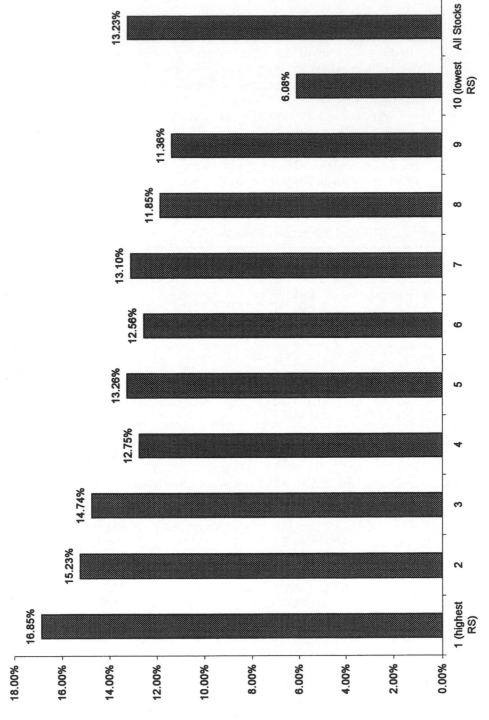

Figure 15-5. Compound return by price appreciation (relative strength) decile, All Stocks universe, 1951–1996.

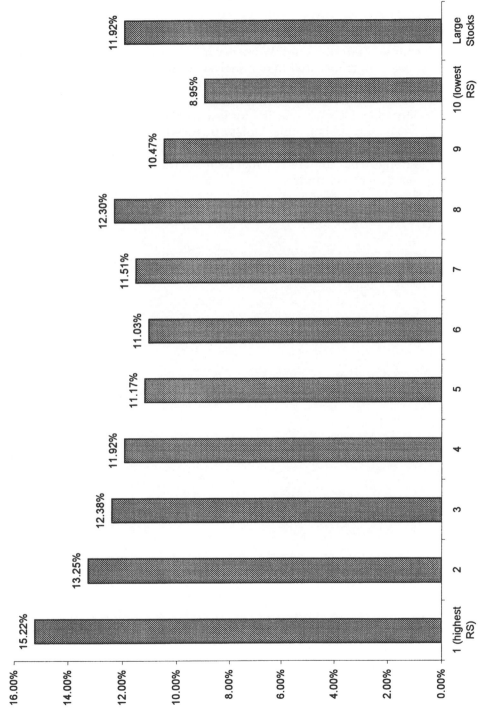

Figure 15-6. Compound return by relative strength decile, Large Stocks universe, 1951–1996.

Implications

Runyon's quote is apt. Winners continue to win and losers continue to lose. Remember that in our analysis losers refer, not to stocks that lost some ground last year, but to the 50 *worst* casualties from the entire universe. Yet the decile analysis shows that investors are best off avoiding stocks in the lowest deciles for last year's price performance.

The advice is simple: Unless financial ruin is your goal, avoid the biggest one-year losers. Buy stocks with the *best* one-year relative strength, but understand that their volatility will continually test your emotional endurance.

16

Using Multifactor Models to Improve Performance

It is not who is right, but what is right, that is important. —Thomas Huxley

Thus far, we've looked only at individual factors, such as low price-to-sales ratios or outstanding relative strength. Now we'll look at buying stocks using two or more criteria. Using several factors can *dramatically* enhance performance or *substantially* reduce risk, depending on your goal. Let's look at how adding factors can improve the performance of the 50 best performing stocks from the All Stocks universe.

Adding Value Factors

Ben Graham said that anyone paying more than 20 times earnings for a stock should prepare to lose money in the long run. What happens if we remove high PE ratio stocks from the All Stocks universe and then buy the 50 biggest winners? Instead of just buying the top 50 relative strength stocks, let's also require that stocks have PE ratios between 0 and 20. Thus, we would start with the All Stocks universe and screen out stocks with PE ratios above 20 or negative PE ratios, *then* buy the 50 with the best one-year price appreciation.

If you invest $10,000 on December 31, 1951 in the 50 stocks from All Stocks with the best price appreciation from the previous year and PE ratios below 20, your investment grows to $22,717,709 by the end of 1996. That's $18,604,003 more than an investment in the 50 biggest winners alone! What's more, this two-factor portfolio has a standard deviation of 24.61 percent, *lower* than the 29.8 percent for the 50 All Stocks winners. The Sharpe ratio for this two-factor strategy is 65, compared with 43 for the 50 best performing stocks from All Stocks.

Risk and return aren't the only things enhanced by this model; the base rates are better as well. The 50 biggest winners from All Stocks with PE ratios below 20 beat the All Stocks universe in 30 of the 45 years of the study, or 67 percent of the time. Over the long term, the results get better, with this strategy outperforming All Stocks in 35 of the 41 rolling 5-year periods and 33 of the 36 rolling 10-year periods. That's a long-term success rate of 92 percent—better than relative strength alone.

What About Other Value Factors?

Adding low PE ratios is just one way to improve performance. Other factors work as well. For instance, if you take stocks from All Stocks with price-to-book ratios below 1 and then buy the 50 stocks with the highest one-year price appreciation, a $10,000 investment made on December 31, 1951 grows to $18,626,247 by the end of 1996, a compound return of 18.21 percent. Risk is lower, with a standard deviation of return of 23.95 percent. Base rates improve, with the strategy beating All Stocks in 33 of the 45 years of the study, 36 of the 42 rolling 5-year periods, and 35 of the 36 rolling 10-year periods. That's 97 percent of the time over all rolling 10-year periods. Table 16-1 summarizes the results for these two strategies.

Price-to-Sales Ratio Better Still

Price-to-sales ratio (PSR) also performs beautifully when joined with relative strength. If you start December 31, 1951 with the All Stocks universe, consider only stocks with PSRs below 1, and *then* buy the 50 with the best one-year price appreciation, your $10,000 investment grows to

Table 16-1. Summary Results for Buying Best One-Year Price Appreciation Stocks with PE Ratios below 20 or Price-to-Book Ratios below 1 from All Stocks Universe, December 31, 1951–December 31, 1996

	All Stocks	50 stocks with PE ratios below 20 (earnings yields >5%) and best 1-year price appreciation	50 stocks with price-to-book ratios below 1 and best 1-year price appreciation
$10,000 becomes	$2,677,557	$22,717,709	$18,626,247
Compound return	13.23%	18.74%	18.21%
Standard deviation of return (risk)	19.51%	24.61%	23.95%
Sharpe ratio	49	65	64
Percent of rolling 10-year periods beats All Stocks	NA	100%	97%

$23,394,653 by the end of 1996, a compound rate of return of 18.81 percent. That's nearly 10 times better than the $2,677,557 you'd earn from an investment in All Stocks. The standard deviation of return of 25.51 percent is higher than All Stocks' 19.51 percent, but lower than the 50 best performers' 29.8 percent. The Sharpe ratio is 64 for this strategy, well ahead of All Stocks' 49. Table 16-2 compares this strategy with the All Stocks universe, and Table 16-3 compares the returns of the two relative strength strategies. Table 16-4 summarizes the returns of the low PSR relative strength strategy.

The consistency of this strategy is amazing, beating All Stocks in 34 of the 45 years of the study, or 76 percent of the time. Over the long term, the record can't get any better: It beat the All Stocks universe 100 percent of the time over all rolling 5- and 10-year periods. Table 16-5 shows the base rates. Figures 16-1 and 16-2 depict the results.

Additional Factors Add Less to Large Stocks

Using multifactor models with Large Stocks does not enhance performance as much as it does with All Stocks. If you start December 31, 1951 and require stocks from the Large Stocks universe to have PE ratios below 20, then buy the 50 with the best one-year price performance, your $10,000 investment grows to $5,761,236 by the end of 1996, a 15.17

Table 16-2. Annual Performance of All Stocks Versus 50 Stocks with PSR below 1 and Then the Best One-Year Relative Strength (RS) from All Stocks Universe

Year ending	All Stocks	Universe = All Stocks PSR <1 top 50 1-year RS	Top 50 PSR <1 best RS relative performance
31-Dec-52	7.90%	7.80%	−0.10%
31-Dec-53	2.90%	6.40%	3.50%
31-Dec-54	47.00%	56.90%	9.90%
31-Dec-55	20.70%	28.80%	8.10%
31-Dec-56	17.00%	30.50%	13.50%
31-Dec-57	−7.10%	−20.10%	−13.00%
31-Dec-58	55.00%	67.50%	12.50%
31-Dec-59	23.00%	32.00%	9.00%
31-Dec-60	6.10%	2.70%	−3.40%
31-Dec-61	31.20%	49.50%	18.30%
31-Dec-62	−12.00%	−13.30%	−1.30%
31-Dec-63	18.00%	31.80%	13.80%
31-Dec-64	16.30%	26.40%	10.10%
31-Dec-65	22.60%	55.10%	32.50%
31-Dec-66	−5.20%	−0.60%	4.60%
31-Dec-67	41.10%	59.90%	18.80%
31-Dec-68	27.40%	46.30%	18.90%
31-Dec-69	−18.50%	−33.60%	−15.10%
31-Dec-70	−5.80%	−5.20%	0.60%
31-Dec-71	21.30%	31.90%	10.60%
31-Dec-72	11.00%	14.60%	3.60%
31-Dec-73	−27.20%	−20.90%	6.30%
31-Dec-74	−27.90%	−23.90%	4.00%
31-Dec-75	55.90%	58.60%	2.70%
31-Dec-76	35.60%	39.00%	3.40%
31-Dec-77	6.90%	24.50%	17.60%
31-Dec-78	12.20%	38.40%	26.20%
31-Dec-79	34.30%	26.30%	−8.00%
31-Dec-80	31.50%	48.50%	17.00%
31-Dec-81	1.70%	−7.70%	−9.40%
31-Dec-82	22.50%	39.50%	17.00%
31-Dec-83	28.10%	35.40%	7.30%
31-Dec-84	−3.40%	−8.20%	−4.80%
31-Dec-85	30.80%	45.20%	14.40%
31-Dec-86	13.10%	19.30%	6.20%
31-Dec-87	−1.30%	−12.90%	−11.60%
31-Dec-88	21.20%	28.00%	6.80%
31-Dec-89	21.40%	30.90%	9.50%
31-Dec-90	−13.80%	−12.10%	1.70%
31-Dec-91	39.80%	43.70%	3.90%
31-Dec-92	13.80%	30.70%	16.90%
31-Dec-93	16.60%	30.40%	13.80%
31-Dec-94	−3.40%	−6.90%	−3.50%
31-Dec-95	27.00%	25.80%	−1.20%
31-Dec-96	18.30%	31.50%	13.20%
Arithmetic average	14.97%	21.74%	6.77%
Standard deviation	19.51%	25.51%	6.00%

Table 16-3. Annual Performance of 50 Stocks with Best One-Year Relative Strength (RS) Versus Low PSR 50 Stocks with Best One-Year Price Appreciation from All Stocks Universe

Year ending	Universe = All Stocks top 50 1-year RS	Universe = All Stocks PSR <1 top 50 1-year RS	Low PSR top 50 1-year RS relative performance
31-Dec-52	3.10%	7.80%	4.70%
31-Dec-53	3.80%	6.40%	2.60%
31-Dec-54	62.30%	56.90%	−5.40%
31-Dec-55	32.00%	28.80%	−3.20%
31-Dec-56	29.20%	30.50%	1.30%
31-Dec-57	−16.50%	−20.10%	−3.60%
31-Dec-58	68.10%	67.50%	−0.60%
31-Dec-59	39.90%	32.00%	−7.90%
31-Dec-60	9.40%	2.70%	−6.70%
31-Dec-61	35.20%	49.50%	14.30%
31-Dec-62	−22.60%	−13.30%	9.30%
31-Dec-63	33.60%	31.80%	−1.80%
31-Dec-64	5.30%	26.40%	21.10%
31-Dec-65	44.40%	55.10%	10.70%
31-Dec-66	−3.90%	−0.60%	3.30%
31-Dec-67	64.30%	59.90%	−4.40%
31-Dec-68	18.40%	46.30%	27.90%
31-Dec-69	−21.90%	−33.60%	−11.70%
31-Dec-70	−26.30%	−5.20%	21.10%
31-Dec-71	39.90%	31.90%	−8.00%
31-Dec-72	20.10%	14.60%	−5.50%
31-Dec-73	−32.10%	−20.90%	11.20%
31-Dec-74	−27.10%	−23.90%	3.20%
31-Dec-75	36.00%	58.60%	22.60%
31-Dec-76	25.30%	39.00%	13.70%
31-Dec-77	22.50%	24.50%	2.00%
31-Dec-78	25.80%	38.40%	12.60%
31-Dec-79	50.90%	26.30%	−24.60%
31-Dec-80	66.00%	48.50%	−17.50%
31-Dec-81	−13.50%	−7.70%	5.80%
31-Dec-82	27.10%	39.50%	12.40%
31-Dec-83	22.80%	35.40%	12.60%
31-Dec-84	−19.50%	−8.20%	11.30%
31-Dec-85	40.00%	45.20%	5.20%
31-Dec-86	14.30%	19.30%	5.00%
31-Dec-87	−3.90%	−12.90%	−9.00%
31-Dec-88	8.10%	28.00%	19.90%
31-Dec-89	39.00%	30.90%	−8.10%
31-Dec-90	−11.90%	−12.10%	−0.20%
31-Dec-91	101.30%	43.70%	−57.60%
31-Dec-92	−7.90%	30.70%	38.60%
31-Dec-93	26.20%	30.40%	4.20%
31-Dec-94	−19.70%	−6.90%	12.80%
31-Dec-95	34.00%	25.80%	−8.20%
31-Dec-96	−7.26%	31.50%	38.76%
Arithmetic average	18.09%	21.74%	3.65%
Standard deviation	29.80%	25.51%	−4.29%

Table 16-4. Summary Return Results for All Stocks and 50 Stocks with PSRs below 1 and the Best Relative Strength (RS) from All Stocks Universe, December 31, 1951–December 31, 1996

	All Stocks	Universe = All Stocks PSR <1 top 50 1-year RS
Arithmetic average	14.97%	21.74%
Standard deviation of return	19.51%	25.51%
Sharpe risk-adjusted ratio	49.00	64.00
3-yr compounded	13.22%	15.48%
5-yr compounded	14.00%	21.29%
10-yr compounded	12.92%	17.08%
15-yr compounded	14.44%	19.53%
20-yr compounded	14.97%	20.74%
25-yr compounded	12.74%	18.24%
30-yr compounded	12.43%	17.56%
35-yr compounded	11.64%	17.53%
40-yr compounded	12.62%	18.09%
Compound annual return	13.23%	18.81%
$10,000 becomes:	$2,677,556.77	$23,394,652.61
Maximum return	55.90%	67.50%
Minimum return	−27.90%	−33.60%
Maximum expected return*	53.98%	72.76%
Minimum expected return**	−24.04%	−29.27%

*Maximum expected return is average return plus 2 times the standard deviation.

**Minimum expected return is average return minus 2 times the standard deviation.

Table 16-5. Base Rates for All Stocks and 50 Stocks with PSRs below 1 and Best One-Year Relative Strength (RS) from All Stocks Universe, 1951–1996

Item	Stocks with PSR <1 and best 1-year RS beat All Stocks	Percent
Single-year return	34 out of 45	76.00%
Rolling 5-year compound return	41 out of 41	100.00%
Rolling 10-year compound return	36 out of 36	100.00%

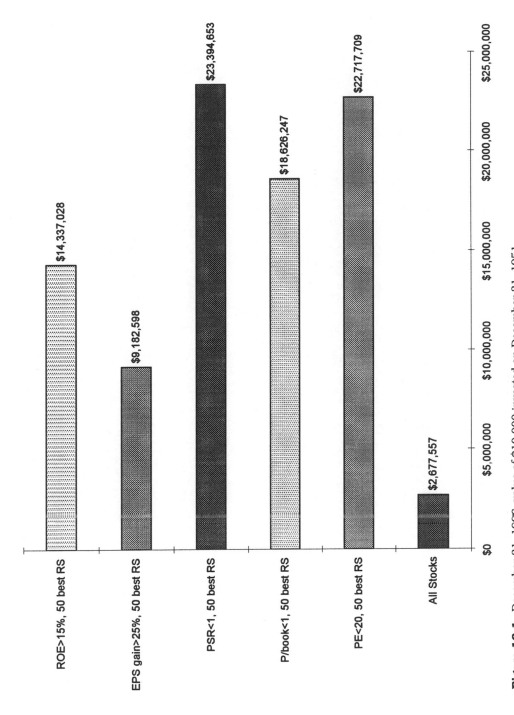

Figure 16-1. December 31, 1996, value of $10,000 invested on December 31, 1951, and annually rebalanced for different multifactor relative strength models using All Stocks as the universe.

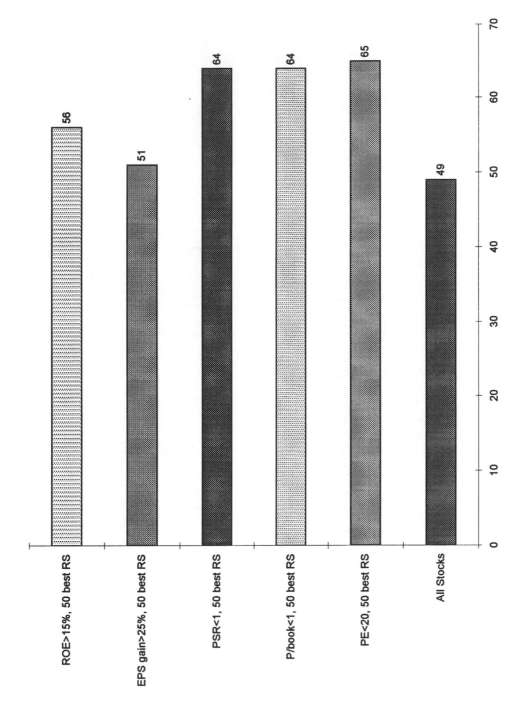

Figure 16-2. Sharpe risk-adjusted return ratios for different multifactor relative strength models using All Stocks as the universe, 1951–1996. (Higher is better.)

percent compound annual return. Risk is relatively low—the standard deviation of 19.05 percent led to a high Sharpe ratio of 60.

Base rates for the strategy are high, beating the Large Stocks universe in 28 of the 45 years of the study, or 62 percent of the time. Longer-term results are even better, with the strategy beating the universe in 35 of the 41 rolling 5-year periods, and 35 of the 36 rolling 10-year periods, or 97 percent of the time.

We were unable to run a test on Large Stocks using price-to-book ratios because Large Stocks rarely trade at price-to-book ratios below 1.

Price-to-Sales Ratio Does Well Too

In the Large Stocks universe, the marriage of low price-to-sales ratios to relative strength does about the same as buying stocks with PE ratios below 20. A $10,000 investment in the 50 stocks from Large Stocks with the best one-year price appreciation and price-to-sales ratios below 1 grows to $5,178,202 by the end of 1996, a compound return of 14.9 percent. The standard deviation of 18.85 percent is virtually the same as for the stocks with PE ratios below 20, possibly because you end up with many of the same stocks in the two portfolios. The Sharpe ratio is 59, considerably better than Large Stocks' 48 and one point behind the best price performers with PE ratios below 20.

Base rates here are not as good as the relative strength stocks with PE ratios below 20. This strategy beat the Large Stocks universe in 29 of 45 years on a year-to-year basis, 32 of the 41 rolling 5-year periods, and 32 of the 36 rolling 10-year periods. Tables 16-6 through 16-8 summarize the returns, which are also charted in Figures 16-3 and 16-4.

What About Growth Factors?

Growth factors work with relative strength too, but the returns are less consistent. For example, if you concentrate on stocks from the Large Stocks universe with PE ratios below 20 *and* positive earnings gains for the year, and then buy the 50 with the best one-year price performance, you will actually earn $1,766,219 *less* than if you buy the low PE, high relative strength stocks alone. The addition of positive earnings gains *hurts* performance in this instance. We'll see in Chapter 19 that higher earnings *can* help, but for now understand that more factors do not necessarily mean better performance.

Table 16-6. Annual Performance of Large Stocks Versus 50 Stocks with PSR below 1 and Then the Best One-Year Relative Strength (RS) from Large Stocks Universe

Year ending	Large Stocks	Universe = Large Stocks PSR <1 top 50 1-year RS	Top 50 PSR <1 best RS relative performance
31-Dec-52	9.30%	13.10%	3.80%
31-Dec-53	2.30%	5.20%	2.90%
31-Dec-54	44.90%	46.60%	1.70%
31-Dec-55	21.20%	23.40%	2.20%
31-Dec-56	9.60%	8.40%	−1.20%
31-Dec-57	−6.90%	−12.10%	−5.20%
31-Dec-58	42.10%	45.40%	3.30%
31-Dec-59	9.90%	8.40%	−1.50%
31-Dec-60	4.80%	0.00%	−4.80%
31-Dec-61	27.50%	25.30%	−2.20%
31-Dec-62	−8.90%	−9.20%	−0.30%
31-Dec-63	19.50%	22.40%	2.90%
31-Dec-64	15.30%	18.60%	3.30%
31-Dec-65	16.20%	28.50%	12.30%
31-Dec-66	−4.90%	−3.60%	1.30%
31-Dec-67	21.30%	30.60%	9.30%
31-Dec-68	16.80%	13.30%	−3.50%
31-Dec-69	−9.90%	−10.40%	−0.50%
31-Dec-70	−0.20%	1.40%	1.60%
31-Dec-71	17.30%	21.70%	4.40%
31-Dec-72	14.90%	11.00%	−3.90%
31-Dec-73	−18.90%	−7.30%	11.60%
31-Dec-74	−26.70%	−21.10%	5.60%
31-Dec-75	43.10%	53.10%	10.00%
31-Dec-76	28.00%	29.20%	1.20%
31-Dec-77	−2.50%	1.50%	4.00%
31-Dec-78	8.10%	16.90%	8.80%
31-Dec-79	27.30%	28.60%	1.30%
31-Dec-80	30.80%	48.30%	17.50%
31-Dec-81	0.60%	−12.50%	−13.10%
31-Dec-82	19.90%	54.10%	34.20%
31-Dec-83	23.80%	22.80%	−1.00%
31-Dec-84	−0.40%	−5.10%	−4.70%
31-Dec-85	19.50%	45.50%	26.00%
31-Dec-86	32.20%	21.00%	−11.20%
31-Dec-87	3.30%	8.80%	5.50%
31-Dec-88	19.00%	22.10%	3.10%
31-Dec-89	26.00%	34.60%	8.60%
31-Dec-90	−8.70%	−6.90%	1.80%
31-Dec-91	33.00%	26.40%	−6.60%
31-Dec-92	8.70%	28.60%	19.90%
31-Dec-93	16.30%	24.90%	8.60%
31-Dec-94	−1.90%	−3.00%	−1.10%
31-Dec-95	28.50%	13.00%	−15.50%
31-Dec-96	18.70%	28.50%	9.80%
Arithmetic average	13.11%	16.44%	3.34%
Standard deviation	16.01%	18.85%	2.85%

Table 16-7. Summary Return Results for All Stocks and 50 Stocks with PSRs below 1 and the Best Relative Strength (RS) from Large Stock Universe, December 31, 1951–December 31, 1996

	Large Stocks	Universe = Large Stocks PSR <1 top 50 1-year RS
Arithmetic average	13.11%	16.44%
Standard deviation of return	16.01%	18.85%
Sharpe risk-adjusted ratio	48.00	59.00
3-yr compounded	14.38%	12.09%
5-yr compounded	13.60%	17.74%
10-yr compounded	13.53%	16.89%
15-yr compounded	15.16%	19.81%
20-yr compounded	14.37%	18.50%
25-yr compounded	12.34%	16.73%
30-yr compounded	11.67%	15.64%
35-yr compounded	10.96%	14.87%
40-yr compounded	11.36%	14.46%
Compound annual return	11.92%	14.90%
$10,000 becomes:	$1,590,667.04	$5,178,201.58
Maximum return	44.90%	54.10%
Minimum return	−26.70%	−21.10%
Maximum expected return*	45.12%	54.15%
Minimum expected return**	−18.91%	−21.26%

*Maximum expected return is average return plus 2 times the standard deviation.

**Minimum expected return is average return minus 2 times the standard deviation.

Table 16-8. Base Rates for Large Stocks and 50 Stocks with PSRs below 1 and Then the Best One-Year Relative Strength (RS) from Large Stocks Universe, 1951–1996

Item	50 stocks with PSR <1 and best 1-year RS best Large Stocks	Percent
Single-year return	29 out of 45	64.00%
Rolling 5-year compound return	32 out of 41	78.00%
Rolling 10-year compound return	32 out of 36	89.00%

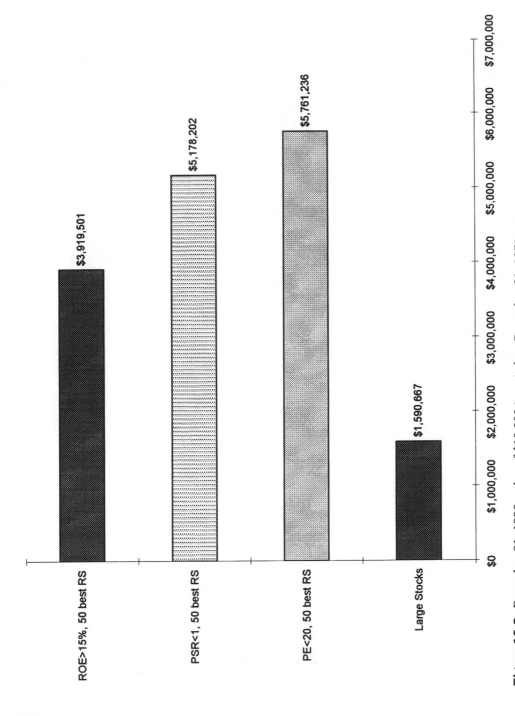

Figure 16-3. December 31, 1996, value of $10,000 invested on December 31, 1951, and annually rebalanced for different multifactor relative strength models using Large Stocks as the universe.

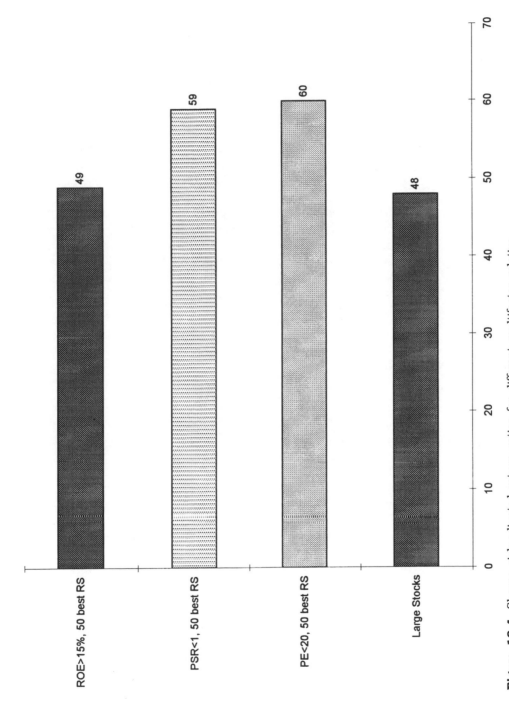

Figure 16-4. Sharpe risk-adjusted return ratios for different multifactor relative strength models using Large Stocks as the universe, 1951–1996. (Higher is better.)

Two Growth Models

While buying stocks with the best one-year earnings gains doesn't beat All Stocks (see Chapter 11), buying stocks with strong one-year earnings gains *and* strong relative price strength handily beats the All Stocks universe. A two-factor model that requires stocks from All Stocks to have one-year earnings gains exceeding 25 percent and then buys the 50 with the best one-year price performance turns $10,000 invested on December 31, 1952 into $9,182,598 by the end of 1996. That's a compound return of 16.77 percent a year, far ahead of All Stocks' 13.35 percent a year. Risk is high, however—the standard deviation for the strategy is 29.18 percent, much higher than All Stocks' 19.7 percent. The strategy's higher return overcomes the risk, pushing its Sharpe ratio to 51, higher than All Stocks' 47. Altogether, its a huge improvement on buying the best one-year earnings gainers or the best relative strength stocks alone.

Again, we weren't able to test this model on the Large Stocks universe because many of the study years did not have 50 Large Stocks with earnings gains above 25 percent.

Return on Equity Does Better Still

Other growth variables work better. In Chapter 14 we saw that buying the 50 stocks from the All Stocks universe with the best ROE didn't beat the market, but adding a high ROE factor to a relative strength model enhances returns even more than the earnings gains model.

If you start on December 31, 1951, require stocks from the All Stocks universe to have a return on equity above 15, then buy the 50 with the best one-year price performance, your $10,000 investment grows to $14,337,028 by the end of 1996, a compound return of 17.53 percent. The result is still considerably behind the returns from buying the 50 best performing stocks with PE ratios below 20.

This strategy is riskier than strategies that buy cheap stocks with strong relative strength, with a standard deviation of 26.99 percent. The Sharpe ratio of 56 is similar to buying the best performing low PE stocks. All base rates are positive, with the rolling 10-year results always beating the universe. Tables 16-9 through 16-11 summarize the findings.

Table 16-9. Annual Performance of All Stocks Versus 50 Stocks with ROE above 15 and Then the Best One-Year Relative Strength (RS) from All Stocks Universe

Year ending	All Stocks	Universe = All Stocks ROE >15 top 50 1-year RS	Top 50 ROE >15 best RS relative performance
31-Dec-52	7.90%	8.2%	0.30%
31-Dec-53	2.90%	1.9%	−1.00%
31-Dec-54	47.00%	71.5%	24.50%
31-Dec-55	20.70%	30.0%	9.30%
31-Dec-56	17.00%	30.8%	13.80%
31-Dec-57	−7.10%	−10.7%	−3.60%
31-Dec-58	55.00%	55.1%	0.10%
31-Dec-59	23.00%	37.5%	14.50%
31-Dec-60	6.10%	22.6%	16.50%
31-Dec-61	31.20%	33.9%	2.70%
31-Dec-62	−12.00%	−17.3%	−5.30%
31-Dec-63	18.00%	19.8%	1.80%
31-Dec-64	16.30%	11.1%	−5.20%
31-Dec-65	22.60%	24.9%	2.30%
31-Dec-66	−5.20%	3.4%	8.60%
31-Dec-67	41.10%	57.4%	16.30%
31-Dec-68	27.40%	39.8%	12.40%
31-Dec-69	−18.50%	−17.5%	1.00%
31-Dec-70	−5.80%	−15.6%	−9.80%
31-Dec-71	21.30%	58.1%	36.80%
31-Dec-72	11.00%	27.0%	16.00%
31-Dec-73	−27.20%	−27.5%	−0.30%
31-Dec-74	−27.90%	−29.8%	−1.90%
31-Dec-75	55.90%	36.3%	−19.60%
31-Dec-76	35.60%	21.6%	−14.00%
31-Dec-77	6.90%	20.6%	13.70%
31-Dec-78	12.20%	26.5%	14.30%
31-Dec-79	34.30%	38.9%	4.60%
31-Dec-80	31.50%	77.7%	46.20%
31-Dec-81	1.70%	−6.0%	−7.70%
31-Dec-82	22.50%	30.9%	8.40%
31-Dec-83	28.10%	21.9%	−6.20%
31-Dec-84	−3.40%	−4.3%	−0.90%
31-Dec-85	30.80%	45.2%	14.40%
31-Dec-86	13.10%	21.2%	8.10%
31-Dec-87	−1.30%	−15.6%	−14.30%
31-Dec-88	21.20%	17.1%	−4.10%
31-Dec-89	21.40%	38.4%	17.00%
31-Dec-90	−13.80%	−11.9%	1.90%
31-Dec-91	39.80%	87.3%	47.50%
31-Dec-92	13.80%	11.5%	−2.30%
31-Dec-93	16.60%	19.9%	3.30%
31-Dec-94	−3.40%	−12.1%	−8.70%
31-Dec-95	27.00%	25.2%	−1.80%
31-Dec-96	18.30%	22.4%	4.10%
Arithmetic average	14.97%	20.61%	5.64%
Standard deviation	19.51%	26.99%	7.49%

Table 16-10. Summary Return Results for All Stocks and 50 Stocks with ROE above 15 and the Best Relative Strength (RS) from All Stocks Universe, December 31, 1951–December 31, 1996

	All Stocks	Universe = All Stocks ROE >15 top 50 1-year RS
Arithmetic average	14.97%	20.61%
Standard deviation of return	19.51%	26.99%
Sharpe risk-adjusted ratio	49.00	56.00
3-yr compounded	13.22%	10.44%
5-yr compounded	14.00%	12.48%
10-yr compounded	12.92%	15.05%
15-yr compounded	14.44%	17.28%
20-yr compounded	14.97%	20.05%
25-yr compounded	12.74%	16.06%
30-yr compounded	12.43%	16.60%
35-yr compounded	11.64%	15.23%
40-yr compounded	12.62%	16.47%
Compound annual return	13.23%	17.53%
$10,000 becomes:	$2,677,556.77	$14,337,028.30
Maximum return	55.90%	87.30%
Minimum return	−27.90%	−29.80%
Maximum expected return*	53.98%	74.59%
Minimum expected return**	−24.04%	−33.38%

*Maximum expected return is average return plus 2 times the standard deviation.

**Minimum expected return is average return minus 2 times the standard deviation.

Table 16-11. Base Rates for All Stocks and 50 Stocks with ROE >15 and Best One-Year Relative Strength (RS) from All Stocks Universe, 1951–1996

Item	50 stocks with ROE >15 and best 1-year RS beat All Stocks	Percent
Single-year return	28 out of 45	62.00%
Rolling 5-year compound return	34 out of 41	83.00%
Rolling 10-year compound return	36 out of 36	100.00%

Large Stocks Less Dramatic

The results are less striking for Large Stocks. Here buying the 50 best one-year price performers that also have a return on equity higher than 15 turns $10,000 invested on December 31, 1951 into $3,919,501, a compound return of 14.19 percent a year. That's double Large Stocks' return over the same period. The standard deviation for the strategy is 22.42 percent, and the Sharpe ratio of 49 is slightly better than Large Stocks'.

Implications

Using multifactor models *dramatically* enhances returns. Whether your focus is All Stocks or Large Stocks, you're better off using several factors to choose stocks. Buying the 50 stocks from All Stocks with price-to-sales ratios below 1 and the best price performance from the previous year takes just a slightly higher risk than buying the 50 stocks from All Stocks with the lowest price-to-sales ratios, yet earns $20 million more over 45 years!

In all likelihood, adding relative strength to a value portfolio dramatically increases performance, because it picks stocks when investors have recognized the bargains and begun buying once again. All the value factors that make them good buys are still in place, but the addition of relative strength helps pinpoint when investors believe the stocks have been oversold.

Adding relative strength also helps growth stocks, but the results aren't uniform. Some growth factors actually reduce the gains from relative strength and should be avoided; others, such as one-year earnings gains above 25 percent and ROEs above 15, are helpful.

17

Two Multifactor Value Models for All Stocks

Great works are performed not by strength, but perseverance.
　　　　　　　　　　　　　　　—SAMUEL JOHNSON

Buying the lowest price-to-sales ratios stocks from All Stocks is the best performing single value factor. It turned $10,000 invested on December 31, 1951 into $8,252,731, with a standard deviation of 25.6 percent. Now let's see if we can enhance returns or reduce risk using several value factors to pick stocks.

Using Several Value Factors

First let's approximate the low price-to-sales stocks returns *without* using price-to-sales ratios as a factor. We'll call this Value Model 1. It requires that stocks chosen from the All Stocks universe meet the following criteria:

1. Price-to-book ratios are below 1.5 (or, as Compustat will calculate it, book-to-price ratios are above .66). This price-to-book ratio is typical for an extreme value stock.

2. Dividend yield must exceed the Compustat average for any given year. This effectively limits us to the upper 20 percent of the database by dividend yield.

3. Price-to-earnings ratios are below the Compustat database average for any given year.

We then buy the 50 stocks with the lowest price-to-cashflow ratios.

The Results

A $10,000 investment on December 31, 1951 (rebalanced annually and time-lagged to avoid look-ahead bias) grows to $8,360,742 by the end of 1996, a compound return of 16.13 percent. This handily beats the All Stocks universe, and is a little more than $100,000 ahead of what we'd earn buying the 50 stocks with the lowest price-to-sales ratios. Risk is also reduced. Here, the standard deviation of return is 23.69 percent, better than the 50 lowest price-to-sales ratios stocks' 25.6 percent. The multifactor portfolios' lower risk translates into a higher Sharpe ratio of 55, compared with 53 for the 50 low price-to-sales stocks. Finally, this strategy's 5-year rolling returns beat those for the low price-to-sales stocks. Tables 17-1, 17-2, and 17-3 summarize the results.

Value Factors Overlap

Importantly, we achieved these results *without* using price-to-sales as a factor. This shows that factors overlap. Many of the stocks with the lowest price-to-sales ratios *also* have low PE ratios, low price-to-book ratios, and high dividend yields. We can slightly reduce risk while maintaining similar returns when we use several factors to choose a portfolio. A variety of value models produce similar results. For example, let low price-to-book ratios be the final factor. Leave low PE ratios out. Require that dividends go up 5 years in a row, and so on. No matter the combination, results are similar, since all models end up choosing similar stocks.

Table 17-1. Annual Performance of All Stocks Versus 50 Stocks from Value Model 1 from All Stocks Universe

Year ending	All Stocks	Universe = All Stocks price-to-book < 1.5 yield > mean, PE < mean top 50 cashflow-to-price	Top 50 relative performance
31-Dec-52	7.90%	10.90%	3.00%
31-Dec-53	2.90%	−4.50%	−7.40%
31-Dec-54	47.00%	70.70%	23.70%
31-Dec-55	20.70%	25.00%	4.30%
31-Dec-56	17.00%	5.90%	−11.10%
31-Dec-57	−7.10%	−13.70%	−6.60%
31-Dec-58	55.00%	74.20%	19.20%
31-Dec-59	23.00%	20.10%	−2.90%
31-Dec-60	6.10%	−1.10%	−7.20%
31-Dec-61	31.20%	30.60%	−0.60%
31-Dec-62	−12.00%	−0.01%	11.99%
31-Dec-63	18.00%	26.70%	8.70%
31-Dec-64	16.30%	22.90%	6.60%
31-Dec-65	22.60%	29.00%	6.40%
31-Dec-66	−5.20%	−4.60%	0.60%
31-Dec-67	41.10%	44.20%	3.10%
31-Dec-68	27.40%	36.90%	9.50%
31-Dec-69	−18.50%	−19.70%	−1.20%
31-Dec-70	−5.80%	1.60%	7.40%
31-Dec-71	21.30%	14.50%	−6.80%
31-Dec-72	11.00%	13.60%	2.60%
31-Dec-73	−27.20%	−18.50%	8.70%
31-Dec-74	−27.90%	−14.30%	13.60%
31-Dec-75	55.90%	84.00%	28.10%
31-Dec-76	35.60%	47.60%	12.00%
31-Dec-77	6.90%	8.10%	1.20%
31-Dec-78	12.20%	4.80%	−7.40%
31-Dec-79	34.30%	23.80%	−10.50%
31-Dec-80	31.50%	10.20%	−21.30%
31-Dec-81	1.70%	4.70%	3.00%
31-Dec-82	22.50%	23.00%	0.50%
31-Dec-83	28.10%	42.90%	14.80%
31-Dec-84	−3.40%	0.08%	3.48%
31-Dec-85	30.80%	32.70%	1.90%
31-Dec-86	13.10%	3.70%	−9.40%
31-Dec-87	−1.30%	15.10%	16.40%
31-Dec-88	21.20%	47.10%	25.90%
31-Dec-89	21.40%	12.90%	−8.50%
31-Dec-90	−13.80%	−21.20%	−7.40%
31-Dec-91	39.80%	47.00%	7.20%
31-Dec-92	13.80%	11.60%	−2.20%
31-Dec-93	16.60%	28.90%	12.30%
31-Dec-94	−3.40%	3.90%	7.30%
31-Dec-95	27.00%	24.50%	−2.50%
31-Dec-96	18.30%	21.90%	3.60%
Arithmetic average	14.97%	18.39%	3.42%
Standard deviation	19.51%	23.69%	4.18%

Table 17-2. Summary Return Results for All Stocks and 50 Stocks from Value Model 1 from All Stocks Universe, December 31, 1951–December 31, 1996

	All Stocks	Universe = All Stocks Value Model 1
Arithmetic average	14.97%	18.39%
Standard deviation of return	19.51%	23.69%
Sharpe risk-adjusted ratio	49.00	55.00
3-yr compounded	13.22%	16.39%
5-yr compounded	14.00%	17.80%
10-yr compounded	12.92%	17.51%
15-yr compounded	14.44%	18.12%
20-yr compounded	14.97%	16.06%
25-yr compounded	12.74%	16.17%
30-yr compounded	12.43%	15.64%
35-yr compounded	11.64%	15.39%
40-yr compounded	12.62%	15.77%
Compound annual return	13.23%	16.13%
$10,000 becomes:	$2,677,556.77	$8,360,741.52
Maximum return	55.90%	84.00%
Minimum return	−27.90%	−21.20%
Maximum expected return*	53.98%	65.77%
Minimum expected return**	−24.04%	−28.98%

*Maximum expected return is average return plus 2 times the standard deviation.

**Minimum expected return is average return minus 2 times the standard deviation.

Table 17-3. Base Rates for All Stocks and 50 Stocks from Value Model 1 from All Stocks Universe, 1951–1996

Item	50 stocks from Value Model 1 beat All Stocks	Percent
Single-year return	29 out of 45	64.00%
Rolling 5-year compound return	32 out of 41	78.00%
Rolling 10-year compound return	32 out of 36	89.00%

A Multifactor Model Using Price-to-Sales Ratios

Let's look at a model that uses low price-to-sales ratios as its final factor. We'll call this Value Model 2. Here, we'll require that stocks from the All Stocks universe meet the following criteria:

1. Dividend yields must exceed the Compustat mean.

2. The stock's price change in the previous year must be positive. (We find this by dividing the current year's price by the preceding year's price so the result is greater than 1.) A positive number guarantees that none of the stocks' prices decreased in the previous year.

We then buy the 50 stocks that have the lowest price-to-sales ratios.

If we start on December 31, 1951, our $10,000 investment Value Model 2 grows to $11,086,291 by the end of 1996, a compound return of 16.86 percent a year. We accomplish this with a standard deviation of return of 22.52 percent, lower than Value Model 1's 23.69 percent. The lower risk and higher return account for the higher Sharpe ratio of 61. Base rates are similar to those of Value Model 1, with the strategy beating the All Stocks universe 89 percent of the time over all rolling 10-year periods. Tables 17-4, 17-5, and 17-6 summarize the results.

Table 17-7 shows compound annual returns by decade for both models. Figure 17-1 charts the results.

Implications

Multifactor models aid risk-adjusted performance. While neither of these models produces returns like those from the low price-to-sales/high relative strength model from Chapter 16, both show that you can enhance returns and reduce the risk of value strategies by adding additional criteria.

Table 17-4. Annual Performance of All Stocks Versus 50 Stocks from Value Model 2 from All Stocks Universe

Year ending	All Stocks	Universe = All Stocks prices up in previous year yield > mean top 50 sales-to-price	Top 50 relative performance
31-Dec-52	7.90%	11.90%	4.00%
31-Dec-53	2.90%	3.60%	0.70%
31-Dec-54	47.00%	66.20%	19.20%
31-Dec-55	20.70%	27.10%	6.40%
31-Dec-56	17.00%	13.50%	−3.50%
31-Dec-57	−7.10%	−17.20%	−10.10%
31-Dec-58	55.00%	43.70%	−11.30%
31-Dec-59	23.00%	18.60%	−4.40%
31-Dec-60	6.10%	−2.40%	−8.50%
31-Dec-61	31.20%	40.90%	9.70%
31-Dec-62	−12.00%	−6.30%	5.70%
31-Dec-63	18.00%	27.40%	9.40%
31-Dec-64	16.30%	23.40%	7.10%
31-Dec-65	22.60%	33.70%	11.10%
31-Dec-66	−5.20%	−12.50%	−7.30%
31-Dec-67	41.10%	54.60%	13.50%
31-Dec-68	27.40%	38.80%	11.40%
31-Dec-69	−18.50%	−26.20%	−7.70%
31-Dec-70	−5.80%	1.00%	6.80%
31-Dec-71	21.30%	23.20%	1.90%
31-Dec-72	11.00%	11.50%	0.50%
31-Dec-73	−27.20%	−19.50%	7.70%
31-Dec-74	−27.90%	−18.50%	9.40%
31-Dec-75	55.90%	72.00%	16.10%
31-Dec-76	35.60%	46.30%	10.70%
31-Dec-77	6.90%	9.30%	2.40%
31-Dec-78	12.20%	9.20%	−3.00%
31-Dec-79	34.30%	41.20%	6.90%
31-Dec-80	31.50%	25.40%	−6.10%
31-Dec-81	1.70%	16.30%	14.60%
31-Dec-82	22.50%	50.00%	27.50%
31-Dec-83	28.10%	36.90%	8.80%
31-Dec-84	−3.40%	5.40%	8.80%
31-Dec-85	30.80%	43.70%	12.90%
31-Dec-86	13.10%	19.60%	6.50%
31-Dec-87	−1.30%	8.20%	9.50%
31-Dec-88	21.20%	26.50%	5.30%
31-Dec-89	21.40%	13.30%	−8.10%
31-Dec-90	−13.80%	−18.20%	−4.40%
31-Dec-91	39.80%	21.20%	−18.60%
31-Dec-92	13.80%	24.60%	10.80%
31-Dec-93	16.60%	27.30%	10.70%
31-Dec-94	−3.40%	1.30%	4.70%
31-Dec-95	27.00%	16.00%	−11.00%
31-Dec-96	18.30%	25.50%	7.20%
Arithmetic average	14.97%	19.06%	4.09%
Standard deviation	19.51%	22.52%	3.01%

Table 17-5. Summary Return Results for All Stocks and 50 Stocks from Value Model 2 from All Stocks Universe, December 31, 1951–December 31, 1996

	All Stocks	Universe = All Stocks prices up in previous year yield < mean, top 50 by sales-to-price
Arithmetic average	14.97%	19.06%
Standard deviation of return	19.51%	22.52%
Sharpe risk-adjusted ratio	49.00	61.00
3-yr compounded	13.22%	13.82%
5-yr compounded	14.00%	18.53%
10-yr compounded	12.92%	13.65%
15-yr compounded	14.44%	18.88%
20-yr compounded	14.97%	19.08%
25-yr compounded	12.74%	17.84%
30-yr compounded	12.43%	17.28%
35-yr compounded	11.64%	16.43%
40-yr compounded	12.62%	16.15%
Compound annual return	13.23%	16.86%
$10,000 becomes:	$2,677,556.77	$11,086,291.30
Maximum return	55.90%	72.00%
Minimum return	−27.90%	−26.20%
Maximum expected return*	53.98%	64.09%
Minimum expected return**	−24.04%	−25.98%

*Maximum expected return is average return plus 2 times the standard deviation.

**Minimum expected return is average return minus 2 times the standard deviation.

Table 17-6. Base Rates for All Stocks and 50 Stocks from Value Model 2 from All Stocks Universe, 1951–1996

Item	50 stocks from Value Model 2 beat All Stocks	Percent
Single-year return	32 out of 45	71.00%
Rolling 5-year compound return	32 out of 41	78.00%
Rolling 10-year compound return	32 out of 36	89.00%

Table 17-7. Compound Annual Rates of Return by Decade

Portfolio	1950s*	1960s	1970s	1980s	1990s**
All Stocks	19.22%	11.09%	8.53%	15.85%	12.78%
Value Model 1	20.07%	14.65%	13.40%	18.23%	14.80%
Value Model 2	18.63%	14.14%	14.46%	23.74%	12.17%

*Returns for 1952–1959.

**Returns for 1990–1996.

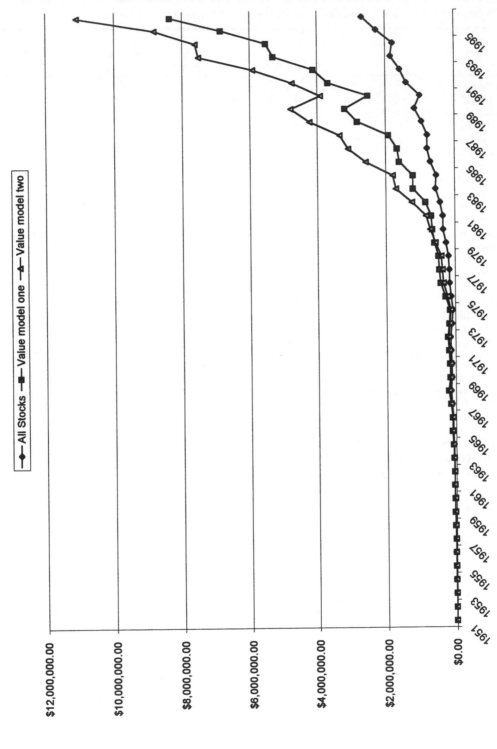

Figure 17-1. Returns for two multifactor value models versus All Stocks, 1951–1996.
Year-end 1951 = $10,000.

18
Finding Value Among the Market's Leaders: A Cornerstone Value Strategy

The best way to manage anything is by making use of its own nature. —LAO TZU

Many investors are uncomfortable with any strategy that has significantly different risks from large cap indexes like the Dow and the S&P 500. They'd love to do better than indexing, but cannot stomach the volatility required to do so. They can't bear a loss in their portfolio when the market is up, much less own stocks that do well in bull markets but get crushed in bear markets. These jittery investors frequently end up in S&P 500 index funds.

An Alternative to Indexing to the S&P 500

There *is* an alternative to indexing to the S&P 500. History shows that a portfolio of market-leading stocks that possess attractive value ratios—particularly those with high dividend yields—consistently beats the market with similar levels of risk. Market Leaders are large, well-known companies with sales well above the average. They usually also have strong cashflows and large numbers of shares available to the public. These market-leading firms are considerably less volatile than the market as a whole. And while we saw in Chapter 9 that buying the 50 stocks with the highest dividend yields alone did not add value to stocks from the All Stocks universe, when combined with large, market-leading firms they improve performance dramatically at risk levels that are virtually the same as the market.

Let's define market-leading stocks. They:

1. Come from the Large Stocks universe

2. Have more common shares outstanding than the average stock in the Compustat database

3. Have cashflows per share exceeding the Compustat mean

4. Have sales 1.5 times the Compustat mean

Finally, utilities are excluded so they don't dominate the list. This greatly limits the number of stocks we can consider. On September 30, 1997, only 570 of the 9889 stocks in the Compustat database met all the requirements. That's just 6 percent of the database!

High PE Ratios Hinder Even Market Leaders

All value factors are useful in sorting out which Market Leaders will do well. As we've seen before, high PE ratios hurt and low ones help the Market Leaders' performance. Tables 18-1 through 18-4 show the results and they are dramatic. A $10,000 investment on December 31, 1951 in the 50 stocks from the Market Leader group with the *highest* PE ratios grew to $1,043,895 by the end of 1996, a compound return of just 10.62 percent. That's behind the $1,590,667 you would earn from an investment in the Large Stocks universe, and way behind the $3,363,529 you'd earn with an investment in the Market Leaders universe. Despite a low standard deviation of 17.23 percent, the poor absolute return

Table 18-1. Annual Performance of Large Stocks Versus 50 Stocks with Highest PE Ratios from Market Leaders Universe

Year ending	Large Stocks	Universe = Market Leaders top 50 highest PE ratios	Top 50 PE ratios relative performance
31-Dec-52	9.30%	15.50%	6.20%
31-Dec-53	2.30%	0.03%	−2.27%
31-Dec-54	44.90%	50.70%	5.80%
31-Dec-55	21.20%	26.60%	5.40%
31-Dec-56	9.60%	13.00%	3.40%
31-Dec-57	−6.90%	−10.00%	−3.10%
31-Dec-58	42.10%	36.70%	−5.40%
31-Dec-59	9.90%	12.50%	2.60%
31-Dec-60	4.80%	−0.01%	−4.81%
31-Dec-61	27.50%	24.10%	−3.40%
31-Dec-62	−8.90%	−13.70%	−4.80%
31-Dec-63	19.50%	23.90%	4.40%
31-Dec-64	15.30%	13.00%	−2.30%
31-Dec-65	16.20%	24.50%	8.30%
31-Dec-66	−4.90%	−1.60%	3.30%
31-Dec-67	21.30%	35.00%	13.70%
31-Dec-68	16.80%	6.80%	−10.00%
31-Dec-69	−9.90%	0.20%	10.10%
31-Dec-70	−0.20%	−6.50%	−6.30%
31-Dec-71	17.30%	27.00%	9.70%
31-Dec-72	14.90%	24.70%	9.80%
31-Dec-73	−18.90%	−14.10%	4.80%
31-Dec-74	−26.70%	−32.90%	−6.20%
31-Dec-75	43.10%	30.10%	−13.00%
31-Dec-76	28.00%	9.20%	−18.80%
31-Dec-77	−2.50%	−12.40%	−9.90%
31-Dec-78	8.10%	12.50%	4.40%
31-Dec-79	27.30%	10.50%	−16.80%
31-Dec-80	30.80%	36.00%	5.20%
31-Dec-81	0.60%	−8.00%	−8.60%
31-Dec-82	19.90%	29.50%	9.60%
31-Dec-83	23.80%	16.90%	−6.90%
31-Dec-84	−0.40	−4.10%	−3.70%
31-Dec-85	19.50%	32.00%	12.50%
31-Dec-86	32.20%	24.00%	−8.20%
31-Dec-87	3.30%	23.50%	20.20%
31-Dec-88	19.00%	19.40%	0.40%
31-Dec-89	26.00%	21.80%	−4.20%
31-Dec-90	−8.70%	−15.50%	−6.80%
31-Dec-91	33.00%	30.50%	−2.50%
31-Dec-92	8.70%	0.01%	−8.69%
31-Dec-93	16.30%	11.00%	−5.30%
31-Dec-94	−1.90%	−3.00%	−1.10%
31-Dec-95	28.50%	15.50%	−13.00%
31-Dec-96	18.70%	18.00%	−0.70%
Arithmetic average	13.11%	12.29%	−0.82%
Standard deviation	16.01%	17.23%	1.22%

Table 18-2. Annual Performance of Large Stocks Versus 50 Stocks with Lowest PE Ratios from Market Leaders Universe

Year ending	Large Stocks	Universe = Market Leaders top 50 lowest PE ratios	Lowest 50 PE ratios relative performance
31-Dec-52	9.30%	15.60%	6.30%
31-Dec-53	2.30%	−0.20%	−2.50%
31-Dec-54	44.90%	51.30%	6.40%
31-Dec-55	21.20%	27.20%	6.00%
31-Dec-56	9.60%	13.30%	3.70%
31-Dec-57	−6.90%	−10.00%	−3.10%
31-Dec-58	42.10%	36.70%	−5.40%
31-Dec-59	9.90%	12.80%	2.90%
31-Dec-60	4.80%	1.10%	−3.70%
31-Dec-61	27.50%	3.60%	−23.90%
31-Dec-62	−8.90%	−4.20%	4.70%
31-Dec-63	19.50%	18.70%	−0.80%
31-Dec-64	15.30%	22.30%	7.00%
31-Dec-65	16.20%	23.30%	7.10%
31-Dec-66	−4.90%	−8.00%	−3.10%
31-Dec-67	21.30%	28.80%	7.50%
31-Dec-68	16.80%	29.60%	12.80%
31-Dec-69	−9.90%	−17.50%	−7.60%
31-Dec-70	−0.20%	7.90%	8.10%
31-Dec-71	17.30%	12.30%	−5.00%
31-Dec-72	14.90%	20.40%	5.50%
31-Dec-73	−18.90%	−10.20%	8.70%
31-Dec-74	−26.70%	−17.10%	9.60%
31-Dec-75	43.10%	88.20%	45.10%
31-Dec-76	28.00%	43.20%	15.20%
31-Dec-77	−2.50%	1.60%	4.10%
31-Dec-78	8.10%	8.20%	0.10%
31-Dec-79	27.30%	28.10%	0.80%
31-Dec-80	30.80%	18.00%	−12.80%
31-Dec-81	0.60%	2.10%	1.50%
31-Dec-82	19.90%	17.40%	−2.50%
31-Dec-83	23.80%	38.80%	15.00%
31-Dec-84	−0.40%	6.10%	6.50%
31-Dec-85	19.50%	37.20%	17.70%
31-Dec-86	32.20%	27.20%	−5.00%
31-Dec-87	3.30%	7.10%	3.80%
31-Dec-88	19.00%	26.90%	7.90%
31-Dec-89	26.00%	24.30%	−1.70%
31-Dec-90	−8.70%	−16.60%	−7.90%
31-Dec-91	33.00%	44.80%	11.80%
31-Dec-92	8.70%	5.20%	−3.50%
31-Dec-93	16.30%	25.80%	9.50%
31-Dec-94	−1.90%	3.70%	5.60%
31-Dec-95	28.50%	34.50%	6.00%
31-Dec-96	18.70%	17.50%	−1.20%
Arithmetic average	13.11%	16.60%	3.49%
Standard deviation	16.01%	20.10%	4.09%

Table 18-3. Annual Performance of 50 Stocks with Lowest PE Ratios from Market Leaders Universe Versus 50 Highest PE Stocks from Market Leaders

Year ending	Universe = Market Leaders top 50 highest PE ratios	Universe = Market Leaders top 50 lowest PE ratios	Lowest 50 PE ratios relative performance
31-Dec-52	15.50%	15.60%	0.10%
31-Dec-53	0.03%	−0.20%	−0.23%
31-Dec-54	50.70%	51.30%	0.60%
31-Dec-55	26.60%	27.20%	0.60%
31-Dec-56	13.00%	13.30%	0.30%
31-Dec-57	−10.00%	−10.00%	0.00%
31-Dec-58	36.70%	36.70%	0.00%
31-Dec-59	12.50%	12.80%	0.30%
31-Dec-60	−0.01%	1.10%	1.11%
31-Dec-61	24.10%	3.60%	−20.50%
31-Dec-62	−13.70%	−4.20%	9.50%
31-Dec-63	23.90%	18.70%	−5.20%
31-Dec-64	13.00%	22.30%	9.30%
31-Dec-65	24.50%	23.30%	−1.20%
31-Dec-66	−1.60%	−8.00%	−6.40%
31-Dec-67	35.00%	28.80%	−6.20%
31-Dec-68	6.80%	29.60%	22.80%
31-Dec-69	0.20%	−17.50%	−17.70%
31-Dec-70	−6.50%	7.90%	14.40%
31-Dec-71	27.00%	12.30%	−14.70%
31-Dec-72	24.70%	20.40%	−4.30%
31-Dec-73	−14.10%	−10.20%	3.90%
31-Dec-74	−32.90%	−17.10%	15.80%
31-Dec-75	30.10%	88.20%	58.10%
31-Dec-76	9.20%	43.20%	34.00%
31-Dec-77	−12.40%	1.60%	14.00%
31-Dec-78	12.50%	8.20%	−4.30%
31-Dec-79	10.50%	28.10%	17.60%
31-Dec-80	36.00%	18.00%	−18.00%
31-Dec-81	−8.00%	2.10%	10.10%
31-Dec-82	29.50%	17.40%	−12.10%
31-Dec-83	16.90%	38.80%	21.90%
31-Dec-84	−4.10%	6.10%	10.20%
31-Dec-85	32.00%	37.20%	5.20%
31-Dec-86	24.00%	27.20%	3.20%
31-Dec-87	23.50%	7.10%	−16.40%
31-Dec-88	19.40%	26.90%	7.50%
31-Dec-89	21.80%	24.30%	2.50%
31-Dec-90	−15.50%	−16.60%	−1.10%
31-Dec-91	30.50%	44.80%	14.30%
31-Dec-92	0.01%	5.20%	5.19%
31-Dec-93	11.00%	25.80%	14.80%
31-Dec-94	−3.00%	3.70%	6.70%
31-Dec-95	15.50%	34.50%	19.00%
31-Dec-96	18.00%	17.50%	−0.50%
Arithmetic average	12.29%	16.60%	4.31%
Standard deviation	17.23%	20.10%	2.87%

Table 18-4. Annual Performance of Large Stocks Versus 50 Stocks with Highest Dividend Yields from Market Leaders Universe

Year ending	Large Stocks	Universe = Market Leaders 50 highest dividend yield	Top 50 dividend yield relative performance
31-Dec-52	9.30%	14.30%	5.00%
31-Dec-53	2.30%	1.20%	−1.10%
31-Dec-54	44.90%	52.50%	7.60%
31-Dec-55	21.20%	28.10%	6.90%
31-Dec-56	9.60%	14.80%	5.20%
31-Dec-57	−6.90%	−13.50%	−6.60%
31-Dec-58	42.10%	44.90%	2.80%
31-Dec-59	9.90%	9.60%	−0.30%
31-Dec-60	4.80%	−0.03%	−4.83%
31-Dec-61	27.50%	24.40%	−3.10%
31-Dec-62	−8.90%	−2.60%	6.30%
31-Dec-63	19.50%	18.80%	−0.70%
31-Dec-64	15.30%	20.30%	5.00%
31-Dec-65	16.20%	17.60%	1.40%
31-Dec-66	−4.90%	−10.20%	−5.30%
31-Dec-67	21.30%	23.70%	2.40%
31-Dec-68	16.80%	26.50%	9.70%
31-Dec-69	−9.90%	−15.00%	−5.10%
31-Dec-70	−0.20%	11.30%	11.50%
31-Dec-71	17.30%	15.80%	−1.50%
31-Dec-72	14.90%	14.00%	−0.90%
31-Dec-73	−18.90%	−5.90%	13.00%
31-Dec-74	−26.70%	−12.30%	14.40%
31-Dec-75	43.10%	58.20%	15.10%
31-Dec-76	28.00%	39.20%	11.20%
31-Dec-77	−2.50%	3.30%	5.80%
31-Dec-78	8.10%	3.30%	−4.80%
31-Dec-79	27.30%	25.60%	−1.70%
31-Dec-80	30.80%	20.30%	−10.50%
31-Dec-81	0.60%	12.80%	12.20%
31-Dec-82	19.90%	19.60%	−0.30%
31-Dec-83	23.80%	38.60%	14.80%
31-Dec-84	−0.40%	4.70%	5.10%
31-Dec-85	19.50%	35.00%	15.50%
31-Dec-86	32.20%	20.60%	−11.60%
31-Dec-87	3.30%	11.60%	8.30%
31-Dec-88	19.00%	26.50%	7.50%
31-Dec-89	26.00%	37.60%	11.60%
31-Dec-90	−8.70%	−7.00%	1.70%
31-Dec-91	33.00%	36.90%	3.90%
31-Dec-92	8.70%	11.60%	2.90%
31-Dec-93	16.30%	20.40%	4.10%
31-Dec-94	−1.90%	4.80%	6.70%
31-Dec-95	28.50%	26.70%	−1.80%
31-Dec-96	18.70%	21.90%	3.20%
Arithmetic average	13.11%	16.68%	3.57%
Standard deviation	16.01%	16.95%	0.94%

accounted for a Sharpe ratio of 40. The strategy beat Large Stocks in just 19 of the 45 years studied, or 42 percent of the time. High PE ratios pulled down even the Market Leaders.

Low PE Ratios Help

Market Leaders with the *lowest* PE ratios tell an entirely different story. Starting December 31, 1951, $10,000 invested in the 50 stocks from the Market Leaders group with the lowest PE ratios grew to $5,266,827 by the end of 1996, a compound return of 14.94 percent. That's $4,222,932 more than the *high* PE group from Market Leaders. The only thing separating the stocks was PE ratio. The risk was higher for the low PE group, with a standard deviation of 20.1 percent, but because of the higher total return, the Sharpe ratio was a decent 56. All base rates are considerably better, with the low PE group beating the Large Stocks universe in 29 of the 45 years studied, or 64 percent of the time. Long-term base rates are also superior, with the low PE Market Leaders beating Large Stocks in 32 of the 42 rolling 5-year periods and 28 of the 36 rolling 10-year periods.

High Yield Works Better Still

The best returns for Market Leaders come from stocks with the highest dividend yields. Buying the 50 stocks from the Market Leaders group with the highest dividend yields does four times as well as an investment in the Large Stocks universe, while assuming very little additional risk.

Starting on December 31, 1951, $10,000 invested in the 50 highest-yielding stocks from the Market Leaders group grew to $6,395,862 by the end of 1996, a compound annual return of 15.44 percent. The remarkable thing here is risk—the standard deviation of 16.95 percent is just slightly higher than Large Stocks' 16.01 percent. Such risk-reward numbers push the Sharpe ratio for the strategy to 67, the highest we've seen thus far!

The most extraordinary thing about this high yield strategy is that the *worst* it ever did was a loss of 15 percent. That's nearly half of Large Stocks' largest annual loss of 26.7 percent. This strategy outperformed Large Stocks in 8 of the 11 bear market years, and *never* had a negative 5-year return. It had only one 10-year period where it failed to beat Large Stocks, then losing to the group by only a minuscule 0.78 percent.

Better in Bull Markets, Too

With such excellent downside protection, you would expect the strategy to perform more modestly in bull markets than Large Stocks. But this strategy *beat* Large Stocks in 9 of the 14 years where market gains exceeded 25 percent! Indeed, in the super bull years of 1954, 1958, and 1975—when Large Stocks gained 40 percent or more—the strategy *always* did better.

These numbers give us outstanding base rates. The high yield strategy beat Large Stocks in 29 of the 45 years of our test, or 64 percent of the time. Over the long term, the news gets continually better, with the strategy beating Large Stocks 85 percent of the time over rolling 5-year periods and all but once over the rolling 10-year periods. Tables 18-5 and 18-6 summarize the returns, and Tables 18-7 and 18-8 show rolling 5- and 10-year compound returns for the strategy versus the Large Stocks universe.

Table 18-9 shows compound annual returns by decade for both groups. Figures 18-1 through 18-4 depict the results graphically.

Implications

Large, well-known market-leading companies are much better investments when they have value characteristics like low PE ratios or low price-to-cashflow ratios, but the best criterion is dividend yield.

The returns from buying the 50 market-leading stocks with the highest dividend yields are so outstanding that this strategy should serve as a cornerstone value strategy for all portfolios. The reasons are numerous. The strategy sticks to large, well-known companies yet does four times as well as the Large Stocks universe while taking virtually the same risk. It has the highest risk-adjusted return of all strategies examined. The *biggest* projected loss is 18.17 percent, lower than the Large Stocks' worst projected loss of 19.73 percent. The maximum projected *gain* for the strategy is 50.82 percent, compared with Large Stocks' 44.97 percent. The strategy's *actual* minimum and maximum returns are even better, with the worst year showing a loss of 15 percent and the best a gain of 58.2 percent. That compares very favorably with Large Stocks' worst loss of 26.7 percent and best gain of 44.9 percent. The strategy does better than Large Stocks in bull *and* bear markets, leading the market in most bull years and providing a cushion in bear years.

Finally, the strategy's high returns coupled with low risk and persistence of returns makes it a natural replacement for anyone indexing a portfolio to the S&P 500 or other Large Stocks-style index.

Table 18-5. Summary Return Results for Large Stocks and Cornerstone Value Strategy December 31, 1951–December 31, 1996

	Large Stocks	Universe = Market Leaders cornerstone value
Arithmetic average	13.11%	16.68%
Standard deviation of return	16.01%	16.95%
Sharpe risk-adjusted ratio	48.00	67.00
3-yr compounded	14.38%	17.41%
5-yr compounded	13.60%	16.81%
10-yr compounded	13.53%	18.32%
15-yr compounded	15.16%	19.89%
20-yr compounded	14.37%	18.05%
25-yr compounded	12.34%	17.58%
30-yr compounded	11.67%	16.52%
35-yr compounded	10.96%	15.26%
40-yr compounded	11.36%	14.76%
Compound annual return	11.92%	15.44%
$10,000 becomes:	$1,590,667.04	$6,395,861.89
Maximum return	44.90%	58.20%
Minimum return	−26.70%	−15.00%
Maximum expected return*	45.12%	50.57%
Minimum expected return**	−18.91%	−17.22%

*Maximum expected return is average return plus 2 times the standard deviation.
**Minimum expected return is average return minus 2 times the standard deviation.

Table 18-6. Base Rates for Large Stocks and 50 Stocks with Highest Dividend Yields from Market Leaders, 1951–1996

Item	50 highest dividend yield stocks beat Large Stocks	Percent
Single-year return	29 out of 45	64.00%
Rolling 5-year compound return	35 out of 41	85.00%
Rolling 10-year compound return	35 out of 36	97.00%

Table 18-7. Rolling 5-Year Compound Returns for Large Stocks and 50 Highest Dividend Yield Stocks from Market Leaders, December 31, 1955–December 31, 1996

5 years ending	Large Stocks	Universe = Market Leaders top 50 dividend yields	Difference
31-Dec-56	16.57%	21.00%	4.44%
31-Dec-57	12.89%	14.44%	1.56%
31-Dec-58	20.55%	22.96%	2.41%
31-Dec-59	14.07%	15.10%	1.03%
31-Dec-60	10.80%	9.53%	−1.27%
31-Dec-61	14.20%	11.31%	−2.90%
31-Dec-62	13.71%	13.98%	0.27%
31-Dec-63	9.84%	9.54%	−0.30%
31-Dec-64	10.90%	11.60%	0.70%
31-Dec-65	13.21%	15.29%	2.07%
31-Dec-66	6.76%	8.01%	1.25%
31-Dec-67	13.05%	13.30%	0.24%
31-Dec-68	12.54%	14.73%	2.19%
31-Dec-69	7.12%	7.03%	−0.09%
31-Dec-70	3.91%	5.86%	1.95%
31-Dec-71	8.37%	11.38%	3.02%
31-Dec-72	7.20%	9.58%	2.38%
31-Dec-73	−0.35%	3.28%	3.63%
31-Dec-74	−4.37%	3.93%	8.30%
31-Dec-75	2.77%	11.50%	8.73%
31-Dec-76	4.58%	15.68%	11.10%
31-Dec-77	1.20%	13.42%	12.22%
31-Dec-78	7.19%	15.56%	8.37%
31-Dec-79	19.70%	24.17%	4.47%
31-Dec-80	17.57%	17.55%	−0.02%
31-Dec-81	12.04%	12.71%	0.67%
31-Dec-82	16.77%	16.06%	−0.71%
31-Dec-83	19.98%	23.09%	3.11%
31-Dec-84	14.24%	18.69%	4.45%
31-Dec-85	12.19%	21.46%	9.27%
31-Dec-86	18.49%	23.09%	4.60%
31-Dec-87	15.01%	21.40%	6.39%
31-Dec-88	14.10%	19.20%	5.10%
31-Dec-89	19.60%	25.90%	6.30%
31-Dec-90	13.33%	16.85%	3.52%
31-Dec-91	13.47%	19.85%	6.39%
31-Dec-92	14.63%	19.85%	5.22%
31-Dec-93	14.10%	18.67%	4.57%
31-Dec-94	8.53%	12.38%	3.85%
31-Dec-95	16.21%	19.55%	3.34%
31-Dec-96	13.60%	16.81%	3.21%
Arithmetic average	11.71%	15.25%	3.54%

Table 18-8. Rolling 10-Year Compound Returns for Large Stocks and 50 Highest Dividend Yield Stocks from Market Leaders, December 31, 1955–December 31, 1996

10 years ending	Large Stocks	Universe = Market Leaders top 50 dividend yields	Difference
31-Dec-61	15.38%	16.05%	0.67%
31-Dec-62	13.30%	14.21%	0.91%
31-Dec-63	15.07%	16.06%	0.99%
31-Dec-64	12.47%	13.34%	0.87%
31-Dec-65	12.00%	12.37%	0.37%
31-Dec-66	10.42%	9.65%	−0.78%
31-Dec-67	13.38%	13.64%	0.26%
31-Dec-68	11.18%	12.11%	0.93%
31-Dec-69	8.99%	9.29%	0.30%
31-Dec-70	8.46%	10.47%	2.01%
31-Dec-71	7.56%	9.68%	2.12%
31-Dec-72	10.09%	11.42%	1.34%
31-Dec-73	5.90%	8.86%	2.95%
31-Dec-74	1.21%	5.47%	4.26%
31-Dec-75	3.34%	8.64%	5.30%
31-Dec-76	6.46%	13.51%	7.05%
31-Dec-77	4.16%	11.48%	7.33%
31-Dec-78	3.35%	9.25%	5.89%
31-Dec-79	6.99%	13.60%	6.61%
31-Dec-80	9.92%	14.49%	4.56%
31-Dec-81	8.25%	14.19%	5.94%
31-Dec-82	8.71%	14.73%	6.03%
31-Dec-83	13.41%	19.26%	5.86%
31-Dec-84	16.94%	21.40%	4.46%
31-Dec-85	14.85%	19.49%	4.64%
31-Dec-86	15.22%	17.78%	2.57%
31-Dec-87	15.89%	18.70%	2.81%
31-Dec-88	17.01%	21.13%	4.12%
31-Dec-89	16.89%	22.24%	5.35%
31-Dec-90	12.76%	19.13%	6.37%
31-Dec-91	15.95%	21.46%	5.51%
31-Dec-92	14.82%	20.62%	5.80%
31-Dec-93	14.10%	18.94%	4.83%
31-Dec-94	13.93%	18.95%	5.02%
31-Dec-95	14.76%	18.20%	3.43%
31-Dec-96	13.53%	18.32%	4.79%
Arithmetic average	11.30%	14.95%	3.65%

Table 18-9. Compound Annual Rates of Return by Decade

Portfolio	1950s*	1960s	1970s	1980s	1990s**
Large Stocks	15.33%	8.99%	6.99%	16.89%	12.61%
Cornerstone value strategy	17.22%	9.29%	13.60%	22.24%	15.66%

*Returns for 1952–1959.

**Returns for 1990–1996.

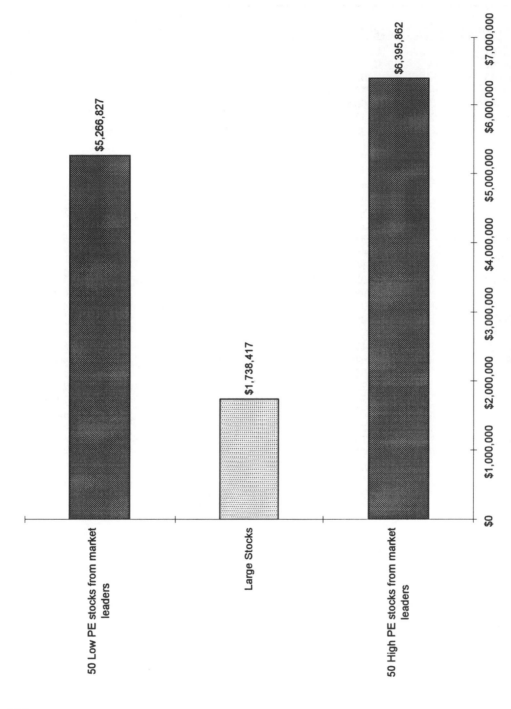

Figure 18-1. December 31, 1996, value of $10,000 invested on December 31, 1951, and annually rebalanced.

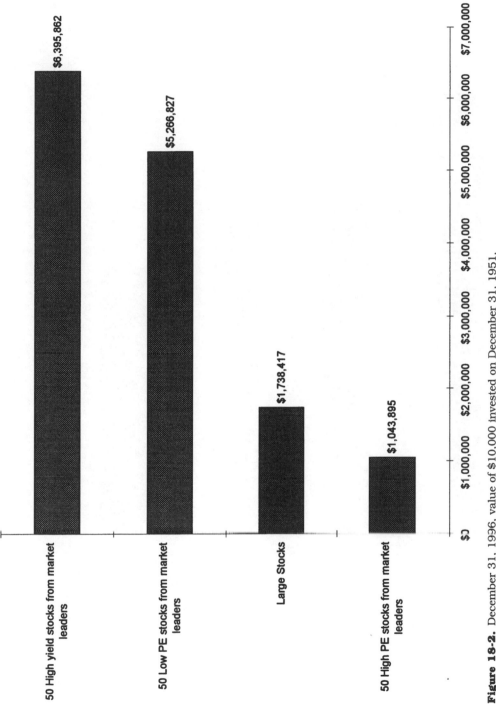

Figure 18-2. December 31, 1996, value of $10,000 invested on December 31, 1951, and annually rebalanced.

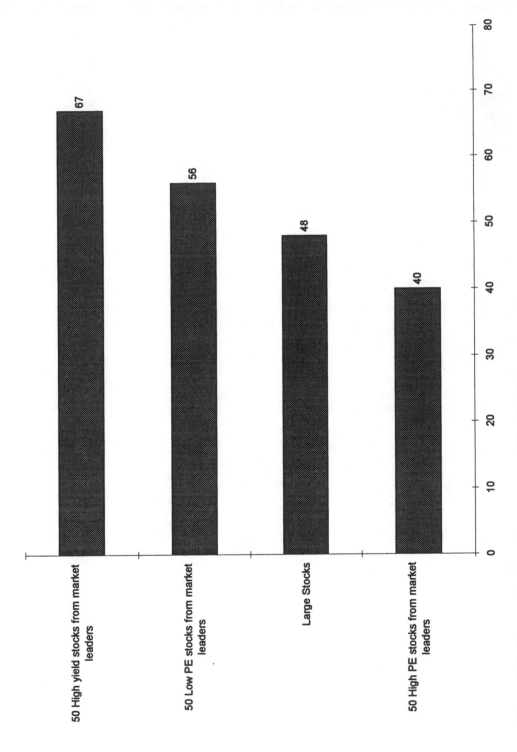

Figure 18-3. Sharpe risk-adjusted return ratios, 1951–1996. (Higher is better.)

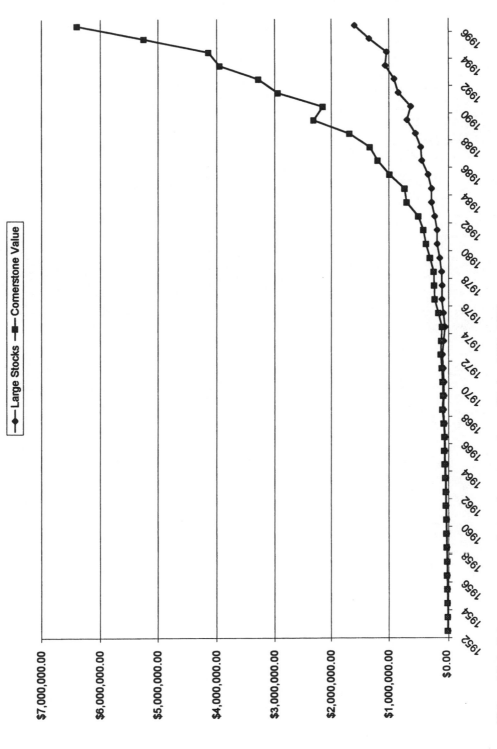

Figure 18-4. Returns on cornerstone value versus Large Stocks, 1951–1996.
Year-end 1951 = $10,000.

19

Searching for a Cornerstone Growth Strategy

Facts do not cease to exist because they are ignored. —ALDOUS HUXLEY

Now let's see if we can find a growth strategy to complement the cornerstone value strategy. With growth strategies, risk is considerably higher. The trick is putting together a portfolio that overcomes its higher standard deviation to provide risk-adjusted returns that compensate for a wilder ride.

The best performing strategy we've seen thus far screens the All Stocks universe for stocks with price-to-sales ratios below 1 and then buys the 50 with the best one-year price performance. (Since we'll be adding earnings variables here and using 5-year earnings gains as well, we'll have to start on December 31, 1954. Therefore, we'll adjust this strategy to the 1954–1996 period.) A $10,000 investment in this strategy on December 31, 1954 grew to $12,999,698 by the end of 1996, a compound return of 18.62 percent. The standard deviation was 25.64 percent and the Sharpe ratio was 61. That's pretty hard to beat. Our objective is to find a growth strategy that offers higher return, lower risk, or better base rates.

Traditional Growth Factors
Fall Short

First let's use a typical group of growth factors coupled with relative strength. We'll call this Growth Model 1 and require stocks to:

1. Come from the All Stocks universe
2. Have 5-year earnings per share growth rates exceeding the Compustat mean
3. Have profit margins exceeding the Compustat mean
4. Have earnings higher than the previous year

We then buy the 50 stocks with the best one-year relative strength.

Starting on December 31, 1954, $10,000 invested in this strategy grew to $6,019,821 by the end of 1996, a compound return of 16.46 percent a year. That's well ahead of a simple investment in All Stocks, where $10,000 grew to $1,640,531 over the same period, with a return of 12.91 percent a year. Growth Model 1's risk is moderate, with a standard deviation of 22.23 percent, not much more than All Stocks' 19.46 percent. That gives it a respectable Sharpe ratio of 57, compared with All Stocks' 44. (Remember we're missing three years of returns here, so the figures are different from those seen earlier.)

On an absolute *and* risk-adjusted basis, this strategy falls far short of the strategy that buys low price-to-sales stocks with the best relative strength, even though we *have* discovered a strategy with a lower standard deviation of return. As mentioned above, $10,000 invested on December 31, 1954 in the 50 stocks with price-to-sales ratios below 1 and the best relative strength grew to $12,999,698 by the end of 1996, more than double the returns of Growth Model 1. Risk is higher, with a standard deviation of 25.64 percent. Table 19-1 summarizes the results.

Higher Earnings More Valuable

You're better off ignoring 5-year compound earnings growth rates and profit margins exceeding the Compustat mean and simply focusing on stocks that have higher earnings than in the previous year without regard to magnitude.

We'll call this simpler strategy Growth Model 2, requiring that stocks:

1. Come from the All Stocks universe
2. Have earnings higher than in the previous year

Table 19-1. Summary Results for Buying Best One-Year Price Appreciation Stocks with Price-to-Sales Ratios below 1 and Those with Higher Earnings from All Stocks Universe, December 31, 1952–December 31, 1996

	All Stocks	Earnings higher than previous year top 50 by 1-year RS	50 stocks with price-to-sales ratios below 1 and best 1-year price appreciation
$10,000 becomes	$2,481,517	$11,210,213	$21,701,904
Compound return	13.35%	17.30%	19.08%
Standard deviation of return (risk)	19.70%	28.34%	25.71%
Sharpe ratio	47	54	63
Percent of rolling 10-year periods beats All Stocks	NA	100%	100%
Best 1-year return	55.90%	96.90%	67.50%
Worst 1-year return	−27.90%	−27.40%	−33.60%

We then buy the 50 stocks with the best one-year price performance.

Since we need only one extra year for the higher earnings, we can start on December 31, 1952. Here $10,000 invested on December 31, 1952 grows to $11,210,213, a compound return of 17.30 percent. That's better than Growth Model 1, but the trade-off is a high standard deviation of 28.34 percent. The risk gives us a Sharpe ratio of 54, and suggests we continue our search for a cornerstone growth strategy. Table 19-2 shows the results.

Table 19-2. Summary Results for Buying Best One-Year Price Appreciation Stocks with Price-to-Sales Ratios below 1 and Cornerstone Growth from All Stocks Universe, December 31, 1952–December 31, 1996

	All Stocks	Cornerstone growth	50 stocks with price-to-sales ratios below 1 and best 1-year price appreciation
$10,000 becomes	$2,481,517.00	$19,748,214.00	$21,701,904.00
Compound return	13.35%	18.82%	19.08%
Standard deviation of return (risk)	19.70%	25.59%	25.71%
Sharpe Ratio	47	63	63
Percent of rolling 10-year periods beats All Stocks	NA	100%	100%
Best 1-year return	55.90%	83.30%	67.50%
Worst 1-year return	−27.90%	−29.10%	−33.60%

Uniting the Two Models for a
Cornerstone Growth Approach

Uniting higher earnings with low price-to-sales ratios results in a strategy that performs virtually the same as low price-to-sales alone while slightly reducing risk. Here, we'll require that stocks:

1. Come from the All Stocks universe

2. Have earnings higher than the previous year

3. Have price-to-sales ratios below 1.5

We then buy the 50 stocks with the best one-year price performance. We increase the price-to-sales minimum to 1.5 to allow more of the "growth" stocks with persistent earnings gains to make the final cut.

A $10,000 investment in this cornerstone growth strategy on December 31, 1952 grows to $19,748,214 by the end of 1996, a compound return of 18.82 percent. That's virtually the same as the return of the 50 best price performers with price-to-sales ratios below 1. It manages this return with a slightly lower standard deviation of 25.59 percent. That gives it a Sharpe ratio of 63, one of the best for all the growth strategies we've examined. Tables 19-3 and 19-4 show the results of the cornerstone growth strategy. All base rates are high: This cornerstone growth strategy beat All Stocks 73 percent of the time annually, 89 percent of the time for rolling 5-year periods, and 100 percent of the time over rolling 10-year periods. It also has better 5- and 10-year base rates than the low price-to-sales high relative strength strategy when compared with the S&P 500. Table 19-5 shows base rates for the strategy, and Tables 19-6 and 19-7 show rolling 5- and 10-year periods.

Table 19-8 shows compound annual returns by decade for All Stocks and the cornerstone group. The results are depicted in Figures 19-1 and 19-2.

Since they are so similar, I expect these strategies to continue to run neck and neck in the future. As we go to press, 1997's returns are just coming in and we see that when 1997 is included, cornerstone growth again nudges ahead of the low price-to-sales, high relative strength strategy, with $10,000 growing to $27.2 million at the end of 1997, compared to $25.2 for the simpler low price-to-sales, relative strength strategy.

Growth Strategies Are Less
Effective with Large Stocks

We won't spend much time reviewing the Large Stocks version of these strategies, since you're much better off using the All Stocks universe

Table 19-3. Annual Performance of All Stocks Versus Cornerstone Growth Strategy Stocks from All Stocks Universe

Year ending	All Stocks	Universe = All Stocks cornerstone growth strategy	Top 50 cornerstone growth strategy relative performance
31-Dec-53	2.90%	0.40%	−2.50%
31-Dec-54	47.00%	56.70%	9.70%
31-Dec-55	20.70%	30.40%	9.70%
31-Dec-56	17.00%	18.00%	1.00%
31-Dec-57	−7.10%	−17.90%	−10.80%
31-Dec-58	55.00%	52.80%	−2.20%
31-Dec-59	23.00%	24.10%	1.10%
31-Dec-60	6.10%	12.60%	6.50%
31-Dec-61	31.20%	51.10%	19.90%
31-Dec-62	−12.00%	−17.20%	−5.20%
31-Dec-63	18.00%	20.80%	2.80%
31-Dec-64	16.30%	30.00%	13.70%
31-Dec-65	22.60%	44.10%	21.50%
31-Dec-66	−5.20%	−0.10%	5.10%
31-Dec-67	41.10%	83.30%	42.20%
31-Dec-68	27.40%	50.50%	23.10%
31-Dec-69	−18.50%	−28.10%	−9.60%
31-Dec-70	−5.80%	−2.60%	3.20%
31-Dec-71	21.30%	32.10%	10.80%
31-Dec-72	11.00%	19.70%	8.70%
31-Dec-73	−27.20%	−27.50%	−0.30%
31-Dec-74	−27.90%	−29.10%	−1.20%
31-Dec-75	55.90%	37.60%	−18.30%
31-Dec-76	35.60%	32.50%	−3.10%
31-Dec-77	6.90%	26.40%	19.50%
31-Dec-78	12.20%	38.30%	26.10%
31-Dec-79	34.30%	38.70%	4.40%
31-Dec-80	31.50%	62.70%	31.20%
31-Dec-81	1.70%	−9.00%	−10.70%
31-Dec-82	22.50%	37.10%	14.60%
31-Dec-83	28.10%	32.70%	4.60%
31-Dec-84	−3.40%	−2.00%	1.40%
31-Dec-85	30.80%	42.50%	11.70%
31-Dec-86	13.10%	17.70%	4.60%
31-Dec-87	−1.30%	−5.40%	−4.10%
31-Dec-88	21.20%	29.70%	8.50%
31-Dec-89	21.40%	23.80%	2.40%
31-Dec-90	−13.80%	−3.30%	10.50%
31-Dec-91	39.80%	51.40%	11.60%
31-Dec-92	13.80%	25.50%	11.70%
31-Dec-93	16.60%	30.30%	13.70%
31-Dec-94	−3.40%	−5.30%	−1.90%
31-Dec-95	27.00%	18.20%	−8.80%
31-Dec-96	18.30%	31.52%	13.22%
Arithmetic average	15.13%	21.72%	6.59%
Standard deviation	19.70%	25.59%	5.89%

Table 19-4. Summary Return Results for All Stocks and Cornerstone Growth Strategy from All Stocks Universe, December 31, 1952–December 31, 1996

	All Stocks	Universe = All Stocks cornerstone growth strategy
Arithmetic average	15.13%	21.72%
Standard deviation of return	19.70%	25.59%
Sharpe risk-adjusted ratio	47	63
3-yr compounded	13.22%	13.76%
5-yr compounded	14.00%	19.21%
10-yr compounded	12.92%	18.27%
15-yr compounded	14.44%	20.31%
20-yr compounded	14.97%	22.45%
25-yr compounded	12.74%	18.13%
30-yr compounded	12.43%	18.54%
35-yr compounded	11.64%	17.79%
40-yr compounded	12.62%	18.25%
Compound annual return	13.35%	18.82%
$10,000 becomes:	$2,481,516.93	$19,748,214.09
Maximum return	55.90%	83.30%
Minimum return	−27.90%	−29.10%
Maximum expected return*	54.52%	72.90%
Minimum expected return**	−24.27%	−29.45%

*Maximum expected return is average return plus 2 times the standard deviation.

**Minimum expected return is average return minus 2 times the standard deviation.

Table 19-5. Base Rates for All Stocks and 50 Stocks Meeting Cornerstone Growth Strategy Criteria from All Stocks Universe, 1952–1996

Item	Cornerstone growth strategy stocks beat All Stocks	Percent
Single-year return	31 out of 44	70.00%
Rolling 5-year compound return	36 out of 40	90.00%
Rolling 10-year compound return	35 out of 35	100.00%

Table 19-6. Rolling 5-Year Returns for All Stocks and Cornerstone Growth Stocks from All Stocks Universe, December 31, 1952–December 31, 1996

5 years ending	All Stocks	Cornerstone growth	Difference
31-Dec-57	14.69%	14.73%	0.04%
31-Dec-58	24.48%	24.78%	0.29%
31-Dec-59	20.12%	19.09%	−1.03%
31-Dec-60	17.07%	15.65%	−1.42%
31-Dec-61	19.78%	21.51%	1.73%
31-Dec-62	18.49%	21.72%	3.23%
31-Dec-63	12.20%	16.13%	3.93%
31-Dec-64	10.95%	17.21%	6.26%
31-Dec-65	14.20%	23.14%	8.94%
31-Dec-66	7.02%	13.36%	6.34%
31-Dec-67	17.61%	32.89%	15.27%
31-Dec-68	19.43%	38.86%	19.43%
31-Dec-69	11.23%	23.35%	12.12%
31-Dec-70	5.52%	14.05%	8.53%
31-Dec-71	10.85%	20.61%	9.75%
31-Dec-72	5.66%	10.76%	5.09%
31-Dec-73	−5.53%	−4.30%	1.23%
31-Dec-74	−7.81%	−4.56%	3.25%
31-Dec-75	1.96%	2.26%	0.31%
31-Dec-76	4.26%	2.33%	−1.93%
31-Dec-77	3.47%	3.45%	−0.03%
31-Dec-78	12.82%	17.71%	4.88%
31-Dec-79	27.77%	34.62%	6.85%
31-Dec-80	23.49%	39.20%	15.71%
31-Dec-81	16.59%	29.13%	12.54%
31-Dec-82	19.81%	31.24%	11.43%
31-Dec-83	23.03%	30.16%	7.13%
31-Dec-84	15.18%	21.43%	6.25%
31-Dec-85	15.06%	18.25%	3.19%
31-Dec-86	17.53%	24.49%	6.96%
31-Dec-87	12.56%	15.59%	3.03%
31-Dec-88	11.32%	15.06%	3.74%
31-Dec-89	16.53%	20.57%	4.04%
31 Dec 90	7.20%	11.57%	4.37%
31-Dec-91	11.84%	17.33%	5.49%
31-Dec-92	15.07%	24.16%	9.08%
31-Dec-93	14.19%	24.27%	10.09%
31-Dec-94	9.09%	17.79%	8.70%
31-Dec-95	17.88%	22.61%	4.74%
31-Dec-96	14.00%	19.21%	5.20%
Arithmetic average	13.17%	19.03%	5.87%

Table 19-7. Rolling 10-Year Returns for All Stocks and Cornerstone Growth Stocks from All Stocks Universe, December 31, 1952–December 31, 1996

10 years ending	All Stocks	Cornerstone growth	Difference
31-Dec-62	16.57%	18.17%	1.60%
31-Dec-63	18.18%	20.38%	2.19%
31-Dec-64	15.44%	18.15%	2.70%
31-Dec-65	15.63%	19.33%	3.71%
31-Dec-66	13.22%	17.36%	4.15%
31-Dec-67	18.05%	27.18%	9.13%
31-Dec-68	15.76%	26.99%	11.23%
31-Dec-69	11.09%	20.24%	9.15%
31-Dec-70	9.78%	18.51%	8.73%
31-Dec-71	8.92%	16.93%	8.01%
31-Dec-72	11.48%	21.32%	9.84%
31-Dec-73	6.22%	15.28%	9.06%
31-Dec-74	1.26%	8.50%	7.24%
31-Dec-75	3.72%	8.00%	4.27%
31-Dec-76	7.50%	11.09%	3.59%
31-Dec-77	4.56%	7.04%	2.48%
31-Dec-78	3.24%	6.14%	2.90%
31-Dec-79	8.53%	13.34%	4.82%
31-Dec-80	12.21%	19.31%	7.10%
31-Dec-81	10.25%	14.95%	4.70%
31-Dec-82	11.34%	16.52%	5.18%
31-Dec-83	17.82%	23.78%	5.96%
31-Dec-84	21.31%	27.85%	6.54%
31-Dec-85	19.20%	28.30%	9.10%
31-Dec-86	17.06%	26.79%	9.73%
31-Dec-87	16.13%	23.17%	7.04%
31-Dec-88	17.03%	22.38%	5.35%
31-Dec-89	15.85%	21.00%	5.14%
31-Dec-90	11.06%	14.86%	3.80%
31-Dec-91	14.65%	20.86%	6.21%
31-Dec-92	13.81%	19.80%	5.99%
31-Dec-93	12.74%	19.58%	6.83%
31-Dec-94	12.74%	19.17%	6.42%
31-Dec-95	12.41%	16.96%	4.55%
31-Dec-96	12.92%	18.27%	5.35%
Arithmetic average	12.51%	18.50%	5.99%

Table 19-8. Compound Annual Rates of Return by Decade

Portfolio	1950s*	1960s	1970s	1980s	1990s**
All Stocks	20.94%	11.09%	8.53%	15.85%	12.78%
Cornerstone growth stocks from All Stocks	20.12%	20.24%	13.34%	21.00%	19.72%

*Returns for 1953–1959.
**Returns for 1990–1996.

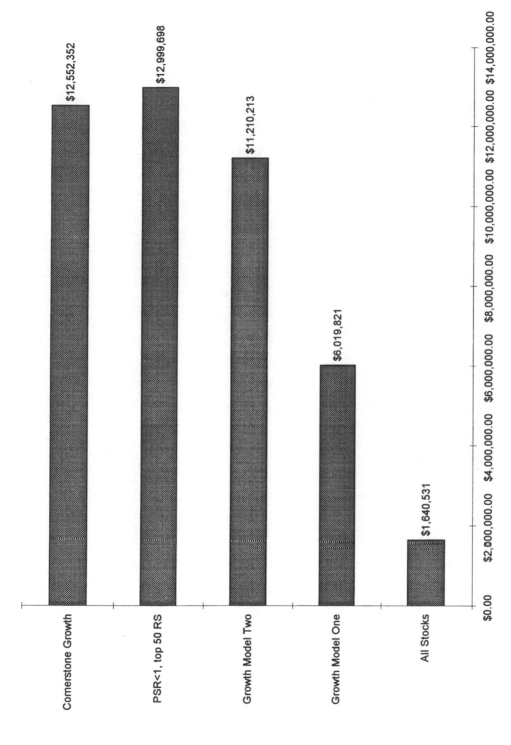

Figure 19-1. December 31, 1996, value of $10,000 invested on December 31, 1954, and annually rebalanced.

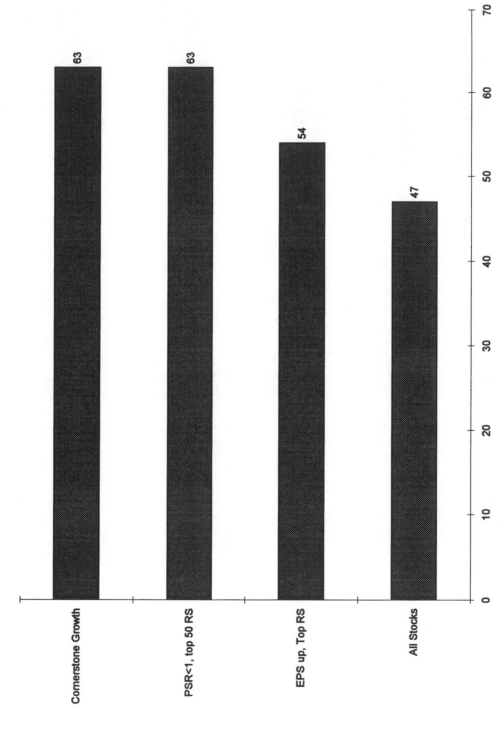

Figure 19-2. Sharpe risk-adjusted return ratios, 1952–1996. (Higher is better.)

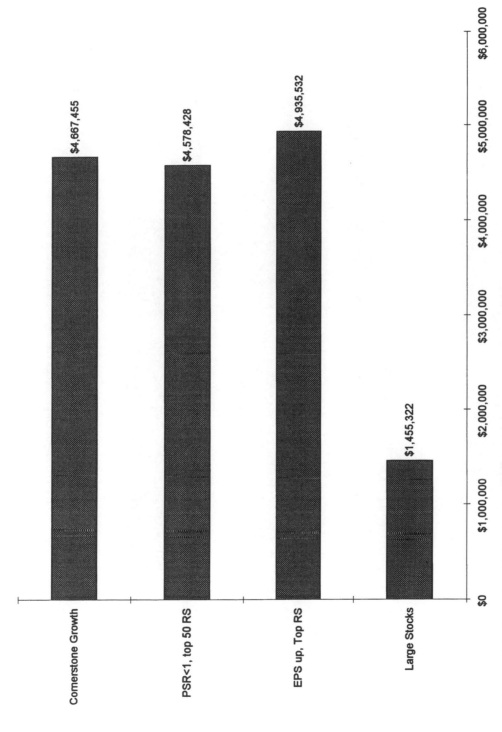

Figure 19-3. December 31, 1996, value of $10,000 invested on December 31, 1952, and annually rebalanced. Strategies are used only on Large Stocks.

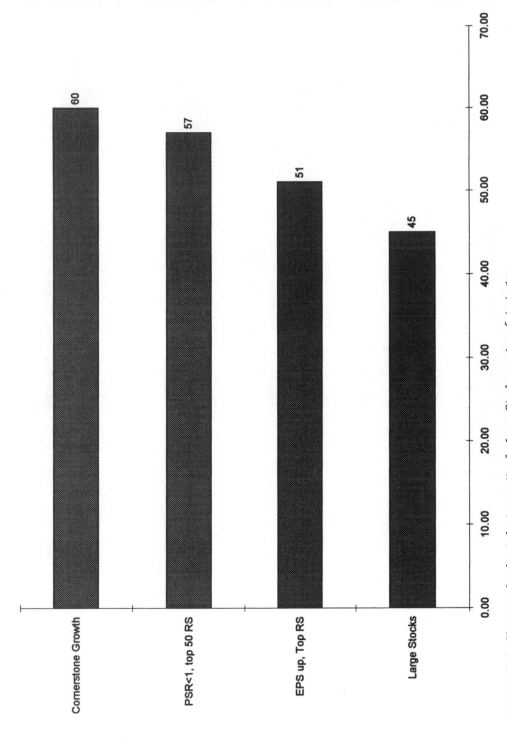

Figure 19-4. Sharpe risk-adjusted return ratios for Large Stocks version of strategies, 1952–1996. (Higher is better.)

when pursuing growth strategies. Figure 19-3 shows the 1996 value of $10,000 invested on December 31, 1952 in the strategies using the Large Stocks universe instead of All Stocks, and Figure 19-4 shows the Sharpe ratios. The strategies all beat the Large Stocks universe handily, yet it's pointless to limit yourself to big companies when buying growth stocks. Unlike the Market Leaders from the cornerstone value strategy, many growth stocks are young, smaller companies that aren't included in the Large Stocks universe. While these smaller stocks are riskier, the difference between the All Stocks and Large Stocks versions of the strategy make it clear that you're well compensated for the additional risk.

Implications

If you can tolerate higher risk, you can beat the market with a strategy like cornerstone growth (see Figure 19-5). It's worth noting that our best growth strategy includes a low price-to-sales requirement, traditionally a value factor. The best time to buy growth stocks is when they are cheap, not when the investment herd is clamoring to buy. This strategy will never buy a Netscape, Cybercash, or Polaroid at 165 times earnings. That's why it works so well. It forces you to buy stocks just when the market realizes that the companies have been overlooked. That's the beauty of using relative strength as your final factor. It gets you to buy just as the market is embracing the stocks, while the price-to-sales constraint ensures that they are still reasonably priced. Indeed, the evidence in this book shows that *all* the most successful strategies include at least one value factor, keeping investors from paying too much for a stock.

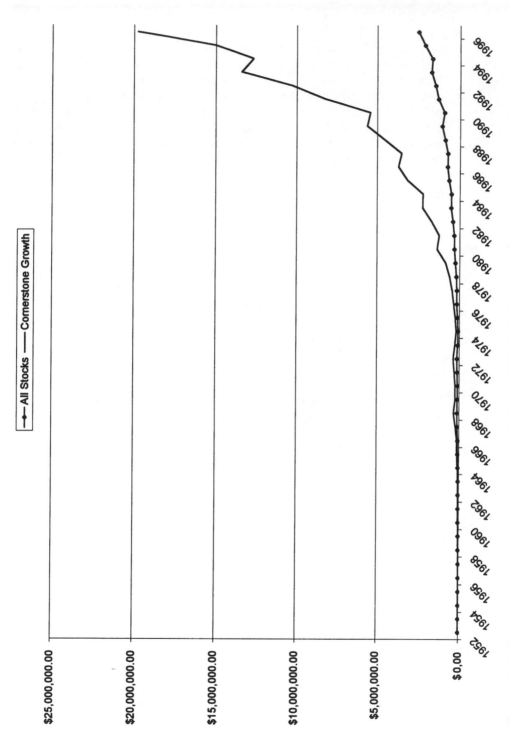

Figure 19-5. Returns on cornerstone growth versus All Stocks, 1952–1996. Year-end 1952 = $10.000.

20

Uniting Strategies for the Best Risk-Adjusted Performance

*What we learn from history is that we do not
learn from history.*
—Benjamin Disraeli

Thus far, we've looked only at results from one style or strategy. Yet the most effective way to diversify your portfolio and enhance risk-adjusted returns is to unite growth and value strategies. Joining growth with value substantially reduces the volatility of growth strategies and increases the capital appreciation potential of less volatile value strategies. It also ensures a diversified portfolio, giving you the chance to perform well regardless of what style is in favor on Wall Street.

Let's look at the returns of a portfolio that unites our cornerstone growth and value strategies. Here we'll start on December 31, 1952 and split a $10,000 investment between cornerstone growth and cornerstone value, investing $5000 in each. We'll rebalance the portfolio annually so it always reflects a 50-50 split between the growth and value strategies.

Obviously, investors who are nearer retirement will allocate less money to the growth strategy and younger investors might allocate more, but the 50-50 mix is a good example to study.

The Results

The united portfolio does almost five times as well as the All Stocks universe. Tables 20-1 and 20-2 compare the results with All Stocks. A $10,000 investment on December 31, 1952 in the combined growth and value cornerstone strategies grew to $11,817,256 by the end of 1996, a compound return of 17.44 percent. (A $10,000 investment in All Stocks grew to $2,481,517 over the same period, a compound return of 13.35 percent.) The amazing thing is that the combined portfolio achieved this performance while taking virtually the same risk as All Stocks! The standard deviation for the united strategies was 19.99 percent, a scant 0.29 percent higher than All Stocks' 19.70 percent. This is extraordinary, accounting for a Sharpe ratio of 68, the highest seen to date.

Uniting the strategies gives us the best chance to beat the market in any given year. Table 20-3 shows the base rates. The combined strategies beat All Stocks in 35 of the 44 years of our test, or 80 percent of the time. Over the longer term, combining the strategies also hits a home run, with the united strategies beating All Stocks in 34 of the 40 rolling 5-year periods and 100 percent of the rolling 10-year periods.

The united strategies do so well in any given year because if one is coasting, the other is often soaring. Consider 1967, a frothy, speculative year. Had you invested only in the market-leading stocks from the cornerstone value strategy, you'd have gained 23.7 percent. That beat Large Stocks' return of 21.3 percent, but did only half as well as the All Stocks gain of 41.1 percent. By adding the cornerstone growth stocks, which soared 83.3 percent, you increase your overall return to 53.5 percent, beating both the All Stocks and Large Stocks groups. That's with *half* your portfolio safely invested in large, conservative market-leading companies paying high dividends.

Conversely, when growth stocks are getting clobbered, the conservative, high-yielding stocks from cornerstone value buffer the portfolio's performance. Cornerstone growth really suffered during the bear market of 1973–1975, but the Market Leaders from cornerstone value fared much better. Splitting your money between the two strategies allowed you to do better than both the Large Stocks and All Stocks universes during the two-year debacle.

Table 20-1. Annual Performance of All Stocks Versus Cornerstone Growth, Cornerstone Value, and Investing 50 Percent in Each Strategy with Annual Rebalancing

Year ending	All Stocks	Cornerstone value	Cornerstone growth	United
31-Dec-53	2.90%	1.20%	0.40%	0.80%
31-Dec-54	47.00%	52.50%	56.70%	54.60%
31-Dec-55	20.70%	28.10%	30.40%	29.25%
31-Dec-56	17.00%	14.80%	18.00%	16.40%
31-Dec-57	−7.10%	−13.50%	−17.90%	−15.70%
31-Dec-58	55.00%	44.90%	52.80%	48.85%
31-Dec-59	23.00%	9.60%	24.10%	16.85%
31-Dec-60	6.10%	−0.03%	12.60%	6.29%
31-Dec-61	31.20%	24.40%	51.10%	37.75%
31-Dec-62	−12.00%	−2.60%	−17.20%	−9.90%
31-Dec-63	18.00%	18.80%	20.80%	19.80%
31-Dec-64	16.30%	20.30%	30.00%	25.15%
31-Dec-65	22.60%	17.60%	44.10%	30.85%
31-Dec-66	−5.20%	−10.20%	−0.10%	−5.15%
31-Dec-67	41.10%	23.70%	83.30%	53.50%
31-Dec-68	27.40%	26.50%	50.50%	38.50%
31-Dec-69	−18.50%	−15.00%	−28.10%	−21.55%
31-Dec-70	−5.80%	11.30%	−2.60%	4.35%
31-Dec-71	21.30%	15.80%	32.10%	23.95%
31-Dec-72	11.00%	14.00%	19.70%	16.85%
31-Dec-73	−27.20%	−5.90%	−27.50%	−16.70%
31-Dec-74	−27.90%	−12.30%	−29.10%	−20.70%
31-Dec-75	55.90%	58.20%	37.60%	47.90%
31-Dec-76	35.60%	39.20%	32.50%	35.85%
31-Dec-77	6.90%	3.30%	26.40%	14.85%
31-Dec-78	12.20%	3.30%	38.30%	20.80%
31-Dec-79	34.30%	25.60%	38.70%	32.15%
31-Dec-80	31.50%	20.30%	62.70%	41.50%
31-Dec-81	1.70%	12.80%	−9.00%	1.90%
31-Dec-82	22.50%	19.60%	37.10%	28.35%
31-Dec-83	28.10%	38.60%	32.70%	35.65%
31-Dec-84	−3.40%	4.70%	2.00%	1.35%
31-Dec-85	30.80%	35.00%	42.50%	38.75%
31-Dec-86	13.10%	20.60%	17.70%	19.15%
31-Dec-87	−1.30%	11.60%	−5.40%	3.10%
31-Dec-88	21.20%	26.50%	29.70%	28.10%
31-Dec-89	21.40%	37.60%	23.80%	30.70%
31-Dec-90	−13.80%	−7.00%	−3.30%	−5.15%
31-Dec-91	39.80%	36.90%	51.40%	44.15%
31-Dec-92	13.80%	11.60%	25.50%	18.55%
31-Dec-93	16.60%	20.40%	30.30%	25.35%
31-Dec-94	−3.40%	4.80%	−5.30%	−0.25%
31-Dec-95	27.00%	26.70%	18.20%	22.45%
31-Dec-96	18.30%	21.90%	31.52%	26.71%
Arithmetic average	15.13%	16.73%	21.72%	19.23%
Standard variation	19.70%	17.14%	25.59%	19.99%

Table 20-2. Summary Return Results for Cornerstone Growth and Cornerstone Value plus Results of Investing 50 Percent of the Portfolio into Each Strategy with Annual Rebalancing, December 31, 1952–December 31, 1966

	All Stocks	Cornerstone value	Cornerstone growth	United
Arithmetic average	15.13%	16.73%	21.72%	19.23%
Standard deviation of return	19.70%	17.14%	25.59%	19.99%
Sharpe risk-adjusted ratio	47	64	63	68
3-yr compounded	13.22%	17.41%	13.76%	15.67%
5-yr compounded	14.00%	16.81%	19.21%	18.12%
10-yr compounded	12.92%	18.32%	18.27%	18.43%
15-yr compounded	14.44%	19.89%	20.31%	20.22%
20-yr compounded	14.97%	18.05%	22.45%	20.53%
25-yr compounded	12.74%	17.58%	18.13%	18.17%
30-yr compounded	12.43%	16.52%	18.54%	17.91%
35-yr compounded	11.64%	15.26%	17.79%	16.88%
40-yr compounded	12.62%	14.76%	18.25%	16.83%
Compound annual return	13.35%	15.47%	18.82%	17.44%
$10,000 becomes:	$2,481,517	$5,595,680	$19,748,214	$11,817,256
Maximum return	55.90%	58.20%	83.30%	54.60%
Minimum return	−27.90%	−15.00%	−29.10%	−21.55%
Maximum expected return*	54.53%	51.01%	72.90%	59.21%
Minimum expected return**	−24.27%	−17.55%	−29.46%	−20.75%

*Maximum expected return is average return plus 2 times the standard deviation.

**Minimum expected return is average return minus 2 times the standard deviation.

Table 20-3. Base Rates for All Stocks and Combined Cornerstone Growth and Value Strategies, 1952–1996

Item	United cornerstone strategies beat All Stocks	Percent
Single-year return	35 out of 44	80.00%
Rolling 5-year compound return	34 out of 40	85.00%
Rolling 10-year compound return	35 out of 35	100.00%

The United Strategy Also
Outperforms Large Stocks

We used the All Stocks universe in our first comparison because it out-performed Large Stocks over time, so it's no surprise that the combined strategies also handily beat Large Stocks. Tables 20-4 and 20-5 compare the united strategies with the Large Stocks universe. In all instances, the combined portfolio did vastly better than Large Stocks. Table 20-6 shows the base rates, with the united growth and value strategy beating Large Stocks in 36 of the 44 one-year periods, and 100 percent of the time over rolling 5- and 10-year periods.

Implications

Table 20-7 compares the returns of the united cornerstone strategies with the All Stocks and Large Stocks universes by decade, and Tables 20-8 and 20-9 show the rolling 5- and 10-year returns versus All Stocks. The results are charted in Figures 20-1 and 20-2. This is truly an impressive strategy. Uniting growth and value stocks is the best way to diversify your portfolio and improve your risk-adjusted return. The 50-50 split is most appropriate for younger investors with average risk tolerance. As retirement approaches, you should reduce the amount of money you allocate to the growth strategy and increase the allocation to the more conservative stocks from cornerstone value. Other than for investors very near retirement, *all* investors benefit from diversifying their investments by style. Even the most aggressive younger investors should have some money in the cornerstone value strategy, bolstering the portfolio during the inevitable periods when larger stocks outperform their smaller brethren from cornerstone growth.

Higher returns at reduced levels of risk are the most important thing that style diversification achieves. Wall Streeters often joke that you should decide how to invest on the basis of whether you want to eat well or sleep well. Splitting your portfolio between growth and value strategies lets you do both, because it provides vastly higher absolute returns than the market at similar levels of risk.

Table 20-4. Annual Performance of Large Stocks Versus Cornerstone Growth, Cornerstone Value, and Investing 50 Percent in Each Strategy with Annual Rebalancing

Year ending	Large Stocks	Cornerstone value	Cornerstone growth	United
31-Dec-53	2.30%	1.20%	0.40%	0.80%
31-Dec-54	44.90%	52.50%	56.70%	54.60%
31-Dec-55	21.20%	28.10%	30.40%	29.25%
31-Dec-56	9.60%	14.80%	18.00%	16.40%
31-Dec-57	−6.90%	−13.50%	−17.90%	−15.70%
31-Dec-58	42.10%	44.90%	52.80%	48.85%
31-Dec-59	9.90%	9.60%	24.10%	16.85%
31-Dec-60	4.80%	−0.03%	12.60%	6.29%
31-Dec-61	27.50%	24.40%	51.10%	37.75%
31-Dec-62	−8.90%	−2.60%	−17.20%	−9.90%
31-Dec-63	19.50%	18.80%	20.80%	19.80%
31-Dec-64	15.30%	20.30%	30.00%	25.15%
31-Dec-65	16.20%	17.60%	44.10%	30.85%
31-Dec-66	−4.90%	−10.20%	−0.10%	−5.15%
31-Dec-67	21.30%	23.70%	83.30%	53.50%
31-Dec-68	16.80%	26.50%	50.50%	38.50%
31-Dec-69	−9.90%	−15.00%	−28.10%	−21.55%
31-Dec-70	−0.20%	11.30%	−2.60%	4.35%
31-Dec-71	17.30%	15.80%	32.10%	23.95%
31-Dec-72	14.90%	14.00%	19.70%	16.85%
31-Dec-73	−18.90%	−5.90%	−27.50%	−16.70%
31-Dec-74	−26.70%	−12.30%	−29.10%	−20.70%
31-Dec-75	43.10%	58.20%	37.60%	47.90%
31-Dec-76	28.00%	39.20%	32.50%	35.85%
31-Dec-77	−2.50%	3.30%	26.40%	14.85%
31-Dec-78	8.10%	3.30%	38.30%	20.80%
31-Dec-79	27.30%	25.60%	38.70%	32.15%
31-Dec-80	30.80%	20.30%	62.70%	41.50%
31-Dec-81	0.60%	12.80%	−9.00%	1.90%
31-Dec-82	19.90%	19.60%	37.10%	28.35%
31-Dec-83	23.80%	38.60%	32.70%	35.65%
31-Dec-84	−0.40%	4.70%	−2.00%	1.35%
31-Dec-85	19.50%	35.00%	42.50%	38.75%
31-Dec-86	32.20%	20.60%	17.70%	19.15%
31-Dec-87	3.30%	11.60%	−5.40%	3.10%
31-Dec-88	19.00%	26.50%	29.70%	28.10%
31-Dec-89	26.00%	37.60%	23.80%	30.70%
31-Dec-90	−8.70%	−7.00%	−3.30%	−5.15%
31-Dec-91	33.00%	36.90%	51.40%	44.15%
31-Dec-92	8.70%	11.60%	25.50%	18.55%
31-Dec-93	16.30%	20.40%	30.30%	25.35%
31-Dec-94	−1.90%	4.80%	−5.30%	−0.25%
31-Dec-95	28.50%	26.70%	18.20%	22.45%
31-Dec-96	18.70%	21.90%	31.52%	26.71%
Arithmetic average	13.19%	16.73%	21.72%	19.23%
Standard deviation	16.18%	17.14%	25.59%	19.99%

Table 20-5. Summary Return Results for Cornerstone Growth and Cornerstone Value plus Results of Investing 50 Percent of the Portfolio into Each Strategy with Annual Rebalancing, December 31, 1952–December 31, 1996

	Large Stocks	Cornerstone value	Cornerstone growth	United
Arithmetic average	13.19%	16.73%	21.72%	19.23%
Standard deviation of return	16.18%	17.14%	25.59%	19.99%
Sharpe risk-adjusted ratio	45	64	63	68
3-yr compounded	14.38%	17.41%	13.76%	15.67%
5-yr compounded	13.60%	16.81%	19.21%	18.12%
10-yr compounded	13.53%	18.32%	18.27%	18.43%
15-yr compounded	15.16%	19.89%	20.31%	20.22%
20-yr compounded	14.37%	18.05%	22.45%	20.53%
25-yr compounded	12.34%	17.58%	18.13%	18.17%
30-yr compounded	11.67%	16.52%	18.54%	17.91%
35-yr compounded	10.96%	15.26%	17.79%	16.88%
40-yr compounded	11.36%	14.76%	18.25%	16.83%
Compound annual return	11.98%	15.47%	18.82%	17.44%
$10,000 becomes:	$1,455,322	$5,595,680	$19,748,214	$11,817,256
Maximum return	44.90%	58.20%	83.30%	54.60%
Minimum return	−26.70%	−15.00%	−29.10%	−21.55%
Maximum expected return*	45.55%	51.01%	72.90%	59.21%
Minimum expected return**	−19.17%	−17.55%	−29.46%	−20.75%

*Maximum expected return is average return plus 2 times the standard deviation.
**Minimum expected return is average return minus 2 times the standard deviation.

Table 20-6. Base Rates for Large Stocks and United Growth and Value Cornerstone Strategies, 1952–1996

Item	United cornerstone strategies beat Large Stocks	Percent
Single-year return	36 out of 44	82.00%
Rolling 5-year compound return	40 out of 40	100.00%
Rolling 10-year compound return	35 out of 35	100.00%

Table 20-7. Compound Annual Rates of Return by Decade

Portfolio	1950s*	1960s	1970s	1980s	1990s**
Large Stocks	14.92%	8.99%	6.99%	16.89%	12.61%
United cornerstone growth and value strategies	17.58%	15.14%	13.91%	21.93%	17.78%
All Stocks	19.00%	11.09%	8.53%	15.85%	12.78%

*Returns for 1953–1959.
**Returns for 1990–1996.

Table 20-8. Rolling 5-Year Returns, United Cornerstone Growth and Value Strategies Versus All Stocks

5 years ending	All Stocks	United cornerstone strategies	Difference
31-Dec-59	20.12%	17.14%	−2.98%
31-Dec-60	17.07%	12.65%	−4.42%
31-Dec-61	19.78%	16.51%	−3.27%
31-Dec-62	18.49%	18.07%	−0.42%
31-Dec-63	12.20%	13.05%	0.85%
31-Dec-64	10.95%	14.61%	3.67%
31-Dec-65	14.20%	19.48%	5.28%
31-Dec-66	7.02%	10.89%	3.87%
31-Dec-67	17.61%	23.36%	5.74%
31-Dec-68	19.43%	26.99%	7.56%
31-Dec-69	11.23%	15.66%	4.43%
31-Dec-70	5.52%	10.54%	5.02%
31-Dec-71	10.85%	16.62%	5.77%
31-Dec-72	5.66%	10.43%	4.77%
31-Dec-73	−5.53%	−0.25%	5.28%
31-Dec-74	−7.81%	−0.03%	7.78%
31-Dec-75	1.96%	7.19%	5.23%
31-Dec-76	4.26%	9.17%	4.92%
31-Dec-77	3.47%	8.80%	5.32%
31-Dec-78	12.82%	17.19%	4.37%
31-Dec-79	27.77%	29.80%	2.02%
31-Dec-80	23.49%	28.65%	5.16%
31-Dec-81	16.59%	21.46%	4.87%
31-Dec-82	19.81%	24.19%	4.38%
31-Dec-83	23.03%	27.11%	4.08%
31-Dec-84	15.18%	20.54%	5.35%
31-Dec-85	15.06%	20.06%	5.00%
31-Dec-86	17.53%	23.88%	6.35%
31-Dec-87	12.56%	18.57%	6.01%
31-Dec-88	11.32%	17.22%	5.90%
31-Dec-89	16.53%	23.33%	6.81%
31-Dec-90	7.20%	14.30%	7.10%
31-Dec-91	11.84%	18.74%	6.89%
31-Dec-92	15.07%	22.10%	7.03%
31-Dec-93	14.19%	21.57%	7.38%
31-Dec-94	9.09%	15.17%	6.09%
31-Dec-95	17.88%	21.21%	3.34%
31-Dec-96	14.00%	18.12%	4.12%
Arithmetic average	12.83%	17.21%	4.39%

Table 20-9. Rolling 10-Year Returns, United Cornerstone Growth and Value Strategies Versus All Stocks

10 years ending	All Stocks	United cornerstone strategies	Difference
31-Dec-64	15.44%	15.87%	0.43%
31-Dec-65	15.63%	16.01%	0.39%
31-Dec-66	13.22%	13.66%	0.45%
31-Dec-67	18.05%	20.68%	2.63%
31-Dec-68	15.76%	19.82%	4.06%
31-Dec-69	11.09%	15.14%	4.05%
31-Dec-70	9.78%	14.93%	5.15%
31-Dec-71	8.92%	13.72%	4.80%
31-Dec-72	11.48%	16.71%	5.24%
31-Dec-73	6.22%	12.55%	6.33%
31-Dec-74	1.26%	7.53%	6.27%
31-Dec-75	3.72%	8.85%	5.13%
31-Dec-76	7.50%	12.84%	5.33%
31-Dec-77	4.56%	9.61%	5.05%
31-Dec-78	3.24%	8.12%	4.88%
31-Dec-79	8.53%	13.91%	5.38%
31-Dec-80	12.21%	17.43%	5.22%
31-Dec-81	10.25%	15.15%	4.90%
31-Dec-82	11.34%	16.24%	4.90%
31-Dec-83	17.82%	22.05%	4.23%
31-Dec-84	21.31%	25.08%	3.77%
31-Dec-85	19.20%	24.28%	5.08%
31-Dec-86	17.06%	22.66%	5.61%
31-Dec-87	16.13%	21.35%	5.22%
31-Dec-88	17.03%	22.06%	5.03%
31-Dec-89	15.85%	21.93%	6.07%
31-Dec-90	11.06%	17.15%	6.09%
31-Dec-91	14.65%	21.28%	6.63%
31-Dec-92	13.81%	20.32%	6.51%
31-Dec-93	12.74%	19.37%	6.63%
31-Dec-94	12.74%	19.18%	6.44%
31-Dec-95	12.41%	17.70%	5.29%
31-Dec-96	12.92%	18.43%	5.51%
Arithmetic average	12.21%	17.02%	4.81%

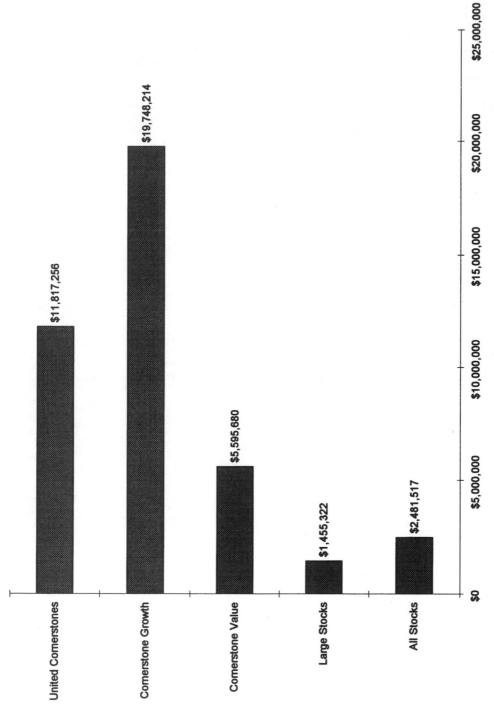

Figure 20-1. December 31, 1996, value of $10,000 invested on December 31, 1952.

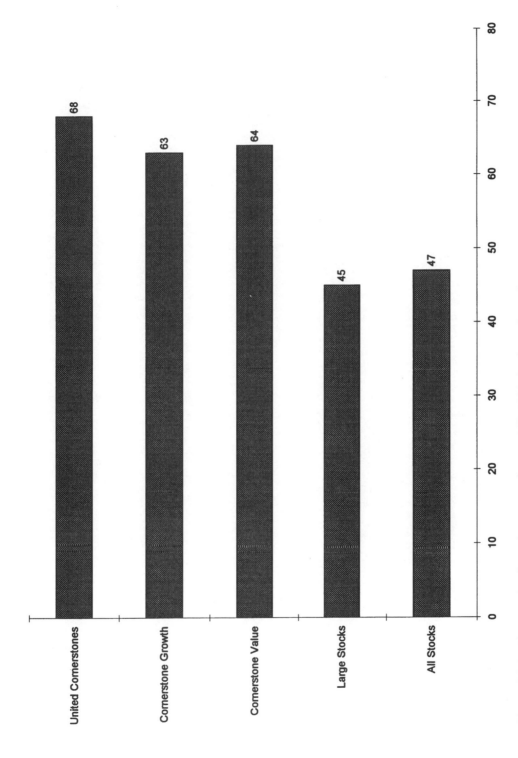

Figure 20-2. Sharpe risk-adjusted return rankings, 1952–1996. (Higher is better.)

21

Ranking the Strategies

*I know of no way of judging of the future but by
the past.*   —PATRICK HENRY

It's time to rank all the strategies' returns on both an absolute and a
risk-adjusted basis. Several of our strategies use 5-year variables, so for
simplicity's sake we'll compare returns starting December 31, 1954.
(Because of the missing three years, the numbers are often different
from those in previous chapters.) We'll also rank only the strategies,
leaving out the deciles for each individual ratio. While the rankings
may differ slightly, the same lessons emerge.

The Results

Our 42 years of data prove that the market follows a purposeful stride,
not a random walk. The stock market consistently rewards some strategies and consistently punishes others. The strategies found near the top
or the bottom of our list possess similar attributes that are easily iden-
tified. Each of the five best performing strategies, for example, includes
a relative strength criterion. All but one of the five worst performing
strategies buy stocks that investors have bid to unsustainable prices,
giving them astronomical price-to-earnings, price-to-book, price-to-
sales, or price-to-cashflow ratios. These factors usually reflect high
hopes on the part of investors. History shows that high hopes are

dashed, and that investors are better off buying reasonably priced stocks with good relative strength.

All the best performing strategies are riskier than the market as a whole, but a handful do *much better* than the market while taking only slightly more risk. Most of the *worst* performing strategies are actually riskier than the best performing strategies. The results prove that the market doesn't always award high returns to portfolios with higher risk.

Absolute Returns

Table 21-1 ranks all the strategies by absolute return, and Figures 21-1 and 21-2 show the five best and worst performers. The low price-to-sales, high relative strength strategy and the cornerstone growth strategy, which buys stocks with persistent earnings gains, low price-to-sales ratios, and strong relative strength, were the best performing of all the strategies. Low price-to-sales, high relative strength turned $10,000 invested in 1954 into $12,999,698, whereas the cornerstone growth strategy nearly duplicated that return, turning $10,000 invested on December 31, 1954 into $12,552,352 by the end of 1996, a compound return of 18.52 percent. Again, note that the top five strategies buy stocks with the best relative price strength. Relative strength is one of the criteria in all 10 of the top performing strategies, proving the maxim that you should never fight the tape.

Fighting the tape leads to our worst performing strategy, which buys the 50 stocks from All Stocks with the worst one-year price performance. A $10,000 investment in these stocks on December 31, 1954 and annually rebalanced was worth just $29,666 by the end of 1996, a pathetic return of 2.62 percent a year! Heed the market's advice and avoid last year's biggest losers.

The other four losing equity strategies buy stocks in which investors' huge expectations have pushed prices to unsustainable levels. This is reflected by the stock's high multiples. With strategies like cornerstone growth available, there's no reason to buy stocks with the highest price-to-earnings, price-to-book, price-to-sales, or price-to-cashflow ratio. The odds for such stocks are about as bad as the story is good. Investors who buy these stocks always brag about the handful that work out and conveniently forget the majority that don't. The evidence is painfully clear: If you habitually buy stocks with good stories but the highest multiples, you'll do much worse than the market.

In the absence of stories, investors look at the base rates. But let one Netscape in the door, and many investors will jettison common sense and sound research, believing it's different this time. It isn't.

Table 21-1. Summary Returns for All Strategies, December 31, 1954–December 31, 1996, Ranked by Absolute Return

Strategy	$10,000 becomes	Compound return	Standard deviation	Sharpe ratio
PSR <1, high rel. str., All Stocks	$12,999,698	18.62%	25.64%	61
Earnings yield >5, high rel. str., All Stocks	$12,570,451	18.52%	24.48%	61
Cornerstone growth, All Stocks	$12,552,352	18.52%	25.41%	61
Pbook <1, high rel. str., All Stocks	$10,258,105	17.95%	23.36%	60
United cornerstone strategies	$7,583,097	17.10%	19.50%	66
ROE >15, high rel. str., All Stocks	$7,582,171	17.10%	26.59%	54
EPS higher than last year, best rel. str., All Stocks	$6,890,629	16.84%	28.19%	52
5-yr EPS ch >mean, Pmargin >mean, EPS higher than last year, best rel. str., All Stocks	$6,019,821	16.46%	22.23%	57
Yield >mean, positive rel. str., lowest PSR, All Stocks	$5,753,941	16.34%	21.98%	52
1-yr EPS ch >25%, high rel. str., All Stocks	$5,578,081	16.25%	28.56%	49
Pbook <1.5, yield >mean, PE <mean, lowest Pcfl, All Stocks	$4,624,623	15.73%	22.85%	52
Low PSR, All Stocks	$4,311,223	15.54%	25.66%	49
$25M <capitalization <$100M	$4,176,424	15.45%	30.44%	44
Market Leaders, low Pcfl	$4,078,918	15.39%	19.00%	57
Cornerstone value	$3,625,789	15.06%	16.47%	62
PE <20, high rel. str., Large Stocks	$3,581,736	15.03%	19.05%	54
Low Pbook, All Stocks	$3,297,096	14.80%	25.17%	46
EPS higher than last year, high rel. str., Large Stocks	$3,191,986	14.72%	21.95%	48
Cornerstone growth, Large Stocks	$3,189,965	14.71%	17.50%	58
Low Pcfl, All Stocks	$3,076,821	14.61%	19.78%	51
Market Leaders, low PE	$3,017,323	14.56%	19.93%	50
PSR <1, high rel. str., Large Stocks	$2,968,702	14.52%	18.86%	54
Low Pbook, Large Stocks	$2,775,184	14.33%	19.40%	52
High 1-yr rel. str., Large Stocks	$2,717,072	14.28%	22.24%	47
1-yr EPS ch >mean, Pmargin >mean, EPS higher than last year, best rel. str., Large stocks	$2,639,136	14.20%	20.19%	47
Low Pcfl, Large Stocks	$2,476,780	14.02%	24.97%	43
High 1-yr rel. str., All Stocks	$2,368,420	13.90%	29.91%	41
Profit Margin >20, best rel. str., All Stocks	$2,230,164	13.74%	23.02%	42
ROE >15, high rel. str., Large Stocks	$2,220,269	13.73%	21.94%	43
Low PSR, Large Stocks	$2,175,915	13.67%	20.36%	47
Low PE, Large Stocks	$2,122,212	13.61%	20.60%	44
$250M <capitalization <$500M	$2,042,964	13.50%	20.92%	46
Small Stocks	$2,022,787	13.48%	21.81%	44
$100M <capitalization <$250M	$2,007,775	13.46%	24.37%	41
Market Leaders	$1,921,677	13.34%	16.59%	50
High yield, Large Stocks	$1,732,216	13.06%	16.63%	50

(Continued)

Table 21-1. Summary Returns for All Strategies,
December 31, 1954–December 31, 1996, Ranked by Absolute Return (*Continued*)

Strategy	$10,000 becomes	Compound return	Standard deviation	Sharpe ratio
All Stocks	*$1,640,531*	*12.91%*	*19.46%*	*44*
High ROE, All Stocks	$1,417,424	12.52%	25.84%	37
$500M <Capitalization <$1B	$1,231,545	12.14%	18.72%	42
Low PE, All Stocks	$1,198,019	12.07%	24.43%	34
Low 1-yr EPS gain, All Stocks	$1,033,974	11.68%	23.42%	36
Capitalization >$1B	$985,177	11.55%	15.77%	41
Large Stocks	*$981,782*	*11.54%*	*15.72%*	*41*
S&P 500	$971,901	11.51%	15.96%	39
Low 1-yr EPS gain, Large Stocks	$889,735	11.28%	17.55%	40
High yield, All Stocks	$840,162	11.13%	20.91%	34
50 highest 1-yr EPS gain, All Stocks	$810,609	11.03%	26.33%	31
High Pmargin, Large Stocks	$716,131	10.90%	15.81%	36
High Pmargin, All Stocks	$691,852	10.61%	20.76%	31
High ROE, Large Stocks	$662,357	10.50%	18.86%	33
High 5-yr EPS gain, Large Stocks	$613,441	10.30%	21.59%	28
Market Leaders, high PE	$599,558	10.24%	16.69%	34
High Pbook, Large Stocks	$583,955	10.17%	23.06%	27
High 5-yr EPS gain, All Stocks	$534,963	9.94%	26.57%	27
High Pcfl, Large Stocks	$488,983	9.70%	22.01%	28
High PSR, Large Stocks	$454,873	9.51%	20.99%	25
High PE, Large Stocks	$429,753	9.37%	20.38%	26
High 1-yr EPS gain, Large Stocks	$400,758	9.19%	18.83%	25
High PE, All Stocks	$368,197	8.97%	26.75%	23
Low 1-yr rel. str., Large Stocks	$367,778	8.96%	19.98%	25
High Pbook, All Stocks	$236,711	7.83%	28.79%	20
High Pcfl, All Stocks	$224,741	7.69%	27.98%	17
Intermediate-term bonds	$152,806	6.71%	6.70%	17
90-day T-bills	$99,854	5.63%	2.71%	0
High PSR, All Stocks	$64,220	4.53%	27.79%	5
Low 1-yr rel. str., All Stocks	$29,666	2.62%	26.33%	−1

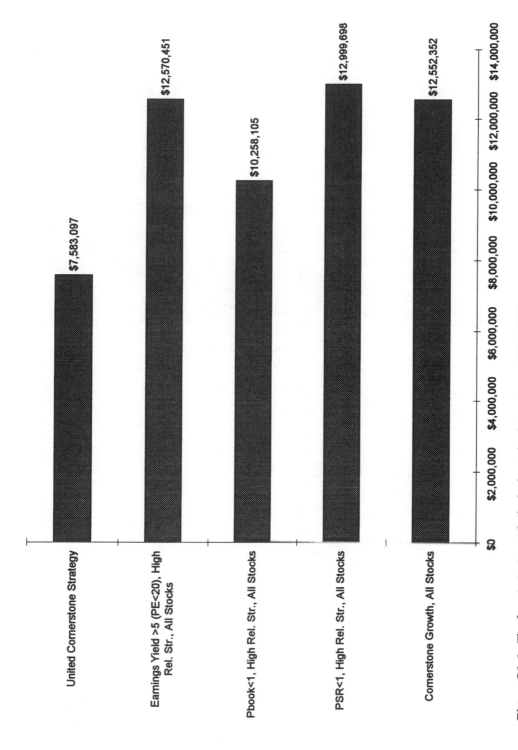

Figure 21-1. The five strategies with the highest absolute returns, 1954–1996.

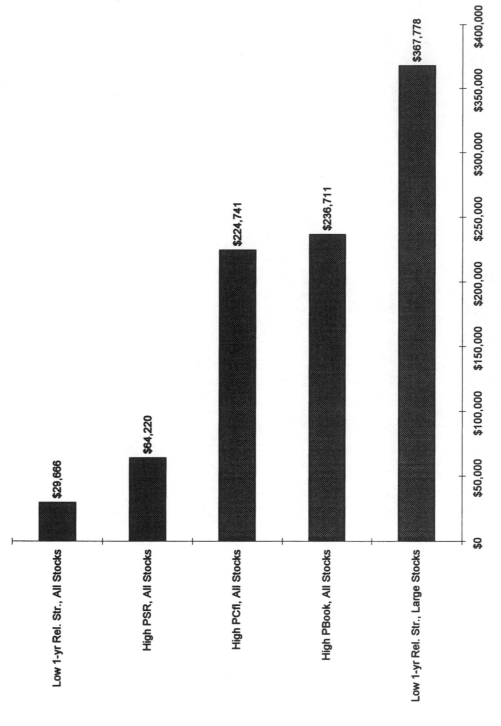

Figure 21-2. The five strategies with the worst absolute performance, 1954–1996.

Risk

Table 21-2 ranks the strategies by standard deviation, and Figures 21-3 and 21-4 show the five strategies with the highest and lowest risk. Buying small stocks in the $25 million to $100 million category is the riskiest strategy, with a standard deviation of 30.44 percent. Such risk is unacceptable, but can be dramatically lowered by adding other factors. Four of the five strategies with the highest standard deviations offer good absolute performance, at least. The other one, high price-to-book stocks, adds insult to injury by giving investors both high risk *and* dismal returns.

All these strategies should be avoided, because the risk is too high. Indeed, you should never use a strategy with an annual standard deviation above 26 percent *unless* its performance is so fantastic that it pushes the Sharpe ratio well above the All Stocks ratio of 44. Unless the potential rewards are vastly higher than the market, the emotional toll of high risk strategies outweighs their benefits. *No one* should invest an entire portfolio in the riskiest strategies, no matter how good their absolute return. You'll capitulate to your fears, usually near a strategy's bottom. This brings nothing but misery and will probably send you into the arms of the nearest S&P 500 index fund. The best use of high risk strategies is to blend them with lower risk ones, bringing overall risk to acceptable levels.

The five equity strategies with the lowest risk all come from the Large Stocks universe. The least risky is the Large Stocks universe itself. This strategy has a standard deviation of 15.72 percent. Of the five lowest risk strategies, only cornerstone value—buying Market Leaders with high dividend yields—*also* provides high absolute returns. The cornerstone value strategy proves that investors needn't take huge risks to handily outperform the market and should be considered by anyone considering a large capitalization index fund.

Risk-Adjusted Return

Table 21-3 ranks the strategies by their Sharpe ratios, and Figures 21-5 and 21-6 show the five strategies with the best and worst risk-adjusted returns. This is the most important table of all, since it puts return into perspective. Buying the 50 stocks from All Stocks with the best relative strength is a good example. This strategy beats All Stocks on an absolute basis, but fails when risk is taken into account. Risk-adjusted returns give you the best indication of whether a strategy is worth the inevitable hills and valleys, and teaches you how to get the most bang for your buck.

Table 21-2. Summary Returns for All Strategies, December 31, 1954–December 31, 1996, Ranked by Risk

Strategy	$10,000 becomes	Compound return	Standard deviation	Sharpe ratio
$25M <capitalization <$100M	$4,176,424	15.45%	30.44%	44
High 1-yr rel. str., All Stocks	$2,368,420	13.90%	29.91%	41
High Pbook, All Stocks	$236,711	7.83%	28.79%	20
1-yr EPS ch>25%, high rel. str., All Stocks	$5,578,081	16.25%	28.56%	49
EPS higher than last year, best rel. str., All Stocks	$6,890,629	16.84%	28.19%	52
High Pcfl, All Stocks	$224,741	7.69%	27.98%	17
High PSR, All Stocks	$64,220	4.53%	27.79%	8
High PE, All Stocks	$368,197	8.97%	26.75%	23
ROE >15, high rel. str., All Stocks	$7,582,171	17.10%	26.59%	54
High 5-yr EPS gain, All Stocks	$534,963	9.94%	26.57%	27
50 highest 1-yr EPS gain, All Stocks	$810,609	11.03%	26.33%	31
Low 1-yr rel. str., All Stocks	$29,666	2.62%	26.33%	−1
High ROE, All Stocks	$1,417,424	12.52%	25.84%	37
Low PSR, All Stocks	$4,311,223	15.54%	25.66%	49
PSR <1, high rel. str., All Stocks	$12,999,698	18.62%	25.64%	61
Cornerstone growth, All Stocks	$12,552,352	18.52%	25.41%	61
Low Pbook, All Stocks	$3,297,096	14.80%	25.17%	46
Low Pcfl, Large Stocks	$2,476,780	14.02%	24.97%	43
Earnings yield >5, high rel. str., All Stocks	$12,570,451	18.52%	24.48%	61
Low PE, All Stocks	$1,198,019	12.07%	24.43%	34
$100M <capitalization <$250M	$2,007,775	13.46%	24.37%	41
Low 1-yr EPS gain, All Stocks	$1,033,974	11.68%	23.42%	36
Pbook <1, high rel. str., All Stocks	$10,258,105	17.95%	23.36%	60
High Pbook, Large Stocks	$583,955	10.17%	23.06%	27
Profit margin >20, best rel. str., All Stocks	$2,230,164	13.74%	23.02%	42
Pbook <1.5, yield >mean, PE <mean, lowest Pcfl, All Stocks	$4,624,623	15.73%	22.85%	52
High 1-yr rel. str., Large Stocks	$2,717,072	14.28%	22.24%	47
5-yr EPS ch>mean, Pmargin>mean, EPS higher than last year, best rel. str., All Stocks	$6,019,821	16.46%	22.23%	57
High Pcfl, Large Stocks	$488,983	9.70%	22.01%	28
Yield >mean, positive rel. str., lowest PSR, All Stocks	$5,753,941	16.34%	21.98%	52
EPS higher than last year, high rel. str., Large Stocks	$3,191,986	14.72%	21.95%	48
ROE >15, high rel. str., Large Stocks	$2,220,269	13.73%	21.94%	43
Small Stocks	$2,022,787	13.48%	21.81%	44
High 5-yr EPS gain, Large Stocks	$613,441	10.30%	21.59%	28
High PSR, Large Stocks	$454,873	9.51%	20.99%	25
$250M <capitalization <$500M	$2,042,964	13.50%	20.92%	46

Table 21-2. Summary Returns for All Strategies,
December 31, 1954–December 31, 1996, Ranked by Risk (*Continued*)

Strategy	$10,000 becomes	Compound return	Standard deviation	Sharpe ratio
High yield, All Stocks	$840,162	11.13%	20.91%	34
High Pmargin, All Stocks	$691,852	10.61%	20.76%	31
Low PE, Large Stocks	$2,122,212	13.61%	20.60%	44
High PE, Large Stocks	$429,753	9.37%	20.38%	26
Low PSR, Large Stocks	$2,175,915	13.67%	20.36%	47
1-yr EPS ch >mean, Pmargin >mean, EPS higher than last yr, best rel. str., Large Stocks	$2,639,136	14.20%	20.19%	47
Low 1-yr rel. str., Large Stocks	$367,778	8.96%	19.98%	25
Market Leaders, low PE	$3,017,323	14.56%	19.93%	50
Low Pcfl, All Stocks	$3,076,821	14.61%	19.78%	51
United cornerstone strategies	$7,583,097	17.10%	19.50%	66
All Stocks	*$1,640,531*	*12.91%*	*19.46%*	*44*
Low Pbook, Large Stocks	$2,775,184	14.33%	19.40%	52
PE <20, high rel. str., Large Stocks	$3,581,736	15.03%	19.05%	54
Market Leaders, low Pcfl	$4,078,918	15.39%	19.00%	57
PSR <1, high rel. str., Large Stocks	$2,968,702	14.52%	18.86%	54
High ROE, Large Stocks	$662,357	10.50%	18.86%	33
High 1-yr EPS gain, Large Stocks	$400,758	9.19%	18.83%	25
$500M <capitalization <$1B	$1,231,545	12.14%	18.72%	42
Low 1-yr EPS gain, Large Stocks	$889,735	11.28%	17.55%	40
Cornerstone growth, Large Stocks	$3,189,965	14.71%	17.50%	58
Market Leaders, high PE	$599,558	10.24%	16.69%	34
High yield, Large Stocks	$1,732,216	13.06%	16.63%	50
Market Leaders	$1,921,677	13.34%	16.59%	50
Cornerstone value	$3,625,789	15.06%	16.47%	62
S&P 500	$971,901	11.51%	15.96%	39
High Pmargin, Large Stocks	$716,131	10.90%	15.81%	36
Capitalization >$1B	$985,177	11.55%	15.77%	41
Large Stocks	*$981,782*	*11.54%*	*15.72%*	*41*
Intermediate-term bonds	$152,806	6.71%	6.70%	17
90-day T-bills	$99,854	5.63%	2.71%	0

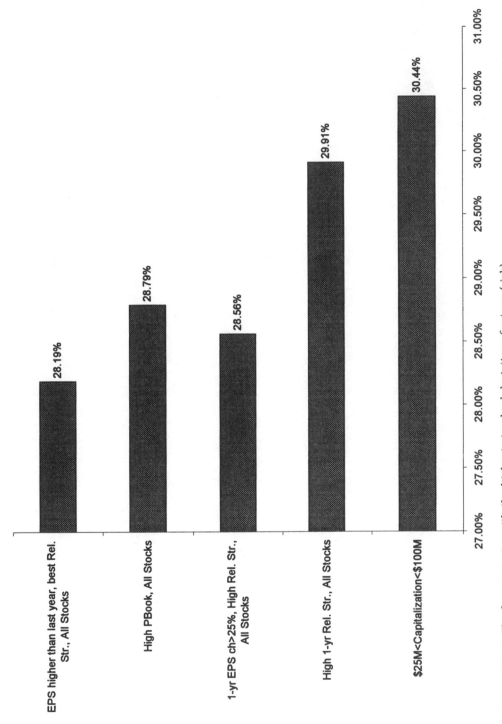

Figure 21-3. The five strategies with the highest standard deviation of return (risk), 1954–1996.

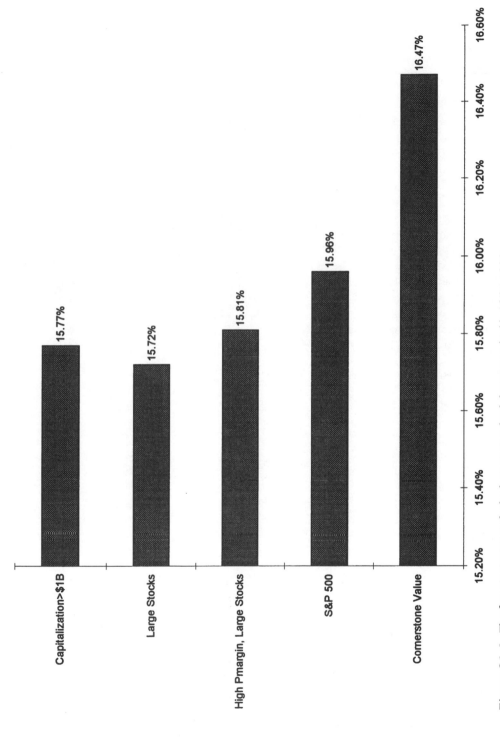

Figure 21-4. The five strategies with the lowest standard deviations (risk), 1954–1996.

Table 21-3. Summary Returns for All Strategies,
December 31, 1954–December 31, 1996, Ranked by Sharpe Ratio.
(Higher is better.)

Strategy	$10,000 becomes	Compound return	Standard deviation	Sharpe ratio
United cornerstone strategies	$7,583,097	17.10%	19.50%	66
Cornerstone value	$3,625,789	15.06%	16.47%	62
PSR <1, high rel. str., All Stocks	$12,999,698	18.62%	25.64%	61
Cornerstone growth, All Stocks	$12,552,352	18.52%	25.41%	61
Earnings yield >5, high rel. str., All Stocks	$12,570,451	18.52%	24.48%	61
Pbook <1, high rel. str., All Stocks	$10,258,105	17.95%	23.36%	60
Cornerstone growth, Large Stocks	$3,189,965	14.71%	17.50%	58
5-yr EPS ch >mean, Pmargin >mean, EPS higher than last year, best rel. str., All Stocks	$6,019,821	16.46%	22.23%	57
Market Leaders, low Pcfl	$4,078,918	15.39%	19.00%	57
ROE >15, high rel. str., All Stocks	$7,582,171	17.10%	26.59%	54
PE <20, high rel. str., Large Stocks	$3,581,736	15.03%	19.05%	54
PSR <1, high rel. str., Large Stocks	$2,968,702	14.52%	18.86%	54
EPS higher than last year, best rel. str., All Stocks	$6,890,629	16.84%	28.19%	52
Pbook <1.5, yield >mean, PE <mean, lowest Pcfl, All Stocks	$4,624,623	15.73%	22.85%	52
Yield >mean, positive rel. str., lowest PSR, All Stocks	$5,753,941	16.34%	21.98%	52
Low Pbook, Large Stocks	$2,775,184	14.33%	19.40%	52
Low Pcfl, All Stocks	$3,076,821	14.61%	19.78%	51
Market Leaders, low PE	$3,017,323	14.56%	19.93%	50
High yield, Large Stocks	$1,732,216	13.06%	16.63%	50
Market Leaders	$1,921,677	13.34%	16.59%	50
1-yr EPS ch >25%, high rel. str., All Stocks	$5,578,081	16.25%	28.56%	49
Low PSR, All Stocks	$4,311,223	15.54%	25.66%	49
EPS higher than last year, high rel. str., Large Stocks	$3,191,986	14.72%	21.95%	48
High 1-yr rel. str., Large Stocks	$2,717,072	14.28%	22.24%	47
Low PSR, Large Stocks	$2,175,915	13.67%	20.36%	47
1-yr EPS ch >mean, Pmargin >mean, EPS higher than last year, best rel. str., Large stocks	$2,639,136	14.20%	20.19%	47
Low Pbook, All Stocks	$3,297,096	14.80%	25.17%	46
$250M <capitalization <$500M	$2,042,964	13.50%	20.92%	46
$25M <capitalization <$100M	$4,176,424	15.45%	30.44%	44
Small Stocks	$2,022,787	13.48%	21.81%	44
Low PE, Large Stocks	$2,122,212	13.61%	20.60%	44
All Stocks	*$1,640,531*	*12.91%*	*19.46%*	*44*
Low Pcfl, Large Stocks	$2,476,780	14.02%	24.97%	43
ROE >15, high rel. str., Large Stocks	$2,220,269	13.73%	21.94%	43
Profit margin >20, best rel. str., All Stocks	$2,230,164	13.74%	23.02%	42

Table 21-3. Summary Returns for All Strategies,
December 31, 1954–December 31, 1996, Ranked by Sharpe Ratio.
(Higher is better.) (*Continued*)

Strategy	$10,000 becomes	Compound return	Standard deviation	Sharpe ratio
$500M <capitalization <$1B	$1,231,545	12.14%	18.72%	42
High 1-yr rel. str., All Stocks	$2,368,420	13.90%	29.91%	41
$100M <capitalization <$250M	$2,007,775	13.46%	24.37%	41
Capitalization >$1B	$985,177	11.55%	15.77%	41
Large Stocks	*$981,782*	*11.54%*	*15.72%*	*41*
Low 1-yr EPS gain, Large Stocks	$889,735	11.28%	17.55%	40
S&P 500	$971,901	11.51%	15.96%	39
High ROE, All Stocks	$1,417,424	12.52%	25.84%	37
Low 1-yr EPS gain, All Stocks	$1,033,974	11.68%	23.42%	36
High Pmargin, Large Stocks	$716,131	10.90%	15.81%	36
Low PE, All Stocks	$1,198,019	12.07%	24.43%	34
High yield, All Stocks	$840,162	11.13%	20.91%	34
Market Leaders, high PE	$599,558	10.24%	16.69%	34
High ROE, Large Stocks	$662,357	10.50%	18.86%	33
50 highest 1-yr EPS gain, All Stocks	$810,609	11.03%	26.33%	31
High Pmargin, All Stocks	$691,852	10.61%	20.76%	31
High Pcfl, Large Stocks	$488,983	9.70%	22.01%	28
High 5-yr EPS gain, Large Stocks	$613,441	10.30%	21.59%	28
High 5-yr EPS gain, All Stocks	$534,963	9.94%	26.57%	27
High Pbook, Large Stocks	$583,955	10.17%	23.06%	27
High PE, Large Stocks	$429,753	9.37%	20.38%	26
High PSR, Large Stocks	$454,873	9.51%	20.99%	25
Low 1-yr rel. str., Large Stocks	$367,778	8.96%	19.98%	25
High 1-yr EPS gain, Large Stocks	$400,758	9.19%	18.83%	25
High PE, All Stocks	$368,197	8.97%	26.75%	23
High Pbook, All Stocks	$236,711	7.83%	28.79%	20
High Pcfl, All Stocks	$224,741	7.69%	27.98%	17
Intermediate-term bonds	$152,806	6.71%	6.70%	17
High PSR, All Stocks	$64,220	4.53%	27.79%	8
90-day T-bills	$99,854	5.63%	2.71%	0
Low 1-yr rel. str., All Stocks	$29,666	2.62%	26.33%	−1

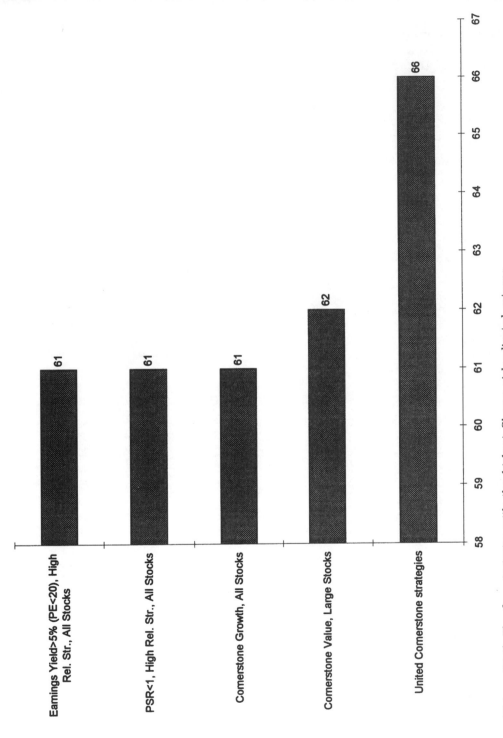

Figure 21-5. The five strategies with the highest Sharpe risk-adjusted returns, 1954-1996.

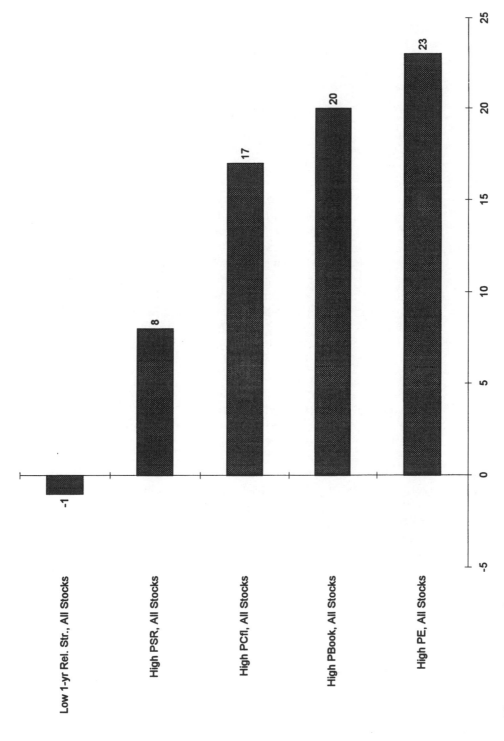

Figure 21-6. The five strategies with the worst Sharpe risk-adjusted returns, 1954–1996.

The united growth and value cornerstone strategies have the highest risk-adjusted return of all the strategies reviewed. This portfolio has a Sharpe ratio of 66, 50 percent higher than All Stocks' 43, yet the risk is the same as for the All Stocks universe. For investors with average risk tolerance, this united strategy is the best way to invest. It covers both growth and value strategies, and is an excellent way to diversify your portfolio.

All the strategies with the best risk-adjusted returns include one or more value criteria. Value criteria act like a chaperone at a party, making sure you don't fall for some sexy stock with a great story. They may keep you from having some short-term fun, but over time they will keep you out of trouble by never letting you overpay for stocks. Except for the stocks selected by the cornerstone value strategy, most of the stocks picked by these top performing strategies aren't household names. The selected stocks are workhorses rather than show horses. There are plenty of buyers for stocks of companies whose activities are continually written up in the major financial publications, and whose officers are treated like celebrities. That's what pushes their prices to levels that end up disappointing their investors. The workhorse stocks selected by most of the strategies with the highest risk-adjusted returns are nonsexy issues like Badger Meter, Inc. Don't look for the CEO on the cover of *Fortune* any time soon!

You will, however, probably find magazine features on companies with the worst risk-adjusted returns. Four of the five worst performing strategies buy stocks with the highest price-to-sales, price-to-cashflow, price-to-book, or price-to-earnings ratios. These glamour stocks command unreasonably high prices for their underlying businesses, and their investors believe that trees really *do* grow to the sky. These companies' prices are based on hope, greed, or fantasies about a future that rarely comes to pass. Nord Resources might be one heck of a mining company, but is it really worth 2120 times revenues? *It* may be, but the class of stocks with these characteristics are *not*, and investors should avoid them.

On a risk-adjusted basis, the *worst* performing strategy is buying the 50 stocks from All Stocks with the worst one-year price performance. The Sharpe ratio is *negative*, because it fails to beat T-bills over the 40 years of our study. If you want to be contrarian, buy stocks with low price-to-sales ratios. Avoid last year's biggest price losers at all costs—their record over the last 40 years is abysmal.

Implications

After weighing risk, rewards, and long-term base rates, the best overall strategy is the united cornerstone growth and value portfolio. Over the 42 years studied, the strategy does nearly five times as well as All Stocks, with an annual compound return of 17.1 percent, some 4.19 percent higher than All Stocks' return of 12.91 percent a year. Yet the risk taken is virtually the same as for All Stocks. It's also extraordinarily consistent, beating All Stocks 80 percent of the time in any given year and 100 percent of the time over rolling 10-year periods.

The united strategy achieves this performance with a portfolio diversified by style, with half its investments in large, market-leading stocks with high dividend yields and half in stocks from All Stocks with persistent earnings gains, low price-to-sales ratios, and good relative strength.

If you use any of the other strategies, stick with the ones with the highest risk-adjusted returns and *always* look at the historical record if tempted to take a chance on a glamour stock trading at high multiples. It won't hurt to be reminded that most of those stocks crash and burn.

22

Getting the Most out of Your Equity Investments

To think is easy. To act is difficult. To act as one thinks is the most difficult of all.
—JOHANN WOLFGANG VON GOETHE

Investors can learn much from the Taoist concept of Wu Wei. Taoism is one of the three schools of Chinese philosophy that have guided thinkers for thousands of years. Literally, Wu Wei means "to act without action," but in spirit it means to let things occur as they are meant to occur. Don't try to put round pegs into square holes. Don't be more clever than you need to be, forever trying to square a circle. Understand the essence of a circle and use it as nature intended. The closest Western equivalent is Wittgenstein's maxim: "Don't look for the meaning: Look for the use!"

For investors, this means letting good strategies work. Don't second-guess them. Don't try to outsmart them. Don't abandon them because they're experiencing a rough patch. Understand the nature of what you're using and let it work. This is the hardest assignment of all. It's virtually impossible not to insert our ego into decisions, yet being dispassionate is the only way to beat the market over time. Following Ockham's Razor—which shows that most often, the simplest theory is the best—is almost impossible. We love to make the simple complex, follow the crowd, get seduced by the story about some hot stock, let our emotions dictate decisions, buy and sell on tips and hunches, and approach each investment decision on a case-by-case basis, with no underlying consistency or strategy. No wonder the S&P 500 beats 80 percent of traditionally managed mutual funds over the long term!

A Taoist story is illuminating: One day a man was standing at the edge of a pool at the bottom of a huge waterfall when he saw an old man tossed about in the turbulent water. He ran to rescue him, but by the time he got there the old man had climbed out onto the bank and was walking alone, singing to himself. The man was astonished and rushed up to the old man, questioning him about the secret of his survival. The old man said that it was nothing special. "I began to learn while very young, and grew up practicing it. Now, I'm certain of success. I go down with the water and come up with the water. I follow it and forget myself. The only reason I survive is because I don't struggle against the water's superior power."

The market is like the water, overpowering all who struggle against it and giving those who work with it a wonderful ride. But swimming lessons are in order. You can't just jump in; you need guidelines. Our study of the last 45 years suggests that to do well in the market, you must adopt the following approach.

Always Use Strategies

You'll get nowhere buying stocks just because they have a great story. Usually, these are the companies that have been the *worst* performers over the last 45 years. They're the stocks everyone talks about and wants to own. They often have sky-high price-to-earnings, price-to-book, and price-to-sales ratios. They're very appealing in the short term, but deadly over the long haul. You *must* avoid them. Always think in terms of overall strategies and not individual stocks. One company's data are *meaningless*, yet can be very convincing. If you can't use strategies and are inexorably drawn to the stock of the day, your returns suffer horribly in the long run. If, try as you might, you can't stick to a strategy, put the majority of your money in an index fund and treat the small amounts you put in story stocks as an entertainment expense.

Use Only Strategies Proven over the Long Term

When I started testing strategies several years ago, I thought a 10-year record was adequate to judge the effectiveness of a strategy. I was wrong. The long-term data prove you need a minimum of 25 years to judge a strategy's effectiveness. More is even better. Buying stocks with high price-to-book ratios appeared to work for as many as 15 years, but the fullness of time proves it's not effective. Many years of data help you understand the peaks and valleys of a strategy. Attempting to use strategies that have not withstood the test of time will lead to great disappointment. Stocks change. Industries change. But the underlying reasons they are good investments remain the same. Only the fullness of time shows which are the most sound.

Invest Consistently

Consistency is the hallmark of great investors, separating them from everyone else. If you use even a mediocre strategy *consistently,* you'll beat almost all investors who jump in and out of the market, change tactics in midstream, and forever second-guess their decisions. Realistically consider your risk tolerance, plan your path, and then stick to it. You may have fewer stories to tell at parties, but you'll be among the most successful investors over the long term. Successful investing isn't alchemy; it's a simple matter of consistently using time-tested strategies and letting compounding work its magic.

Always Bet with the Base Rate

Base rates are boring, dull, and very worthwhile. Knowing how often a strategy beats the market and by how much is one of the most useful pieces of information available to investors, yet few take advantage of it. You now have the numbers. Use them.

Never Use the Riskiest Strategies

There is no point in using the riskiest strategies. They will sap your will and make you abandon them, usually at their low. Given the number of highly effective strategies, always concentrate on those with the highest risk-adjusted returns.

Always Use More Than One Strategy

Unless you're near retirement and investing only in low risk strategies, always diversify your portfolio by strategy. How much you allocate to each is a function of risk tolerance, but you should always have some growth and some value guarding you from the inevitable flow of fashion on Wall Street. Unite strategies so your portfolio can do much better than the overall market without incurring more risk.

Use Multifactor Models

The single-factor models show that the market rewards certain characteristics while punishing others. Yet you're much better off using several factors to build your portfolios. Returns are higher and risk is lower. You should always make a stock pass several hurdles before investing.

Insist on Consistency

If you don't have the time to build your own portfolios and prefer investing in mutual funds, buy only those that stress consistency of style. Many fund managers follow a hit-or-miss, intuitive method of stock selection. They have no mechanism to reign in their emotions or ensure that their good ideas work. All too often their picks are based on hope rather than experience. You have no way to know exactly how they are managing your money, or if their past performance is due to a hot hand unguided by a coherent underlying strategy.

Don't bet with them. Buy one of the many funds based on solid, rigorous strategies. I started a fund company because of the power of this research. O'Shaughnessy Funds offer several of these best performing strategies as strategy indexes, invested in stocks that meet the strategy's selection criteria with no ability to override it. As more and more research comes out, I expect that there will be other fund companies that also invest using a disciplined, consistent strategy that works well over long periods of time. If your fund managers don't clearly define their investment style, insist that they do. You should expect nothing less.

The Stock Market Is Not Random

Finally, the data prove the stock market takes purposeful strides. Far from chaotic, random movement, the market consistently rewards specific strategies while punishing others. As Ben Graham requested, we now know the historical behavior of securities with defined characteristics. We must let history be our guide, using only those time-tested methods that have proven successful. We know what is valuable and we know what works on Wall Street. All that remains is to act upon this knowledge.

Appendix: Research Methodology

As a rule, I always look for what others ignore.
—MARSHALL McLUHAN

Data

Annual data come from Standard & Poor's Compustat database, including the research data file. The research file contains information on all companies removed from the database. Compustat PC Plus designates these files *C and *R. All data from 1950 through 1974 were uploaded to O'Shaughnessy Capital Management PCs from Compustat's mainframe. We accessed subsequent years using various Compustat PC Plus dataplates on CD.

Time Horizon

We examined the 46 years from December 31, 1950 to December 31, 1996. The use of time lags (to avoid look-ahead bias) forced us to start most tests as of December 31, 1951. Tests with 5-year inputs, such as 5-year earnings per share growth rates, required a starting point of December 31, 1954. After 1994, real-time data were used from actual Compustat databases, so no time lags were required. Thus, all returns since December 31, 1994 are for real-time portfolios.

Universe

We include only stocks that could actually be purchased without a tremendous liquidity problem. We review both the "average" stock in the universe and large stocks in the universe. We set a market capitalization of $150 million as a minimum for all stocks after consulting with institutional traders. Inflation has caused a tremendous shift in nominal values since 1950, so we deflated the current value of $150 million back to 1950. We used a five-year average of the deflated value of $150 million in each year and switched it every five years. Thus, these were the capitalization minimums:

December 31, 1951–December 31, 1954	$27 million
December 31, 1955–December 31, 1958	$27 million
December 31, 1959–December 31, 1963	$28 million
December 31, 1964–December 31, 1968	$31 million
December 31, 1969–December 31, 1973	$34 million
December 31, 1974–December 31, 1978	$44 million
December 31, 1979–December 31, 1983	$64 million
December 31, 1984–December 31, 1988	$97 million
December 31, 1989–December 31, 1993	$117 million
December 31, 1994–December 31, 1996	$150 million

All stocks with a deflated market capitalization in excess of $150 million are included and are designated All Stocks in the book.

We also wanted to look at returns for which large stocks—the group from which many money managers select—were the universe. A simple way to achieve this was to require a stock's market capitalization to exceed the mean in any given year (Large Stocks). Generally, stocks with market capitalization in excess of the mean accounted for the upper 16 percent of the database by market capitalization, and stocks with market capitalization in excess of a deflated $150 million accounted for the upper 50 percent of the database.

Returns

Returns are calculated annually using the following formula:

$$\text{Total return} = (\text{PRCC[1y]}/\text{PRCC} - 1) + (\text{DVPSX[1y]}/\text{PRCC})$$

where PRCC[1y] = year-end price of stock one year ahead of date of test

PRCC = price of stock at beginning of period when it qualified for inclusion in the portfolio

DVPSX[1y] = dividend actually paid in year of test

As an example, consider Company XYZ, a stock that qualified for a low price-to-earnings screen on December 31, 1960. Total return for the period December 31, 1960 through December 31, 1961 would be calculated thus:

$$\text{PRCC (price on December 31, 1960)} = \$10.00$$

$$\text{PRCC[1y] (price on December 31, 1961)} = \$15.00$$

$$\text{DVPSX[1y] (Dividend actually paid in 1961)} = \$1.00$$

Thus:

$$(\$15.00/\$10.00 - 1) + (\$1.00/\$10.00) = 0.5 + 0.1 = 0.60$$

The result is a gain of 60 percent for the year.

For 1994 forward, we use the actual total return as calculated by Compustat's total return function. (TRT1y) returns were done on a year-by-year basis, and each year of the series was inspected for outliers. All portfolios, except those in Chapter 4, contain 50 stocks. If a return for an individual stock was extreme or inconsistent with other data, it was removed. Since the dividend was not reinvested monthly for the 1951–1994 period, returns are slightly understated.

All stocks were equally weighted by dollar amount. Thus, if IBM was one selected stock and Terra Industries another, each would have the same amount of dollars invested. (i.e., if we bought 10 stocks and invested a total of $100,000, $10,000 would be invested in each.) Portfolios were not adjusted for any factor such as beta, industry, or geographical location.

Returns differ somewhat depending upon which Compustat dataplate (CD) you use. This happens because Standard & Poor's Compustat continually updates the data. A study to see if any material difference in returns occurred because of such an irregularity found that over time, it was a wash.

Data Definitions

Annual data were lagged a minimum of 11 months to account for reporting delays and to avoid look-ahead bias. We used periods ranging from 11 months to 15 months because of the year-end, calendar nature of our data and in order to include stocks with fiscal years that were not December 31. Since we were making trading decisions only each December 31, we had to decide what data were available *at that time.* Using several current Compustat data CDs, we studied when information became available in real time and applied it to the historical record. Each data item's time lag is consistent with what we found examining current databases. Since 1994, all data are real time, so no time lags were required.

Here are the definitions of items, followed in parentheses by their Compustat descriptor and time-lag information for the 1951–1994 period. For all years after 1994, results and tests were done in real time, so no time lag was used.

Sales: Annual net sales, time-lagged by 15 months. (SALE[@yr(-15m)])

Common shares outstanding: The net number of all common shares outstanding at year end, excluding Treasury shares and scrip. Adjusted for splits, lagged by 15 months. (CSHO[@yr(-15m)])

Common equity liquidating value: The common shareholders' interest in a company in the event of liquidation of company assets. Common equity is adjusted by the preferred stockholders' legal claims against the company. We used this as a proxy for book value. Time-lagged by 15 months. (CEQL[@yr(-15m)])

Income before extra items: The income of a company after all expenses, including special items, income taxes, and minority interest but before provisions for common and or preferred dividends. Does not reflect discontinued operations. Time-lagged in larger formulas. (IB)

Annual dividend per share by ex-date: Lagged by 11 months. DVPSX represents the cash dividends per share adjusted for all stock splits and stock dividends. This item excludes payments in preferred stock. All extra dividends are included. The current sources for the data are Interactive Data Service, Inc. and Standard & Poor's *Dividend Record*. (DVPSX@yr(-11m)])

Annual earnings per share, excluding extraordinary items: Not restated, but adjusted by the adjustment factor for each year. Represents primary earnings per share before extraordinary items and discontinued operations. Time-lagged by 15 months. (EPSPX[@yr (-15m)])

Calendar year closing price: Not lagged. (PRCC)

Pretax income: Operating and nonoperating income before provisions for income tax and minority interest. Specifically excludes income from extraordinary items and discontinued operations. Annual, lagged in larger formulas. (PI)

Adjustment factor: Ratio used to adjust all share data for splits. (AJEX)

Depreciation-amortization: Noncash charges for obsolescence and wear and tear on property. Annual figure. (DP)

Formulas

All formulas use the above items as well as common ranking and averaging techniques. Most common formulas establish an average or rank items in descending order. Here are the definitions:

Averages.   Averages are established using the @CAVG(X,SET) function. The function calculates the average value of an item or expression (*x*) over a set. This function returns a decimal. Thus to obtain, for example, the average market capitalization of all the stocks in the Compustat database, the formula would be: @CAVG((PRCC*CSHO[@yr(-15m)])), @SET(*C + *R,@ISVALUE((PRCC*CSHO[@yr(0m)]))). This tells the computer to calculate the average market capitalization for all items in the active (*C) and research (*R) databases that *have* a value for market capitalization—that is, the computer determines whether data exist for an item (@ISVALUE). The same @CAVG, @SET, and @ISVALUE formula is used to find the database average for all items, such as price-to-earnings and price-to-book ratios.

Ranking.   Items, such as the top 50 by dividend yield or the top 50 by sales-to-price ratio, are ranked using Compustat's @RANK(X,SET) function. This function determines the relative rank of an entity in any item or expression (*x*) in a set. Entities are ranked in descending order. This function returns an integer. Thus to get the top 50 stocks by price appreciation, the formula would read: @RANK((PRCC/PRCC[1y]), @SET(*C + *R))<51.

The @SET(Base set, condition) selects entities for a set within an expression by analyzing a set (Base set) according to the predetermined criterion.

Sample formula.   Here's a sample formula that returns the 50 best performing stocks from All Stocks that also have price-to-sales ratios below 1:

$$@IF(PSR1\#AND\#MK1\#AND\#@RANK((PRCC/PRCC[-1]),@SET$$
$$(*C + *R,PSR1\#AND\#MK1))<51,1.0,.0)$$

where PSR1 = (PRCC/(SALE/CSHO)[@yr(15m)])<1 establishes a
           price-to-sales ratio less than 1 and
     MK1 = (PRCC*CSHO[@yr(-15m)])>117 establishes that all
           market capitalizations must exceed 117 million

The 1.0,.0 at the end simply tells the program to include a stock if it meets all the criteria and to exclude it if not. The <51 says we just want the top 50 by price appreciation.

Here are the formula definitions followed by the code written for Compustat PC Plus:

Market capitalization: 12/31/yy price times common shares outstanding, lagged by 15 months. (PRCC*CSHO[@yr(-15m)])

Return on equity: 100 times (IB divided by CEQL), lagged by 15 months. (100*(IB/CEQL)) used as (ROE[@yr(-15m)])

Annual indicated dividend yield: DVPSX, lagged by 11 months, divided by PRCC. (DVPSX[@yr(-11m)]/PRCC)

Pretax profit margin: 100 times (PI divided by SALE), lagged by 15 months, called PPM. (PPM[@yr(-15m)])

Sales-to-price ratio: Annual sales per share, lagged by 15 months, divided by year-end price. ((SALE/CSHO)[@yr(-15m)]/PRCC)

Price-to-sales ratio: Year-end price, divided by annual sales data per share, lagged by 15 months. ((PRCC/(SALE/CSHO)[@yr(-15m)]))

One-year earnings per share gain: Change in earnings per share compared with the year-earlier figure, lagged by 15 months. (EPSPX/EPSPX[1y])[@yr(-15m)]. Worst earnings per share changes were found using the inverse: (EPSPX[1y]/EPSPX)[@yr(-15m)].

Earnings-to-price ratio: The inverse of the price-to-earnings ratio, with earnings lagged by 15 months. (EPSPX[@yr(-15m)]/PRCC)

Price-to-earnings ratio: (PRCC/EPSPX[@yr(-15m)])

Book-to-price ratio: The inverse of the price-to-book ratio, with book value lagged by 15 months. A simple book value was calculated by dividing common equity liquidating value (CEQL) by common shares outstanding. ((CEQL/CSHO)[@yr(-15m)]/PRCC)

Price-to-book ratio: ((PRCC/(CEQL/CSHO)[@yr(-15m)]))

Cashflow: Income before extraordinary gains, which represents the income of a company after all expenses except provisions for common and preferred dividends plus depreciation, lagged by 15 months, called CFL. (CFL = (IB + DP), CFL[@yr(-15m)])

Cashflow-to-price ratio: Cashflow, from above, divided by common shares outstanding, divided by price. ((CFL/CSHO)[@yr(-15m)]/PRCC)

Price-to-cashflow ratio: ((PRCC/(CFL/CSHO[@yr(-15m)]))

One-year sales gain: Change in sales compared with the year-earlier figure, lagged by 15 months. (SALE/SALE[1y])[@yr(-15m)]. Worst one-year sales gains were obtained using (SALE[1y]/SALE)[@yr (-15m)].

Five-year compound growth rate for earnings per share: Uses a Compustat function—@CGR—to calculate the five-year compound growth rate for earnings per share. The function returns a percent. The first and last observations must be positive. (((@CGR(EPSPX,-5,0)[@yr(-15m)])

Five-year compound growth rate for sales: Uses a Compustat function—@CGR—to calculate the five-year compound growth rate for sales. The function returns a percent. The first and last observations must be positive. ((@CGR(SALE,-5,0)[@yr(-15m)])

Annual relative strength: Excludes dividends and uses simple share price appreciation. (PRCC/PRCC[1y]). Worst annual price appreciation is obtained by dividing this year's closing price by the previous year. (PRCC[1y]/PRCC)

Taxes, Commissions, and Market Impact Costs

These costs are not included, but a real-time use of the strategies reveals that market impact and commissions are minimal. Taxes would reduce the returns according to the tax rate faced. Since all the strategies are rebalanced annually, a taxable investor would pay at the 28 percent capital gains tax rate on all gains and would presumably sell all losses for short-term capital losses to be reported against ordinary income.

Bibliography

Ambachtsheer, Keith P. "The Persistence of Investment Risk," *Journal of Portfolio Management*, Fall 1989, pp. 69–72.

Arnott, Robert D., Kelso, Charles M., Jr., Kiscadden, Stephan, and Macedo, Rosemary. "Forecasting Factor Returns: An Intriguing Possibility," *Journal of Portfolio Management*, Fall 1990, pp. 28–35.

Banz, R., and Breen, W. "Sample-Dependent Results Using Accounting and Market Data: Some Evidence," *Journal of Finance*, September 1986, pp. 779–793.

Barach, Roland. *Mind Traps: Mastering The Inner World of Investing*. Dow Jones-Irwin, Homewood, IL, 1988.

Basu, S. "The Relationship Between Earnings Yield, Market Value, and Return for NYSE Common Stocks: Further Evidence," *Journal of Financial Economics*, June 1983, pp. 129–156.

Bell, David E., Raiffa, Howard, and Tversky, Amos. *Decision Making: Descriptive, Normative, and Prescriptive Interactions*. Cambridge University Press, Cambridge, England, 1988.

Bernstein, Peter L. *Capital Ideas: The Improbable Origins of Modern Wall Street*. The Free Press, New York, 1992.

Bjerring, James H., Lakonishok, Josef, and Vermaelen, Theo. "Stock Prices and Financial Analysts' Recommendations," *Journal of Finance*, March 1983, pp. 187–204.

Blakney, R. B. *The Way of Life: A New Translation of Tao Te Ching*. New American Library Publishing, New York, 1983.

Bogle, John C. *Bogle on Mutual Funds: New Perspectives for the Intelligent Investor*. Irwin Professional Publishing, New York, 1994.

Brandes, Charles H. *Value Investing Today*. Dow Jones-Irwin, Homewood, IL, 1989.

Brealey, Richard A. *An Introduction to Risk and Return from Common Stocks*, 2nd ed. MIT Press, Cambridge, MA, 1993.

Brealey, Richard A. "Portfolio Theory Versus Portfolio Practice," *Journal of Portfolio Management*, Summer 1990, pp. 6–10.

Brock, William, Lakonishok, Josef, and LeBaron, Blake. "Simple Technical Trading Rules and the Stochastic Properties of Stock Returns," *Journal of Finance*, December 1992, pp. 1731–1764.

Brown, John Dennis. *101 Years on Wall Street: An Investor's Almanac*. Prentice Hall, Englewood Cliffs, NJ, 1991.

Brown, Stephen J., and Kritzman, Mark P., CFA. *Quantitative Methods for Financial Analysis.* Dow Jones-Irwin, Homewood, IL, 1987.

Brown, Stephen J. (Leonard Stear School of Business, NYU), and Goetzmann, William N. (Yale School of Management), "Performance Persistence," *Journal of Finance, 1995,* First Draft: November 1992, Current Draft: September 30, 1994.

Brush, John S., and Boles, Keith E. "The Predictive Power in Relative Strength and CAPM," *Journal of Portfolio Management,* Summer 1983, pp. 20–23.

Brush, John S. "Eight Relative Strength Models Compared," *Journal of Portfolio Management,* Fall 1986, pp. 21–28.

Casti, John L. *COMPLEX-ification, Explaining a Paradoxical World Through the Science of Surprise.* HarperCollins Publishers, New York, 1994.

Chan, Louis K., Hamao, Yasushi, and Lakonishok, Josef. "Fundamentals and Stock Returns in Japan," *Journal of Finance,* December 1991, pp. 1739–1764.

Chan, Louis K. C., and Lakonishok, Josef. "Are the Reports of Beta's Death Premature?" *Journal of Portfolio Management,* Summer 1993, pp. 51–62.

Chopra, Navin, Lakonishok, Josef, and Ritter, Jay R. "Measuring Abnormal Performance: Do Stocks Overreact?" *Journal of Financial Economics,* November 1992, pp. 235–268.

Cottle, Sidney, Murray, Roger F., and Block, Frank E. *Graham and Dodd's Security Analysis,* 5th ed. McGraw-Hill, New York, 1988.

Coulson, Robert D. *The Intelligent Investor's Guide to Profiting from Stock Market Inefficiencies.* Probus Publishing Company, Chicago, IL, 1987.

Dawes, Robyn M. *House of Cards: Psychology and Psychotherapy Built on Myth.* The Free Press, New York, 1994.

Dewdney, A. K. *200% of Nothing: An Eye-Opening Tour Through the Twists and Turns of Math Abuse and Innumeracy.* John Wiley & Sons, New York, 1993.

Dreman, David N. *Psychology and the Stock Market.* Warner Books, New York, 1977.

Dreman, David N. *The New Contrarian Investment Strategy.* Random House, New York, 1980.

Dreman, David N. "Good-bye EMH," *Forbes Magazine,* June 20, 1994, p. 261.

Dreman, David N. "Nasty Surprises," *Forbes Magazine,* July 19, 1993, p. 246.

Dreman, David N. "Chronically Clouded Crystal Balls," *Forbes Magazine,* October 11, 1993, p. 178.

Dunn, Patricia C., and Theisen, Rolf D. "How Consistently Do Active Managers Win?" *Journal of Portfolio Management,* Summer 1983, pp. 47–50.

Ellis, Charles D., and Vertin, James R. *Classics: An Investor's Anthology.* Dow Jones-Irwin, Homewood, IL, 1989.

Ellis, Charles D., and Vertin, James R. *Classics II: Another Investor's Anthology.* Dow Jones-Irwin, Homewood, IL, 1991.

Fabozzi, Frank J., Fogler, H. Russell, and Harrington, Diana R. *The New Stock Market: A Complete Guide to the Latest Research, Analysis, and Performance.* Probus Publishing Company, Chicago, IL, 1990.

Fabozzi, Frank J. *Pension Fund Investment Management.* Probus Publishing Company, Chicago, IL, 1990.

Fabozzi, Frank J., and Zarb, Frank G. *Handbook of Financial Markets: Securities, Options, and Futures.* Dow Jones-Irwin, Homewood, IL, 1986.

Faust, David. *The Limits of Scientific Reasoning.* University of Minnesota Press, Minneapolis, 1984.

Ferguson, Robert. "The Trouble with Performance Measurement," *Journal of Portfolio Management,* Spring 1986, pp. 4–9.

Ferguson, Robert. "The Plight of the Pension Fund Officer," *Financial Analysts Journal,* May/June 1989, pp. 8–9.

Fisher, Kenneth L. *Super Stocks.* Dow Jones-Irwin, Homewood, IL, 1984.

Fogler, H. Russell. "Common Stock Management in the 1990s," *Journal of Portfolio Management,* Winter 1990, pp. 26–34.

Freeman, John D. "Behind the Smoke and Mirrors: Gauging the Integrity of Investment Simulations," *Financial Analysts Journal,* November/December 1992, pp. 26–31.

Fridson, Martin S. *Investment Illusions.* John Wiley & Sons, New York, 1993.

Givoly, Dan, and Lakonishok, Josef. "Financial Analysts' Forecasts of Earnings: Their Value to Investors," *Journal of Banking and Finance,* December 1979, pp. 221–233.

Gleick, James. *Chaos: Making A New Science.* Viking Penguin, New York, 1987.

Guerard, John, and Vaught, H. T. *The Handbook of Financial Modeling.* Probus Publishing Company, Chicago, IL, 1989.

Hackel, Kenneth S., and Livnat, Joshua. *Cash Flow and Security Analysis.* Business-One Irwin, Homewood, IL, 1992.

Hagin, Bob. "What Practitioners Need to Know About T-Tests," *Financial Analysts Journal,* May/June 1990, pp. 17–20.

Harrington, Diana R., Fabozzi, Frank J., and Fogler, H. Russell. *The New Stock Market.* Probus Publishing Company, Chicago, IL, 1990.

Haugen, Robert A., and Baker, Nardin L. "Dedicated Stock Portfolios," *Journal of Portfolio Management,* Summer 1990, pp. 17–22.

Hoff, Benjamin. *The Tao of Pooh.* Penguin Books, New York, 1982.

Ibbotson Associates. *Stocks, Bonds, Bills, and Inflation 1995 Yearbook.* Ibbotson Associates, Chicago, IL, 1995.

Ibbotson, Roger G., and Brinson, Gary P. *Gaining the Performance Advantage: Investment Markets.* McGraw-Hill, New York, 1987.

Ikenberry, David, Lakonishok, Josef, and Vermaelen, Theo. "Market Under Reaction to Open Market Share Repurchases," July 1994, unpublished.

Jacobs, Bruce J., and Levy, Kenneth N. "Disentangling Equity Return Regularities: New Insights and Investment Opportunities," *Financial Analysts Journal,* May/June 1988, pp. 18–38.

Jeffrey, Robert H. "Do Clients Need So Many Portfolio Managers?" *Journal of Portfolio Management,* Fall 1991, pp. 13–19.

Kahn, Ronald N. "What Practitioners Need to Know About Back Testing," *Financial Analysts Journal,* July/August 1990, pp. 17–20.

Keane, Simon M. "Paradox in the Current Crisis in Efficient Market Theory," *Journal of Portfolio Management,* Winter 1991, pp. 30–34.

Keepler, A. Michael. "Further Evidence on the Predictability of International Equity Returns," *Journal of Portfolio Management,* Fall 1991, pp. 48–53.

Keppler, A. Michael. "The Importance of Dividend Yields in Country Selection," *Journal of Portfolio Management,* Winter 1991, pp. 24–29.

Klein, Robert A., and Lederman, Jess. *Small Cap Stocks: Investment and Portfolio Strategies for the Institutional Investor.* Probus Publishing Company, Chicago, IL, 1993.

Knowles, Harvey C. III, and Petty, Damon H. *The Dividend Investor.* Probus Publishing Company, Chicago, IL, 1992.

Kritzman, Mark. "How to Detect Skill in Management Performance," *Journal of Portfolio Management,* Winter 1986, pp. 16–20.

Kuhn, Thomas S. *The Copernican Revolution: Planetary Astronomy in the Development of Western Thought.* Harvard University Press, Cambridge, MA, 1957.

Kuhn, Thomas S. *The Structure of Scientific Revolutions.* University of Chicago Press, Chicago, IL, 1970.

Lakonishok, Josef, Shleifer, Andrei, and Vishny, Robert W. "Contrarian Investment, Extrapolation, and Risk," working paper, June 1994.

Lee, Wayne Y. "Diversification and Time: Do Investment Horizons Matter?" *Journal of Portfolio Management,* Spring 1990, pp. 21–26.

Lerner, Eugene M. and Theerathorn, Pochara. "The Returns of Different Investment Strategies," *Journal of Portfolio Management,* Summer 1983, pp. 26–28.

Lofthouse, Stephen. *Equity Investment Management: How to Select Stocks and Markets.* John Wiley & Sons, Chichester, England, 1994.

Lorie, James H., Dodd, Peter, and Kimpton, Mary Hamilton. *The Stock Market: Theories and Evidence.* Dow Jones-Irwin, Homewood, IL, 1985.

Lowe, Janet. *Benjamin Graham on Value Investing: Lessons from the Dean of Wall Street.* Dearborn Financial Publishing, Chicago, IL, 1994.

Lowenstein, Louis. *What's Wrong with Wall Street.* Addison-Wesley, New York, 1988.

Maital, Shloml. *Minds, Markets, and Money: Psychological Foundation of Economic Behavior.* Basic Books, New York, 1982.

Malkiel, Burton G. "Returns from Investing in Equity Mutual Funds 1971–1991," Princeton University Press, Princeton, NJ, 1994.

Martin, Linda J. "Uncertain? How do you Spell Relief?," *Journal of Portfolio Management,* Spring 1985, pp. 5–8.

Marcus, Alan J. "The Magellan Fund and Market Efficiency," *Journal of Portfolio Management,* Fall 1990, pp. 85–88.

Mattlin, Everett. "Reliability Math: Manager Selection by the Numbers," *Institutional Investor,* January 1993, pp. 141–142.

Maturi, Richard J. *Stock Picking: The 11 Best Tactics for Beating the Market.* McGraw-Hill, New York, 1993.

McElreath, Robert B., Jr., and Wiggins, C. Donald. "Using the Compustat Tapes in Financial Research: Problems and Solutions," *Financial Analysts Journal,* January/February 1984, pp. 71–76.

Melnikoff, Meyer. "Anomaly Investing," in *The Financial Analyst's Handbook,* ed. Sumner N. Levine. Dow Jones-Irwin, Homewood, IL, 1988, pp. 699–721.

Murphy, Joseph E., Jr. *Revised Edition: Stock Market Probability.* Probus Publishing Company, Chicago, IL, 1994.

Newbold, Gerald D., and Poon, Percy S. "Portfolio Risk, Portfolio Performance, and the Individual Investor," *Journal of Finance*, Summer 1996.

Nisbett, Richard, and Ross, Lee. *Human Inference: Strategies and Shortcomings of Social Judgment*. Prentice Hall, Englewood Cliffs, NJ, 1980.

O'Barr, William M., and Conley, John M. *Fortune and Folly: The Wealth and Power of Institutional Investing*. Business-One Irwin, Homewood, IL, 1992.

O'Hanlon, John, and Ward, Charles W. R. "How to Lose at Winning Strategies," *Journal of Portfolio Management*, Spring 1986.

Oppenheimer, Henry R. "A Test of Ben Graham's Stock Selection Criteria," *Financial Analysts Journal*, September/October 1984, pp. 68–74.

O'Shaughnessy, James P. "Quantitative Models as an Aid in Offsetting Systematic Errors in Decision Making," St. Paul, MN, 1988, unpublished.

O'Shaughnessy, James P. *Invest Like the Best: Using Your Computer to Unlock the Secrets of the Top Money Managers*. McGraw-Hill, New York, 1994.

Paulos, John Allen. *Innumeracy: Mathematical Illiteracy and Its Consequences*. Hill and Wang, New York, 1989.

Perritt, Gerald W. *Small Stocks, Big Profit*. Dearborn Financial Publishing, Chicago, IL, 1993.

Perritt, Gerald W., and Lavine, Alan. *Diversify Your Way to Wealth: How to Customize Your Investment Portfolio to Protect and Build Your Net Worth*. Probus Publishing Company, Chicago, IL, 1994.

Peter, Edgar E. *Chaos and Order in the Capital Markets: A New View of Cycles, Prices, and Market Volatility*. John Wiley & Sons, New York, 1991.

Peters, Donald J. *A Contrarian Strategy for Growth Stock Investing: Theoretical Foundations and Empirical Evidence*. Quorum Books, Westport, CT, 1993.

Pettengill, Glenn N., and Jordan, Bradford D. "The Overreaction Hypothesis, Firm Size, and Stock Market Seasonality," *Journal of Portfolio Management*, Spring 1990, pp. 60–64.

Reinganum, M. "Misspecification of Capital Asset Pricing: Empirical Anomalies Based on Earnings' Yields and Market Values," *Journal of Financial Economics*, March 1981, pp. 19–46.

Schwager, Jack D. *Market Wizards: Interviews with Top Traders*. Simon & Schuster, New York, 1992.

Schwager, Jack D. *The New Market Wizards*. Harper-Collins Publishers, New York, 1992.

Sharp, Robert M. *The Lore and Legends of Wall Street*. Dow Jones-Irwin, Homewood, IL, 1989.

Siegel, Jeremy J. *Stocks for the Long Run*. Irwin Professional Publishing, Burr Ridge, IL, 1994.

Siegel, Laurence B. *Stocks, Bonds, Bills and Inflation 1994 Yearbook*. Ibbotson Associates, Chicago, IL, 1994.

Smullyan, Raymond M. *The Tao Is Silent*. Harper & Row, New York, 1977.

Speidell, Lawrence S. "The New Wave Theory," *Financial Analysts Journal*, July/August 1988, pp. 9–12.

Speidell, Lawrence S. "Embarrassment and Riches: The Discomfort of Alternative Investment Strategies," *Journal of Portfolio Management*, Fall 1990, pp. 6–11.

Stumpp, Mark, and Scott, James. "Does Liquidity Predict Stock Returns?" *Journal of Portfolio Management*, Winter 1991, pp. 35–40.

Thomas, Dana L. *The Plungers and the Peacocks: An Update of the Classic History of the Stock Market*. William Morrow, New York, 1989.

Tierney, David E., and Winston, Kenneth. "Using Generic Benchmarks to Present Manager Styles," *Journal of Portfolio Management*, Summer 1991, pp. 33–36.

Train, John. *The Money Masters*. Harper & Row, New York, 1985.

Train, John. *Famous Financial Fiascos*. Clarkson N. Potter, New York, 1985.

Train, John. *The New Money Masters: Winning Investment Strategies of: Soros, Lynch, Steinhardt, Rogers, Neff, Wanger, Michaelis, Carret*. Harper & Row, New York, 1989.

Treynor, Jack L. "Information-Based Investing," *Financial Analysts Journal*, May/June 1989, pp. 6–7.

Treynor, Jack L. "The 10 Most Important Questions to Ask in Selecting a Money Manager," *Financial Analysts Journal*, May/June 1990, pp. 4–5.

Trippe, Robert R., and Lee, Jae K. *State-of-the-Art Portfolio Selection: Using Knowledge-Based Systems to Enhance Investment Performance*. Probus Publishing Company, Chicago, IL, 1992.

Tsetsekos, George P., and DeFusco, Richard. "Portfolio Performance, Managerial Ownership, and the Size Effect," *Journal of Portfolio Management*, Spring 1990, pp. 33–39.

Twark, Allan, and D'Mello, James P. "Model Indexation: A Portfolio Management Tool," *Journal of Portfolio Management*, Summer 1991, pp. 37–40.

Valentine, Jerome L., CFA. "Investment Analysis and Capital Market Theory," *The Financial Analysts*, Occasional Paper Number 1, 1975.

Valentine, Jerome L., CFA, and Mennis, Edmund A., CFA. *Quantitative Techniques for Financial Analysis*. Richard D. Irwin, Homewood, IL, 1980.

Vandell, Robert F., and Parrino, Robert. "A Purposeful Stride Down Wall Street," *Journal of Portfolio Management*, Winter 1986, pp. 31–39.

Vince, Ralph. *The Mathematics of Money Management*. John Wiley & Sons, New York, 1992.

Vishny, Robert W., Shleifer, Andrei, and Lakonishok, Josef. "The Structure and Performance of the Money Management Industry," in the *Brookings Papers on Economic Activity*, Microeconomics, 1992.

Watzlawick, Paul. *How Real Is Real? Confusion, Disinformation, Communication*. Vintage Books, New York, 1977.

Williams, John Burr, Ph.D. "Fifty Years of Investment Analysis," *The Financial Analysts Research Foundation*, 1979.

Wood, Arnold S. "Fatal Attractions for Money Managers," *Financial Analysts Journal*, May/June 1989, pp. 3–5.

Zeikel, Arthur. "Investment Management in the 1990s," *Financial Analysts Journal*, September/October 1990, pp. 6–9.

Index